RECONVERGENCE

A POLITICAL ECONOMY OF TELECOMMUNICATIONS IN CANADA

THE HAMPTON PRESS COMMUNICATION SERIES
International Communication
Richard C. Vincent, supervisory editor

Goodbye, Gweilo: Public Opinion and the 1997 Problem in Hong Kong
L. Erwin Atwood and Ann Marie Major

Democratizing Communication?: Comparative Perspectives on Information and Power
Mashoed Bailie and Dwayne Winseck, eds.

Global Productions: Labor in the Making of the "Information Society"
Gerald Sussman and John A. Lent, eds.

Reconvergence: A Political Economy of Telecommunications in Canada
Dwayne Winseck

forthcoming

U.S. Glasnost: Missing Political Themes in U.S. Media Discourse
Johan Galtung and Richard C. Vincent

Towards Equity in Global Communication: MacBride Report Update
Richard C. Vincent, Kaarle Nordenstreng, and Michael Traber, eds.

Political Economy of Media and Culture in Peripheral Singapore
Kokkeong Wong

RECONVERGENCE

A POLITICAL ECONOMY OF TELECOMMUNICATIONS IN CANADA

DWAYNE WINSECK

CARLETON UNIVERSITY

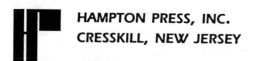

HAMPTON PRESS, INC.
CRESSKILL, NEW JERSEY

Library of Congress Cataloging-in-Publication Data

Winseck, Dwayne Roy, 1964-
    Reconvergence : a political economy of telecommunications in Canada / Dwayne Winseck.
        p.   cm. – (The Hampton Press communication series)
    Includes bibliographical references and indexes.
    ISBN 1-57273-144-3. – ISBN 1-57273-145-1 (pbk.)
    1. Telecommunication–Canada. 2. Telecommunication policy – Canada. 3. Telecommunication–Canada–History. I. Title.
II. Series.
    HE7815.W56 1998
    384'.0971–dc21   98-7414
                                                                  CIP

Hampton Press, Inc.
23 Broadway
Cresskill, NJ 07626

BRIEF CONTENTS

CONTENTS

PREFACE

The time frame of this study, 1846 to 1996, corresponds to the 150-year history of electronic communication in Canada. This study offers a political economic analysis of that history, from the introduction of the telegraph in 1846 by a group of merchants from Hamilton, Niagara Falls, and St. Catherines, to the intense and urgent pressures now emanating from the corporate boardrooms of Canadian telephone companies and online media providers, the corridors of political power in Ottawa, and from citizens, public interest groups, and users across the country, aimed at ushering in and shaping the latest incarnation of electronic communication: information highways.

Whereas much telecommunications-related writing is steeped in the perspectives of engineers, economists, and policy experts, this book links telecoms to a discussion of politics and economics in Canada and to the role of communication in a democratic society. The focus is on how business, government, and people shape technologies into viable media systems that realise some ideals about how communication should serve society while letting others disappear from view.

Thinking about the interaction among telecoms, business, government, and people brings us into the arenas where decisions about *telecoms* policy are made. An historical examination of telecoms policy is essential for understanding the nature of communication in modern societies, providing an enduring record and source of data on telecoms development. Telecoms policy is also a key location where relations among business, government, people, and technologies are structured and the balance between visions of information as either a commodity or a public good contested and inscribed in regulations and laws.

Policy decisions made now will have a crucial impact on future network evolution, adjacent communication services, and the economy as a whole. From an economic point of view, the role of telecoms in the Canadian economy is substantial, representing about 3% of the Gross National Product in the early to mid-1990s compared to about 2.25% in Organisation for Economic Cooperation and Development (OECD) countries (Industry Canada, 1995; Mansell, 1993). Telecoms systems also provide the infrastructure of social communication in countries. Once again, comparative figures show that there is near universal access to basic telephone service and high levels of access to some of the newer communication services in Canada. There are nearly 59 main telephone lines per 100 people in Canada compared to 45 per 100 in the United States and about 43 telephone lines per 100 people in the OECD countries as a whole (OECD, 1995; Stats Can., 1996).

However, the analysis presented in this book suggests that there are several reasons not to be sanguine about the state of telecoms availability in Canada. First, there are cleavages between those who have and do not have access to basic telephone services that closely follow lines of socioeconomic class: for example, whereas 99.9% of the highest income households have basic telephone service, for those below the poverty line the figure is just over 86% (Stats Can., 1994a). Second, disparities in access are more striking for "new media"—cable television, computers, and the Internet. For instance, although computer networking is still a minor, but rapidly growing, area of communication (7.4% of homes have networked computers), differences in access are stark. People with the highest income are nearly seven times as likely to use the Internet from home as those with incomes below $15,000, although important differences are also tied to the presence of children in the house, education levels, and gender (Stats Can., 1996d). Finally, universal service was achieved under different conditions from those that are now taking hold and from when the Canadian Radio-television and Telecommunications Commission (CRTC) and telecoms policy was aimed at expanding universal service as part of public interest objectives. In contrast, recent efforts aim to narrowly tailor the concept as part and parcel of wider efforts to redefine communication and information as commodities.

Although access to communication services is a key consideration in this book, it is not the main aspect in the political economy of telecoms that is pursued. In my view, universality cannot be thought of only in terms of trying to get everybody hardwired to the newest electronic gadgetry. The issues are more profound than this. Although it is important to emphasise the need to uncouple access to communication resources from social and economic inequalities, it is just as crucial to stress the quality of mediated communication, people's ability to participate in the processes that shape new and old means of communication, and that the concepts of universality and communication should remain rooted in the public good factors inherent in information as well as to citizenship and democracy.

Ultimately, these considerations are connected to telecoms policy decisions, who makes them, and for what purposes. Telecoms policy and regulatory analysis focuses on the decisions, choices, and policies that affect the *design, ownership, and control* and *uses* of communication systems. The aim of policy and regulatory analysis is to ask about the representativeness, power, and responsibility of those who act on new communication systems. It is also to draw on the normative ethics of democratic theory that require responsibility and power to be transparent, accountable, legitimate, and otherwise in the public interest. The consistent foregrounding of the links between telecoms, power, and democracy distinguishes this book from others that fail to look historically at where new media come from or how the gap between an invention and its realisation in a functioning system is shaped by political and economic forces bent on ensuring that new media serve some needs and interests better than others.

Whether links between responsibility, accountability, and media development are realised is largely determined by how telecoms policy represents various interests and value positions. A crucial issue is whether telecoms policy mediates and tempers relations of power between institutions, technology, and people or functions to shield the communication industries, technology, and power from critical analysis and competing visions about how communication should be organised and used in society. Which of these prospects prevails depends on whether telecoms policy is guided primarily by an interest in creating/expanding information markets or a normative interest in realising the public good qualities inherent in information and fortifying the historical ties between communication, citizenship, and human rights.

Several chapters discuss how telecoms policy is currently overwhelmed by efforts to expand information markets, create "national champions," and bootstrap citizens into the information age and on to "information highways." It is shown that a corollary of these efforts is the emergence of a strong state driven more by industrial policy concerns than a desire to include citizens in the processes that influence the design of new media in Canada. The strong state is evident in many new Cabinet powers available under the *Telecommunications Act* (1993); unprecedented levels of government intervention *before, during,* and *after* Canadian Radio-television and Telecommunications Commission (CRTC) regulatory hearings; and the consolidation of federal jurisdiction over telecoms, among other things.

As much as new media are the outcome of dynamic technological changes and digitisation, it is an inescapable fact that government *choices* to remove media cross-ownership laws, raise limits on ownership concentration, and subsidise the nascent information infrastructure are fundamentally directing the course of media evolution. In my view, we therefore need to consider the political economy of telecoms policy as well as the legal, organisational, functional, and technical aspects of media reconvergence. Such a perspective illuminates the fact that new media and "information highways" could follow many potential evolutionary trajectories, but that government and industry are busily orienting the new technologies exclusively toward *commercially viable modes of media evolution.*

A key factor structuring the book's contents is the recognition that telecoms policy reform has passed through two quite distinct stages. The first stage, often misnamed deregulation, was mainly driven by large business groups such as the Canadian Banking Association, the Canadian Business Telecommunications Alliance, the Information Technology Alliance of Canada, and so on, who sought competition, a broader range of telecoms services at lower prices, and the removal of telecoms from the public arena, as organised under the auspices of the CRTC. This phase of regulatory liberalisation was primarily directed at achieving change *within* telecoms, and it dominated the regulatory agenda from the late 1970s until the 1990s. Parts of Chapters 1, 2, and 5 analyse these efforts, and they are the chief focus of Chapter 6.

Just as important as these groups' efforts to obtain regulatory liberalisation *within* telecoms were attempts emerging in the mid-1990s to revise regulations, institutional arrangements, and technologies *across* the communication industries as a means of fueling media reconvergence and "information highways." This second prong of telecoms policy reform is as crucial as the first. Rather than being driven mostly by large business user groups, it has been mainly motivated by telecom providers, the computer industries, and, crucially, the Canadian government. All three, especially members of Stentor (a consortium of the main telephone services providers) and the Canadian government, have gone so far as to claim a link between national economic, political, and cultural survival and the rapid development of the information highway.

Of course, such claims are hype. They are also propagandistic in that they obscure the history of media development and sanction the turning over of command and control of media evolution to the State and corporations by appealing to people's fears and well-documented anxieties about the future. *Reconvergence: A Political Economy of Telecommunications in Canada* challenges such claims, perhaps most importantly by revealing the extent to which telecoms networks have always served as platforms for a diverse array of content services. This is made particularly clear in Chapter 3's account of the telegraph and how this system supported the rise of the press and a plethora of "online" services in North America and parts of Europe. The role of telecoms in journalism and information services is shown to have been so extensive as to have caused the Supreme Court of Canada (1882/83) to call for telecoms to be regulated as "electronic publishers," not "common carriers"—a condition that persisted for several decades and was revised only after another bout of regulatory intervention. The history of media divergence—telecoms, publishing, broadcasting—that has shaped our (mis)understanding of modern media is shown to stem from corporate collusion, politics, and regulatory regimes that had little to do with underlying technological considerations.

Chapters 1 and 2 present a descriptive and theoretical overview of media divergence and of the nature and functioning of the communication industries and telecoms policy in general. Details of the media divergence thesis are introduced in Chapters 3, 4, and 5 in which separation of telecoms from the press, online services, and broadcasting is traced not to technological developments but to regulatory interventions, the natural monopoly view of telecoms, corporate covenants, and government actions that, post hoc, legislated media divergence from about the mid-1940s until the 1990s. Just as this history is shown to have created separate media sectors and regulatory traditions, I argue for the need to look at the economic, political, and legal factors leading to reconvergence today.

Chapters 6 and 7 show that new organisational patterns for electronic media are being sought through telecoms policy reform, promotion of strategic rivalry *across* the media, global "free trade" regimes, and advocacy of information highways. While the issues remain unsettled, it is argued that the government's new regulatory regime and commitment to global trade regimes—CUFTA, NAFTA, and WTO— indicate a shift from restricting media reconvergence toward permitting, if not promoting, this aim. At stake are crucial issues about whether telecoms providers should have "media freedoms" akin to the political democratic freedoms of individual citizens, and how answers to this impinge on the evolution of an appropriate network infrastructure, cultural policy, and people's freedom to produce, distribute and consume the "new" online media.

Although the structure of new media has yet to be stabilised, Chapter 7 suggests that there are at least three potential "models" that may come to characterise the "new" online media environment: (a) an expanded "free lunch," mass media version that is subsidised by advertising, service providers' collection of personal information made easier by weak privacy laws, and "stupid" user/network interfaces; (b) a "luxury good" model based around "information *suburbs*"(as opposed to

FOREWORD

VINCENT MOSCO

Over the past 15 years the world has experienced a massive transformation in telecommunications and electronic media. Nowhere has this transformation been more profound and more powerful than in Canada. This is primarily because the commitment to a public service model of telecommunications was widely established in Canada. Specifically, this meant universal access to low-cost and efficient telephone service across the vast Canadian landscape; tens of of thousands of skilled, well-paid, unionized jobs; and a firm government policy that regulated dominant monopoly corporate providers and permitted government ownership in provinces that dominant companies refused to wire for universal service. As Dwayne Winseck skillfully demonstrates in this exhaustive political economy of Canadian telecoms, this public service model was not easily won, nor easily sustained. Building on the work of Dallas Smythe and Robert Babe, Winseck demonstrates that considerable political mobilization was necessary to keep the system focused on serving the public interest. Moreover, the system sometimes tilted overwhelmingly in favor of dominant interests led by Bell Canada and its provincial telephone carriers so that what at times looked like a widely beneficial social contract would at other times appear to be a cosy arrangement for a government-backed national monopoly.

In spite of the problems, the public service model was successfully extended from telecommunications to electronic media with the creation of the Canadian Broadcasting Corporation and with smaller but no less vital institutions like the National Film Board, Telefilm Canada, and the Canada Council. Communication and culture also received institutional support in government with creation of the Ministry of Communication. Canada was a model of balance between public service and private market approaches to electronic media, especially in comparison to the United States. With its anemic public broadcasting system and a telecommunications system run almost entirely by and for AT&T, the United States was for many Canadians the negative inspiration for a uniquely Canadian approach to balance and fairness. Combined with a distinctly Canadian system of universal access to health care, public education, unemployment insurance, old-age pensions, and social welfare, this country become an international model for its ability to sustain a robust welfare state.

But much of this has now changed with the fundamental restructuring of the Canadian political economy. This resulted from intense corporate pressure to cut government spending and streamline social welfare programs, from continental and global trade agreements, and from the creation of a world economy policed by the United States and global trade organizations like the World Trade Organization, the World Bank, and the International Monetary Fund. This has certainly left its mark on the communication sector. With the disappearance of the Department of Communication, curiously just at the time that the dominant discourse invokes the Age of Communication, the policy vacuum has been filled by an Industry Ministry whose mandate is to promote the market in every facet of social life. Industry Canada and the no longer even formally independent regulator, the Canadian Radio-television and Telecommunications Commission, have implemented a strategy that has eliminated most public interest regulation, transferring billions of dollars from residential customers to monopoly telephone companies in order to lower long-distance charges—a demand pressed most forcefully by Canadian and foreign, mainly American, large business users—and made it easier for telecom companies to shed tens of thousands of jobs. Changing regulations, euphemised as a procompetitive strategy, have left the industry with an unregulated monopoly in control of local markets and competition provided in the long-distance markets, not by the hoped for Canadian alternatives but from the branch plants of American giants AT&T and Sprint. The CBC has been cut to the bone and the rest of the national cultural apparatus has also felt the axe. The government waxes triumphant because the federal budget is now balanced. but the social and cultural system that gave Canada its genuine triumphs is in shambles. The health care and public education systems are in crisis and the pressures to privatise mount. A model unemployment security system has been reduced substantially in spite of an unemployment rate consistently in the 8%-10% range. The new Employment Insurance system is a model of Orwellian discourse. As a result of this transformation, many Quebeckers who once leaned in favor of staying within the Canadian federation because the social and economic benefits outweighed the strong call of Quebec nationalism now question the benefit of a united country that has given up on most of the institutions that made it a nation.

In this time of genuine transformation and upheaval, it is more important than ever to have the benefit of scholars who can grasp both the broad sweep of history and complex, fine detail—what the philosopher William James referred to as society's many "coercive facts." In *Reconvergence*, Dwayne Winseck demonstrates that he is such a scholar, someone who possesses what I would like to call, in a variation on C. Wright Mills' description of the model sociologist, *the political economic imagination*. In brief, the political economic imagination is comprised of four characteristics: a sense of history, the social totality, moral philosophy, and praxis.

Winseck treats a topic that is rife with ahistorical accounts. It is safe to say that most treatments of contemporary communication and information technology, afflicted with what the social historian David Nye calls the "technological sublime," regard developments in computers and telecommunications as embodiments not of historical processes but of a break with history, the creation of a new age as different from what came before as the New Testament is from the Old in the Christian Bible. As one of the premier prophets of this new age, Nicholas Negroponte, of MIT's famed Media Lab, announces, where we were once atoms living in physical space, we must now learn to be digital, to live in cyberspace. One of the sacred words of these new age prophets is *convergence*, the technical magic of new technologies coming together in multiple seamless networks that integrate the production, distribution, and reception of digital flows of print, audio, and video material. Among the numerous contributions that he makes to our historical understanding of the transformation in telecommunications, Winseck's historical account of the many convergences and reconvergences that mark the development and application of communication technology in Canada stands out. Convergence is neither natural nor new. It is rather the process of an accumulation of political decisions that brought together and separated numerous communications instruments over the course of history. The coming together of computers and telecommunications today is just the latest version of a specific type of convergence, given form and power by the social choices embodied in the neoliberal business agenda that now governs so much of Canadian society.

Winseck matches this sharp historical sense with an appreciation for the social totality of which choices about telecommunications are one, albeit integral, component. Specifically, this means taking account of the technological, economic, political, social, and indeed cultural milieux out of which specific technologies like the telegraph and telephone emanate and specific forms of convergence emerge. Eschewing the understandable but restrictive tendencies to an instrumentalism that would see forms of convergence resulting solely and simply from the interests of, say, Bell Canada, Winseck is aware that social formations are complex and dynamic, comprised of numerous conflicting forces and tendencies that are positioned all over the social and political map. What emerges from this analysis is a sense of the social whole riven with conflicts and contradictions, at times loosely and at times tightly integrated with changing centers of continental and global power.

The political economic imagination is more than a sense of how to examine social life. It has been imbued, from the time of Adam Smith and Karl Marx, with a clear sense of the need for moral philosophical critique. For Smith, it was the vestiges of feudal social practices and the excesses of capitalist individualism; for Marx, the exploitation of labor and the contradiction between unprecedented wealth accumulated alongside unprecedented squalor. Winseck demonstrates this dimension of the political economic imagination by providing details about the social consequences of Canada's unravelling social contract in telecommunications, charting the gap between what the "communication revolution" has meant for business users operating in Canada (lower rates, customized service) and for residential users who have paid the price in higher rates and reduced regulatory protections so that major banks, mass retailers, and other large users can enjoy a Made-in-America telecommunications. The ultimate irony for average Canadians is that they are left with a system that is arguably less just and fair than even the American. This is because the United States was able to accomplish the breakup of its largest provider, AT&T, thereby severing the link between local and long-distance service providers. Canada has retained its fully integrated telecommunications monopoly, Bell Canada, which remains dominant in local and long-distance markets, and has strengthened the monopoly by providing it with controlling interests in Canadian satellite and global telecom provision. The ironic injustice of a Canadian communication landscape marked more than ever by large monopolies in newspapers (Hollinger), book publishing (Chapters), cable (Rogers), and other media amid all the rhetoric about competitive market forces is not lost on Winseck.

Finally, Winseck has a strong sense of praxis, of the recognition that research and social intervention are intimately connected so that research is not simply the task of describing the world but of pointing the way to changing it. Winseck does this by chronicling the interventions of public interest and social advocacy groups who have tried, with occasional success, to slow or even constrain the seemingly inevitable march to a transformation in telecommunications. Moreover, he provides us with detailed policy recommendations that would guide the return to a distinctively Canadian communication system. In this respect, Winseck provides perhaps his best service, not only suggesting entry points for genuine social intervention but inspiring us to believe, even in these times when the climate for democracy is as cold as an Ottawa winter, that it is more that worth the effort.

1 INTRODUCTION TO THE HISTORY AND POLITICAL ECONOMY OF TELECOMS AND MEDIA RECONVERGENCE

INTRODUCTION

This book takes a broad look at telecoms. In my view, the topic is vital in an era in which discussions of media convergence around some form of integrated networks are widespread, popular imaginations of 'information highways' abound, and quite massive changes in the nature of telecoms policy often proceed along fixed ideological lines with little consideration to the breadth of issues involved.

This chapter begins by defining telecoms, discusses why this is an important area to study, and identifies some of the issues addressed by telecoms policy. The next section introduces several key historical concepts found in the telecoms literature: common carriage, natural monopoly, universal service, and different approaches to setting prices. The section indicates that although telecoms are often thought of in narrow technological and economic terms, it is an area pregnant with issues relating to power, politics, and democracy. I suggest that these factors have shaped the history of telecoms in Canada and elsewhere and continue to do so in the emerging contexts of network convergence, "information highways," and regulatory liberalisation.

THE SOCIAL AND ECONOMIC SIGNIFICANCE OF TELECOMS

Telecoms are wire- or radio-based communication networks that carry information—regardless of whether that information is voice, data, television, computer-enhanced services, and so on—from one point to another without editorial intervention. From telegraphs to broadband communication networks, telecoms have provided essential infrastructures for commerce, administration, the mass media, and communicative interaction between people separated by time and space. The centrality of even simple technologies to Canadian social life has been underscored across the century, as Canadians have consistently been among the world's most extensive users of the telephone.

Canada offers an excellent opportunity for studying telecoms, providing a record of how interactions among technology, economics, and government policy over the last 150 years have been consistently and deliberately guided to produce one of the most ubiquitous electronic communication systems in the world. Telecoms are the cornerstone of this system, providing telephone and more advanced services to 99% of Canadian homes, a rate higher than the United States (94%) and equaled only by Sweden and Norway. As a point-to-point, two-way communication system, telecoms are important supplements to pervasive patterns of mass-mediated communications delivered to 72.4% of Canadian homes by cable television systems and to 99% of the population by conventional over-the-air television (Industry Canada, 1995, p. 1). They also support more recent forms of electronic communication, most notably the Internet.

As a distinct economic sector, the communication industries are a central dimension of national economies. The communication industries—telecoms, computers, and broadcasting (cable and over-the-air)—account for approximately 6% of the gross domestic product (GDP), have annual revenues of approximately $33 billion (cnd), and employ 258,000 people. Economic growth in computers (7%) and telecoms (8.8%) is significantly higher than in the rest of the economy (5%). Telecoms are the most significant segment of the communication industries. They are nearly two and a half times as large as the computer, broadcasting, and cable sectors combined, contribute 3% to GDP, have revenues of $16.5 billion, and employ 126,000 people (Industry Canada, 1994a, pp. 3-10; 1995, pp. 1-4). Because of such facts, telecoms have surged to the top of economic policy agendas.

Telecoms policy is more than just another aspect of industrial policy, however. Telecoms have a significance that goes beyond the economic because of the historical relationship between communication and democracy, a status reflected in, for example, the second clause of the Canadian *Charter of Human Rights*, the First Amendment to the *United States Constitution*, Article 10 of the *European Convention on Human Rights*, and Article 19 of the United Nation's (1948) *Universal Declaration of Human Rights*. Telecoms policy builds on these values by, for example, promoting increased access to communications media and reasonable prices. Another regulatory concept, *common carriage*, prevents telecoms providers from exerting influence or editorial control over the content/messages flowing through their networks, a requirement that erects a defence against government or corporate censorship (Noam, 1994). The aim of common carriage is to sever mediated communication from the potentially distorting influence of ownership and control, a point unique to telecoms that is returned to often in this volume.

By mediating relationships among technology, industry, and society, policy stamps its imprint on the evolution of telecoms networks. Telecoms policy has traceable consequences for:

- who pays what for monthly telephone service
- the structure of the communications industries
- the relationship between information distribution and content production
- the rate of technological innovation and implementation
- the division of regulatory and policymaking powers among different levels of governments
- the balance between economic imperatives and social needs
- the balance between citizens' and corporate rights to freedom of expression
- the scope of universal service

Despite the eclipse of the "natural monopoly" concept and the onslaught of regulatory liberalisation, telecoms policy is as consequential as ever. Stentor's[1] proposal to eliminate measures preventing telcos from delivering information and video services in return for commitments to develop integrated broadband networks (IBNs), or so-called "information highways" is an example of this point, and is discussed repeatedly throughout this volume. This confronts the Canadian Radio-television and Telecommunications Commission (CRTC) with the option of using regulatory policy to *prevent, permit* or *promote* these far reaching proposals (Elton, 1992, p. 382). Although each choice entails a different degree of regulatory involvement, none eliminate the regulator or government's role in making policy decisions that will affect telecoms for years to come.

MAJOR PLAYERS IN CANADIAN TELECOMS

Most of the 61 telecoms carriers in Canada are privately owned and regulated by the federal regulatory agency, the CRTC. The Manitoba Telephone Service (MTS), Saskatchewan Telephones (SaskTel), and the Thunder Bay Telephone Company remain as reminders of an earlier era when public ownership and provincial or even municipal regulation was a more prominent feature of the telecoms landscape in Canada. The

Telecommunications Act (1993) and recent court decisions have brought these companies and independent telcos under federal jurisdiction and, hence, the regulatory authority of the CRTC. These independent telcos have been crucial forces in realising the goal of universal service by providing services to remote and rural areas found unprofitable by the members of Stentor or would-be competitors. The main providers and general conditions of the telecoms industry are outlined in Table 1.1.

As Table 1.1 indicates, despite the diverse number of companies in the Canadian telecoms industry, control over the telecoms system (77.2%) mainly rests with the 10 members of the Stentor consortium. Even within this consortium, the industry is very concentrated, with Bell Canada accounting for almost 44% of the entire industry's revenues. To the extent that competition exists within telecoms, it is mainly on the margins with a small number of competitive long distance suppliers (AT&T/Unitel, Sprint Canada, Westel, Telroute) and a large number of resellers[2] recently permitted entry by a series of CRTC decisions (CRTC, 1990, 1992a). Competitors garner only about 10% to 15% of telecoms revenues, although this may increase as the effect of the CRTC decisions mentioned earlier take root.

For much of this century, the telecoms industries in Canada have been governed by their status as *common carriers*, a belief that telecoms were *natural monopolies*, and *public interest-oriented regulation* by a semi-autonomous regulatory agency (now the CRTC). These factors have left an indelible imprint on the evolution of telecoms and continue to set the baseline for discussions about the future of the industry, the role of policy, and the contributions telecoms can make to economic welfare, social interaction, and democratic communication. The next sections survey these principles and consider their future viability.

THE COMMON-CARRIER CONCEPT

The *Railway Act* (the guiding legislation for telecoms in Canada from 1906 until 1993) and the *Telecommunications Act* (1993) define telecoms as point-to-point communication systems offering carriage to all forms of information. These definitions distinguish telecoms from other forms of electronic communication in two important ways. First, the emphasis on point-to-point communication distinguishes telecoms from electronic mass media which distribute messages from one point to a large number of receivers—the so-called mass audience. Second, telecoms rest on the separation of carrier and content supply functions, unlike the electronic mass media. This separation is known as the *common-carrier principle*.

The idea that common carriage should apply to telecoms did not automatically apply to the first technological innovations in the field. Courts in North America were reluctant to apply the common-carrier principle to telegraphy because information and communication were intangible and thus not encompassed by the idea of services assumed by definitions of common carriage (Baxter vs. Dominion Telegraph Co., 1874/1875). The Supreme Court of Canada in *Dominion Telegraph Co. v. Silver et al.* (1882/1883) also found that telecoms and the press should be regulated by the same laws. This changed in the first decade of the 20th century, however, in response to complaints by news agencies that some telegraph companies were charging discriminatory rates between their own wire services and those of others (Babe, 1990, Board of Railway Commissioners, 1910; Nichols, 1948). As chapter 3 shows, the history of Canadian telecoms has oscillated between common carriage (1846-1870), a hybrid electronic publishing/common-carriage model (1870-1910), common carriage (1910-1994),[3] and back to a hybrid electronic publishing/common-carriage/broadcasting model at present.

The view of telephone systems as common carriers evolved piecemeal through regulatory interpretations of the *Railway Act*, amendments to this Act, and changes to the laws governing major telecoms providers in Canada such as Bell Canada and BC Tel. Until recently, the common-carrier concept prevented carriers from influencing the messages flowing through their networks and required them to offer *nondiscriminatory access* to their system on the basis of "*just and reasonable*" rates (Canada, 1979, s. 320; 1993a, s. 33). In return, policies and laws limited carriers' liability for messages communicated through their networks (Canada, 1979, s. 381; Department of Communication, 1971a). As section 5 of the *Bell Canada Act* unequivocally states, the company "shall neither control the contents nor influence the meaning or purpose of the message emitted, transmitted or received" nor "be the holder of a broadcast licence" (Canada, 1968, p. 46). The *Telecommunications Act* (1993) extends these provisions to all carriers under federal jurisdiction, although it allows the CRTC to grant waivers to such a policy—an issue discussed further later (Canada, 1993a, s. 36).

According to Noam (1994), such policies created a communications system that is decidedly different from the mass media. Access to the mass media is discretionary, with the conditions of access governed, for the most part, by private contracts and responsibility for content enforced through libel, indecency, and slander laws. According to some critics, under these conditions media freedoms belong to those who own the media because citizens' access to the media is entirely dependent on owners' discretion (although this "freedom" is qualified by the cultural-policy orientation of the broadcast regulatory regime, public access cable channels, and a minimal right of public access to over-the-air broadcast facilities) (CRTC, 1971a, pp. 16-19; Juneau, 1972). In contrast, the common-carrier principle prevents private arrogation of freedom of expression by erecting barriers to censorship by the state and private interests. Table 1.2 presents the differences between the competing network access regimes for telecoms and the electronic mass media.

Table 1.2. Electronic Media: Common Carriage versus Contract Carriage.

Comparative Focal Points	Telecoms	Electronic Mass Media
Type of Communication	Point to Point	Point to Multipoint
Direction of Communication	Two-way and interactive	One-way and relatively passive
Network Architecture	Switched and Narrowband	Unswitched and broadband
Focus of Regulation	Structure	Structure and Content
Policy Goals	Economic welfare, social interaction, free flow of information	Cultural identity, national sovereignty and freedom of expression
Justification for Regulation	Natural Monopoly	Spectrum Scarcity
Network Access	Nondiscriminatory, common carrier	Discretionary, private contracts
Financing	Regulated tariffs	Advertising and some user fees
Carrier Responsibility for Message	Limited	Libel, slander, etc.

THE NATURAL MONOPOLY CONCEPT

Historical Origins

The natural monopoly view stemmed from the observation that in most countries, or regions within a country, one firm controlled the supply of telecoms services, from the manufacture of equipment to the telephone in people's homes. Yet, as Chapter 4 shows, competitive and independent telephone systems thrived from about 1893 until 1920. It was only after a series of efforts to establish dominance within telecoms and several regulatory decisions after 1915 that the Bell Telephone Company of Canada and six other telcos were able to consolidate control over the industry (Board of Railway Commissioners, 1916a). Thereafter, the theory of natural monopoly became unassailable in telecoms policy circles. The main explanations for this exceptional view was that the *underlying technical characteristics* of telecoms inexorably lead to "*natural market failure*" (Wilson, 1992, p. 348; emphasis added).

According to Babe (1990), three arguments supported the idea that telecoms were unable to sustain a competitive industry structure: economies of scale, the need for systems-wide cross-subsidies to bring about universal service, and systems integrity. The high cost of constructing universal telecoms networks created enormous economic barriers to market entry. Besides, it was thought inefficient to duplicate networks, especially because economies of scale meant that extending existing networks to embrace additional subscribers was cheaper than reaching these same people through the construction of competing networks. Thus, a single network served the public interest because the declining cost of serving additional subscribers meant that total average costs for all subscribers would decline. This also enhanced the value of the telecoms network for all users, as additional subscribers were potential communicative partners for everyone else connected to the network. As a framework for harmonising divergent interests, the natural monopoly concept appeared to be a good one.

The final, major argument supporting the natural monopoly concept was that of systems integrity. According to the telcos, the complex technical nature of the technologies involved, and the importance of uninterrupted telecoms services to the public, required unified, end-to-end control of the network by one company. Representatives of Bell Canada put the case at Senate hearings this way:

> [t]he company feels very strongly that it should have complete control over the system, firstly in order to protect the equipment . . ., and, secondly, in order to make sure that the fringe operations, which sometimes can become the most lucrative operations, are not taken away from it to the detriment of the subscriber. (Canada, Standing Committee on Transport and Communications, House of Commons, 1967, p. 66)

Bell had put forth similar arguments since at least 1905 (Canada, Mulock Committee, 1905, p. 622) in its unending efforts to cloak the monopolistic structure of the telecoms industry in a shroud of technological necessity.

Another strategy was to present the possibility of competition as unfair, in the sense that competitors would only enter the most profitable areas—a process known as "cream-skimming"—thereby undercutting the telcos' ability to use revenues from these areas to subsidise unprofitable rural and remote areas. Once again, natural monopoly aligned the telcos with the public interest through recourse to the goal of universal service. Yet, as Babe (1990) observes, the position ignored the independent telcos—about 1,400 in 1915—who drew their existence from Bell and the other large telcos' failure to serve remote areas.

Strategic Interests and the Division of the Communication Industries

Critics argue that the natural monopoly explanation is historically inadequate and based on reasons that are neither necessary nor of the magnitude claimed. Even recent studies commissioned by the CRTC have been unable to *conclusively* determine if natural monopoly conditions prevail in telecoms (1992a, pp. 18-40). Other studies suggest that corporate size in telecoms has not led to innovation and universal service but to efforts to snuff out new technologies and competitors threatening the monopoly/oligopoly network operators (Babe, 1990; Davis, 1994; Mansell, 1993; Schultz & Janisch, 1993).

In contrast to natural monopoly explanations, it is necessary to consider how the entire communications system has been historically shaped through extensive struggles among civic associations, labour unions, farmers, independent telephone companies, large corporations, and government agencies. One intense period in telecoms politics coincided with the flourishing of competitive and independent telcos (circa 1893-1920), briefly described earlier, and drew its energies from the fact that the institutional organisation of the communications industries was still undetermined and up for grabs.

This quickly abated once control in the communication industries was consolidated on the basis of powerful ties between the media industries and the Canadian government, and between the Canadian communications system and its U.S. counterpart. Besides adopting the natural monopoly concept as the cornerstone of telecoms policy, the most significant outcome of this historical period was the segregation of North American communication industries among telephony, telegraphy, publishing, and broadcasting. This was not due to technical requirements of different media, but to struggles for dominance in subsectors of the communications field involving skirmishes over patents, restrictive covenants, and the subsequent legal frameworks that protected these exercises of corporate power.[4] One key record of this history is the 1926 *Consent Agreement*, which resulted in, among other things, AT&T leaving broadcasting and telegraphy in return for promises from General Electric, Western Union, Westinghouse, Zenith, and RCA to stay clear of the telephone business (United States Senate, 1926, p. 5480).[5] Given the early integration of the Canadian communications industries into that of the United States through ownership, extensive patent agreements, and corporate director interlocks, a similar situation came to define conditions in Canada.

As Babe stresses, the division of the communications industries and separate legal regimes developed for each thereafter resulted from

> collusive and restrictive covenants on the part of Canadian [and US communication] firms, certainly not from either a general principle that content should be separated from carriage or the premise that broadcasting and telephony used radically different types of apparatus. . . . In fact, the opposite was the case: the two fields diverged through corporate agreement. (1990, p. 205)

Without these practices, the issue of media convergence now so prominent might have been settled in the 1920s and 1930s instead of the 1990s: The Bell Telephone Company might have developed on its early trials with radio to become not only the dominant telephone company in Canada but also the largest commercial broadcaster. For their part, policymakers duly noted that these dealings violated anti-trust laws, then adopted them as the basis for the United States' *Communications Act of 1934* and, in Canada, to continue separately regulating telecoms under the *Railway Act* and broadcasting through a series of legislation leading up to the *Broadcasting Act of 1991*.

By the end of the 1920s the natural monopoly concept underpinned the position of the major telephone companies *within* telecoms while corporate agreements secured their positions *across* the divided communications industries. But, could such arrangements last, especially in the face of an onslaught of technological innovations such as cable television? The short answer is yes, until a more compelling alignment of strategic interests was constructed! That compelling alignment of interests is taking shape now, amid the experimental use of new technologies such as the Internet and jostling amid strategic interests over institutional boundaries and telecoms policies that will govern the convergence of IBNs, ownership and control of the emerging networks, and conditions for offering services on the so-called "information highways." This is discussed later and in detail in the latter half of the book.

In the 60- to 70-year span between segregation of the communications field and the current period of reconvergence, a penumbra of policies inhibited media convergence, cross-media ownership, and the delivery of information services that seemed to cross imaginary technological boundaries. The CRTC regularly put forth policy statements and decisions disallowing telcos from holding a cable television licence, preventing the undue reliance of cable television systems on the telcos, and hindering efforts by the publicly owned provincial telecoms companies, SaskTel and MTS, to provide cable television services (CRTC, 1969; 1976a; 1977a). In addition, Parliament amended the *Bell Canada Act* (1968) to prohibit the telco from exercising editorial influence over information flowing through its network or holding a broadcasting license (Canada, 1968, s. 5). Although digitisation, computerisation, and visions of "wired cities" animated public discourse about communication during the late 1960s and 1970s, barriers between the media industries were not being eroded, but reinforced! The telcos acquiesced willingly. As Bell chairperson A. J. de Grandpré stated, the company did not want to be a broadcaster, cable television operator, or "to control in any way the contents of the message . . . . [T]he telephone companies wanted to be common-carriers, pure and simple . . . (Canada, Standing Committee on Transport and Communications, House of Commons, 1967, p. 65).[6] Chapter 5 shows that Bell not only acquiesced to regulatory reinforcements of the maginot line but actively enforced the lines itself by prohibiting cable systems leasing its facilities "from offering any . . . network or point-to-point communications" (CRTC, 1977a, p. 71).

Faced with the option of preventing, permitting, or promoting network convergence, most institutional actors involved in telecoms policy chose the first option: There were to be no breaches in the regulatory walls separating electronic communications media. The parallels between these actions shaping network convergence and broadband communications from the 1960s until quite recently and the earlier efforts to stabilise the institutional boundaries between telecoms and the then-new technologies of broadcasting could not be more striking.

THE STATE, TELECOMS POLICY, AND RECONCILING COMPETING INTERESTS

The natural monopoly concept *within* telecoms, and government-sanctioned corporate agreements structuring institutional arrangements *across* the communications industries, meant that any remaining role for communication markets was purely residual. In the place of communication markets there developed the concept of public-interest based regulated industries.[7] Whether publicly or privately owned, Canadian telcos across the country were brought under the supervision of provincial or federal regulatory agencies. In Manitoba, MTS was supervised by the provincial Public Utilities Commission after 1912; in Saskatchewan, SaskTel came under the oversight of the government of the day. In those areas under federal jurisdiction, companies such as Bell and BC Tel[8] fell under the regulatory authority of, first, the Board of Railway Commissioners (BRC), followed by the Canadian Transport Commission (CTC), and finally the CRTC after 1976.

More important than who regulated who is that the transition from competitive telephone systems to the monopoly provision of telecoms services early in the 20th century dissolved the possibility for the industry to claim that communication markets could adequately represent the public interest. According to classical economic theory, competitive markets accomplish two things: efficient allocation of economic resources as well as fair access to goods and services. The natural monopoly concept displaced both goals. As Macpherson (1985) explains,

> with the twentieth-century decline of competition the market could no longer claim exemption from non-market ethical standards . . . . Moreover, the state, which now shares the allocative function [of markets], must, in so far as it is a democratic state, claim that its . . . policies are based on the public interest. (p. 15)

Within the context of telecoms, the state stepped into the regulatory and ethical void created by "market failure" through the use of policies designed to secure what markets no longer could: efficiency, social justice, and the public interest. This was done through the common-carrier principle, rate regulation, universal service goals, and balancing citizens' and corporate rights to freedom of communication. Although in some way these measures did check potential abuses of monopoly power, they also raised the spectre of an economic and/or legitimation crisis (Habermas, 1975) as the state became torn between promoting economic accumulation versus using telecoms policy to expand citizen's rights. This placed tensions between economic rights and human rights at the heart of telecoms policy. Should telecoms policy secure the economic value of information or serve as an instrument for expanding the concept of democratic communication? Irresolvable in theory, the tension is preserved in the transient balancing of interests and rights obtained through the politics and power relations endemic to telecoms policy. This point is illuminated later in reference to three key areas of telecoms policy: pricing, universal service obligations, and the concept of "freedom of expression" that held sway in media policy in the 1970s and into the 1980s.

Telecoms Pricing Policy: Myths, Class, and Power

One of the most salient issues in telecoms policy is pricing. It is also one of the most complex areas, in which extensive political issues are easily obscured by economic and scientific models designed to distribute costs across various users and to promote competing policy ends such as universal service, growth in the electronic services industry, and international competitiveness.

Telecoms policy has conventionally employed "rate of return" regulation to set monopoly telecoms operator's (TO's) profits in the absence of competition. Ideally, rate setting by regulators balanced the interests of the TOs in a reasonable profit and users' interests in, and legislative requirements for, "just and reasonably" priced telecoms services. Of course, these competing interests, and the fact that what was "just and reasonable" was a malleable concept, meant that rate setting was inherently political. Many also claimed that "rate of profit" regulation contains incentives for telecoms companies to "gold plate" their networks because they can easily pass the costs of doing so through regulators and onto users. Yet, it is also true that regulators did supervise construction plans to avoid overbilling and to ensure that network construction was reasonably balanced across geographical and economic zones. The aim was to avoid exacerbating geographic and class divisions.

Currently, rate-of-profit regulation is being replaced by "price cap"[9] regulation. Price caps are positively perceived by many regulators and TOs because they allow the TOs some flexibility in setting prices across a range of services, so long as they do not surpass the "ceiling price" for the whole "basket of communication services" covered by the price-cap plan. Several issues are important here: The main concern relates to the size of telcos' profits under this regulatory regime verses the rate-of-profit regime, how broadly the "basket of services" is defined, how stringent the "price-cap ceiling" is in relation to the consumer price index (CPI), the effects of price-cap regulation on network investment, the ability of TOs to assign high prices to services in the basket where competition is weak and demand inelastic (e.g., local service where research shows an insensitivity to price changes), and low prices to services where competition is strong and price elasticity high.

Price-cap regulation has been welcomed by the TOs, especially because their profits have risen from 8% to 12% under rate-of-profit regulation to between 15% and 20% during the transition to the price-cap regime to be implemented in 1998 (*Globe and Mail Report on Business,* 1996, p. 162; Industry Canada, 1995, p. 4). Despite this benefit, the price-cap approach pits the telcos, who have an interest in narrowly defined "service baskets," against users and those interested in social justice, who seek broader definitions. Also, price caps contain incentives to reduce investment in network development and to reduce the workforce in order to increase profits for shareholders, setting the interests of telecoms workers against those of the companies (Carsberg, 1987; Hills, 1991, p. 8). Thus, in contrast to efforts to harmonise competing interests under rate-of-profit regulation, price caps contribute to a complex system of class conflict. In contrast to much of the literature on deregulation, this *expands the role of the state*, as regulators such as the CRTC become embroiled in the mediation of conflict through the telecoms policy process.

The complexity of pricing policy issues is made all the greater by the range of "subsidy myths" in popular circulation. At one end of the spectrum is the widespread argument that there has historically been a cross-subsidy from long-distance services to local services. The effect of this subsidy was/is to artificially inflate the price of long-distance services and underprice local services, which was, in effect, a hidden income transfer from business users dependent on long-distance communications to local users. On the other hand, William Melody argues that the subsidy was the other way around. Melody claims that networks were built to the exacting demands of heavy-volume users for data communications and to access long-distance networks, regardless of whether residential users required these capabilities. Because local users were paying for "gold-plated" network designs that outstripped their requirements they were subsidising big business (Melody, 1982, cited in National Anti-Poverty Organization, 1987). The elaborate nature of the evidence and models underlying both conclusions leads some to conclude that the economic theories used to justify pricing decisions are "fairy tales" reflecting and serving the balance of power prevailing in policy circles at any given point in time (Rideout & Mosco, 1997).

Other important issues in telecoms pricing are emerging as regulators revisit the controversy between flat-rate and measured-service pricing. Flat-rate pricing sets fees for a period of service irrespective of telecoms facilities usage, whereas measured service is charged according to how much one uses communication facilities. Because it is insensitive to usage, flat-rate pricing is thought to encourage communication and thus to enhance social interaction and further goals of democratic communication. Furthermore, flat-rate pricing may spur the development of electronic network services because large amounts of time and vast fluctuations in the volumes of information involved in a telephone conversation, the delivery of a large document or a video feed, can easily outstrip small users' ability to pay when charged on a volume sensitive basis (Connell, 1994, p. 244). Recently, local users and network service providers in Germany derided substantial local rate increases, claiming this would dampen the growth of electronic network services dependent on local network access points.

Universal Service

Pricing policy is closely linked with universal service goals. Universal service is often claimed to be one of the most important objectives of telecoms policy—historically, politically, and in terms of the legitimacy of the regulatory framework. The basic goal of universal service is to allow all people access to broadcasting, telephone, and more advanced network technologies. In Canada, these objectives have historically been pursued through provisions in the *Railway Act*, which required all telephone rates to be "just and reasonable" and "not unjustly discriminatory or unduly preferential" (Canada, 1979, sec. 320). Similar clauses are included in the new *Telecommunications Act* (1993).

Universal service is influenced by available communication technologies, social and political factors, and assumptions in the theory and praxis of democracy prevailing during any point in time. The concept is derived from premises in democratic theory that link access to information to effective citizenship. Over time, universal service has expanded from concerns with literacy to include education, access to libraries and government information, and broadcasting and telecoms. Universality underpins *representational aspects* of democracy by providing access to broadcasting agencies who, at least in theory, function on behalf of citizens (e.g., "fourth estate" notions). Moreover, universality contributes to *participatory dimensions* of democracy, as telecoms networks facilitate communicative interaction within civil society, bypassing representative/mediated channels of bureaucratic public service and commercial media (such as the CBC and commercial media such as CanWest and CTV networks in Canada). As Hills (1993a) notes,

> democratising telecommunications can play a part in facilitating the interchange of information between citizens. It is no coincidence that where civil and political rights have been denied, although . . . centralised broadcasting systems used for propaganda have been well developed, . . . telecommunications have remained undeveloped . . . . Telecommunications enable citizens within a democracy to receive information on which to determine their . . . political interests and the right to communicate and join with others to further their interests. (pp. 21-23)

The centrality of universal service to Canadian telecoms policy has extended telecoms services to 98.7% of the population, one of the highest rates in the world. However, more detailed analysis reveals that only 86% of people below the poverty line ($10,000) have telephone service and that universal service remains an elusive goal with respect to long-distance service, cable television, computers, and computer networking (Statistics Canada, 1994c, Table 3; 1996f, Table 1). As the comparative analysis of access to media technologies and services presented in Figure 1.1 suggests, divisions between "information rich" and "information poor" closely parallel income distribution in the country.

As broader changes in the Canadian economy eliminate the historical tendency for income gaps to narrow (Love & Poulin, 1991, pp. 4.1-4.11), and an expanding range of telecoms network services become available, important questions arise about the future of universal service. Given these trends and the longstanding commitment of critical communication researchers to democratic communication, a key issue in research and public policy proceedings is how universal service should be defined. Those most concerned about the growing gaps between the "information rich" and the "information poor" argue for an expansive definition of universal service, that is, one that encompasses convergence between computers and telecoms, whereas most policymakers and participants in the communication industries argue for narrowing the concept (Bangemann, 1994; CRTC, 1994a, pp. 133-138; NAPO, 1987; Norman, 1995, p. 2; Rideout & Mosco, 1997). Current trends in telecoms policy point toward a significant narrowing of the concept. The CRTC narrowed the concept of universal service in its long-distance competition decision and in a subsequent decision in which it adopted the Bell Canada-inspired redefinition of "basic" services as "utility" services (CRTC, 1992a, 1994a, pp. 133-138).[10] Elsewhere, German communication ministers announced that citizens should understand universal service as a very narrow concept and not as "a luxury system" (Norman, 1995, p. 2). The European Union's *Bangemann Report* (1994) on the information society makes a similar point.

Of course, proponents of such measures would not agree that they are aiming to narrow the range of communication services available to citizens. Rather, regulatory policy is seen as objectively drawing lines between *basic services* that fall under regulatory jurisdiction and other *value-added* services that are subject to market regulation.[11] Yet, as Mansell (1988) notes, "such distinctions are static and arbitrary" (p. 245). The basic controversy is whether universal service "should be extended to newer services," not where regulatory lines should be drawn on the basis of supposed technical considerations. The crucial point is that all communication services "add value" (p. 246), and policymakers are in the business of deciding just how much of that value citizens will receive, at what cost, and under what terms.[12] Services defined as "value-added," and thus falling outside the scope of universal service obligations, are made available primarily on a "pay-per" basis, thus directly linking access to information to income (Mosco, 1989).

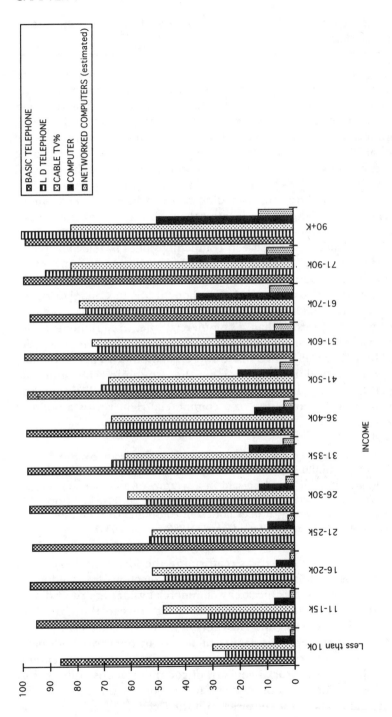

Figure 1.1. Universal service measures for communication technologies in Canada (1995)

Source: Statistics Canada (1994c, 1996f)

Freedom of Expression, the Economic Value of Information, and the Crisis of Democracy

As the earlier discussion of pricing and universal service indicates, telecoms policy remains captive to cross-cutting pressures to realise the economic value of information versus efforts to expand the historical link between communications and democracy. Despite being riddled with such conflicts, the natural monopoly-based telecoms policy regime did partially harmonise the interests of monopoly TOs, labour unions, large users, and citizens. Furthermore, the common-carrier policy, CRTC restrictions on cable/telco cross-ownership, and prohibitions against Bell and other telcos holding a broadcasting or cable licence staked out an ambitious concept of the public interest that constrained the concept of information/communication as a commodity.

The balance struck between competing values by telecoms policy reflected more general shifts in the Canadian political economy, other areas of media policy, and the courts. Indicative of more general trends in how communications issues were being thought about, Canadian courts continued into the 1980s to reaffirm freedom of expression as a political right of citizenship, rather than a commercial one. In arguments about the relationship between competing values in communications policy, the Ontario High Court of Justice made two crucial points. First, the court declared that in "a democratic society the economic realm must be subordinate to the political realm." Second, the court distinguished between freedom of expression as a commercial right versus a political and civil right, stating:

> Pure commercial speech says nothing about how people are governed, or how they should govern themselves. Indeed, it stands outside of public discourse: it could be said in a tyranny or a democracy, a monarchy or a society without a government at all. Providing no support to a democracy, it does not claim constitutional protection. (Klein and Law Society of Upper Canada, 1985, pp. 523, 534)

Essentially, the court was reaffirming the idea that there are a hierarchy of values covered by Constitutional protections for freedom of expression, and that in this hierarchy commercial values are subordinate to political and civil ones. Similarly, in an address to the Canadian Association of Broadcasters, the chairperson of the CRTC, Pierre Juneau (1972) stated that when the rights of media owners to freedom of expression came into conflict with those of citizens, the latter should prevail. For Juneau, the crucial concern of communications policy has to be with "the freedom of people, that's the important principle that we have been talking about for centuries, not the freedom of opinion of the owners of the transmitters and their small group of employees" (p. 47). Although neither of these examples, nor any other 'freedom of expression' case law in Canada, explicitly references telecoms policy, their ranking of speech rights is consistent with the balancing of interests achieved through the common-carrier principle, that is, the subordination of telcos' editorial discretion to the rights of those whose information is carried over telecoms networks.[13] Current trends toward removing regulatory and legislative restrictions on network reconvergence suggests that the link among telcos, the common-carrier principle, and freedom of expression is poised to become a major issue in telecoms policy. For now, we can note that by the 1980s, communications policy—through pricing, universal service obligations, and the balancing of freedom of expression values—had moved from the theoretical possibility of the state stepping in to fill the ethical void opened by "natural market failures" early in the century toward an expansive conception of citizens' communication rights in practice.

For some, the inclination of telecoms policy toward political and civil rights suggested that it had been diverted from its original mission toward a far more expansive social policy agenda. As the Canadian communications policy analysts Richard Schultz and Hudson Janisch (1993) argue, telecoms policy departed from limiting potential abuses by monopoly TOs, "to pursue a wider political agenda through regulatory means" (p. 9). As a result, markets were seen to be overrun by political and bureaucratic considerations, and the benefits of new telecoms technologies as not being passed on to major users and the economy as a whole. This was particularly problematic in the context of long-term declining rates of growth for the Canadian economy. In contrast to a decline in rates of economic growth from about 6% during the 1950s and 1960s to 3% or less from the mid-1970s onwards, the information and communications sectors, except broadcasting, were growing at a rate of around 8% per annum (Industry Canada, 1995, pp. 1-4; Magdoff, 1992, p. 48). Coupled with the thesis that industrially based economies were being transformed into information economies, these rates of growth suggested that the social policy orientation of telecoms policy might be hindering economic recovery.

From a different perspective, Macpherson (1985) argues that what was really at stake was a trade off of civil and political rights for promises of renewed economic growth. In order to reinstate the priority of economic objectives, state policies needed to be depoliticised and disconnected from their normative roots and the acquiescence of citizens to this narrowing of the political sphere obtained through promises of higher material standards of living (Habermas, 1975). With respect to telecoms, it meant stripping communication of its public interest connotations and links to theories of democracy.

REGULATORY LIBERALISATION, RECONVERGENCE, AND REINSTATING THE ECONOMIC VALUE OF INFORMATION

During the 1980s and 1990s the boundaries of state action and telecoms policy have been redrawn to expand the role of information/communication markets, rebalance the prices of telecoms services for large and small users, ensure that competition works, and to enforce a narrow concept of the public interest. These processes of regulatory liberalisation began in Canada in earnest in the 1980s, with the goal of removing services from the natural monopoly framework and public interest-oriented regulation. As the decade progressed, the CRTC allowed private lines used to supply competitive data services to be interconnected with the telecoms network, completely eliminated the telcos' monopoly over equipment attached to the network, adopted distinctions between basic and enhanced services that limited the scope of monopoly services while expanding competitive markets, and accepted the principle of long-distance competition (CRTC, 1979, 1982a, 1984, 1985). The Commission extended this approach during the 1990s by allowing resellers to offer local and long-distance services, approving facilities-based competition in local and long-distance telephone service, and adopting a new regulatory framework (CRTC, 1990, 1992a, 1994a). By the mid-1990s, these actions had created one of the most competitive-oriented telecoms systems in the world, at least in theory if not in practice.

A corollary of expanded communication markets is the narrowing of universal service and public interest concepts. For its part, as noted earlier, the CRTC restruck the balance between economic imperatives and civic values by redefining "basic services" as "utility services" and by promoting distinctions between these and "enhanced" services. The telecoms sections of the NAFTA and the World Trade Organisation's General Agreement on Trade in Services (GATS) adopt similar distinctions. As a result, there are a paucity of regulated basic/utility services, on the one hand, and an expansive range of enhanced "information age" services delivered on the basis of commercial transactions, on the other, such as e-mail, voice mail, electronic data bases, Internet access, electronic newspapers, and video-on-demand (Canada, 1992; CRTC, 1994a, pp. 133-138; TNC, 1993). These distinctions remove new media and "enhanced services" from the scope of public interest-based regulation and ultimately contribute to a condition in which, as Richard Schultz and Hudson Janisch (1993) suggest, "social policy concerns largely disappear from the forefront of public debate" (p. 9).

Such attempts to depoliticise and narrow the scope of telecoms policy are often confused with deregulation—the reduction/elimination of regulations and laws governing the sector. For supporters of these initiatives, deregulation is not a reflection of transformations in the political economy of telecoms but the natural outcome of changing technology. Government reports, industry statements, academic writing, policy position papers by telecoms labour unions, and the popular press all suggest that telecoms policy is "rapidly being undermined by technological change" (Addy, 1994, p. 2), and "that all markets will be competitive in the not-too-distant future" (Schultz & Janisch, 1993, p. 7). However, such views overlook the ever-prominent role of the CRTC, an expanded role for Industry Canada, increasing attention to the sector by the Minister of Consumer and Corporate Affairs, greater reliance on the *Competition Act* and *Merger Enforcement Guidelines*, and higher levels of direct ministerial intervention in telecoms policy then ever (Addy, 1994; Canada, 1993a; CRTC, 1994a, p. 67; MacDonald's record, 1988, p. 1; Schultz & Janisch, 1993). Given these developments, rather than speaking of deregulation, it is more appropriate to speak of regulatory liberalisation—a process changing the focus of telecoms policy from protecting natural monopolies, industry boundaries, and balancing competing interests, toward expanding markets, insuring that competition works and reconciling the contradictory interests among historically dominant TOs, new competitors, and large users.

Changes in telecoms policy are most evident in the evolving approaches to media reconvergence and to "information highways." One encapsulation of possible approaches to these developments is provided by the United States' *White Paper on Communications Act Reform*—a document that appears to have influenced the CRTC's thinking for its *Competition and Culture on Canada's Information Highway* (CRTC, 1995a). According to the U.S. *White Paper*, policy for broadband communications networks should be guided by the following five principles:

- Private investment
- Competition
- Open access to . . . consumers and providers
- Universal service to avoid creating a society of information "haves" and "have nots"
- Flexibility, so that the newly adopted regulatory framework can keep pace with the rapid technological and market changes that pervade the telecoms and information industries (US, 1994a, p.1).

Although most of these principles have been incorporated into Canadian telecoms policy through the CRTC's *Regulatory Framework Review* decision (CRTC, 1994a) and its *Competition and Culture* document (CRTC, 1995a), Commission policy on Integrated Broadband Networks (IBNs) is still unfolding, and key regulatory issues have yet to be resolved satisfactorily. A key question that the CRTC has had to face is whether or not policy should prevent convergence, permit it, or take an active promotional role toward this possibility as part of larger industrial and social policy initiatives (Elton, 1992, p. 382). None of these options presented itself as the best one—each involved different trade-offs—nor could any of them lead to state withdrawal from telecoms.

The Legal and Regulatory Prerequisites of Media Reconvergence

The eclipse of the natural monopoly regulatory regime means that there are no longer any vested interests served by continued segregation. Stentor members have gone from wanting only to be common carriers to advocating network competition and media reconvergence. Stentor members sought reinterpretations to the *Telecommunications Act* (1993) immediately after it became law and persistently petitioned the CRTC to exempt them from common-carrier status so that they could offer a range of information and video services. They also proposed the Beacon Initiative, a plan to invest $8.5 billion in interactive IBNs to be available to 80% of Canadian homes by the year 2005 in return for government pledges to remove restrictions on cross-media ownership and the telcos' ability to obtain broadcast licences, to become multimedia content producers, and to offer any other online service (Anderson, 1994, p. A15; CRTC, 1994a; Cohen, 1993; Stentor, 1994; Surtees, 1994b, p. A13).

These proposals were brought to a head in series of events between 1994 and 1996. At this time, the CRTC and government announced measures that, basically, removed all *legal and regulatory* barriers to reconvergence and/or set the criteria under which telcos could become involved in broadcasting, cable television, electronic publishing, and so on (Canada, 1996a, 1996b; CRTC, 1994a, 1995a, 1995b). An extensive discussion of these decisions, events, and issues is provided in Chapter 7, and to a lesser extent in the chapters before and after it. Meanwhile, however, the details involved will be postponed to get a better grasp of the factors precipitating the metamorphosis in Canadian media policy, the range of choices that were available to policymakers, and the context within which media reconvergence needs to be situated.

Stentor's initiatives, and the government's accommodation of these proposals, would have been wholly out of place a decade ago. However, in a short time[14] such overtures came to be seen as sensible in light of popular musings about information highways, the perception that information services are key to economic recovery, and prevalent criticisms that cable systems were abusing their monopoly position. With respect to the latter point, it has long been clear that cable operators have used their local monopoly positions to exact rate increases in excess of price rises for regulated telecoms services and other items charted by the consumer price index (Royal Task Force on Broadcasting, 1985, pp. 562-569; Stats Canada, 1995d, Table 3). Although this seldom meant more then empty admonitions for the cable operators to quit abusing their positions, the balance may have shifted as content providers, including the largest press interests such as Southam, and specialty program suppliers, experienced difficulty getting cable distribution. In addition, the telcos argued that the CRTC's "asymmetrical regulatory policy," which kept them out of cable but allowed cable operators into telecoms, reinforced cable monopolies and propped up artificial competition (Stentor, 1994, 1995).

Another argument was that regulatory barriers to media convergence and the supply of content services by the telecoms carriers had to be removed so that they would have the additional revenue sources needed to finance new broadband networks. As a CRTC-commissioned study on network convergence noted, the development of IBNs:

> will not be possible without significant new revenue sources. . . . [O]nly the delivery of interactive entertainment broadband video services, some only conceptually defined, others yet to be invented or identified, are likely to generate a sufficiently broad based consumer demand to produce the incremental revenues required to deploy [IBNs] to the home. (Comgate, 1991, p. 35)

Martin Elton (1992), however, claims that network competition may lead to even more colossal monopolies across the telecoms and cable industries, that the link between network modernisation and content as revenue sources may not be as tight as contended, and that IBNs are unnecessary for all but the most demanding users. Although there is an explosion in the range of network information services, most of these services can be made publicly available using less grandiose technologies such as Integrated Services Digital Networks (ISDNs).[15] Such observations suggested caution before universal freedom of expression values embodied in the common-carrier principle were traded off in return for financing network technologies that may mainly serve particular institutional interests.

Despite these warnings, the CRTC and government have promoted media reconvergence and the delivery of information and video services by the telcos. After an early period of caution, the CRTC removed restrictions on the telcos' ability to offer information services, allowed exemptions for telcos to deliver "cable-like" programming on an "experimental basis," permitted telecoms services to be offered by cable network operators, and set out the preconditions for telco/cable competition and cross-ownership. Furthermore, the acceptance of a spate of mergers and acquisitions across the communications industries suggests that government policy is not only permitting network reconvergence but actively promoting it (CRTC, 1994a, pp. 46-53; 1995a, pp. 10-25).

Mergers and Acquisitions as Communication Policy for the Information Age

The promotional approach to media reconvergence has helped to fuel acquisitions across the media industries. In the wake of these trends, the number of independent telcos continues to decline and extensive cross-cutting links between telecoms carriers, broadcasting, new media, and other industries have been created. Typifying the trend, Bell Canada Enterprises (BCE) bought part ownership of the direct-to-home satellite service, ExpressVu. It also started Multi-Media Incorporated (MMI), in conjunction with other members of Stentor, as a means of developing content to be delivered over the emerging broadband networks once they are in place (Anderson, 1994, p. A15; Surtees, 1994b, p. A13). The same carriers have also moved into online publishing and internet access since November 1995, with Sympatico/MediaLinx.

Another telecoms provider, Rogers/Unitel (cable television, broadcasting, telecoms), recently acquired MacLean-Hunter (publishing and broadcasting). Similar patterns have consolidated control in the cable industry among three players: Rogers, Videotron, and Shaw.

Despite widespread belief that such trends put the prerequisites for convergence and IBNs in place, they do not guarantee success. Immediately after acquiring MacLean-Hunter, long-standing difficulties in telecoms forced Rogers and CNCP to sell their shares in Unitel to AT&T and three of Canada's five biggest banks—Royal Bank, Toronto-Dominion, and Bank of Nova Scotia. Whether specific deals succeed or fail, the belief that cross-media alliances are a prerequisite to success in the new telecoms has proved resiliently triumphant. As an executive stated in discussions of the aborted merger between Bell Atlantic and TeleCommunications Inc., the largest cable operator in the United States, the deal was "a perfect information age marriage, . . . *a model* for communications in the next century," combining the companies' activities in telecoms, publishing, film, video, cable, and so on, with emerging services such as video-on-demand, home banking, and electronic data bases, among others (quoted in Morley & Robins, 1995, p. 14; emphasis added). Using the same logic, but with a nationalist twist for good measure, the CRTC approved Rogers takeover of MacLean-Hunter, arguing it ensured "Canadian stories, ideas and values . . . for the electronic information highway" (Dalglish & Fulton, 1994, p. 44).

The CRTC's permissive approach to cross-media ownership is bolstered by its reliance on the weak tests of concentration, vagaries, and omissions included in the *Mergers Enforcement Guidelines* and competition law (CRTC, 1994a, pp. 64-69). The effect of these features is to reinforce the enduring tendency in Canada for government policies to support "national champions." As a commentator on the *Telecommunications Act* stated, "'competitiveness' at the domestic level may require a number of industry participants, while 'competitiveness' at the international level may require significant concentration at home" (Romaniuk, 1992, p. 21).

Historically, analysts have accepted that a *potential* for abuse of market power existed when one firm controlled over 10% of a market, less then four firms controlled 35%, and/or less then eight firms had a 50% market share (Atkin, 1994, pp. 336-337). The *Mergers Enforcement Guidelines*, in contrast, uses the comparatively weak benchmark figure of "35% market control" by one firm to establish a case that a merger *could* lead to excessive market control. Mergers and acquisitions falling beneath the threshold will usually be approved, whereas those exceeding the benchmark should be avoided.

This benchmark is not only weak but plagued with three other problems. First, there is a *lack of clarity* about what 35% control of a market means. Are markets defined by sector, technology, or geography? If sector-based definitions are assumed, as the CRTC does in the *Competition and Culture on Canada's Information Highway* document (1995), the acquisition of a television station by Bell Canada Enterprises, to use a not too far-fetched hypothetical example, could be seen as diversifying control *within* the television "market." However, this does not measure diversity *across* the media or the economy as a whole. The "35% standard" also fails to distinguish between network providers and content providers. Whereas the standard may not pose problems for telecoms networks that are properly regulated and governed by the common-carrier principle, 35% control of all online services, electronic newspapers, or broadcasting by one firm is surely unacceptable. Second, the regulator can grant *exemptions* to these standards altogether if the (ill-defined) benefits of technological innovation and global competitiveness are perceived to outweigh the costs of regulation (Addy, 1994; CRTC, 1994a, pp. 64-69; Schultz & Janisch, 1993, p. 16). Finally, competition law and guidelines for mergers and acquisitions *omit* communication policy's stress on pluralism, diversity, universal service, and other goals that further the values of democratic communication. In fact, in reviewing recent takeovers within the newspaper industry, for example, members of the Liberal government have gone so far as to claim that the impact of mergers on content, diversity, and media freedoms are irrelevant (Mosco, 1997) to considerations under the *Mergers Enforcement Guidelines* and the *Competition Act.*[16]

It appears that concentrated ownership is to broadband networks what restrictive covenants and dormant antitrust laws were to early broadcasting and telecoms history. Although there may not be any consent agreements, and arguments about system integrity, economies of scale, and cross-subsidy have lapsed, three claims are being pressed into service to sanction media concentration: concentration is needed to build IBNs, to sustain technological innovation, and to compete globally.

Competition, Open Networks and Technological Solutions to Market Power

Ownership concentration may be offset by decisions introducing competition into the industry and the use of "open network architectures" to allow interconnection between competitors and the networks of the historically dominant TOs. As a result of these measures, there is an emerging range of new competitive and private networks, content providers and service providers, Internet Service Providers (ISPs), and resellers offering telecoms and network-based content services. Although still small relative to the industry as a whole, some of the new players have formed coalitions to influence changes in telecoms policy and to curtail the powers of the TOs (Bouwman & Latzer, 1994, p. 162). Rather than relying on the traditional politics of telecoms policy, these "new coalitions" have sought regulatory policies that embed possibilities for competition in the design of media technologies. These include, for example, proposals for Comparably Efficient Interconnection (CEI), Open Network Architecture (ONA), and Open Systems Architecture (OSA). These proposals have also gained favour among some regulators, as they can coincide with their interest in finding technical solutions to an acutely political issue in telecoms policy: market power (CRTC, 1994a, pp. 34-50; Mansell, 1993).

"Open networks" attempt to solve such problems by separating telecoms networks into various components, functions, and services, unbundling the network services costs from general tariffs and requiring that these separate aspects be made available to all on an "as needed" basis. In theory, this helps wrestle control of telecoms networks away from dominant TOs, who have historically refused network interconnection to would-be competitors, offered services on an "all or nothing basis," and denied access to network functions required by competitors. Open network protocols limit the scope of network monopolies by allowing interconnection and delineating services that are to be made available according to commercial criteria versus terms defined by regulation.

Yet, as Mansell (1993) indicates, these solutions cannot eliminate contests by strategic interests to control the organisation, design, and uses of the new telecoms. Instead, open network policies move the politics of telecoms policy into the frontiers of technology design, as incumbent TOs seek to embed most network functions, services, and intelligence into equipment under their control, while others try to remove functions, services, and intelligence from the TOs' networks and toward competitive service providers, peripheral computers, and so on.

To be sure, the legalisation of competition in telecoms and greater reliance on ONA, CEI, and so on have contributed to the spread of new competitors where before there were none. Competitive networks and online new media services are taking hold. As they do, the previously stable boundaries between the media industries are being erased and the "natural monopoly" of telecoms is yielding to a view of the telecoms environment as consisting of "multiple tiers" and a "network of networks" (Noam, 1994). The emerging system consists of interconnecting, interoperable, and competitive networks organised into a *tiered hierarchy* of infrastructure providers, access providers, content suppliers and packagers, and users. Figure 1.2 provides one way of viewing the emerging telecoms network-based media environment. It also indicates that many of these "new services" are not so new but have historical antecedents in an earlier era of "electronic publishing."

As Figure 1.2. indicates, near the bottom of the telecoms system hierarchy there are monopoly and competitive network suppliers.[17] Examples of these are the traditional TOs and new competitive networks where infrastructure competition is allowed, as in Canada, the United States, the United Kingdom and Japan.[18] Moving upwards, there are those who mediate relations between network and content sources (access providers and content packagers/information wholesalers),[19] such as ISPs, information wholesalers who package content from numerous sources, and resellers. This tier includes access networks/service providers such as America Online/Bertelsmann; Compuserve; Europe On-Line; Istar; Prodigy; Sympatico/MediaLinx; Wincom; the Calgary, Ottawa, and Vancouver Freenets, among others; and network management services offered by resellers such as Call Net. In Canada, this is a diverse group, including 400 ISPs and 150 resellers (Cyberspace Research, 1996; Industry Canada, 1995, p. 3). However, the future viability of this tier is in jeopardy, as telcos reorganise access to needed network functions, search for a feasible commercial model for IBN deployment, and offer their own ISP packages. At the same time, software providers such as IBM and Microsoft are bundling Internet access and content sources into software as part of their efforts to overcome the formidable barriers to broadband media. Chapter 7 shows how these practices are part of a deeper struggle amid vested interests to transform online mediaspaces into workable commercial markets. It is suggested that two approaches are being used to try to surmount economic, social, and cultural barriers to the viability

Institutional Users	**Residential Users**
Very heterogenous needs	Access to appropriate technology and services

Content Providers/Information Retailers

Contemporary: press (Southam, Thompson, institutional and residential network users, web sites (personal nonprofit groups, Sympatico/MediaLinx, AOL/Bertelsmann), online data base providers (Infomart/Dialog, Stats Can), mass media (CBC, CTV), public libraries, and so on.

Historical: telephone and telegraph users, telegraph journalists, metropolitan press, stock markets (London, New York, Toronto Stock Exchanges), churches, political groups, Parliament, gambling houses, and so on.

Major Policy Concerns: Free speech; editorial autonomy; access to distribution; diversity; balance of commercial and noncommercial content; timeliness; authenticity; citizens access to "essential information," ability to produce and receive information; whether to finance from user fees, advertising subsidy or government subvention; public good versus commodity view of information (e.g., intellectual property right/copyright regime).

Content Packagers/Information Wholesalers

Contemporary: information brokers (AFP, AP, AP/Dow Jones, Bloombergs, CP, Infomart/Dialog, UPI, Reuters), online service providers (AOL/Bertelsmann, Compuserve, Europe On-line, IBM/Southam, Prodigy, Sympatico/Medialinx), online libraries, and so on.

Historical: information agencies (AP, CP, Extel, Gold & Stock, Reuters, United Press, Western Assoc. Press), online service providers (Central News, Cochrane News, Electric News, Electrophone, Telephone Hirmondo).

Major Policy Concerns: Ability to influence content providers; vertical integration with providers and distributors; exclusive access packages; editorial power over content reaching users; exclusive rights versus public right to access info; financing of content production and distribution; privacy of users; nondiscriminatory access to carrier networks; interconnectivity with other network, service and content providers.

Access Providers

Contemporary: Internet service providers (ISPs) (AOL, Compuserve, FreeNets, Istar, Hook-up, Sympatico/MediaLinx, Wincom), bandwidth wholesalers/resellers, and network management.

Major Policy Concerns: integration with networks and content providers, access to carriage and content, privacy of users, public access, new media freedoms.

Network Infrastructure Providers

Contemporary: Wire and wireless network providers, broadcasters, cable television, LANS, MANs, mobile communications, satellite, telecoms, (Stentor members, private networks, cable/broadcast companies, and so on).

Historical: Telegraph and wireless point-to-point and broadcasting media (American Telegraph Co., CP, Canadian Northern, Dominion Telegraph, Great NorthWestern, Montreal Telegraph Company, Western Union, and so on).

Major Policy Concerns: Universality in terms of price and coverage, responsiveness to user needs, interconnection with other network and content providers, nondiscriminatory access, vertical integration, public infrastructure.

Equipment Providers

Contemporary: network and CPE equipment such as Northern Telecoms, Ericsson, Siemens, but also computer firms such as Hewlett Packard, IBM, Microsoft, SystemHouse, and so on.

Historical: Vertically integrated with TO, or separate; for example, Bain, House, Morse, and Cook and Wheatstone telegraph sending and receiving equipment.

Major Policy Concerns: vertical integration; interconnectivity, patents, location of intelligence/functionality.

Figure 1.2. Telecoms-network based media

of online media and IBNs: extending the advertising-subsidised, "free lunch" mass media model to online mediaspaces, or the marketing of computer communications and IBNs as "luxury goods." Neither, it is argued, adequately realises the communicative potential of new media. Basically, I suggest that the needs of most commercial interests, cultural/content producers, and users are being subordinated to a "gold-rush" mentality and strategic interests fostered by governments, infrastructure providers, and only the most discriminating of large users bent on implementing a communication system that most do not need or want. Addressing the discrepancies between what vested interests are offering and what most users want, the final chapter proposes another model based on more appropriate ISDN technology, a more sensitive approach to media freedoms, and the use of communication policy and competitive forces to achieve a broader set of aims than is currently offered.

Finally, near the top of the model are content providers and users, including telephone subscribers, electronic data base providers, newspapers, academic journals, libraries, and so on. This tier consists of a large, diverse, and expanding range of services, as there were at least 2,745 Canadian-based world-wide web sites by early 1996. The range of content providers is also structurally diverse, including 930 research and education-based sites, 1,671 privately-owned sites, and 144 government-affiliated sites (Cyberspace Research, 1996). As Chapters 7 and 8 show, the future of this currently vibrant area of communicative interaction depends on which model of media evolution—the "free lunch" mass media, "luxury good," or the proposed "exemplary media system" (see Chapter 8)—prevails.

From Common Carriage to Freedom of Expression Rights for Telcos?

Media reconvergence challenges the existence of common-carriage principles in telecoms policy. Telcos are increasingly functioning simultaneously as bandwidth retailers/wholesalers (carriers), content providers (publishers), and audiovisual producers and distributors (broadcasters), and this has brought formerly distinct media policy traditions into collision. In the wake of these processes, the common-carriage principle is withering (Noam, 1994) and the telcos are becoming endowed with media freedoms that allow them greater ability to pick and choose who can access the PTN. Yet, even as they begin offering content services and editing "online mediaspace," the telcos will continue to confront vestiges of common carriage embedded in the CRTC's video-dial-tone platform and interconnection policy, among other places. As such, telcos *do not* have unbridled editorial rights and media freedoms. The key issue now, however, is to define just where the telcos' media freedom ends and others' right to access the PTN begins. The remainder of this chapter addresses these issues.

In the abstract, telecoms policy can treat the common-carrier principle in one of three ways. The first is to import the principle wholesale into the emerging telecoms network-based media environment. This would maintain separations among the TOs, content providers, content packagers, access providers, and so on. This approach would bar the telcos from influencing messages flowing through their networks. An alternative is to relax the common-carrier principle to allow telcos to offer content, video, and interactive services over a portion of their networks. In this approach, policymakers can agree to turn over some editorial discretion to the telcos in return for commitments from them to develop IBNs that meet specified telecoms policy aims. This approach was favoured in the United States by public interest groups such as the Electronic Frontier Foundation (1994), who argued that it "permits . . . a band of channels to be controlled by the network operator, but also for a common carriage connection that is open to all who wish to speak, publish and communicate on the digital information highway" (p. 2). Although this approach was included in early legislative approaches in the United States to replace the *Communications Act of 1934*, it fell in favour of giving U.S. telcos near unbridled discretion to manage access and use of the PTN (Senate Committee on Commerce, Science, and Transportation, 1996; US, 1991).

Although these three approaches are all theoretical possibilities, in the real world the range of choice has been narrowed by CRTC decisions, the probable reluctance of cable networks and new access providers to relinquish control over contents scheduling, and developments in the United States that may impact on telecoms policy by way of example and/or through the trade regimes established by the NAFTA and GATS. As indicated earlier, the CRTC eroded much of the common-carrier principle by allowing TOs to offer whatever information services they wanted and by setting nominal preconditions to be met before telcos could become broadcast undertakings or programmers. It is also unlikely that common-carrier principles can withstand network, regulatory and industry convergence, as the cable industry and new media providers—Prodigy, Sympatico/MediaLinx, and so on—show reluctance to relinquish editorial freedoms just because they share a regulatory regime with telecoms providers (Noam, 1994, pp. 435-436).

The CRTC (1995a) has chosen to apply cultural policies to "broadcast-like" services offered by telecoms carriers such as VOD and NVOD (pp. 30-42), but it is questionable whether this approach can be sustained over time.[20] Although the telcos acquiesced to this effort, it is not hard to imagine a time in the near future when cultural policy aims begin to look like another state-imposed burden that carriers are fond of complaining about (Schultz & Janisch, 1993, pp. 7-13). Such resistance may be galvanised all the more if the TOs are joined by cable and broadcasting industries that see a possible way out of their obligations to further cultural policy objectives. There are currently several factors that suggest the remaining distance between the TOs and freedom of expression rights may be traversed in the near future.

First, in contrast to the court decision and statements by the CRTC introduced earlier, Canadian courts have recently decided that commercial speech is covered under the "freedom of expression" clause of the Charter (Festinger, 1994, p. 19). As a result, economics are no longer subordinate to politics, and the divide between citizen's and corporate rights to freedom of expression narrowed. Second, recent decisions in the United States argue that the First Amendment prevents Congress from abridging citizens' right to freedom of expression, but places no onus on telcos to carry content provided by others (Barron, 1993, p. 381). This suggests that the common-carrier principle is at odds with the First Amendment. Another court decision extended this reasoning by declaring that restrictions on telco/cable cross-ownership "deprived telephone companies of the editorial judgement, control and discretion that is the essence of their First Amendment rights" (emphasis added, (United States Court of Appeals [4th Circuit], 1994, p. 12; emphasis added). Until recently a similar challenge in Canada was possible on grounds that the *Telecommunications Act* and *Bell Canada Act* restrictions preventing telcos from influencing content or from holding a broadcasting or cable licence curtailed their freedom of expression rights embodied in the *Canadian Charter of Rights and Freedoms* (Canada, 1987b, s. 7; Canada, 1993a, s. 36). In September 1996, however, the Chretien government averted this by introducing legislation to remove the "offending provisions" from existing laws (Canada, 1996b).

Despite variations in the paths taken to the same ends (e.g., courts versus Parliament), it is possible that the U.S. cases can still provide examples for Stentor members and others searching to remove the remaining limits to "media freedoms" found in the new regulatory regime. In conjunction with the NAFTA and GATS sections on telecoms and computer services, these examples may provide a vehicle for further expanding the scope of "media freedoms" and "electronic publishing" in the Canadian telecoms policy regime—prospects treated at some length in Chapters 6 and 7. The NAFTA and GATS regimes are relevant because their distinctions between basic and enhanced services result in enhanced services falling beyond the reach of domestic telecoms policies. Yet, in the context of IBNs and media reconvergence, in which telecoms networks carry streams of digital content—voice, data, video, television programming—how can unregulated enhanced services be distinguished from regulated broadcasting services? If such distinctions cannot be made, how does the CRTC apply cultural policies in a digital communications environment? Unless the CRTC can come up with a sound basis for distinguishing between digital streams—and there will be enormous pressures from the United States' government, U.S.-based telcos, Canadian TOs, and others not to make such distinctions, and sanctions used according to terms set out in the Free Trade Agreement if it does—NAFTA and GATS could prevent regulation of *all* forms of enhanced services carried over telecoms networks, whether data, online information services, Internet access, or television programming. Hence, there would be de facto freedom of expression for Canadian telcos.

CONCLUSION: THE TECHNOLOGICAL POTENTIALS AND SOCIOPOLITICAL REALITIES OF THE NEW TELECOMS

There are strong parallels between efforts to stabilise the new telecoms and the historical propensity of policymakers to sanction alliances between communications, the state, and corporate power during the formative years of broadcasting and the telephone. During the 1920s, policymakers realised that agreements to carve up the communications industries among a small number of major players "were clearly violating the Clayton anti-trust and the Sherman anti-trust laws" (US, 1926, p. 548). However, rather than pursuing the implications of such observations within parameters established by law, or in relation to the potentials of the new technologies demonstrated by citizens groups, labour unions, educators, and churches, the agreements were sanctioned as a means of bringing new media into the prevailing institutional organisation of power. These moments parallel contemporary developments in which weak anti-trust laws and new justifications support high levels of concentration in certain areas of the new telecoms.

There are also parallels between the "technological necessity" arguments used to legitimate natural monopolies and current attempts by the CRTC to don the mask of technological determinism to conceal the political issues involved in drawing boundaries between communication services made universally available to citizens and those excluded from public service obligations. The essential issue is whether universal service will be expanded to encompass the increased importance of communication in contemporary society and the capacities of the new technologies, or curtailed so that most services are defined as "information age" luxuries.

Despite the prevalent belief that telecoms policy is ruled by deregulation, the CRTC and other agencies maintain considerable power on the basis of their ability to *define things*. This source of institutional power is visible in how universal service is defined, as well as in the CRTC's role in defining the 'basket of services' covered by price caps regulation, the terms of network convergence, what constitutes competition, who is and is not a legitimate participant in regulatory hearings, the scope of the *Broadcast Act*'s cultural policy provisions, and so on.

Contemporary analysis of telecoms policy needs to consider these historical parallels and the continued role of regulation in the current period of radical experimentation with the new telecoms media. The crucial questions are: does current experimentation register a permanent expansion in democratic communication? Or, is this a transient moment occurring in the interval between the emergence of a new media system and its ultimate stabilisation within the prevailing political and economic matrix of society once divergent visions of the future give way to a viable commercial *model of* communications evolution? Are today's civic networkers, electronic bulletin board posters, FreeNets, and ISPs the modern incarnations of yesterday's demolished "radio movement" (McChesney, 1997),[21] this time exploring the bounds of media freedom through the new telecoms? Ultimately, as Nicholas Garnham (1995) states, how such issues are resolved will depend on the "levels of concentration, the role of advertising finance, patterns of consumption, and . . . the nature of regulation" that come to define the institutional boundaries of the new telecoms (p. 25).

Finally, the extent to which new media can be linked to democracy depends on the balance struck between telcos' claims to "media freedoms" and common carriage. The disappearance of common carriage altogether would invite the editorial discretion and power relations of the mass media into the new telecoms, thereby undermining much of the potential for a new regime of decentralised "electronic publishing." Considered in this light, it is incumbent on us to consider, to recall Pierre Juneau, whether it is citizens' rights to freedom of expression that are central to democratic theory, or, as a new regime of media freedoms for telcos would suggest, that we are still really talking about the "freedom of a small number of media owners"? These are the issues covered in the subsequent chapters.

ENDNOTES

1.   The Bell Canada-led consortium of 10 regional telecoms companies (telcos).
2.   Resellers buy transmission and other services in volume—essentially on a wholesale basis—from the telcos and resell these services to users who

would not otherwise qualify for the "quantity discounts" offered by the telcos to large users. By pooling together several small- to medium-size users, resellers can sell, for example, long distance services to small- and medium-size users at a price somewhere between usual customer rates and the prices charged to large users.

3.   Subsequent chapters provide the details that help bring about a more nuanced picture. For example, as will be seen, the "electronic publishing" model emerged earlier than 1870 in England, while also beginning to wobble and disintegrate about a decade before being basically eliminated in Canada in 1910. The same applies to common carriage, which, as Chapters 5 and 7 show, began to teeter near the end of the 1960s, was significantly dented in the 1980s, and finally turned into a residual part of the telecoms policy regime in 1994-1995.

4.   Although the details of these arrangements are presented in Chapters 3, 4 and 5, a cursory survey of the key issues is presented here.

5.   These agreements not only divided the communications industries among the major industry players but, as Barnouw (1982) notes, created the terms and conditions under which telephone systems (mainly AT&T), for example, would provide long distance services to the broadcast companies eager to establish their national networks.

6.   A similar statement by the head of a large Canadian telecoms provider today would be impossible. The interesting questions are why this is so and what has happened in the intervening 25 to 30 years to change the circumstances so radically. Although it is tempting to suggest technology, especially digitalisation, it should be clear by now that technological factors offer little power to explain the institutional structure of the Canadian communications industries.

7.   Although the natural monopoly doctrine was a major prop on which subsequent regulatory frameworks were articulated, regulatory initiatives were hastened along and shaped by the intense politics of telecoms that had begun to emerge in the 1890s. This "politics of telecoms" was united by a confluence of a wide range of factors that united independent telcos and a broad array of groups. The Canadian court's nullification of key Bell patents in 1885 and the expiration of Bell patents in the United States in 1893 and 1894, as well as the company's failure to develop a universal network, opened the way for independent telcos, although they were continuously confronted by Bell's efforts to scuttle these competitive possibilities. In addition, Trade and Labour Councils, provincial and municipal governments, and others who saw the social utility of telephones being undermined by Bell and the other dominant telcos in western Canada, organised to push for reform and regulation of the telephone system. These initiatives reached their apogee in the massive inquiry conducted by the Mulock Committee in 1905, which was followed by the beginnings of a federal regulatory regime developed under the *Railway Act* and overseen by the Board of Railway Commissioners, as well as the establishment of public ownership in the prairie provinces between 1905 and 1909 (Babe, 1990; BRC, 1908; Canada, Mulock Committee, 1905).

8. As discussed further in Chapter 4, BCTel did not come under federal regulatory authority until electing to do so in 1917 (Bernard, 1982, p. 74).

9. Price cap regulation involves three main ingredients: (a) a "basket of services", (b) the setting of prices for services within this basket on the basis of a formula that is pegged to the retail price index (RPI), and (c) a target set by regulators according to which the price of services should move in relation to the RPI (usually expressed as X%). From a users' point of view, important considerations are how many services are contained within the basket and whether service prices decline at a rate fast enough vis-à-vis the RPI to account for increases in technical and economic efficiencies characteristic of the telecoms industries. In the United Kingdom the "basket of services" was initially narrowly defined, excluding the cost of initiating telephone services and operator assistance, for instance, and prices set according to an "RPI-3%" formula. Later, the regulator, OFTEL, expanded the range of services in the basket and made the price target a more stringent "RPI-8%" (Carsberg, 1987, pp. 237-240; Hills, 1991, p. 8).

10. This latter term redefines basic services to exclude from regulation long-distance services, access to the long-distance network, the installation of wiring and telephone service, and other features formerly part of the "basic services" category. As a consequence, such services are withdrawn from regulatory oversight and disassociated from goals of universal service, among others (CRTC, 1994a, p. 15). Here, one cannot help but note the contrast between the promises of information abundance, on the one hand, and the narrowing of even a basic range of services made universally available to citizens on a guaranteed basis, on the other. This is discussed again in a later section.

11. These distinctions are based on different criteria and varying terminology in different countries or regions. Thus, *basic* and *enhanced/value added services* are terms used in Canada and the United States. Europe prefers to use the terms *reserved* and *nonreserved services*, and Japan distinguishes between Type 1 and Type 2 services. Despite different terminology, the distinctions are always predicated on technological or market considerations that are considered to be "objective." Yet the fact that practices vary so widely across countries and regions, and in accord with different policy priorities, gives the lie to the claim of objectivity. Such line drawing will increasingly play a major role in the politics of telecoms policy.

12. Ironically, recent regulatory initiatives simultaneously eliminate the antiquated technological basis for separate regulatory systems for telecoms, broadcasting, cable television, and publishing (as shown in the following sections as well as in later chapters), while reinforcing or creating other technologically specific regulatory concepts. This "new technological determinism" mystifies the role of technology, industry, and government in reconfiguring the communications environment and, in doing so, performs an ideological function by obscuring the existence and exercise of power (see Babe, 1990, for a discussion of the mythology of technology in Canadian policymaking historically).

13. This was not a new idea associated with the spread of social welfare democracy, as critics are inclined to suggest. Rather, it reflected

longstanding tensions between the incorporation of corporate actors into the legal theory of liberal democracy near the end of the 19th century as "legal persons" in possession of extensive property rights but *without* the civil and political liberties associated with real citizens. In this light, attempts by corporate actors to obtain "freedom of expression" rights are directed at restriking the terms of this "historical accommodation" between corporate capital and democracy. These ideas are discussed at length in the next chapter.

14. In Chapter 7, I argue this short period of time may have been as little as one or two years and certainly not more then four or five. As noted there, the new *Telecommunications Act* (1993) and *Broadcasting Act* (1991) both carried on the history of legislating media divergence, and during hearings on the telecoms act only SaskTel and labour unions took issue with this. Their proposals to allow reconvergence to facilitate IBNs were dismissed without comment (Canada, 1993a; Canada, Proceedings of the Standing Senate Committee on Transport and Communications, 1992).

15. The difference between IBNs and ISDNs relates largely to the capacity and speed of the two networks. Although definitions differ regionally, in North America the IBN standard applies to networks capable of transmitting 1.44 Mbits/second, whereas ISDN networks have two 64kbits/second channels and one 28 kbits/second signalling channel (altogether 156kbits/second). Thus, ISDN networks have considerably less capacity than IBNs but far more than traditional telephone networks. Whether or not IBN is needed more than ISDN really hinges on whether policy favours promoting an additional mass media distribution system, eg. carrying video, pay-per TV, cable television, and so on, because most other services, like the Internet, transactional services for banking from home, email, and so on, can be more than adequately served by ISDN. These issues provide the core of Chapters 7 and 8.

16. As communications are treated more and more within the framework of industrial policy, competition policy and antitrust law, communication policy loses its ability to make the kind of relevant distinctions that are being called for here. In the hands of the Minister of Consumer and Corporate Affairs, Industry Canada, the *Competition Act*, and the *Merger Enforcement Guidelines* economic considerations become overriding imperatives (Addy, 1994; Canada, 1993a; CRTC, 1994a, p. 67; Schultz & Janisch, 1993), as concern with other values disappears. This is very much what was meant during the earlier discussion of attempts to uncouple expansive concepts like information/communication from their political and normative roots.

17. The bottom area, Equipment Providers, is not considered in this book, except incidentally.

18. Although network competition also occurs between the telcos and cable providers, the scope of this competition remains rather limited in Canada because of the recent use of an assymetrical regulatory framework that allows cable to compete in telecoms, but not vice versa, an implicit historical quid pro quo between the telcos and cable providers to stay out of one anothers' core service areas (see Chapters 4 and 5). As a result of these

industrial arrangements and regulatory policies, different functions have been embedded in telecoms and cable technologies over the course of their separate evolutionary paths. Telecoms networks are switched, two-way, intelligent but narrowband, whereas cable is unswitched, one-way, stupid but broadband. These different characteristics mean that each network is good in its respective field, but weak across existing media boundaries. These technical differences will have to be overcome for full-scale telco/cable interoperability, although the telco and cable companies are already making modifications in anticipation of changes in current regulatory policies as well as struggling to piece together bits and pieces from one anothers' networks to help them fill in "missing links" to their "broadband initiatives." Open network architecture helps allow interconnection between both networks.

19. The concept of *information wholesalers* is one that I have become familiar with through conversations with Oliver Boyd-Barrett. Boyd-Barrett's (1980) work on global news agencies shows the crucial role played by these intermediaries regarding content production, distribution and consumption since the middle of the last century.

20. Whether or not cultural policies will actually be applied to the new telecoms will be a crucial issue in the future politics of telecoms regulation. As the following discussion indicates, it is likely to be very difficult to apply cultural policies to telecoms providers in the face of restrictions in NAFTA and GATS.

21. McChesney uses the term *radio movement* to describe the diverse and large number of individuals and various civic groups who were experimenting with radio broadcasting prior to being pushed to the very margins of broadcasting in the United States by the adoption of the *Radio Act* (1927); the network system of advertising-financed, privately owned corporate media; and a weak public interest standard that regulators have, for the most part, been loathe to give any substantive meaning to ever since.

2 COMMUNICATION, REGULATION, AND MODERN SOCIETIES

INTRODUCTION

The previous chapter argued that the historical divergence of communication media along technical lines was contrived. It was suggested that distinctions between telecoms and other media, and the evolution of separate regulatory traditions for each, represented the outcome of strategic rivalry, collusion, and post hoc explanations aimed to "naturalise" the established state of affairs.

This chapter extends this thinking by trying to explain the origins of media regulation. It is argued that media regulation has much less to do with specific technologies and issues of scarcity than commonly assumed. Instead, the origins of regulation are traced to broad changes in modern societies, the birth of new commercial organisations (corporations), protection of the quality of communication, and attempts to structure relations of power among governments, business, and people (Hoffman-Riem, 1996).

It is claimed that modern societies have multiple ways of structuring relationships and solving problems. Government intervention is one mode of steering social relationships and attending to the problems arising from within and without complex societies. Markets and economic transactions provide another means of regulating behaviour and coordinating action, as well as exercising power and steering people, organisations, and society in particular directions. Knowledge and experts, and in particular what counts as valid and invalid knowledge, are also key factors shaping the course of events in modern societies. Finally, people, politics, and communication *can* play a crucial role in trying to orient the actions of governments, markets, and experts, as well as legitimating the actions that are taken on their behalf by other actors. This chapter suggests that the key issues confronting societies as they determine how new media will be developed and used are whether the system will be regulated by bureaucratic, commercial, technocratic, or communicative principles (Galtung, 1994; Habermas, 1987).[1]

Three inferences for how we think about communication, technology, society, and policy are derived from these observations. First, we need to look at how new media create potentials for action, while focusing on how economics, politics, people, and knowledge interact to "choose between the alternatives" (Mody, Bauer, & Straubhaar, 1995, p. xx). Second, it is pointless to conceptualise telecoms politics within the narrow confines of "dichotomous thinking—to regulate or not to regulate" (Mosco, 1988, p. 107). Third, we need to see societies as thoroughly and irrevocably "policy-determined," either by commission (regulation) or omission (regulatory liberalisation) (Offe, 1996, pp. ix, 75).

Telecoms actors draw on such "problem solving resources," interact in strategic rivalry, and act within an economy consisting of an oligopolistic/monopolistic core, a public sector, and a competitive fringe—not perfect competition—to shape the evolution of successive communications media. Even more abstractly, these actors and interactions are captured within a matrix of tensions set up by, on the one hand, "modernity's" promise of flexibility, dynamic change, and freedom and, on the other, the subordination of these potentials to various actors' attempts to control the economic, political, social, and cultural environment.

THE IDEA OF MODERNITY

The idea of *modernity* refers to the historical movement of societies toward greater complexity as well as the separation of different spheres of life out from under the control of one overarching source of authority. Modernity is usually seen as successive waves of social change and differentiation. As Tomlinson (1991) summarises, through differentiation "the church was separated from state, law from morality, state from civil society, there was a division of labour in the production process and so on" (p. 132). Such ideas were also captured by the late 19th-century sociologist Ferdinand Tonnies, who identified "modern societies as differentiated, associational . . . and structured by three principles: markets, states and public opinion" (German original translated and quoted in Keane, 1991, p. 21). More recently, the prominent British sociologist, Anthony Giddens (1993), described modern societies as complex, differentiated, and consisting of many overlapping and shifting relationships. However, beneath this diversity, he claims there are reasonably stable "principles of organisation" that show up as a "clustering of institutionalised practices across space and time . . . . These structural relationships need to be examined as conditions of system reproduction. They help to pick out basic features of the circuits of reproduction" (pp. 131-132).

Social differentiation, principles of organisation, and problem solving are difficult ideas to grasp at first. However, they can be depicted and related to communication issues in ways that are helpful for thinking about communication, policy, technology, and society in broad social and historical context. Doing so, it is offered, makes it easier to free ourselves from the blinders of dichotomous thinking. Figure 2.1 represents communication media within modern societies as consisting of various actors—states, capital, and civil society—who use numerous methods to coordinate action and solve problems—communication/legitimacy (axis 1), economics/money (axis 2), law/bureaucracy (axis 3), and knowledge/expertise (axis y). The remainder of this chapter discusses how some of the issues that can be derived from this visual representation can help us to think about the political economy of communication in societies like Canada.

COMMUNICATION, MODERNITY, AND MEDIA FREEDOMS

Western sociology, philosophy, and communication theory have an enduring fascination with the historical processes that led to social differentiation between the church, state, economy, and civil society. The historical process is crucially tied up with issues about media freedoms and the spread of the printing press, literacy, and so on. It is well noted that the church spent years trying to suppress printing technology and literacy to maintain a monopoly over knowledge, and hence a powerful grip on people's lives. Yet, such resistance proved futile. As the church lost its monopoly over knowledge, new forces of social and political organisation were emerging: the modern state, public opinion, and free markets.

As Tonnies (quoted in Keane, 1991) remarked near the end of the 19th century: "In the last century, the Christian religion has lost what public opinion has gained" (p. 21). At the same time that the church was losing its grip on absolute power, writers like John Locke, John Stuart Mill, Jean Jacques Rousseau, Tonnies, and others were describing the nascent antithesis between public opinion and despotic governments. Despite pressures for media freedoms since the 15th and 16th centuries, in the mid-19th century John Stuart Mill (1859/1947) still had to query

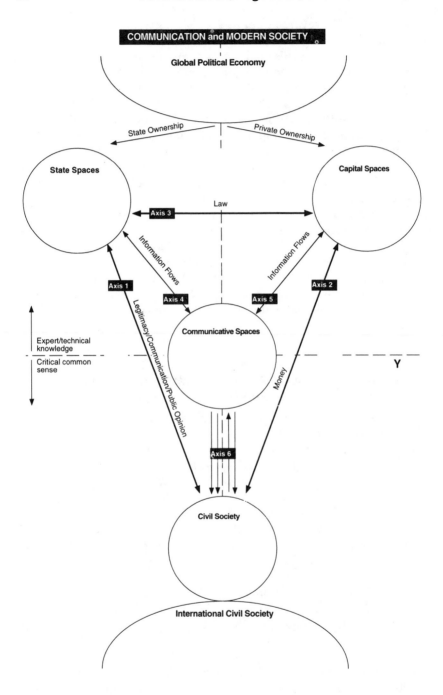

Figure 2.1. Communication and modern society

modern societies' commitment to "the 'liberty of the press' as one of the securities against corrupt or tyrannical government" (p. 15). Not content with affairs in his native England and elsewhere, Mill went on to adumbrate, once again, why "freedom of the press" was the foundation of a civilised society and individual liberty. Ferdinand Tonnies (1887/1955) was somewhat more sanguine in his assessment, claiming that "the State already depended on . . . public opinion . . . to determine what laws will be decreed or maintained, what domestic or foreign policy will be pursued" (p. 221).

The emerging idea of media freedoms was rooted in a new understanding of individuals and efforts to establish an ethical basis for controlling authority, as well as a broad concept of property that would secure the autonomy of the individual. Modern individuals were seen as distancing from, and reflecting on, traditional values, customs, and other ethical constraints. As Herbert Marcuse (quoted in McCarthy, 1993) claimed, posttraditional citizens "examined and judged everything," and could "act in accordance with their insights" (p. 142).

"Liberty of the press" theories were drawn directly from these ideas. As John Stuart Mill (1859/1947) wrote,

> The liberty of . . . publishing opinions may seem to fall under . . . *that part of the conduct of an individual which concerns other people,* but, being almost of as much importance as the *liberty of thought itself,* and resting in great part on the same reasons, is practically inseparable from it. (p. 12; emphasis added).

Mill's ideas are notable for the extent to which he acknowledged the tension in liberal theories between the emphasis on individual rights *and* the social nature of communication that also merits protection from the distorting influences of power. In the end, Mill came down on the side of individual human rights as the warrant for "liberty of the press," like so many of his contemporaries. Why he rejected the other possible line of defense are not clearly stated, and the conundrum merely raised in passing. However, it can be noted that contemporary debates about whether media freedoms are part of individual liberties or a broader public good are hung up on the same impasse, so it is not surprising that Mill faired no better on the issue (Garnham, 1990; Kelley & Donway, 1990; Lichtenberg, 1990).

Nonetheless, this particular way of anchoring liberty of the press was consistent with a view of rights as the "natural property" of individuals. From the classical liberal point of view, communication and language were the transmission belts between consciousness and the outside world and, as such, should be protected from external interference. This point of view was also grounded in a broad concept of property derived from the work of John Locke. According to Locke (1689/1963), property encompassed *"Life, Liberty and Estate"* (p. 367; emphasis added). In Locke's (1689/1963) view, "Freedom . . . and uncontrouled [sic] enjoyment of all the Rights and Privileges of the Law of Nature" are given at birth. The only proper role of "Power [the State] . . . in any political society is . . . to preserve property" (p. 367).

Although some contemporary philosophers see Locke as providing a basis for deregulation and more secure property rights, such views fail to recognise that he did not distinguish property rights (a right to things) from human rights (immaterial in nature): they were two sides of the same coin. Both sides of the classical conception of property inform the tradition of media freedoms, although society has changed so dramatically that it is hard to read a basis for modern conceptions of media freedom back to these sources.

This link between consciousness, autonomy, property, and political critique is present in the record of media freedoms. This can be seen from the historical and geographical spread of measures implemented to secure such aims, from the *French Declaration of the Rights of Man and the Citizen* (1789), the U.S. First Amendment (1791), Article 19 of the United Nations' *Universal Declaration of Human Rights* (1948), and to the formalisation of such rights in the *Canadian Charter of Human Rights and Freedom* (1982) (the latter had largely been adhered to through common-law practice during the present century). Thus, as the French *Declaration of the Rights of Man and the Citizen* (1789) states:

> the unrestrained communication of thoughts and opinions being one of the most precious rights of man, every citizen may speak, write, and publish freely, provided he is responsible for the abuse of this liberty in cases determined by law. (quoted in Barbrook, 1995, p. 10)

Almost two centuries later, the *Canadian Charter of Human Rights and Freedoms* set out a more ambitious, less encumbered conception of media freedoms, stating:

> Sec. 2. Everyone has the . . . freedom of thought, belief, opinion and expression, including freedom of the press and other media of communication; (Sec. 1) . . . subject only to such reasonable limits demonstrably justified in a free and democratic society. (Canada, 1993)

According to Barbrook (1995), the "political rights of media freedom were dependent on the natural right of the property ownership of printing presses" (p. 17). Economic rights allowed people to own printing presses, whereas political rights allowed them to publish freely

(p. 8). A very important condition of these freedoms, as will be shown shortly, was that they applied only to people, to printer-journalists, not to companies or to other organisations (p. 14). As discussed next, one key moment in the evolution of modern societies was the birth of the corporation, and the subsequent dislodging of property from its Lockean moorings, as well as concerns with consciousness as the property of the individual. Contemporary difficulties with understanding media freedoms turns on the problematic relationship among corporate property, consciousness, and Lockean property.

In the meantime, further attention will be given to the links between property, consciousness, and media freedoms. Habermas's (1989) wide-ranging historical and theoretical work on communication, the public sphere, and society is helpful in this respect. As Habermas notes, the conjoined nature of property rights and media freedoms allowed the press to turn from being

> merely a seller of new information . . . [to] become a dealer in public opinion. Publishers provided the commercial basis for the newspaper without, however, commercialising it as such. The press remained an institution of the public itself, operating to provide and intensify public discussion, no longer a mere organ for the conveyance of information. (p. 234)

In the general scheme of things, the media were Janus-faced entities; commercial enterprises as well as places where ideas were shared and the exercise of authority pacified, legitimated, and hence, at least in theory, rendered democratic (Thompson, 1995, p. 56). In addition to congealing economic, political, and civil liberties under one umbrella, the press relied on a diverse source of revenue: reader fees, patronage, and advertising revenues (Smythe, 1977, p. 17). As such, the structural diversity of modernity—citizens, the state, and capital—were united by the press, a feature Habermas (1989) argues allowed the media to be linked to each yet autonomous from all: the ideal public sphere.

The democratising trends associated with the new media were evident not only in the structure of the "public sphere," but also in what was published. At the beginning of the 18th century in Europe, nearly 90% of all books were in Latin and circulated among small groups of intellectuals. One hundred years later, only 20% of books were written in Latin and the rest in popular languages with much wider circulation (Christians, 1995, p. 75).

Media economics also favoured the democratisation of communication, rather than worked against it. In addition to the diverse sources of financing just mentioned, Thompson (1995) notes that during the formative years of the modern media industries publishing houses were quite small, often employing the owner/publisher and fewer than 10 workers (p. 56). Similar conditions prevailed in Canada and the United States. Prior to the last half of the 19th century, a newspaper was commercially viable in North America with between 300 and 400 readers (Innis, 1951, p. 158). According to de Sola Pool (1983), "5,000 copies was considered a good circulation for an American newspaper" (p. 18). A commercially viable newspaper cost about $10,000 in Canada at the time (Kesterten, 1967, p. 22). Media production and media freedoms, as such, were still the property of individuals. This was about to change, though, and theories of media freedoms rendered immensely more difficult to comprehend.

THE RISE OF THE MODERN CORPORATION AND THE DEMISE OF THE JOURNALIST-PRINTER OF MEDIA FREEDOM THEORIES

Economic conditions in the press changed rapidly after the mid-19th century, with the rise of the advertising-supported penny press, the industrialisation of media production, and the invention of the modern corporation. This is not the place to recite the economic history of the press, although it can be noted in passing that the U.S.-based *Hutchins' Report* did recount this history and how the rise of corporate media precipitated the demise of journalist-printers. According to the *Hutchins' Report*, by the 1940s starting a newspaper in large urban areas of North America required between $5 and $10 million, whereas beginning operations in a mid-size city cost about $1 million (Liebling, 1961, p. 32).

de Sola Pool (1983) claims that changing media economics merely reflected broader changes in the economy brought about by the industrial revolution. As industrialisation percolated into the media industries, the press began using assembly line production to standardise the production of newspapers. In de Sola Pool's view, this had benign, even beneficial effects, as the cost of media consumption fell and the number of readers increased dramatically.

Changes in the press no doubt corresponded to broader changes in society. Such changes were also related to the rise of the telegraph, the first electronic medium, during the late 1830s and early 1840s in England, and mid-1840s in Canada and the United States (Kieve, 1973; Thompson, 1947). In turn, the telegraph was symptomatic of industrialisation and the emergence of the corporation. Prior to the 1850s, there was no such thing as a corporation (Smythe, 1981). As such, it had to be created. As Chapter 3 shows, much of this "creativity" took place within the realm of telecoms, as telegraph companies pushed the frontiers of organising capital on unprecedented levels and pleaded with governments to sanction this new legal form and to give generous subsidies.

The corporation did not have many advocates to begin with, even encountering staunch resistance among those who were otherwise erstwhile supporters of capitalism such as the leading London-based journals, *The Times* and the *Economist* (Kieve, 1973, pp. 46-48; Thompson, 1947, pp. 198-202). Carey (1989) refers to the conjunction of telegraphy, the corporation, and social change as follows:

> the telegraph was a new and distinctively different force of production that demanded a new body of law, economic theory, political arrangements, management techniques, organisational structures, and scientific rationales with which to justify and make effective the development of a privately owned and controlled monopolistic corporation. (p. 205)

As Chapter 3 recounts in detail, from 1850 to the middle of the 1880s corporate organisations consolidated their control over the new media. These new corporate-controlled telegraph systems bore names like American Telegraph Company, Anglo-American Telegraph Company, Canadian Pacific Telegraph Company, Dominion Telegraph Company, Montreal Telegraph Company, and, of course, Western Union. The rise of corporate forms in telegraphy was not unique, though, and was soon followed by similar patterns in telephony, with the rise of the American Telephone and Telegraph Company (AT&T), the Bell Telephone Company of Canada, and so on.

These trends matched, and perhaps even led, processes of consolidation in other areas of the economy. According to economic historian, William Carroll (1986), corporations became prominent features on the Canadian economic landscape between the 1870s and 1910. He traces the rise of this new feature of Canadian history to several intense phases of consolidation in the periods 1882-1886, 1908-1913, and 1921-1930. As Chapters 3 and 4 show, there is close overlap between these dates and patterns observable in the economic history of Canadian telecoms.

The new telegraph agencies, and subsequently the telephone companies, straddled the North American continent, and from the 1860s onwards, crossed the Atlantic and other oceans as well. These continental information networks harmonised markets, coordinated the dispersed agencies of the state, and provided a metaphor for a nascent national, even transnational, culture. The networks connected urban centres and stock markets, helped coordinate production and consumption, and merged the press and telegraph into a continental system of "electronic publishing" (Blondheim, 1994; Carey, 1989; Thompson; 1947). As Flichy

(1995) notes, in France, in 1851, stock market information accounted for around 38% of all telegraph messages and about 60% of telegraph traffic in Belgium. Telegraph networks linking Montreal and Toronto were similarly busy passing economic information back and forth. These features revealed the enduring close links among telecoms, the press, and economic information that persist to this date. Such issues are returned to on several occasions in the following chapters.

The new electronic media encountered several problems, both from within the media industries—publishing, telegraphs, and telephones—and from without. The press and other content sources incessantly complained of abuses by those who controlled the distribution networks, while the telegraph and telephone companies battled for several years, mainly between 1878 to 1890, over the lines that would divide their empires. The history of these skirmishes are recounted in Chapters 3 and 4. For the moment, attention is focused on the challenges leveled first at the rise of the corporation and second at how the new electronic media were being organised and regulated.

One of the more scathing critics of the rise of the modern corporation was Thorsten Veblen. In contrast to explanations that focused on the "necessity" of the corporation as a response to industrialisation and the needs of mass production, Veblen (1924) retorted:

> the corporation is . . . not an industrial appliance. It is a means of making money, not of making goods . . . . It is only since the dominant interests of the civilised nations has shifted from production for a livelihood to investment for a profit, that this principle of net gain has come to stand out naked and unashamed, as the sound and honest rule that should govern and limit the production of goods for human use. The corporation incorporates this underlying principle of business enterprise more singly and adequately than any form of organisation that had gone before. (pp. 85-86)

Veblen's critique fit the telegraph well, as it was there that the modern corporation first came into its own. The critique of political economists like Veblen, Marx, and others was shared by those who were concerned about the interconnections among "overcapitalised" telegraph companies, the rise of stock markets, and flows of information that supported speculative financial trading (Kieve, 1973; Thompson, 1947). Speculative financial trading by telegraph was also of deep concern to members of the London Stock Exchange (as discussed in Chapter 3). In Fall 1893, for instance, the London Stock Exchange and the *Financial Times* were abuzz with efforts to remove the Exchange Telegraph

Company from the exchange building on the grounds that it supported rogue traders whose speculative activities eroded public confidence in the stock market. The Exchange Telegraph Company was temporarily removed. It was only readmitted after suitable regulatory arrangements were set up amid the Committee of the Stock Exchange and the Exchange Telegraph Company to keep "rogue speculators" away from telegraph-based "online" information services (*Financial Times*, 1893; Scott, 1972, pp. 15-25).

CHALLENGES TO LIBERAL PHILOSOPHICAL AND LEGAL PRINCIPLES

Corporations were admitted into modern societies as "legal persons," which meant that the new economic actors enjoyed property rights but not political or civil rights. The limited legal standing of corporations was also evident in the fact that, especially in telecoms, they required a government charter to commence business. Charters, as Macpherson (1985) notes, simultaneously sanctioned a new way of organising commerce but also narrowly circumscribed corporate "rights." Moreover, charters did not give corporations unbridled property rights, but a right to a revenue for a fixed period of time.

Canadian telegraph and telephone companies were all given conditional charters before beginning business, and they were subject to government reviews of their profit and capitalisation levels. The Dominion Telegraph Company was chartered in 1868, The Bell Telephone Company of Canada in 1880, the Canadian Pacific Telegraph Company in the same year, and so on (see Chapters 3 and 4). Similar practice prevailed in the United States and the United Kingdom. In the latter, telegraph-based online content services—parliamentary information, press services, stock market information, and so on—were licensed by the Post Office to use certain facilities and to draw an income, but not to permanent existence (Post Office, 1879, File 1; Post Office, 1882-1907, File VI, pp. 1-6; United Kingdom, 1868, section 16). Similar practices also prevailed for the distribution of licenses to radio and television broadcasters that gave them the right to temporarily use the radio spectrum, in theory, for a fixed period of time.

The tenuous toe-hold of corporations in modern society was not so much a constraint on capitalism/free markets, but a reflection of transformations in the liberal concepts of property and economic organisation, *in progress*. Again, Veblen's (1924) comments on the matter were incisive, as he looked aghast at attempts to fit corporate entities into legal and philosophical regimes constructed for another time and place:

> Habits of thought have . . . not been displaced and shifted forward to a
> new footing in law and morals in anything like the same measure in
> which men have learned to use new ways and means in industry . . . .
> [O]pinionated persons are quite able to believe that no substantial
> change need take place . . . in that range of habitual "action patterns"
> in which law and morals are grounded . . . . [This] overlooks the service
> rendered by legal fiction and constructive precedents, of course . . . .
> [Laws] were framed by the elder statesmen of the eighteenth century;
> whereas the new industrial order . . . is created by the technicians of the
> twentieth century. There is accordingly a discrepancy between the run
> of material facts in the present and the canons of law and order as
> stabilised in the eighteenth century. (pp. 205-207)

Obvious strains on laws and morals framed in the past and actions
in the present were evident in the organisation and uses of the new
electronic media. In this area, the state was variously called on to establish
a publicly owned telegraph monopoly, to legalise private monopolies,
and/or to regulate the interactions between the telegraph, the press, and
other early "online" information services providers. The close knit links
between the telegraph, the press, and "online" content services in Canada
and the United States from the outset (about 1846) and somewhat later in
the United Kingdom (about 1855) posed perplexing challenges between
the old and new ways of doing things that coexisted uncomfortably at the
time. As new ways of doing things with electronic media confronted old
habits, several questions were pushed to the fore.

The first dealt with whether or not corporations had
consciousness or a mind. The issues came to a head before the Supreme
Court of Canada in 1882 in a case involving the Dominion Telegraph
Company and charges of libel for news stories produced and distributed
by its news service. The conundrum was a "catch-22" situation. To preserve
the philosophical boundaries between corporate "legal persons" and real
citizens—consciousness—would mean that corporations could not be
held responsible for libelous content; however, to make them responsible
for media content would erode the key principle that had kept them from
claiming all the rights of citizenship. In other words, if corporations had a
mind, and in liberal theory the protection of consciousness was the
rationale for media freedoms, the corporation, too, would be all that
much closer to possessing press/media freedoms.

The Supreme Court rejected the Dominion Telegraph Company
lawyers' claim that "the corporation has no mind," but did not deal
directly with the broader issues of media freedom raised (*Dominion
Telegraph Co. vs. John Silver and Abraham Martin Payne*, 1882/1883, pp. 260-
261). However, it was clear that the axis dividing corporations from media
freedoms had shifted from the realm of philosophical anchors to the

politics of judicial activism and expediency. It would only be a matter of time before the opaque divisions between legal people and real people would disappear in a fog of historical amnesia, and, therefore, for media freedoms to be allocated wholly according to political considerations rather than philosophical and ethical principles. These conditions underpin current thrusts by media and telecoms corporations to gain a broader swath of media freedoms than hitherto possible, as discussed in later chapters.

This Supreme Court decision, as well as others occurring in Canada, the United States and the United Kingdom at around the same time (as discussed more fully in the next chapter) was even more interesting in that it brought the telegraph and the press under much the same legal framework. As such, these decisions inaugurated the first phase of "electronic publishing." As the Supreme Court of Canada noted:

> It has been suggested that the transmission of news for publication in newspapers is not within the legitimate business for which telegraph companies are incorporated. I fail to appreciate . . . this objection; as newspapers are now a necessity, so at this day is telegraphic news. . . . No newspaper published in a city such as *St. John* could exist as a leading influential journal without telegraphic news. To say that the transmission of such news by telegraph companies . . . is not a legitimate branch of their business . . . is to ignore what is presented before our eyes every day when we take up a morning or evening paper . . . . It would seem that *telegraph companies are similar to . . . publishers.* (*Dominion Telegraph Co. vs. John Silver and Abraham Martin Payne*, 1882/1883, pp. 257-258, 261; emphasis added).

The important point to note is that legal opinion did not draw stark lines between different means of communication, underscoring the point made at the outset of this chapter about media regulation not being tied to particular technologies. According to legal opinion between about 1870 and 1910, telegraph operators offering press-like services were regulated in a manner analogous to the press—both bore responsibility for content (*Baxter vs. Dominion Telegraph Co.*, 1874/1875, pp. 470-483; *Dominion Telegraph Co. vs. John Silver and Abraham Martin Payne*, 1882/1883, pp. 238-276; de Sola Pool, 1983).

Where distinctions were made, they were between private and public services, and/or between active and passive uses of the telegraph. When telegraph companies played an active role, for example, in collecting and distributing a news service, they had to adhere to strict standards of responsibility and were regulated in a manner analogous to the press. When they played a passive role, as in transmitting messages for others, they were treated as common carriers, carrying messages in the order they were received and bearing little responsibility for content. This hybrid regulatory regime, thus, treated telegraph companies both as "electronic publishers" and as common carriers, depending on the function served. Technical-based distinctions only came later. The details of this mode of regulation is discussed in Chapter 3, and once again in Chapter 7, in which it will be argued that current policy is shifting back to this hybrid form of media regulation.

It is hard to grasp precisely why issues of media freedom were never directly raised or resolved, especially because critiques of telegraph abuses were made on these grounds. Despite the lack of concrete answers to this issue, some reasonable conjecture is possible. One reason might have been due to the fact that most cases in this area dealt with libel and involved commercial interests. In contrast, media freedom in liberal theory dealt with state interference with communication. Moreover, even though media freedoms were predicated on the protection of private actors from state interference, corporations had just been legalised by governments. As such, it was unlikely that the new economic actors would rush to "bite the hand that sustained them." Furthermore, in the context of widespread commercial and popular antagonism to corporations, such actors depended on the state for whatever political legitimacy they could muster (Kolko, 1963, pp. 14-17; Veblen, 1924).

Finally, large corporations in the telecoms industry were not trying to keep governments at bay. Rather they leaned on them not only for their life and legitimacy, but for subsidies, protected monopolies, and, under certain conditions, for governments to take them over outright. All of these forms of business/government interaction are prominent features of telecoms history in Canada, the United Kingdom and the United States. Details of protected monopolies, public ownership, and subsidies follow in the next two chapters, so only some broad points will be made about the origins of media regulation to help further the present discussion.

In 1861, no less a supporter of capitalism then J. L. Ricardo (son of the economist David Ricardo) invited the English government to take over the largest telegraph company in the country, the Electric Telegraph Company, of which he was the chairman (Flichy, 1995, pp. 52-53; Kieve, 1973, pp. 120-121). In Canada, the General Manager of Canadian Pacific's Telegraph Department, Sir Sandford Fleming (1880), an instrumental figure in the history of Canadian telecoms, spoke of two options to develop a national telegraph system (despite the longstanding existence of several other companies):

> 1. To complete it as a Government work, and operate it directly under a Department, as in Great Britain, France and other countries with uniform low scales of charges.

2. To transfer the [existing] 1,200 miles constructed to some company which would undertake to complete and operate the whole line [to the Pacific] on conditions to be determined. (p. 30f)

These are not atypical examples but enduring features of media evolution in North America and elsewhere. The Bell Telephone Company also developed its telephone system under a very favourable charter, as Chapter 4 indicates. Similar interactions between government and industry shaped the development of broadcasting in North America. Although the Canadian government assumed a leading role in broadcasting after 1932, a strong role for the private sector has always been retained. In the United States, private, commercial interests were given a more prominent role in broadcasting, although this was no less "political" for all that. There the state played a key role in allocating rights and resources to create a commercially viable, but politically docile, "broadcast system." Vested interests in the United States made sure that the new media extended commerce, not radical politics. As Zenith chairman W. G. Cowles argued before a 1926 Hearing on Radio Matters, broadcasting should be controlled by national corporations with

> the privilege of refusing . . . all controversial matter, whatever its nature, whether it be religious, politics, or anything . . . in the nature of controversy . . . unless Bolshevist propaganda have a better chance in this country then ever before. All radical thinkers . . . will fill the air with their efforts to poison the minds of those without formed opinion. (U.S. Senate, 1926, p. 12499)[2]

Given such sentiments, and that the *Radio Act of 1927* and the *Communications Act of 1934* did little more than ratify plans for electronic media drawn up by private industry, it is not surprising that broadcasting developed as a poor supplement to democratic politics in the United States. Across the political spectrum, it has been broadly acknowledged that education, labour, religious, and other nonprofit groups got far less than a fair allocation of radio frequencies (Barnouw, 1982; McChesney, 1990; de Sola Pool, 1983, p. 125).[3] As de Sola Pool (1983) noted, once "technical order" and a "stable industry structure" were set, labour-affiliated stations found themselves sharing frequencies with up to 11 others, or their signals jostling for space with the more powerful channels of, for example, Westinghouse (p. 125). Although labour unions and others were incensed, the National Association of Broadcasters gloated that the new law contained "every major point we asked for . . ." (McChesney, 1990, p. 7).

NEOLIBERALISM, THE NEW SOCIAL CONTRACT, AND PEOPLE

The extension of economic rights to corporations in the 19th century, as Macpherson (1985) writes, coincided with promises of improved material well-being for more people as well as the expansion of civil and political rights *within the bounds of the social welfare State*. Rights went from the "first principles" of classic liberalism to the trade-offs of the jointly managed (state and corporations, and to a lesser extent, trade unions) social welfare economy of industrial capitalism. This involved not regulation, or deregulation, but all four modes of intervention mentioned at the beginning of this chapter: government intervention, market regulation, technocratic management, and deference to citizens and democratic processes so long as these did not cut too deeply into economic accumulation, governability, and the civil liberties of property owners.

As C. B. Macpherson, T. H. Marshall (1950), and other political theorists have noted, during the 20th century citizenship came to rest on three kinds of rights: socioeconomic, political, and civil. Socioeconomic rights are rights to a modicum of welfare guaranteed by the state (Marshall, 1950, p. 11; Macpherson, 1985, pp. 22-23). Macpherson (1985) describes them as:

> the right to work; the right to equal pay for work of equal value; the right to social security against the consequences of illness, old age, death of the breadwinner, and involuntary unemployment; the right to an income consistent with a life of human dignity; the right to rest and leisure . . . and to education. (p. 22)

Political rights were those such as voting, which gave citizens "a voice in the control of the state" (Macpherson, 1985, p. 23). Only after corporations were legalised and given the right to own property were citizens given political powers free of connections to property ownership or gender. Citizenship and voting rights for Canadian men were severed from property ownership requirements in 1885, and it was not until 1918 that women could vote in national elections. In the provinces, these changes took even longer (Jackson & Jackson, 1990, p. 462; Khan & McNiven, 1991, p. 168). Civil liberties differed from political rights in that they supported individual freedoms and empowered people "against the State" (Macpherson, 1985, p. 23).

It was only a relatively short step from strengthening people's "voice in the control of the State" to arguments that this required access to the resources necessary to support informed participation in public affairs. As a result, citizens gained the right to receive information, although this was not to be misconstrued as the ability to use modern means of communication to disseminate information. The right to receive information was evident in the development of universal, publicly funded education since the end of the 19th century, public libraries, and national information and statistical agencies, among other things. Public libraries, for instance, were established in Canada between 1883 and 1903, and in the United States (1902) and the United Kingdom at about the same time.[4]

It did not take long for the idea of the right to receive information to be extended to include the right to receive telecoms services, first for the telegraph, then for telephony, and finally for broadcasting. In the United Kingdom, part of the reason for nationalising the telegraph service initially was to make it universally available (United Kingdom, 1868, p. 503). This did not, of course, mean that every home should have a telegraph connection. It meant that the telegraph should be geographically ubiquitous, even if this was uneconomic, and that service should be available on demand at affordable rates. To this end, enormous subsidies were given for public use of the telegraph (Fleming, 1902). The interest in a universal telegraph system was also linked to the availability of the press and the forging of a national political culture— also matters that were hugely subsidised by the state under the concept of *political enfranchisement*. Similar ideas underwrote cheap telegraph rates for the press in Canada as well (BRC, 1910; 1914; Fleming, 1902; Post Office, 1876).

Similar considerations also informed telecoms, and later broadcasting, policy. This was visible in the intense telecoms politics in Canada between about 1893 and 1915. Some of the ingredients of the universal service concept were outlined in Chapter 1, and will be discussed in greater historical detail in Chapter 4. For the moment we can note that such ideas were embedded in provisions in the *U.S. Communications Act of 1934* requiring that broadcasting and telecoms service be made universally available "so far as practicable" (Mueller, 1993). Universal service, of course, was also linked to perceptions that telecoms systems were instrumental to the development of countries' economic and social infrastructure (Mansell, 1993). Others spoke of using new media to forge nationally based universal languages (standardisation of regional dialects), universal technical standards for interoperable systems, universal standard time set by instantaneous communication across the country, and universal nationally based communicative spaces (Flichy, 1995, pp. 10-36). Thus, the concept of universal service encompassed political economic, sociocultural, technical, and geographic dimensions, and should not be narrowly construed.

Recent critiques of universal service by Mueller (1993) and Schultz and Janisch (1993) are right to argue that too many scholars have misinterpreted the concept and tied it too narrowly to the natural monopoly regulatory regime. However, their interpretations too narrowly tie the concept to telephony and fail to see its earlier history in telegraphy, the press, and the transformation of liberal politics that brought about, among other things, a limited political right of information access as a quid pro quo for citizens' acquiescence to the sweeping social, political, economic and legal transformations in society that have been described in this chapter. Schultz and Janisch's (1993) argument that universal service is merely a by-product of activist bureaucrats completely ignores this social and historical context.

Moreover, these critiques miss the point altogether that a right to information and telecoms services is a poor approximation of a potentially much richer concept of media freedoms. As Ruggles (1994) states, "expressive rights in the electronic media are not incorporated into the package of civil, political and social rights of citizenship enjoyed in North America" (p. x).

Citizens may have the right to access information, and government officials can measure and worry about the availability of telephones, televisions, newspapers, computers, and so on, but in the end, as de Sola Pool (1983) states in reference to the United States, "the First Amendment should be read as permitting unrestrained expression by publishers rather than requiring a fair, publicly organised forum" (p. 133). The same applies elsewhere, as well, as Garnham (1990) reminds us when he states:

> We would find it strange now if we made voting rights dependent on purchasing power or property rights; yet access to the mass media, as both channels of information and forums of debate, is largely controlled by just such power and rights. (p. 111)

KNOWLEDGE, EXPERTS, AND THE POLITICS OF TELECOMS POLICY

This idea of modern liberalism as a trade-off (Macpherson, 1985) is buried in contemporary telecoms politics and policy. Instead of sorting out the convoluted history of modern capitalism and democracy, telecoms analysts, by and large, argue within the debilitating confines of regulation/deregulation, or tackle policy issues as if they are mostly technical in nature. This is understandable given media researchers enduring commitment, as one of the "founding fathers" of communication research, Paul Lazarsfeld, candidly acknowledged, to conducting inquiry and "criticism within the present framework of the [communications] industry" (quoted in Hardt, 1992, p. 77). Although critical and comparative research has revealed that there are many ways to organise media systems to supplement a democratic way of life, such inquiry has largely been pushed to the margins of communication policy (Schiller, 1989; Smythe, 1981).

Telecoms policy is usually, as Porat (1978) describes, about "technology, prices, law and public opinion" among those with a material interest in regulatory proceedings (p. 12). The policy process, in North America anyway, is not closed but open to various groups who, as Noll and Owen (1983) argue, enter the regulatory process to represent specialised interests. These groups, according to Noll and Owen's analysis, enter policy proceedings on the basis of "self-interest" and the "size of the stakes involved," tend to shift alliances depending on the issues at hand, and are equally able to shape the policy agenda and outcomes (pp. 41-43). Commenting on this "public interest" view of policy politics in general, Hayek (1986) argues that the disruptive forces of free markets prevent "power blocs" from forming over the long run and that the guiding logic is strategic self-interest. According to Hayek, it is impossible for public policy processes to be guided by ideas of "social or distributive justice, since consensus about what such concepts mean can never exist" (p. 26).

Even though policy processes may be characterised by interest group politics, it is also true that one of the most powerful forces shaping the policy process is the belief that key issues can be solved by science and technique. Experts have long claimed to have special insights into what human purposes new technologies should serve. Media historian Carolyn Marvin (1988) quotes an early electrical engineer to indicate the degree to which technical thinking has colluded with media politics: "No other man in the world has such stern and unceasing discipline, and so it comes about that no other man is so safe a moral guide as the engineer, with his passion for truth and thinking straight" (p. 32).

Such sentiments were arguably buttressed by the natural monopoly regime that has characterised so much of 20th century telecoms history. These arrangements came to be legitimated on the grounds that monopoly and vertical integration in telecoms, although undermining the allocational efficiency of competition in the short term, compensated for this in the long term by producing greater dynamic efficiencies. Bauer and Steinfield (1994) note that advocates of regulated monopolies believed that "innovation is best facilitated under conditions of imperfect competition that enable innovating firms to earn temporary innovation premiums through their market power" (p. 21). As such, competition was intentionally inhibited to foster "a better environment for planning and innovation . . . . Part of the reason for creating giant firms is precisely to afford insulation from market pressures to allow long-term, major innovation" (Sayer, 1995, p. 138). This stress on long-term planning and the suppression of uncertainty meant not only that regulation shielded monopoly telephone providers from competition but that the overall context of telecoms was governed by systems planning, technical knowledge, and experts.

These views gained strength in the mid to late 1960s in response to the increasing complexity—technological, economic, and political—of communications. At the time much hope was fixed on computer-based and other expert-system approaches to objectively solve the problems brought up by the ever-more complex context of telecoms. The Chief of the Economic Studies Division of the FCC, Boyd Nelson (1969), held out hope that politics and intransigent policy positions would yield once scientific studies

> discovered the best evidence . . . . There would be little concern with the age-old arm-twisting arts . . . . [T]he agency would make its underlying data and other supporting material available for criticism and its experts might be made available for questioning as a means of pointing up . . . the weaknesses of the model . . . . Other experts might propose modifications of the model, relying always on its own experts (perhaps including outside consultants) for technical advice . . . . Best of all perhaps would be an informal type of proceeding open to all persons having either a financial or an intellectual interest. A record should be kept and made available to the public. (pp. 337-338)

Although obviously there is a considerable need to build a robust body of knowledge on which to base communication policy, this is different from attempting to depoliticise public life. The approach advocated by Boyd seemed to ignore this link among knowledge, technology, and politics, and in doing so, limited citizens' presence in telecoms policy. More attention seemed to be focused on models and what the experts thought than what the issues were, what people wanted to do with the new media, and other salient points.

The transformation of political issues into technical ones is not unique to telecoms. Jurgen Habermas argues that this reflects a general tendency to subordinate substantive democracy to "limited democracy." He claims that the greatest threat to modern society is the incessant reduction of all issues to the formal, technical needs of administrative problem solving. The consequent excessive stress on formal rules, procedures and transparency, and the objectivity of administration/law, Habermas (1984/1987) states, "has defused the explosive contents of modernity" (p. 320). Habermas (1984/1987) goes on to argue that this is done through a rather blatant, albeit unreflective and naïve, disregard for what is so unique about modern societies: the fact that the entire social and political order is "in principle open to criticism and in need of justification" (p. 260). In his view, democracy should rely on standards of what should be done through communication in the public sphere, not only formal rules and procedures guiding the interaction among the major constituents of modernity—state, capital, people, and media. In a democracy, communication would be elevated as a means of steering the political, economic, and technical spheres of society, not subordinate to their "logics."

Yet this is exactly the point contested by neoliberal theorists and those of "limited democracy." These theorists argue for clear-cut rules, boundaries, and ideas about rights and freedoms, and the uncoupling of markets, science, and technology from normative constraints (Hayek, 1986; Kelley & Donway, 1990; Weber, 1946). Habermas (1984/1987), in contrast, claims that this drains law, politics, and economics of their practical and ethical content as they are overwhelmed by competitive struggles over the levers of power, self-interest, and success. As politics, law, and economics escape public communication and people's understanding, they become linked to instrumental action, power, and technical knowledge rather than any idea of what is right, just, and good. After a while, nobody believes that the society in which they live is the best it could be, but hope that it can continue to "deliver the goods" or lapse into alienation in the face of an apparent absence of imaginable or possible alternatives.

Table 2.1 tries to summarise these competing views. It suggests that at least three different theoretical views of democracy can be imagined and have been relied on at various times by communication policy analysts. The three perspectives are: theories of "limited democracy" relied on by liberal theorists; a theory of "communicative democracy" derived from Habermas' work, among others; and an intermediary view referred to as "pragmatic democracy" that is culled from the long-standing efforts of experts to address the "public interest" in communication policy.

CRISIS OF DEMOCRACY OR BUSINESS AS USUAL?

The idea that communications policy is an exercise in expert-based problem solving has been strongly challenged since the late 1960s. One main criticism has been that alliances among regulators, governments, and industry have sacrificed public policy to "extra-parliamentary political processes" (Held, 1987, p. 216).

In Canada, several factors coalesced to produce a more robust telecoms politics. First, there began to be increased unease with Bell and

Table 2.1. The Three Faces of Democracy.

Type of Democracy	Limited Democracy	Pragmatic Democracy	Communicative Democracy
Orientation to Rules	High	Moderate	Low
Value Given to Social Change	Low	Moderate (w. represent democracy)	High (fundamental to democracy)
Citizen Participation	Limited, representative, and periodic	Regular, but expert/elite guided	Extensive communicative interaction
View of Technology	Neutral/evolutionary	Malleable and possibly liberating	Expression of power, but contestable
Orientation to Power	Limited/state-centric	Conciliatory	Focus of critique
Nature of Rights/Freedom	Negative freedoms	Mixed negative and positive freedoms (social contract)	Mixed (focus on equitable distribution and realisation in praxis)
Value Given to Economic Change	High/superordinate	Resigned/control in public interest	Subordinate to reflexive praxis
Understanding of Communication	Commodity/entertain. Political knowledge Watchdog representative	Empathy/reciprocity. Soc/psychological dev. Social integration Mediated participation	Legitimate and mediate power Participatory/media access Form of soc/pol critique Reflexive, critical and transformative
Orientation to Knowledge	Specialist/expert	Public interest-oriented experts	

other Trans Canada Telephone System (TCTS) members' use of the regulatory process to thwart competition and push through a spate of rate increases (Babe, 1990; Surtees, 1994a). Second, there was growing concern that limiting the policy process only to those with a 'material or intellectual interest' was at odds with democratic politics. These trends percolated through to telecoms policy proceedings in several key instances, some of which included a Canadian Transport Commission (CTC) decision in 1975 refusing support for greater public participation in its hearings, the transfer of telecoms regulation to the CRTC in 1976, and that agency's subsequent announcement that it would take a broad view of the "public interest" (CTC, 1975; CRTC, 1976a).

Some saw these as attempts to democratise communication, policy, and society. Others, however, saw the attempts to revitalize people's involvement in politics and public life as a "crisis of democracy." In the mid-1970s, several leading academics, business leaders, and government officials from Canada, Europe, Japan and the United States—the so-called Trilateral Commission—began to investigate and report on the problems of political governance in the industrial democracies. According to the Trilateral Commission, regulated markets and representative democracy were producing an excess of politics and demands among citizens that business and government were incapable of satisfying. Crozier, Huntington, and Watanuki (1975), the authors of the report, put matters this way:

> the advanced industrial societies have spawned a stratum of value-oriented intellectuals who . . . devote themselves to the derogation of leadership, the challenging of authority, and the unmasking and delegitimation of institutions, their behaviour contrasting with that of the increasing numbers of *technocratic and policy-oriented intellectuals.* In an age of widespread . . . education, the pervasiveness of the mass media, and displacement of manual labour by clerical and professional employees, this . . . challenge to democratic government is . . . as serious as those posed . . . by the aristocratic cliques, fascist movements and communist parties (pp. 6-7; emphasis added).

These ideas were familiar to Canadian policymakers at the time, as two consecutive chairs of the CRTC, the soon-to-be Minister of Communications, Francis Fox, and several members of the print and broadcast media contributed to Trilateral Commission work (Crozier et. al., 1975, introductory note, pp. 209-211). Illustrating the extent to which "crisis of democracy" thinking penetrated regulatory affairs, the CTC rejected citizens' efforts to liberalise the politics of telecoms policy. According to Commissioner John Gray (CTC, 1975):

> Citizens' groups may quite unwittingly and with the best of intentions, by fostering unjustified public non-confidence in regulatory tribunals over the long run do more serious injury to the public interest than they do good. . . . When this situation exists there is a danger that the regulated industry may become a poor investment, receiving less income than it requires to meet expenses and provide a reasonable profit. The industry may become unable to attract capital. . . . It may be impossible . . . to plan for future expansion and eventually the public finds itself deprived of service. . . . (p. 71)

The trade-off between economic welfare and political participation discussed earlier could hardly be put more starkly. Yet, such views were typical for the time. In fact, they reflected the enduring antimony between capitalism, communication, and democracy. As Max Weber (1946) argued, democracy should be seen only as a means for people to periodically select and change leaders, to confer political legitimacy, and as an efficient means of steering society, the economy, and government bureaucracy.

When the CRTC took over the telecoms policy agenda from the CTC in 1976, it attempted to introduce a more open approach that supported competition in the public interest, in contrast to the technocratically oriented monopoly regime of its predecessor (Babe, 1990; CRTC, 1976; Roman, 1990). However, it was stymied from the outset by the intrusive hand of the emerging strong state that was bent on realizing its own particular version of competition, as reviewed in Chapters 5 and 6, as well as by academic critics who saw the Commission as pursuing an activist agenda of unsanctioned social policies and transfers of wealth that should be brought out into the open and eliminated (Janisch, 1986; Rowley, 1983, p. 30; Schultz & Janisch, 1993, p. 9). To avoid a continuation of this "excessive democratic drift," some advocated constitutional reform to relieve government and "free markets" of "intense and strident societal pressures" (McKay, 1983, p. 100; also see Hayek, 1986, pp. 24-27; Rowley, 1983, pp. 53-61).

This situation has changed. As Chapters 5, 6, and 7 demonstrate, the state has freed telecoms politics from the binds of the more democratic policy process that flourished under the CRTC's new mandate between 1976 and the early 1980s. Whereas the CRTC, even as early as 1969, saw itself mediating among industry, new technology, and the public, rather than slavishly tying itself to an agenda wholly set by business and "technological imperatives" (CRTC, 1969, p. 36), now its mission seems mainly to be to construct markets, shield new media from public service obligations, and to sell its policy outcomes to the public as in the "consumers interest."[5]

One big change in telecoms policy is that the focus has switched from selling the "natural monopoly" regime to convincing people that the future lies in embracing information highways for which there is little demonstrable demand (Canada, 1996a; CRTC, 1994a, 1995a, 1995b). As David Johnson, chairperson of the Information Highway Advisory Council (IHAC), noted during a recent speech, the task of government and industry is to get Canadians onto the information highway as fast as possible (see also, Canada, 1996, p. 24). Another study prepared for the government, and reported in *Computing Canada*, notes that "government and corporations *must assist the consumer's desire* to have a flexible and responsive communications environment . . . . [T]he Canadian mindset may dictate whether they win or lose on the information highway" (quoted in Shoesmith, 1995, p. 1; emphasis added). It is clear from this and other American, European, and Japanese reports that information highway/society initiatives seek more than just new technologies, data flows, and economic arrangements; they seek the hearts and minds of those who will inhabit the new world information order (Bangemann, 1994; US, 1994a). Whether such social engineering efforts are proper activities for democratic governments, however, is another issue altogether, and one addressed at great length in Chapter 7.

TELECOMS AND THE THEORY OF LEGITIMATION CRISIS

The Three Sector Model of the Economy

Generally speaking, there are two ways of dealing with an "overloaded social system." The first is to expand the capacity of existing institutional arrangements to deal with the issues being pressed; for example, by opening telecoms policy even further to a wide array of interests. A second option is to render regulation less susceptible to "systems overload." Telecoms policy over the last 15 years or so has relied more heavily on this latter option, substituting regulation by the market and technical expertise for politically organised methods of solving communication policy problems and issues (Mosco, 1988).

Although this shift was no doubt connected with "crisis of democracy" theories, its more overt connections were to new technologies—computers, satellites, microwave—and the competitive telecoms policy agenda first promoted in the United States and to ever-wider circles thereafter. The shift was anticipated by a series of "little bangs" that introduced competition on the margins of the industry—

microwave, customer premises equipment (cpe), data communication—from the 1950s onward. Changes to the natural monopoly telecoms policy regime gained much more momentum after the AT&T divestiture decision in 1982 that vastly expanded network infrastructure competition. This created intense pressures to establish similar conditions worldwide (Jussawalla, 1989; p. 7; Porat, 1978, p. 13).

The advent of competition in telecoms is usually attributed to technological change and the need to eliminate government intervention in the economy. Regulation is thought to have been predicated on a specific technological base and is often seen as a transient political response to peculiar conditions. In contrast, "deregulation is presented as non-political and an inevitable result of technological progress" (Hills, 1986, p. 4). In addition, economic growth has led to the view that it is no longer necessary for governments to pool together scarce resources as a means of furthering technological innovation and meeting social policy aims. In addition, markets are seen as more transparent devices for solving problems than government-organised solutions.

The trend toward competition, however, is neither straightforward nor unproblematic. The first problem is with what is meant by competition. The analysis in this book shows that there are at least three approaches to competition: niche, network services-based, and infrastructure competition.

For the most part, competition starts in niche areas such as data communications, cpe, microwave, and so on, and then gravitates toward network services and, in some cases, to the network core. This is not always true, however. France, for example, as will be seen, has been far more eager to allow niche competition than in the other areas. The German approach, as in Canada until the early 1990s, has promoted network services competition. The United States and the United Kingdom have embraced network competition the longest (OECD, 1995a). As shown in Chapter 6, Canada adopted infrastructure competition with the introduction of long-distance competition in 1992 (CRTC, 1992a). Approaches to competition also depend on whether governments prevent, permit, or promote media reconvergence.

Despite the varying approaches to competitive telecoms policies, an impressive body of evidence exists to show that competition does not conform to the expectations of economic theory—at least in its idealised form. This applies where experience is long and tested, as in the United States, or where it is of more recent vintage, as in Canada. Evidence in the United States from 1988 to the present shows competition to be settling into an oligopoly shared among AT&T (60-65% market share), BT/MCI, and Sprint. The latter two share 25% to 30% of the market, whereas 200 to 500 other companies scramble for the left over 5% to 10% (Mosco, 1990a, p. 43; Trebing, 1995, p. 317). Trebing (1995) analysed market dominance, profits, and price leadership in the United States and concluded that there are no signs of "workable competition" (p. 317). By mid-1996, Noll saw a possible return to the old Bell System, only this time "with a Bell West, a Bell East and centrally-based Ameritech in a quandary as to whether to join the West or the East, or to act as the glue containing all into a single maxi-Bell" (p. B-9). As most analysts persist to defy the real world, Noll (1996)

> continued to wonder whether the provision of telecoms services is a natural monopoly after all, and competition . . . contrived. Monopoly is not inherently evil. What can be evil is unregulated, unfettered monopoly, and this . . . is what seems to be evolving at the local Baby Bell level. (p. B-9)

Similar trends are apparent in the United Kingdom, where talks of a merger between Cable and Wireless (the second largest operator in the United Kingdom and among the largest telcos in the world) and BT were called off only to be upstaged a few months later by the BT/MCI merger announcement. The sale of Rogers' and CP's shares in the major—and until then, solely owned by Canadian interests—long-distance competitor, Unitel, to AT&T, the Bank of Nova Scotia, Royal Bank, and Toronto Dominion Bank, also marked the capitulation of competition in Canada to the oligopolistic telecoms market. So, too, has the set-up between Call-Net and its U.S. partner, Sprint. As BT (1990) recently acknowledged, "the world-wide telecommunications infrastructure will likely be managed by perhaps only four or five large providers" (quoted in Webster, 1995, p. 88).

It is quite clear that rather than conforming to the ideals of "perfect competition," the reality of telecoms is that of oligopolistic and strategic rivalry alongside pockets of competition. This is close to a model of the "late capitalist" economy developed by Jurgen Habermas, J. K. Galbraith, and Claus Offe, among others. According to these authors, the competitive ideal has been displaced by a three-sector economy consisting of an oligopoly/monopoly core, a public sector, and a competitive fringe.[6]

Applying this view to telecoms is not necessarily a radical step, but one that would have gained the assent of erstwhile champions of competition up until, perhaps, a decade ago. Even de Sola Pool (1983) accepted that, "the degree of monopoly is likely to remain significant in transmission plants. . . . As such, common carrier principles, including compulsory non-discriminatory access, will continue to be appropriate . . . , [although] electronic publishing should be fully unregulated" (p. 218).

The view that competition in certain areas of telecoms is yielding to strategic and oligopolistic rivalry is widely held, although interpretations about what this means and what should be done about it differ widely (Mansell, 1993). Some argue that it does not matter, so long as the benefits of competition can be obtained some other way, for example, by just the threat of competition. As the communication economist Meheroo Jussawalla (1989) claims, "Contestability theory . . . shows that some of the values of the competitive process can be preserved in a market with a small number of large firms—in particular, a monopolist with several small potential rivals" (p. 23).

Yet, such explanations seem to force reality to fit preconceived theoretical notions, rather than to deal squarely with the problem of "market failure." As will be seen in Chapter 6, this problem seems to befuddle the CRTC and Canadian policymakers as they proliferate a variety of new terms to describe less-than-real competition. In contrast, Mansell (1993) takes a less sanguine view of how imperfect telecoms markets interact on the basis of power, the control of technological design, and access to the PTN, among other things, to produce suboptimal outcomes for society in general. In addition, she sees strategic rivalry as pitting those in the oligopolistic core against one another, as well as against others in the competitive fringes, over issues about who will be price makers and price takers, and who will control the benefits and uses of new technical innovations. Those in the competitive fringes also seek to position themselves opportunistically as well as defensively alongside the expansionist ambitions of the dominant core telecoms providers (Mansell, 1993; Melody, 1994; Offe, 1984; pp. 43-44).

The Role of the State

Divergent approaches to competition and the existence of strategic rivalry suggests that the role of the state in telecoms policy has been changed, not abandoned. Theories of deregulation typically overlook this fact. As this chapter has suggested, it is a mistake to speak of regulation and deregulation. Far from passively withdrawing from telecoms markets, as Mody and Tsui (1995) point out, government actors are among the most forceful advocates of regulatory liberalisation and privatisation. In fact, as Pettrazinni (1993) indicates, the more far-reaching the changes to the telecoms policy regime sought, the more determined the exercise of state power must be. As the U.S. *White Paper* (1994a) on communication policy reform states, "when national interests are at stake," the federal government will need to be able to preempt lower level governments in "a few key areas" (p. 3). As Chapters 5, 6, and 7 illustrate, one of the paradoxes of regulatory liberalisation is the emergence of the strong state in telecoms policy.

The idea that governments will no longer intervene in markets and media politics is a fiction. In capitalist societies, governments regularly intervene in the economy so long as this does not unduly interfere with economic growth, does not single out specific private interests for unjust treatment, is consistent with maximising tax revenues, and can be sold to the public as in their best interest. The political theorist, Martin Carnoy (1984), argues that among all of these concerns, "economic accumulation is the most powerful constraint on . . . the policy-making process" (p. 134). This emphasis on the promotion of economic accumulation can be seen in the three main types of state intervention that take place.

There are those that intend to correct market shortcomings through investments, technology policy, "cultural adjustment" strategies, tax credits, cash infusions, joint projects, and so on. Then there are initiatives that create or expand private markets such as infrastructure projects paid for out of public budgets, arms,[7] space programs, commercialisation and privatisation of communication/information resources, and technology-push programs (information highways). At the very least, telecoms markets require governments to create

> proper political and legal institutions that are . . . guaranteed by the State. It is only State actions that secure rights of property, freedom of exchange, the sanctity of contract, and the prohibition of practices that interfere with the free market. (Horwitz, 1991, p. 58)

Finally, there are global planning initiatives. Interventions of this latter type, as Hawkins (1995) suggests, harness the "shallow" (goods, information, and services) and "deep" (laws, institutions, infrastructure) resources of a country to the dynamics of the global economy (p. 5). Cox (1992) similarly notes that one of the major new roles for contemporary governments is to recalibrate "national economic practices and policies to the perceived exigencies of the global economy" (pp. 30-31). In the Canadian context, the CUFTA, NAFTA, and GATS agreements, all of which cover communication issues, exemplify this new mode of government intervention. The different modes of government intervention in telecoms policy are summarised in Table 2.2.

ACCUMULATION, LEGITIMACY AND THE CRISIS OF COMMUNICATION

Governments play a key role in managing the economy, politics, and public life on a daily basis. Habermas (1975) and Offe (1984) are keen to analyse how this is done, on the one hand, without unduly interfering with economies that are still based primarily on market distribution and

Table 2.2. Modes of Government Intervention in Telecoms Policy.

Approach to Network Access	Approach to Media Reconvergence	Approach to Network Comp.	Regulating the General Political Economy
Common carrier	Prevent	Niche	Correct market defects
Partial relaxation/ Hybrid	Permit	Network-based services	Create/expand markets
Contract carriage	Promote	Infrastructure	Global planning

Note: Obviously, this is not an exhaustive list of the ways in which governments, technology, and markets interact. It, does, however, consolidate many of the points raised thus far in Chapters 1 and 2. Moreover, the table gives an idea of the many possible combinations of different regulatory logics, thus underscoring the futility in trying to reduce complexity to a simple-minded regulation/deregulation opposition.

private ownership, while on the other, retaining governments' need for political legitimacy. Governments, thus, depend on legitimacy that is generated through the political process, while the scope of their action is still linked to the needs of a privately owned economy and dependent on the economy for tax revenues (Offe, 1984, p. 121). These conditions create crisis potentials for governments because they are simultaneously torn between promoting the general conditions of economic accumulation and trying to maintain political legitimacy in the eyes of citizens, or the electorate. The problems are made all the more difficult, as the vast changes to the market, the state, and civil society described earlier mean that there are no "first philosophical principles" left to guide the state's actions.[8] As such, decisions depend on the transient balance of political forces.

Habermas' (1975) position on these developments has been incisive in several ways. In contrast to the Trilateral Commission's emphasis on the crisis of governance, Habermas (1975) argues that modern societies contain the potential for an economic, political, and/or cultural crisis. The possibility of an economic crisis arises because although governments may seek to promote general processes of economic accumulation, particular capitalists always try to shape policy agendas and outcomes in their favour. Specific attempts to tie public policy to private agendas become rampant, as business interests try to "win the regulatory game," and there are always some interests capable of claiming that one or another policy is a grievous instance of "appropriation without compensation"[9] whenever things do not turn out in their favour. In addition, coupling the polity and the economy threaten a rupture between the private interests the government strives to further and the general interests it claims to embody (legitimation crisis) (Habermas, 1975, p. 39).

Finally, attempts to legitimate the integration of the state, economy, and technology are based on promises of higher levels of material comfort for people in general. This presumes that the idea of citizenship can be reduced to material interests, consumer choice, and post-hoc ratification of governments and their industrial policies through the vote. Moreover, it presumes that the promise to "deliver the goods"—abundant consumer marketplaces—can be redeemed, a promise now fading in the face of falling incomes, greater income gaps between rich and poor, and the lowering of expectations about what constitutes the "good life" (cultural crisis) (Barlow, 1996; Galbraith, 1992; Love & Poulin, 1991).

This thesis has been pursued recently by Galbraith (1992) and by Canadian writers and social critics such as Barlow (1996) and McQuaig (1995). These authors claim that a political culture based on strident self-interest is emerging in which the rich buy themselves out of publicly funded education, media and health systems, and establish their own private enclaves filled with the essential agencies of social, cultural, and physical reproduction. As Barlow (1996) observes:

> In the name of "choice", governments are openly discussing publicly-funded-for-profit schools, allowing unprecedented corporate intrusions in the classroom, and attacking teachers and other front-line educators as adversaries of "advancement" . . . . Everyone is a consumer; students, parents, and those who will enjoy the final product—value added children whose . . . utility in the world of work can and must be measured. Proponents of this ideology insist that liberty and democracy require the unlimited right to consumer choice, even if it will destroy the public systems upon which Canada was built. Public schools do not preach competition; established to meet collective goals of democracy and equality, they have little in common with the . . . theology of . . . consumerism and competitiveness that characterises the global economy. (p. 2)

The same logic that is restructuring the broader political and economic culture also extends to telecoms policy decisions, in which calls to promote cultural pluralism, media access, and diversity of ownership collide with intense efforts to deepen and extend markets and to liberate new media from any public service obligations whatsoever (CRTC, 1995a; European Commission, 1996; Hitchens, 1997; Horwitz, 1991; US, 1996).[10] As these changes percolate through society, "the ability to pay criterion is becoming the standard of information access" (Schiller, 1986, p. 38), the burden of paying for the telecoms network is shifted onto smaller users (Hills, 1986, p. 203), and domestic space, leisure time, and public life harnessed to new information markets through the commercialisation of telecoms, broadcasting, and public information (Smythe, 1981). The trends are also visible in public, university, and corporate libraries, where new information-technology rich facilities often have fewer staff, shorter hours, expensive user fees, and librarians whose task is as much to police access to information as it is to encourage it.[11]

SUMMARY COMMENTS

As the following chapters show, these arguments are not antithetical to the advent of competition and a greater role for the "market" in telecoms and content services. As will be seen, competitively provided online information services commingled with public service goals as early as the late 19th century. The same can be said about telephone development in Canada and elsewhere (Babe, 1990; Davis, 1994; Mueller, 1993), as shown in Chapter 4. It is only when market power is liberated from furthering the human condition, shielded from public voice and potential critiques of power through recourse to philosophical discourses no longer appropriate for our times, and buttressed by the strong state, that "competition" becomes grotesque.

The point continued throughout this book is that it is no longer possible, nor desirable, to interpret telecoms policy within the framework offered by liberal theory. Through vast transformations in modern societies that are fundamentally connected with the history of telecoms, the foundations of liberalism have been swept away. The fact that these vast sweeping changes have dissolved natural rights and led to societies that are completely and irrevocably "policy determined" is neither a good thing nor a bad thing. It does mean, however, that attempts to rely on "free markets" or liberal visions of the state for a recipe for what should be done to develop, organise, and use existing and new means of communication are irrelevant at best, ideological at worst. In terms of the latter, the antiquated discourse of liberalism provides a recipe for "limited democracy" that works primarily to shield social institutions, new media, and power from people.

Despite its progressive role in expanding the scope of civil liberties, political freedoms, and democratic societies, liberal theory had its faults. One is that although it beneficially located the philosophical basis for regulating the distorting influence of the state on people's communicative acts squarely in the mind, it also glossed over the fact that communication is a social act as well. In addition, whereas liberalism properly provided people with a voice to control the state, no such communicative powers were given with respect to corporations (nor could they have been because the corporation had yet to be invented). As such, it properly protected people from the intrusive hand of the state but denigrated efforts to create fairly organised systems of communication as well. Media regulation needs to be concerned more about the quality of communication in general, and not just with civil liberties (Hoffman-Riem, 1996). This, of course, has been done for much of the last 150 years, but its origins and rationale have been opaque.

Second, the discourse of liberalism overemphasised the negative impact of the state on private life, and thus ignores distinctions between legitimate and illegitimate efforts to improve society by way of democratic means. Moreover, the tendency to dichotomise the world into capital versus the state fails to see that societies regulate their affairs and solve problems through markets, political arenas, expert knowledge, and people talking about what needs and should be done. As such, there are at least four modes of regulation, not one.

Politics has become a system of trade-offs (Macpherson, 1985), the precise balance of outcomes regulated by the interaction of markets, expertise, and government intervention. Although it is possible to expand the role of people, politics, and communication in defining the types of societies where we might want to live, it seems that regulatory collusion among markets, experts, and governments has been bent on removing issues from the public agenda and limiting democracy. The rest of this book discusses this enduring historical tension between the reality of media, technology, and society, on the one hand, and what people have consistently tried to do with the means of communication at their disposal, on the other.

ENDNOTES

1. Mosco (1988) has also developed similar ideas, noting that societies possess several methods for "processing social claims": the market (economic power), representation (political power), social control (cultural power), and expertise (technocratic power) (pp. 108-110).

2. Cowles' views were not atypical among the leading voices influencing the development of the new media and journalism in the United States at the time. The leading American political and journalism theorist, Walter Lippman (1956) argued, "The people have acquired power which they are incapable of exercising, and the governments . . . have lost powers which they must recover . . . . Where mass opinion dominates the government, there is a morbid derangement . . . [that] brings about the enfeeblement, verging on paralysis, of the capacity to govern" (p. 19).

3.   Barbrook (1995) notes similar features in France, where, after an early period of experimentation with radio by individuals and various collectives, radio was soon handed over to "responsible" industrial concerns, and later to the government (p. 46). The events in Canada around this period are discussed in Chapter 5.

4.   Canadian public libraries have roots in professional and trade libraries set up in Newfoundland in 1827. The first public libraries were established in Ontario with the *Free Libraries Act.* British Columbia followed several years later (1891), whereas Quebec waited until 1960 before establishing similar facilities (Morton, 1975, pp. 1-3). Funding was a perennial issue during the early years, often resulting in the libraries relying on outside benefactors such as Andrew Carnegie, and later, the Rockefeller Foundation (Myrvold, 1986, pp. 67-68).

5.   Whether by coincidence or design, Canadian political scientists observe a return to "democratic normalcy," as citizens report greater feelings of alienation, powerlessness, negativity, and a lack of trust in politics (Clarke, LeDuc, Jenson, & Pammett, 1991, pp. 25-43).

6.   Throughout this study, a combination of Concentration Ratios and the Herfindahl-Hirshmann Index, as well as criteria set out in the *Mergers Enforcement Guidelines* referred to in the previous chapter, is used to evaluate the presence or absence of competition. A strict interpretation of market power is assumed to have *prima facia* support when one firm controls more than 10% of a market, 3 firms 25%, and 8 firms 50% (Atkins, 1994). A less restrictive measure is where 35-40% of a market is controlled by one firm (Trebing, 1995, p. 317). Measures are based on profits, market share, and share of users "controlled" by firms. "Sectors," by and large, conform to the division of the telecoms-based media universe outlined in Figure 1.2 in Chapter 1: network infrastructure, access providers, content packagers, and content providers. The scope of private and public ownership is also compared and contrasted historically according to each sector's share of revenues, profits, and subscribers.

7.   Note the relationship here between military research and expenditures and every new major adjunct to communication markets in the past 150 years: telegraphy, broadcasting/wireless, computers, Internet, microwave, mobile phones, satellites, digitisation, video cameras, and so on (Babe, 1990; Flichy, 1995; Garnham, 1990; Mosco, 1989). All have a crucial military lineage.

8.   Resorting to the "first principles" of liberalism is almost completely out of the question because it would involve abolishing the corporation—an unlikely prospect.

9.   This particular phrase has an enduring life in telecoms history. It was raised early in the debates about the nationalisation of telegraphy in England, before "satisfactory" arrangements were arrived at. Theodore Vail, of U.S. Bell, and C. F. Sise, of the Canadian Bell System, often leaned on the phrase to claim grievous injustice every time government policy did not bend completely to their whims. Surtees (1994a) also reminds us that Bell Canada's de Grandpré regularly used the phrase during the 1970s and 1980s as regulatory policy begin to shift from protecting monopoly to eroding it. Stentor (1992) also used it to challenge the interconnection

provisions of the CRTC's 1992 decision opening up long-distance competition.

10. Barlow (1996) refers to telling a example of what this means in practice. As she notes, the introduction of commercial communications media into school curricula in the United States—for example, Whittle Communications' Channel One—means contractually locking classrooms into one-way flows of advertising-supported "educational" programs. Contracts require that "90% of the children in a school must watch the programmes 90% of the time; each programme must be watched in its entirety . . . and the teacher does not have the right to [interrupt or to] turn it off (p. 8). So much for "media literacy" programs and realising the potential of new patterns of communication that are technically possible.

11. During research for this book I found that Stats Canada charged $60 to start up their CANSIM data bank, Bell Canada had just begun a $50 user charge to access its archives, and Investment Canada, because it had bought into a private commercial data (U.S.-based) service, could not provide access to data on Canadian telecoms that policymakers themselves were able to use to inform policies affecting this area.

3 TELECOMS AND ONLINE NEWS AND CONTENT SERVICES FROM 1840 TO 1910: THE TELEGRAPH IN CANADA, THE UNITED STATES, AND EUROPE

INTRODUCTION

The origins of telecoms in Canada can be traced back 150 years to the introduction of the telegraph. By looking at the telegraph, we can readily see many of the same issues that perplex Canadians today, particularly with respect to how a wide array of potential options for media development are winnowed down to one or two dominant "models." The historical connections between telegraphy, the press, and other content producers illuminates the origins of common carriage, electronic publishing, and how a variety of interactions between people, governments, and industry, on a local and global level, shape the evolution of new media systems. With some minor tinkering, the history of the telegraph and electronic publishing can still be enormously instructive for choices about telecoms and information production, distribution, and consumption today.

A LONG BIRTH

The telegraph emerged without clear uses in mind or a system of organisation. In Canada the telegraph was relegated to the margins, despite widespread sensitivity to the need for speedier flows of information within the country, as well as to and from the United States, Britain, and elsewhere. Exemplifying such concerns, a Government Post Office report from 1863 stressed the need for more efficient communication and quoted several articles from the popular press to this effect. Attention was given to the benefits of improved transportation routes, cheaper postal rates, and press subsidies allowing newspapers to be carried through the public mails at greatly reduced costs (Dewe, 1863, p. 12), but little thought was given to how the telegraph might enhance communication. This was despite the fact that it had already found stable patterns of organisation in the United States, England, France, and elsewhere.

Although the postponed introduction of telegraphy in Canada was unusually long, delayed introduction of new innovations in communication, or new technical systems in general, was the norm rather than the exception, and not just in Canada. In Great Britain, Francis Ronalds demonstrated a feasible electric telegraph to the Royal Navy in 1816 but was turned down because of the Navy's recent investments in a semaphore telegraph network introduced to England from France. Presentations were also given to the French government but spurned for similar reasons and because the telegraph was seen as inferior to the semaphore system in place since 1794 (Kieve, 1973, pp. 16-17). Even though Samuel Morse in the United States developed a telegraph system comparatively later, and the environment there was generally considered more hospitable to new mechanical innovations than in Europe, his system met with a similar fate. Morse had to wait until 1843 and 1844 before his system was commercialised, despite having demonstrated its effectiveness in 1837.

The eventual transition of the telegraph from the margins of commercial, political, and public life to an organised system of communication cannot be separated from the evolution of four other agencies of 19th century capitalism: railways, the bureaucratic state, stock markets, and the press. It was not one institution and set of interests alone that impressed themselves on the technology equally at all places and times, as Winston's (1996, pp. 68-69) claim that telegraphy emerged to serve the signalling, controlling, and safety needs of the railways seems to suggest. Despite the persistent metaphor between transportation and electronic communication in the field of media studies, it was only in England during the boom years of the railway between 1837 and 1848 that the telegraph was called into service primarily to meet railway needs. Even in that country by the mid-1850s it was clear that the needs of the railways pressed less urgently on the telegraph companies. More and more, English telegraph companies were relying on revenues from international communication and the press and even beginning to generate their own news and specialised financial and political information services delivered "online" to various subscribers (Kieve, 1973, pp. 47-49).

In France and Germany, in contrast, the telegraph passed immediately into the hands of the state, serving to tie the peripheral regions into the centre and to forge a national political culture with the state at its apex. As French Interior Minister Lacave-Laplagne frankly declared in 1847, "the telegraph is an instrument of politics, not of commerce" (Kieve, 1973, p. 46; author's translation). Early attempts by Morse to develop a telegraph line in cooperation with a private French railway company were blocked and the telegraph reserved for the exclusive use of the government. Only in November 1850 were reforms introduced to liberalise French telecoms and open up this new means of communication to the general public. The likely sources for the liberalisation of control lie in the revolution of 1848 and, more importantly, in the fact that trading between the Stock Exchanges in London and Paris became possible several months earlier with the laying of a cable connecting England and France (Attali & Stourdze, 1977, p. 101). Table 3.1 illustrates the varied uses (by percentage) to which the telegraph was put in Britain, France, and the United States within a few years of its inception.

Table 3.1. Communication by Telegraph: Britain, France, and the United States.

Country	Stock Market	Trade	Family	Other
Britain (1854)	50	31	13	6
France (1851)	38	28	25	9
USA (1845)	28 (est.)	32	15 (est.)	25 (press)

Source: Blondheim (1994), Flichy (1995), and Kieve (1973).

Although the aspect of political domination loomed large in the telecoms systems of France and Germany, it was also present to a lesser extent in England, the United States, and Canada. In each place, the legal framework allowed governments to take over telegraph systems to eliminate public disorder or to restore "normalcy" during periods of strife. The British government relied on the telegraph considerably during the 1840s in its efforts to pacify public dissent. In 1848, it temporarily took over the English Telegraph Company's network as part of its efforts to stifle the populist, working-class uprisings organised and led by the Chartists across the country. Telegraphic communication between the Chartists was blocked, the movement of troops was coordinated by telegraph, and attempts to establish hegemonic interpretations of the events were undertaken, as citizens were denied access to the network and government reports of the events were distributed by wire to the country's press (Mather, 1953, pp. 40-53). The role of the state in England was enlarged significantly in 1863, albeit in a different direction, as legislation was enacted to regulate the privately owned telegraph system. In 1868 the scope of state action expanded again as the government introduced an Act allowing it to assume ownership of most telegraph networks in 1870, a point returned to later.

Direct relationships between the telegraph, government, and politics in the United States were generally weaker than elsewhere. To be sure, there were subsidies. However, these were minuscule and of short duration. There was even a brief period of government ownership during early periods of experimentation with the new technique and later during the Mexican and Civil Wars; however private ownership was quickly restored after each war. A more influential impression on the telegraph in the United States occurred when proceedings from the two major parties' political conventions in 1844 were reported by telegraph to an eager audience waiting at one end of the line in Washington and to a broader public via telegraphic news reprinted in the press. Likewise, the amount of information circulated by telegraph from the beginning of the Mexican War in 1846 reinforced perceptions of the telegraph's social significance at a time when there was a lack of confidence about its utility. Although such events highlighted the telegraph's importance, they did not facilitate government ownership or detailed regulatory intervention during the early years of technical and organisational innovation. The comparably weaker connection between government and the telegraph was confirmed in 1844-45 when the U.S. government turned down opportunities to buy exclusive rights to the Morse patents for $100,000. At the same time, the government privatised an experimental line it had operated between Baltimore and Washington after only one year of service, despite enduring calls by Morse and the Post Office to operate the telegraph as a government monopoly and an extension of the postal service (Blondheim, 1994, pp. 32-34; Thompson, 1947, pp. 33-34).

Just as the telegraph was used by the English government to quell the Chartists, the federal government of Canada employed it to quash the rebellious actions of the Metis and Louis Riel. Despite such superficial similarities, the role of the Canadian state in the development of the telegraph was unique, differing from and residing somewhere between the model of the strong state projected by France and Germany and the less interventionist model of state-economy-communication relations typical in England and the United States. It was probably closer to the U.S. and (before government ownership) English examples insofar as takeovers of the telegraph for the government's exclusive use remained the exception rather than the rule and were typically short term. However, the Canadian model was distinct from that of Great Britain and the United States in several respects.

For one, the idea of U.S. political and cultural imperialism was already openly discussed in certain official circles from at least the 1860s and, as will be seen further, was raised more than once to justify one plan or another regarding how the telegraph in Canada should be owned, organised, regulated, and used (Colonial Office and Authorities of Canada and British Columbia, 1864-66, pp. 12-16; Fleming, 1882, 1902; Pacific Cable Committee, 1899, pp. 5-6). Acting somewhere between the poles of benign neglect and moderate doses of state intervention, Canadian governments limited themselves to establishing a general legal regime, granting charters to individual companies and resisting proposals such as that by the Atlantic and Pacific Telegraph and Transit Company in 1863 to license companies to build networks along certain routes in return for a rate of profit guaranteed by government (4-5%), annual subsidies, and a protected monopoly (Colonial Office and Authorities of Canada and British Columbia, 1864-66, pp. 12-16, Innis, 1923/1972, pp. 39-43). Circumstances differed between Canada and the United States, however, on the state's role vis-à-vis telecoms policy, as indicated by the first Canadian telecoms law, the *The Electric Telegraph Companies Act of 1852* (hereinafter, referred to as *The Electric Telegraph Act*, Province of Canada, 1852). In itself, the fact that legislation was introduced at all was unusual and significant. The telegraph law predated similar efforts in England 11 years later, and in the United States, where it was not until 1914 that the government extended its regulatory authority to encompass telecoms matters. Moreover, sections of the 1852 telegraph law, although quite liberal in orientation, at least envisioned the possibility of government assuming ownership of the telegraph network at some point in time and under certain conditions.

TELECOMS AND THE NEWS: THE MARITIME PROVINCES AND MEDIA GLOBALISATION IN THE 19TH CENTURY

The passage of the *Electric Telegraph Act* signaled the emerging salience of telecoms in Canada. Rens (1993) argues that the new law was so favourable that it ushered in a new wave of telegraph companies in Canada and rapid expansion of the telecoms network. The new telecoms law cleared the way for anyone to develop telecoms networks, a measure that led to rapid expansion of the network but at the cost of harnessing the telegraph system to the needs of the press, telegraph companies, and the political economy of the United States and England. Thereafter, three features in particular impressed themselves on the evolution of telegraphy in Canada: the close alignment between the growth of telegraph networks and the needs of the press in the United States; a shift from "methodless enthusiasm" toward "consolidation" (Thompson, 1947); and the mediation of developments in Canadian media by the competing pulls of continentalism, imperialism, and, much later, nationalism.

Just prior to the Act, the telegraph system had begun to emerge in earnest; thereafter it began to explode along the corridor running between the Maritime provinces, Montreal, and Toronto. In 1846, several merchants from St. Catherines, Hamilton, and Niagara Falls endeavored to construct a telegraph system connecting Buffalo and New York to Toronto. A year later, Orton Woods, brother-in-law of Ezra Cornell, one of the leading figures in the Western Union company of the United States, began to organise the Montreal Telegraph Company to serve commercial interests in Canada, and perhaps those of the press as well (Thompson, 1947, pp. 241, 253). Given the close ties—financial, organisational, and familial—between the new company and Western Union, the effort was also an early attempt by Western Union to extend its influence into Canada. In the same year, Frederick. N. Gisborne established the British North American Telegraph Company, with plans to link together Quebec, Nova Scotia, New Brunswick, and, later, Newfoundland. The company, however, was unable to survive a cut-throat price war with the Montreal Telegraph Company, and in 1856 the British North American Telegraph Company was absorbed by the Montreal Telegraph Company. The latter was better connected, financially better endowed, and, crucially, able to subsidise competition with revenues gained from its monopoly lines (Babe, 1990, p. 38). A few years after Gisborne's failed venture, the Great North Western Telegraph Company (1859) obtained a charter, set up operations in Toronto, and harboured ambitions to initiate telegraphic communications west of Lake Superior (Innis, 1923/1972, pp. 38-39; Nichols, 1948, p. 10). Nonetheless, the scope of the telegraph system in Canada remained skeletal, with 1,500 kilometres of network in place by 1852, in comparison to 36,000 in the United States, 3,800 kilometres of line under the control of just one of the main companies in Britain, the Electric Telegraph Company (1851), and 5,000 in France (1852) (Flichy, 1995, p. 52; Kieve, 1973, p. 53; Thompson, 1947, pp. 241).

The obsession of the American press and telegraph organisations with the speed and volume of news and information flowing into and out of the United States drove each of these agencies up the Maritime coast and, from 1849 onwards, into Nova Scotia, New Brunswick, Newfoundland, and Prince Edward Island. The ties between the press and the telegraph were clear in the United States from the first attempts to commercialise the telegraph in the mid-1840s. Newspaper publishers were among the first and most generous investors in setting up telegraph operators, providing the largest source of revenue, and establishing organisations such as the Associated Press (AP) (1846) to exploit the potentials of electronic communication for the print media. In return, the press gained access to a relatively cheap, quick, and quite reliable means for producing and distributing news, transmission privileges, and subsidised press rates (Blondheim, 1994, pp. 41-45; Thompson, 1947, pp. 217-225). In short, the link between the telegraph and the press stemmed from shared uses of a new technology, cross-ownership, functional interdependence, and, from about 1870 onward, harmonisation of a legal regime around a hybrid telecoms/publishing model—a point returned to later.

These arrangements left an indelible impression on the Canadian mediascape. The ensuing strategic rivalry among the press and telegraph agencies inclined the communication industries in Canada, the United States, and England toward monopoly and/or oligopoly. Yet, before this, news brokers were driven by competition to push further north in their efforts to get information more quickly into Boston, New York, Philadelphia, and Washington. Capturing the news in Canadian provinces and forwarding it by way of a patchwork of telegraph networks to the press and emerging news cooperatives, such as Associated Press, was up to 48 hours quicker than waiting for information from Europe to reach ports in the United States (Thompson, 1947, p. 299). This emphasis on speed did not stem mainly from the competitive nature of the media, but from the fact that the value of news did not yet reside in information per se. Because there was still no copyright in news, the economic value of the transactions lay mostly in the ability to arbitrage differences in time. Time, not information, was money. Once differences in time were eliminated by the telegraph, the economics of newsgathering tilted away from competition toward monopoly and from realising the commodity value of time differences to attempts to secure the commodity value of information itself. For the time being, however, news was not a commodity, and the idea that its property value could be secured by copyright laws remained a foreign one—a point returned to later (Nichols, 1948; Post Office, 1876, pp. 190-192).

Under the competitive conditions prevailing in North America between 1847 and 1852 (Thompson, 1947, p. 259), a great number of companies sprang up in the Canadian Maritime provinces. Some were partially Canadian-owned such as the New York, Newfoundland, and London Telegraph Company incorporated in 1854 in Newfoundland; the New Brunswick Telegraph Company; and the Nova Scotia Telegraph Company (1849), the first government-owned telecoms network in Canada. By 1859, many of the small telegraph systems had combined to form the Great North Western Telegraph Company. Within a decade, the Dominion Telegraph Company (1868) started operations from Montreal and began challenging the larger Montreal Telegraph Company throughout Quebec, parts of Ontario, and much of the Maritimes for control of telegraphs and newswire services in Canada (Babe, 1990, p. 47; Nichols, 1948, p. 10).

However, the period was one of transition. Strategic rivalry was already leading to the disappearance of smaller independent networks and their absorption into more tightly knit organisations. More than once, the New Brunswick Telegraph Company and the government-owned Nova Scotia Telegraph Company found themselves in compromising alliances with several Boston-based newspapers, as well as the Associated Press. Heavily reliant on these users for revenues and granting them privileged transmission rights as a result, the Canadian-based telegraph companies often encountered no-win situations. They were identified as targets of criticism by the rising antimonopoly forces and attacked by rivals trying to break the Associated Press stranglehold on foreign news, while also coveted by the substantial backers of the Associated Press in the U.S. telegraph industry who were desirous of bolstering their own positions across the entire Maritime mediascape. During the 1850s, a series of transactions led to almost all companies in the Canadian Maritime provinces, including the Nova Scotia Telegraph Company, coming under the control of the American Telegraph Company (ATC) (Blondheim, 1994, pp. 151-163; Thompson, 1947, pp. 226-240). In central and parts of eastern Canada, the Montreal Telegraph Company also went on an acquisitions spree, purchasing the Toronto, Hamilton & Niagara Electric Telegraph Company, the Montreal & Troy Telegraph Company, the Vermont & Boston Company, Prescott & Montreal Telegraphs (all in 1852), and a few years later, the British North American Telegraph Company (1856) (Babe, 1990, p. 45).

Over a course of many twists and turns, the attempts of ATC and the Montreal Telegraph Company to consolidate control over telegraphy in North America became aligned with a broader effort to bolster AP's monopoly over information flows coming into North America from abroad. To this end, a far-reaching initiative was undertaken by ATC, the Canadian Frederick Gisborne, and the British and Irish Magnetic Telegraph Company to build a trans-Atlantic cable (Kieve, 1973, pp. 106-110; Thompson, 1947, pp. 299-301, 306-307, 335). The initiative was driven purely by the aim of achieving unassailable monopoly over telegraphy and news in North America and by a desire to diminish the monopoly over foreign news held by Reuters in Great Britain. The result was the New York, Newfoundland and London Telegraph Company. The new trans-Atlantic project linked together two of the largest telegraph companies in the United States and England, the interests of the Associated Press, and a Canadian able to turn pressures on the Newfoundland legislature into what must have been one of the most favourable pieces of legislation to monopoly ever produced. In 1854, after a few ensuing machinations, the company emerged as the Anglo-American Telegraph Company, the company responsible for constructing the first successful trans-Atlantic cable in 1865. The company was authorised to raise unlimited capital in Newfoundland, New York, and London. More importantly, the legislature barred anyone else from operating in, or landing a telegraph cable at, any point in Newfoundland for the next 50 years (*Direct United States Cable Co. v. Anglo-American Telegraph Company et. al.*, 1877). The company also received an annual subsidy of £14,000 from the British government (Kieve, 1973, p. 108).

The effects of the Anglo-American Telegraph Company reverberated well beyond Newfoundland and deep into Canada. Over time, it came to own the telegraph system on Prince Edward Island. The shockwaves were delivered deeper into Canada primarily through the medium of the Montreal Telegraph Company, whose line to Halifax was connected with Anglo-American by way of a complex web of relations between it, the American Telegraph Company (whose partial ownership of Anglo-American gave it exclusive rights to forward trans-Atlantic traffic through the Maritimes and into the United States), and Western Union (see the map of telegraph systems in Canada, Nova Scotia and the United States in 1853).[1] Throughout the 1850s and 1860s, the ties between Montreal Telegraph Company, Western Union, and American Telegraph Company had become more intimate, not least because of their joint membership in the cartel-like arrangements of the North American Telegraph Alliance[2] begun in 1857 (Montreal Telegraph Company was given entry one year later), and became even moreso in 1866 when Western Union finally swallowed the ATC. By 1865, there were only three companies remaining in the United States. A year later Western Union had eliminated even these companies, and as a result achieved an almost complete monopoly over the telegraph industry in the United States, except for a few small would-be competitors here and there.

Two companies that stood outside these arrangements were the American Union Telegraph Company and the Dominion Telegraph Company. Prevented from interconnecting with any of the other major telegraph companies in North America by the cartel arrangements of the North America Telegraph Association, American Union and Dominion Telegraph aligned themselves with each other, a competitive trans-Atlantic telegraph company, and, later, news services that had sprung up to challenge the AP monopoly. As links with the Dominion Telegraph Company in Canada and the Direct United States Cable Company (another trans-Atlantic cable operator) were put in place, American Union set out to challenge Western Union and AP's stranglehold over telegraphy and news in North America and the 50-year monopoly over landing rights that had been granted by the Newfoundland government to Anglo-American (by that time under the partial control of Western Union by way of its acquisition of the American Telegraph Company) (*Direct United States Cable Co. v. Anglo-American Telegraph Company et. al.*, 1877).

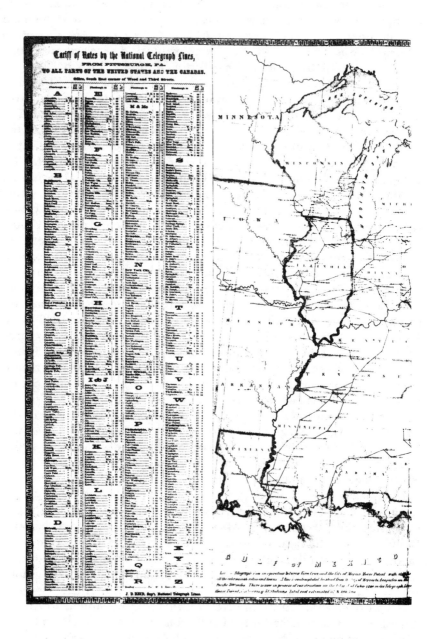

Map of telegraph systems in Canada, Nova Scotia,

and the United States in 1853

In 1874, Direct United States Cable began offering services in competition with the Anglo-American system, a prospect made ever more difficult by costly and ultimately unsuccessful litigation against the latter's legislated monopoly over optimum areas of the Canadian coastline, as well as its exclusive interconnection rights with Western Union in the United States and the Montreal Telegraph Company in Canada. In the ensuing rivalry between the two transnational alliances, the Dominion Telegraph Company was given exclusive rights to carry Direct's traffic in Canada and also to distribute the National Associated Press news service linked to Direct and its U.S.-based counterpart, the American Union Telegraph Company. Although the manoeuvers loosened the monopolistic grip of Western Union and Associated Press in the North American context, the irony is that the Canadian mediascape became more tightly tied to the United States as afterward even more U.S.-based content producers were distributed in Canada, for example, National Associated Press, the forerunner of the later United Press service (Blondheim, 1994, pp. 163-164; Rens, 1993, p. 32).

At best, these arrangements were examples of strategic rivalry between mismatched competitors. The final demise of even this superficial appearance of competition is nonetheless quite interesting, not least because of its connections to Canada and for what it reveals about future relations between different areas of the communication industries. Essentially, by the second half of the 1870s, the arrangements had created a duopolistic telegraph industry in Canada shared between the Montreal Telegraph Company and Dominion Telegraph Company, with a smattering of companies fragmented and offering services on the peripheral and competitive fringes of the telegraph industry. The arrangements are particularly interesting because they not only united Canadian interests with American interests, but telecoms with the press; the Montreal Telegraph Company was allied with Western Union and Associated Press, whereas the Dominion Telegraph Company was attached to the American Union Telegraph Company and the nascent United Press. These arrangements came to a head over a short period of time, mainly between 1878 and 1881.

In this time span, the two ostensibly Canadian companies engaged in ruinous price wars. This occurred not only as the companies were trying to further expand the range of news and information services they delivered to subscribers but also as they attempted to expand into the nascent field of telephony. The ensuing price wars brought network expansion in telegraphy to a standstill and led to a stillbirth in each company's efforts to provide telephone services. With respect to this latter point, the Montreal Telegraph Company had acquired rights to the Edison telephone patents and Dominion to the patent rights of Bell. Patents in hand and networks essentially already in place, competitive "local telephone exchanges were opened in Montreal, Quebec City, Ottawa, Saint Johns (New Brunswick), Halifax and several other locations in Ontario" (Rens, 1993, p. 32; author's translation). However, after exhausting themselves through competition, both companies were forced to abandon their telephone systems to the Bell Telephone Company in 1880. Another result of this disastrous bout of strategic rivalry was Western Union's acquisition, via a circuitous route, of Dominion Telegraph in 1881.

For the next three years Western Union and its close affiliate, the Great North Western Telegraph Company, enjoyed an almost complete monopoly over telegraphy and delivery of Associated Press' "online" news service, after which the entry of the Canadian Pacific Railway and Telegraphy Company created a duopoly in transmission and news services, as it acquired the rights of the former Dominion Telegraph Company to deliver the United Press' "online" news service in Canada (Nichols, 1948, pp. 10-12; Rens, 1993, pp. 53-55). In addition, and crucially, given that each of these had been offering telephone services, the episode of ruinous competition between the Montreal and Dominion telegraph companies clearly demonstrated that telegraphy and telephony were not separate arts requiring distinct systems of organisation, but diverged as a result of strategic rivalry, the fruits of which accrued to the Bell Telephone Company of Canada. The possibility of dissolving these boundaries arose later that year when the Canadian Pacific Railway and Telegraph Company's (CP) enabling charter authorised it to operate in all areas of telecoms. Rather than risk yet another bout of "ruinous competition," however, Bell and CP promptly agreed to divide the field between themselves and to share their network resources. This was the first phase of media divergence in the Canadian context and it occurred *despite* the inherent compatibility between telephony and telegraphy and a legal framework that anticipated their interoperability, not separate development.[3]

GOVERNMENT-OWNED TELEGRAPHS AND THE PRICE OF LEGITIMACY

The exhaustion of competition through strategic rivalry and various anticompetitive practices offered the Canadian state a legitimate pretext to step into telecoms, either through government ownership or regulatory intervention. Despite such possibilities, neither course of action was adopted with any vigor. This was very different to what had occurred from the outset in France and Germany, and from the arrangements put into place in Great Britain under similar circumstances (discussed later). Even though the *Electric Telegraph Act (1852)* in Canada offered the potential for strong state intervention, the political economy of a (neo-) colonial state and the strength of transnational capitalism constrained such possibilities. The only direct forms of state intervention were limited to the temporary ownership of the Nova Scotia Telegraph Company by the provincial colonial government of Nova Scotia in 1849, the Newfoundland colonial government's protection of the Anglo-American Telegraph Company's monopoly, meagre efforts to extend the telegraph to remote areas, and administration of a legal framework designed more to secure investments than to promote public communication.

Conditions differed in Great Britain. As in North America, three companies—the Electric Telegraph Company, Magnetic Telegraph Company, and United Kingdom Electric Telegraph Company—had gained control over the general telegraph service by the mid-1860s. Two other specialised services operated on the margins: Reuters Telegram Company, with its own network to bring news into the country as part of its efforts to solidify a monopoly over foreign news and to reduce its dependency on the networks of the big three; and the Universal Private Telegraph Company, who offered private networks to the banking, finance, commercial, and later, the press communities. However, there was widely held opinion that these companies' control over the industry and attempts to branch out further into news and information services was beginning to interfere with development of the core network as well as with the needs of various users, most notably the press.

The *Times*, an influential London-based newspaper, also complained that the telegraph companies were promoting the emergence of a new business entity—the limited liability corporation. The concern was that corporations separated ownership from responsibility and capitalisation from productive property, which the *Times* felt would be detrimental to investors—although the concern was applicable to how corporations related to society in general (see footnote 4, below; Kieve, 1973, p. 47). Also signaling that the new media would be the child of Parliament and the courts as much as anything else, in 1862 alone, for example, the Electric Telegraph Company spent £6,000, the Magnetic £1,957, and the United Kingdom Electric Telegraph Company, the new comer against whom the two others were spending their money, spent £11,709 petitioning Parliament or pursuing law suits, mostly over patents. The press, despite receiving reduced rates, also criticised the companies bitterly for excessive rates and flocked to the new United Kingdom Electric Telegraph Company (1860) for its flat rate pricing scheme and cheaper tariffs. Moreover, exclusive agreements between the Electric, the Magnetic, and Reuters reproduced monopolistic trends found in the United States and threatened to reinforce the dominance of the latter company over the flow of international news, political reports, and market information into the country. Even the Edinburgh Chamber of Commerce, that "authoritative exponent of commercial opinion," advocated government ownership, after a study it sponsored concluded that rates were excessive, service unreliable, and networks not as available as they should be (Kieve, 1973, pp. 61-71). By this point, the broad consensus was that the choice was not whether "free trade" in telecoms could prevail, but whether the solution would be regulation of oligopolistic markets or government ownership.

The *Telegraph Acts* of 1868 and 1869 saw the country follow the latter course of action. In the preamble to the *Telegraph Act* (1868), the government made its position clear:

> Whereas the Means of Communication by Electric Telegraphs within the United Kingdom of Great Britain and Ireland are insufficient, and many important Districts are without any such Means of Communication . . . it would be . . . [a] great advantage to the State, as well as to Merchants and Traders, and to the Public generally, if a cheaper, more widely extended, and more expedient System of Telegraphy were established . . . , and to that end it is expedient that Her Majesty's Postmaster General be empowered to work Telegraphs in connexion with the Administration of the Post Office. (United Kingdom, 1868, p. 503)

There are several key aspects of the act, four of which stand out in particular:

- The generous terms given to the companies bought out (*Telegraph Act*, 1868, sections 8 to 10).
- The inclusion of press subsidies and flat rate, distance insensitive pricing for public telegraph service (*Telegraph Act*, 1868, section 16; *Telegraph Act*, 1869, preamble).
- The possibility of competition with the Post Office in the area of private networks and licensing requirements for those offering "online" information services over private networks or lines leased from the Post Office (*Telegraph Act*, 1868, section 16; *Telegraph Act*, 1869, section 5).
- A broad definition of telegraphic communication (*Telegraph Act*, 1868, section 3; *Telegraph Act*, 1869, section 3).

The Post Office acquired the lines of the Electric Telegraph Company, Magnetic Telegraph Company, United Kingdom Telegraph Company, Reuters Telegram Company, and Universal Private Telegraph Company. The price paid was generous. Each company received a sum equal to 20 years of profit. Reuters was exceptionally lucky because its telegraph system was not originally on the list of companies to be acquired by the government. It only became so after Julius Reuters intervened to convince the government that his company's network should also be bought along with the others. In the end, Reuters' telegraph lines were bought for five times what the system had cost to erect just two years prior to the government "takeover." The price paid each company is listed in Table 3.2 (Read, 1992, pp. 49-50). Although some argued the government could have built a new network from scratch for about £2 million, the cost of acquiring the networks at the time of purchase was almost three times that amount and grew even larger as the magnitude of Post Office miscalculations continued to pile up over the years. Moreover, focusing on just economic costs ignores the idea that the state also had to buy itself out of a potential legitimation crisis brought on by the knowledge that nationalisation decisively shifted the boundaries between state and capital in the world's leading free market economy. It did this by diffusing the costs across the general public, amortising the expense over time, and liberally dispensing "benefits for everyone": cash for the telegraph companies, subsidies for the press, cheaper rates and universal service for the public, and, for the few leftover doubters, room for action on the competitive fringes left outside the Post Office monopoly.

Table 3.2. Cost of Telegraph Nationalisation in England

Names of Telegraph Companies with whom arrangements have been made pursuant to the Telegraph Acts	Amounts Payable to Telegraph Companies under the Telegraph Acts		
	£	s.	d.
The Electric Telegraph Company	2,938,826	9	0
The British and Irish Magnetic Telegraph Company, Ltd.	1,243,536	0	0
Reuter's Telegram Company	726,000	0	0
The United Kingdom Electric Telegraph Company, Ltd.	562,264	9	11
The Universal Private Telegraph Company	184,421	10	0
The London and Provincial Telegraph Company	60,000	0	0
	5,715,048	8	11

Source: Public General Statutes (1869), "An Act to alter and amend," (1868), United Kingdom (1869).

Contrary to conventional wisdom, the *Telegraph Act did not* give the Post Office a monopoly over all means of electronic communication, nor did the Post Office necessarily covet such a goal, as later events with respect to the telephone (as discussed in footnote 3) demonstrate so clearly. Several companies were explicitly excluded from the scheme, namely, the Anglo-American Telegraph Company, American Telegraph Company, and others primarily engaged in international communication. The lines of railway companies were also left mainly intact, although there were provisions for the Post Office to acquire these should the need arise. In addition, private networks were allowed to remain, so long as they were for intracompany use or had obtained a licence from the Post Office to offer services to the public.

Some argued that government ownership meant abandoning liberal capitalism. However, this was no more true than the damage wrought on liberal philosophy by the earlier rise of corporations, the impact of overcapitalisation[4] as "watered-stock" lost all relation to productive inputs—land, labour, and machines—and as the decisive battles for industrial supremacy occurred as often in the courts and political spheres as they did under the pressures of competitive markets. Essentially, the English government bought itself out of a legitimation crisis and saved some semblance of liberal political theory by limiting its hegemony to the communicative space of the nation, although only temporarily, and by leaving areas such as private networks and global communication for private enterprise.

The excessive cost of assuming government ownership of the telegraph in England must have looked positively daunting to any others contemplating public ownership of telecoms. There can be little doubt that such concerns influenced decisions in Canada where, as we have seen, legal potential and economic realities could have easily legitimated a policy of government ownership had there not been such a weak state and pronounced lack of political will. In addition to these conditions, possibilities in Canada were circumscribed by the fact that the telecoms system was tied—organisationally, technically, functionally, and even, politically and legally—to conditions south of the border. Despite numerous investigations by the U.S. government into how Western Union and the Associated Press combined to restrain trade across the communication industries as a whole and to make absolute nonsense out of Constitutional guarantees of freedom of communication, nothing was done (Blondheim, 1994, p. 151). Thus, the daunting experience of England with public ownership; the political, economic, and ideological constraints imposed by network integration with the United States; and an ineffectual state more eager to grant charters, administer an "investment friendly" telecoms law, and, as in Newfoundland especially, to protect the nascent monopoly/oligopolistic structure of the communication industries, meant that any flirtations with public ownership of telecoms would be just that.

COLONIALISM, GLOBAL COMMUNICATION, AND THE STATE

Of course, this does not mean that there were no forces supportive of publicly owned telegraph systems in Canada during the period under review (1840-1910); there were. As already mentioned, public ownership was briefly introduced in Nova Scotia, and the *Electric Telegraph Act* (1852) anticipated such a possibility. The most notable forces pushing public ownership were an odd mixture of Canadian nationalism, British imperialism, and the indubitable Sir Sandford Fleming, a perennial and influential exponent of a global imperial communications network, and later promoter of public ownership of the means of electronic communication. The seeds of this potent mixture were visible by 1862, as a few members of the British political elite promoted the idea, with the help of Sandford Fleming, that the Canadian government license and give favourable terms to the Atlantic and Pacific Telegraph and Transit Company to extend the telegraph network west of Lake Superior and on to British Columbia. The project was promoted as serving "Canadian and Imperial interests," inhibiting Americanisation and the "incalculable mischief" that might cause, and even ensuring a passage to China and the rest of Asia (Colonial Office and Authorities of Canada and British Columbia, 1864-66, pp. 7-12).

This initiative, although never implemented, was to be based on state subventions for a privately owned network[5] but did not propose government ownership. It did, however, call for an expanded role for the state in telecoms matters—granting of monopoly rights, guaranteed profits, and outright subsidies—and marked the emergence of a view that the telegraph was not only a "weapon of commerce" but an "instrument of politics" as well. Even though Canada may have been more aligned with the United States in commercial affairs, it remained tied to the orbit of English political affairs. As such, it is not surprising that the emerging telecoms policy environment in Canada contained elements from both contexts. In the present case, there were strong parallels to the situation in Britain, where the government relied heavily on the Electric International Telegraph Company (later Cable and Wireless) during the 1870s and 1880s to rapidly build an imperial network to link London to Delhi, Hong Kong, Rangoon, Shanghai, Singapore, Sydney, and other outposts of the colonial empire. The emergence of the "All Red" project in the 1880s indicated a further shift toward a government-owned global telecoms network, something that came to dominate Sandford Fleming's

(1882) animated talk of global communications, despite his appointment as General Manager of telegraphs at the new privately owned Canadian Pacific Railways and Telegraph Company. Fleming explicitly and relentlessly argued for a government-owned, "All-Red" network to be built entirely across British land to counter U.S.-based Western Union's efforts to bring a line across the Bering Straight into Russia and afterwards down the Asian coast of the Pacific.

The arguments and discussions about the "All Red" network were not just pitched in the realm of high colonial politics. The project was also directed at reigning in the increasing power of the Electric International Telegraph Company (EITC) and Reuters, on the one hand, and the Anglo-American Telegraph Company (AATC) and Associated Press, on the other,[6] to control the international flow of information and to set tariffs so high that they inhibited the "free flow of knowledge" between the people of the British colonies. From 1880 until the turn of the century, the benefits of a publicly owned global communications network competing with the EITC and AATC monopolies were continuously extolled. Fleming was near the forefront of most of these discussions, whether in the numerous pamphlets he published on the matter, as a representative of the Canadian government, or in his presentations to the Pacific Cable Committee in 1896 at which the "All Red" project was finally approved. Before the latter committee, Fleming went well beyond the realpolitik of colonialism and global communication to argue that "cheaper telegraph communication would benefit the whole world, and not just Canada, Britain and Australia alone" (Pacific Cable Committee, 1899, p. 26).

Although Fleming was prone to confusing colonial paternalism with his own humanism, his presentations always contained a critique of how the potential of "the telegraph, . . . the most perfect means yet discovered for the free interchange of knowledge" was hindered by overcommercialisation and monopoly (Fleming, 1902, p. 8). Although some of Fleming's points may seem a bit naïve in hindsight, the critical edge to his argument stood out in stark relief alongside the unrelentingly myopic views of his peers at the Pacific Cable Conference. In contrast to Fleming, they queried the justice of having Canadian, Australian, and British citizens subsidise a humanitarian-oriented mission without any promise of material benefit in return. Apparently the issues were resolved satisfactorily, as the Canadian, British, and Australian governments finally constructed and completed the "All Red" network in 1902, a move that, among other things, strengthened the role of the Canadian state in telecoms affairs—national and international.

MEDIA CONVERGENCE AND "ONLINE" SERVICES IN AN AGE OF ELECTRONIC COMMUNICATION: THE PAST AS PROLOGUE TO THE FUTURE?

The decision by the Canadian government to limit its initiatives to meaningful subventions in support of the "All Red" global communications network, but not to directly commandeer the national telecoms infrastructure, once again distinguished the Canadian model of telecoms from circumstances in the United States, England, France, and Germany. The "All Red" project in tandem with the *Electric Telegraph Act (1852)* and the liberal regime for licensing telecoms providers illustrated that the role of the Canadian state in telecoms policy would not include extensive and direct intervention (the "European model") nor total neglect (the "U.S." model').

Other actions taken during the period under discussion (1840-1910)—either through commission or omission—also left an indelible impression on the evolution of telecoms, indeed the communication industries as a whole, in Canada. Another consideration that defined telecoms and the media industries in this period stemmed from the fact that neither the *Electric Telegraph Act* nor any of the enabling charters granted to various telegraph companies prevented these companies from operating across various media boundaries. The relevant parameters were defined loosely by the bounds of electronic communication and by the commonsense idea that all media were in the business of conveying information from one point to one or more other points. Neither of the charters granted to the Bell Telephone Company (1880)[7] and to the Canadian Pacific Railway and Telegraph Company (1880) prevented them from operating in all spheres of electronic communication. The charter of the Grand Trunk Pacific Telegraph Company (renewed in 1906) was quite clear and specific on the matter:

> The Company may establish, construct or acquire . . . and may maintain and operate any . . . telegraph or telephone, or any system of wireless telegraphy, or of signaling or of other electric or magnetic communication, from and to any places in Canada or elsewhere, and establish offices for the transmission and reception of messages or communications. (Canada, 1906, p. 128)

These provisions are typical of all charters granted to Canadian telecoms companies. There were simply no distinctions drawn along technical lines between various means of communication, nor were then any measures, such as the doctrine of common carriage, that prevented telecoms providers from becoming fully involved in the provision of news and other information services. As such, technical, organisational, functional, and legal convergence across a range of activities dealing with the production, distribution, and storage of information characterised the history of the telegraph and early press in Canada.

From the outset, telegraph operators doubled up as reporters and journalists. In his history of the Canadian Press wire service, Nichols (1948) refers to news wire services delivered to the press by the Montreal Telegraph Company (1846) and the Great North Western Telegraph Company (1847)[8] since their inception. As he states:

> the newspapers and the telegraphs were closely knitted in mutually advantageous business; they were complementary to each other. The newspapers needed the telegraph companies' services, the telegraph companies not only needed the business but found they could carry it at a fraction of commercial rates and show some profit. (p. 11)

Given the close ties between the Montreal Telegraph Company and the Great North Western Telegraph Company with Western Union in the United States, and therefore to Associated Press, it is likely that the Associated Press news wire service was also being offered, certainly by the early 1850s, if not sooner, into Canada (Nichols, 1948, pp. 5-11; Rens, 1993, p. 34). The same is also true for an "online" information company known as Gold and Stock, a company with which Western Union was affiliated by 1868. By 1871, Gold and Stock delivered an "online" information service of stock quotes, gold prices, and other data pertinent to commodity trading to about 800 subscribers from various banks and brokerage houses (Thompson, 1947, pp. 444-445). References in leading Canadian court cases of this time involving the telegraph also identified the existence of a longstanding news reporting and information brokerage service being offered by the Dominion Telegraph Company, as well as similar services being offered by Western Union affiliates and other independents (*Dominion Telegraph Co. v. Silver et al.*, 1882/83, pp. 238-239). Also, as mentioned earlier, it appears that the Dominion Telegraph Company distributed the wire services of the U.S.-based National Associated Press (the precursor to United Press) for a short period between 1874 and 1881, when it was acquired by Western Union. A few years later (1884), Canadian Pacific (CP) began carrying the United Press newswire service, only to drop it a decade later on learning that the "rival news service" was a sham and under the control of Associated Press. After dropping the counterfeit agency, CP and Associated Press signed (on January 2, 1894) a contract to "collect, distribute and exchange news for publication in newspapers in the United States [and] Canada, . . . and to deliver news reports . . . to no other parties for use within . . . Canada, the British provinces of North

America [or] the United States" (contract reproduced in full in BRC, 1910, p. 270). It is probable that CP's ability to obtain rights to the news service resulted from the loosening relations between Associated Press and Western Union during the late 1870s and 1880s, and because only CP's telegraph network crossed the country, whereas the Western Union/Great North Western Telegraphs partnership went only as far as Winnipeg in the west (Nichols, 1948, p. 12; Rens, 1993, p. 48).

In England, convergence between telecoms and various "online" news and specialised wire services was also occurring, but through different means. The telegraph system moved closer toward the press and away from the railways between the mid-1850s and 1870. The new orientation was exemplified in 1854, when the Electric Telegraph Company began to offer a telegraph news service to 120 members of the provincial press and to deliver a variety of other information services to subscribers, including parliamentary news, commercial reports, and stock exchange prices, as well as sport, racing, and gambling information (Kieve, 1973, p. 71). However, once these services were combined with the Reuters' foreign news services in the 1860s, the provincial press and proponents of government ownership intensified their efforts to undo what appeared to be an emerging media monopoly among the big three telegraph providers, a few members of the London press, and Reuters.

The three most influential results in terms of the discussion at hand are the formation of a telegraph-news cooperative in 1865—the Press Association—among the provincial press; state ownership of the telegraphs; and, a brief flourishing of independent "online" information services. The intimate link between these developments is underscored by provisions in the 1868 and 1869 *Telegraph Acts*, which instituted generous press subsidies and measures that allowed publishers to establish and receive licences for private networks.

> it shall be lawful for the Postmaster General . . . to make . . . Arrangements with the Proprietor and Publisher of any public registered Newspaper, or the Proprietor or Occupier of any News Room, Club or Exchange Room, for the Transmission . . . of . . . Telegraphic Communications at Rates not exceeding One Shilling for every Hundred Words transmitted between the Hours of Six p.m. and Nine a.m. and at Rates not exceeding One Shilling for every Seventy-five Words transmitted between the Hours of Nine a.m. and Six p.m. to a single Address, with an additional Charge of Twopence for every Hundred Words, or Twopence for every Seventy-five words, as the case may be . . . . [T]he Postmaster General may from Time to Time . . . let to any such Proprietor, Publisher, or Occupier the special use of a Wire . . . for the purposes of such Newspaper, News Room, Club, or Exchange Room at a rate not exceeding Five hundred Pounds per *Annum*. Provided that no . . . undue Preference [be given] in respect of

such Rates over any other such Proprietor, Publisher or Occupier. (section 16, Telegraph Act (1868); United Kingdom, 1868, pp. 514-515)

The new telecoms law strengthened the nascent bonds among the telegraph, press, and other information services in several ways: it subsidised rates for a broad class of content providers and users, including the press, news rooms, clubs, and so on. The rate structure also conformed to the economics of "broadcasting," as distribution costs fell by almost 85% after reaching the first subscriber.[9] The new law also allowed private networks to be set up and, just as importantly, subsidised as well as licensed them. A cynical interpretation might dismiss these as the cost the state incurred for buying off the press in its efforts to wrestle control of the telegraph out of the hands of the private sector monopolies and into its own. Although such an explanation offers some purchase on reality, it does not address other significant points worthy of consideration.

The English provincial press no doubt found the promise of cheaper rates and the liberalised access to private networks good grounds for supporting the new telecoms law. Yet, the press and government officials also argued that the press was an educational institution, responsible for informing the public and forging a national political culture and, therefore, deserving of special consideration (e.g., Post Office, 1876, pp. 180-181).[10] In response to critics of the subsidy's negative impact on the Post Office deficit, the Director of Telegraphs, Sir William Preece, stated that this was irrelevant:

[t]his of course means no more than that the government are persuaded of the educational value of the press, that it gives a sum equal to this large shortage in the shape of a bonus to the newspapers. It is another form of applying the principle of aiding in the diffusion of newspaper information, which in Canada and the United States is done by nominal charges for transportation. (quoted in Fleming, 1902, p. 6)[11]

The situation after government ownership was an improvement on previous experience. Telegraph networks were extended to areas unserved in the past, and the distance-insensitive pricing regime defined a national electronic communicative space that was, from the perspective of availability and cost, far more available than ever before. The number of messages sent expanded by 50% within two years of nationalisation (Kieve, 1973, p. 178). A member of a Select Committee inquiry into the press subsidy in 1876 also claimed—perhaps overstating his case and turning a blind eye to more critical issues about the potential homogenizing effects of the telegraph and subsidy on the political culture—that "the rise of the modern provincial press . . . is mainly a creation of the telegraph. [It] . . . has given a powerful impulse to provincial journalism . . ." (Post Office, 1876, p. 183). To be sure, these improvements in communication were happening in the midst of an administrative and financial nightmare—a point returned to later. Putting this aside for a moment, though, it can be seen that the range of information sources offered over the telecoms network proliferated, as the Post Office adhered more strictly to the principles of "first come first serve," the requirement to avoid giving "undue preference" to network users, and a more open framework for licensing private networks and "online" information service providers.

In addition to strengthening the provincial press and the news wire service of the provincial papers, a range of specialised private networks and news agencies were brought into existence. By 1872 the Exchange Telegraph Company (Extel) was licensed to run a private network over the Post Office telegraph system for the purpose of offering specialised information, news, and entertainment services to subscribers mainly from the financial community, but also from the press and various clubs, news rooms, and so on, that received these kinds of services (Post Office, 1870-1880, File I, pp. 1-11).[12] The new company distributed prices, quotes, and other stock-related data obtained under exclusive license from the London Stock Exchange to brokers, traders, and other subscribers. In return for a monthly fee, subscribers were connected to Extel's private network; received equipment to receive, record, and transcribe the electronically broadcast data that came in several times a day; and, most importantly, were granted the privilege to obtain information over which Extel held a monopoly by way of exclusive privileges granted by the Committee of the Stock Exchange (1873). In addition to exclusive rights to distribute information by telegraph from the London Stock Exchange, over time the company established connections with the New York Stock Exchange and Paris Bourse (1874), Dow Jones (1885), and various others. By the mid-1880s Extel offered a wide range of financial information services, general news, political reports, international news, legal reports, and entertainment services to 600 or more subscribers (Post Office, 1882-1907, File VI, pp. 1-3; Scott, 1972, pp. 15-25).

Of course, Extel was not the only "online" information service provider. An 1876 Post Office Select Committee Report identifies a burgeoning "information market," and other sources corroborate this with references to companies such as the Electric News Company, Central News, MacMahon's Telegraph News Company, Cochrane News Service, Gregory News Service, the Howard, London and Manchester Press Agency, and so on. During the period between 1879 and 1881, the Post Office was particularly liberal in licensing new content providers, as

MacMahons, Central News, and a few other services were brought into existence. Such liberality did not, however, extend to all aspects of the new burgeoning field of "online" service providers, as certain companies, for example, MacMahons, were, at least temporarily, prohibited by the Post Office from offering stock market quotes, most likely as a means to protect its earlier licensee, Extel (Post Office, 1879-1881, File 1, p. 6). Thus, in some ways, the Post Office was actively regulating the content of "online" service providers, not directly on political grounds but on commercial ones.

Although the Post Office encouraged some competition, Extel, for example, complained bitterly that it "had now licensed [too] many rival institutions". Given that the Post Office's policy had caused Extel "to fight for its living," the company reasoned that it could legitimately petition for lower telegraph rates (Post Office, 1882-1907, File VI, p. 18). After failing to get the Post Office more deeply involved in regulating competition, Extel embarked on an ambitious project of eliminating competitive threats to its profit margins on its own terms. As had been the case in North America, a host of practices surfaced to replace the dynamic "electronic information market" with a more placid and controllable one. One effort of this ilk was the attempt to create a cartel arrangement among the dominant telegraph-news agencies to restrain the downward pressure of competition on prices (Scott, 1972, pp. 29-34). Another more ambitious method was the elimination of competition through mergers and acquisitions. This path was pursued with some vigor by Extel in the early 1880s, as it acquired MacMahons (1882), Central News (1884), and Electric News (1884). The Post Office stood idly by as the mergers and acquisitions proceeded apace, stating that it would only require Extel to revise its license to take account of its new possessions (Post Office, 1882-1907, File VI, p. 4).

Perhaps the most significant and enduring impact on the long-term development of telegraph-news agencies stemmed from actions taken by the Committee of the London Stock Exchange and Extel to create a monopoly over electronic news and information flows from the Stock Exchange.[13] Although many tried to erode the information monopoly, either through attempts to establish competing services, or by piracy or legal challenges, they failed to get Extel and the Stock Exchange to yield their control over information. The courts were unhelpful in the matter, as they validated monopoly information rights, outlawed information piracy, and embarked on a radical program to reconstruct and expand copyright law to ensure that property rights to information became inviolate.[14] In one instance, the Court of Appeals stated matter of factly that the Stock Exchange and Extel were fully "entitled to limit the supply of . . . information . . . as they thought fit" (*Exchange Telegraph Company Limited v. Gregory & Co.*, 1895, p. 157). Information scarcity, not abundance, was the aim and source of profit, and the courts wasted no time in reinforcing this trend, despite the fact that government ownership of the telegraph, the press subsidy, and policies supportive of universal service were legitimated on the grounds of increasing access to the means of communication and information, not limiting it. The Post Office was also of little help in these matters, despite the fact that it licensed Extel and could attach certain obligations to its licenses so long as they remained consistent with the *Telegraph Acts*. However, its primary interest was policing the boundaries between its monopoly over public telegraph services and the ill-defined scope of private telegraphy and competition, rather than devising an expansive concept of public communication. It is also probable that the Post Office sought to avoid any appearance of using licensing powers to abuse "electronic publishers," a prospect given prominence by the controversies spawned by government ownership and, especially, the press subsidy (Post Office, 1876, p. 182).

FROM COMMON CARRIAGE TO ELECTRONIC PUBLISHERS AND BACK AGAIN: TELECOMS AND TURN-OF-THE-CENTURY COMMUNICATION LAW

As the press and telegraph became more closely knit together, jurisprudence began to rely less and less on the transportation analogies used earlier to elaborate the doctrine of common carriage. After a short period of usefulness, the common-carrier principle in telecoms matters was pushed aside as the courts increasingly turned to laws governing the press for guidance, in particular, those regulating issues of libel.

As the bottleneck through which various content providers had to pass, especially under conditions of oligopoly or monopoly, fair network access was a prerequisite to the healthy development of "information markets" and a democratic political culture. However, for a long time, those who controlled the distribution network combined with content providers to secure an advantage over would-be competitors. For example, from its inception in 1849, the Nova Scotia Telegraph Company generally adhered to "first come, first serve" principles, but on several occasions it did collude with certain content providers so that they had priority access to the network to ensure a temporal advantage over rival news and information providers. Of course, Western Union and Associated Press were incessantly engaged in such activities during the last half of the 19th century, each agreeing to avoid competing in the others' line of business and to give advantage to one anothers' services over that of would-be rivals (Blondheim, 1994, pp. 156-163; Thompson, 1947, pp. 229-236). Similar conditions also arose around the turn of the century in relations between Canadian Pacific Telegraphs, Associated Press, and attempts by western newspapers to organise a competing wire service—a point returned to later.

At best, only partial aspects of the common-carriage principle prevailed within the mature structure of the telegraph industry and were only meekly enforced through a combination of self-regulation and weak legislation. The concept did not mean, as it has come to in the 20th century, a rigid separation between carriers and content providers and "just and reasonable rates." At most, it meant that access should be given on a "first come, first serve" basis and that all users should be served under comparable conditions. Moreover, after a brief flirtation with the concept as a principle of telecoms law during the early evolution of the telegraph system, the courts largely abandoned it as the art and social relations of telegraphy were consolidated and shifted from affiliations with the railways and into the ambit of the communication industries. The common-carrier principle first lost its lustre in the United States and shortly afterwards in Canada and England. By 1874, it had become unremarkable for Canadian courts to state that "telegraph companies cannot be treated as analogous to or co-extensive with that of a common carrier" (*Baxter v. Dominion Telegraph Co.*, 1874/1875, p. 470). A few years later, the Supreme Court of Canada confirmed this idea (*Dominion Telegraph Co. v. Silver et al.*, 1882/1883, pp. 258-261).

Why were the courts so keen to reject common carriage? And, what were the implications of this, especially for a certain view of history that assumes an unproblematic historical analogy between telecoms and transport and uses this to buttress the supposed naturalness of the separation of media along technical lines into telecoms, broadcasting, and publishing?

The courts were not obscure on these questions, offering two key reasons for treating telecoms essentially the same as publishers. In the first instance, as just indicated previously, the courts argued that the analogy between telegraphs and transport was all wrong. In making the point, one Canadian court drew on a colorful and illustrative quote from a recent decision in the United States in support of its position:

> I cannot refrain from observing here, that the business . . . of transmitting ideas from one point to another, by means of electricity operating upon an extended insulated wire, and giving them expression at the remote point of delivery, by certain mechanical sounds, or by marks, or signs indented, . . . is so radically and essentially different . . . in its nature. . . , its methods, and agencies from the business of transporting merchandise and material substances from place to place by common carriers, that the peculiar and stringent rules by which the latter is controlled and regulated,

can have very little just and proper application to the former. And all *attempts heretofore made by Courts to subject the two kinds of business to the same legal rules and liabilities will, in my judgment, sooner or later, have to be abandoned, as clumsy and undiscriminating efforts and contrivances to assimilate things which have no natural relation or affinity whatever, and at best but a loose or mere fanciful resemblance.* (quoted in *Baxter v. Dominion Telegraph Co.*, 1874/1885, p. 482; emphasis added)

The key point here is that it was the link between telecoms, transport, and common carriage that the court rejected, not the affinity between telecoms, ideas, and other available means of communication. Contemporary thinking about communication media turns these ideas upside down, as it reverses the logic and finds the same thing judges over 100 years ago were dismissing as "clumsy" and "fanciful," that is, facile grounds for distinctions between the means of communication. The ideas expressed in this case are not unique, but a type of reasoning shared by Canadian, U.S. and British telecoms law—each cross-referenced the other.[15]

The second reason for rejecting the common-carrier principle was that the telegraph system was so closely aligned with the press, and general issues relating to publishing so pertinent, that it made little sense to distinguish between two aspects of the same process: communication. The courts argued that it was especially important to treat telegraph operators as publishers, otherwise a lack of liability for the content produced by telegraph-news services would lead to irresponsibility and, more seriously, libelous content being distributed to subscribers, the media, and the general public. This also led to esoteric arguments about whether corporations had a conscience, and depending on the answer to this, whether and how they could be held responsible for content distributed by electronic communication. To head off these questions, telegraph providers were, essentially, defined as "electronic publishers." Because the issues are so at variance with contemporary common-sense, as well as so clearly stated by the courts, its worthwhile to introduce another quote at length, this time by the Supreme Court of Canada:

To exempt telegraph companies from liability as now claimed would be to clothe them with an irresponsible power for the perpetration of injustice and wrong wholly opposed to every principle of law or right.

I am at a loss to understand how a newspaper proprietor can be liable for the publication of a libel and the party who prepares the libel and delivers it at the office of the newspaper for publication, and without whose acts no publication of the libelous matter could take place, can escape an equal liability with the printer or publisher of the paper; *they are all engaged in one and the same transaction, viz.:*

collecting, transmitting and publishing matter collected, the aid and participation of all being necessary to the publication.

In *communications especially designed for the press, we see no reason why they should not stand on the same footing as publishers.* But *in strictly private messages the reason for so stringent a rule does not obtain,* perhaps should not be applied at all. (*Dominion Telegraph Co. v. Silver et al.,* 1882/1883, pp. 259, 261-262; emphasis added)

It is important to stress that this was not just a decision made on the margins of Canadian society, but by the Supreme Court. The idea of media convergence was not just a quaint idea, but the law of the land, just as it was in other Anglo-Saxon countries as well. In addition, it is interesting to note that the issues turned on the problem of libel, that "Achilles heal" of the "freedom of the press" tradition. As such, these cases brought telecoms into the ambit of issues relating to power and freedom of the press, issues that the Supreme Court did not fail to attend to—albeit in somewhat different words—in comments about the need to constrain irresponsible journalism and its supposed nefarious impact on business and the economy in general (*Dominion Telegraph Co. v. Silver et al.,* 1882/1883, p. 258).

A final point to observe about this and other decisions is that although they certainly aligned telecoms with publishing, they did not dispense with the common-carrier principle altogether, as noted in the earlier quote. Instead, it can be argued that a hybrid telecoms/publishing model was constructed. In matters of a public nature, and where the telegraph provider played an active editorial role in producing the contents distributed to others, they would be treated in a manner analogous to the press. However, in matters of a private nature and when telegraph operators played a passive role and did not editorially intervene, for example, in transmitting personal messages for others, the lower standards of content responsibility associated with common carriage applied. Thus, distinctions were not erected along technical lines. Different approaches were taken depending on the type of service involved, whether it was public or private in nature, and, lastly, whether or not the telegraph provider played an active or passive function in the communication process.[16]

THE DEATH OF "ELECTRONIC PUBLISHING" AND THE RETURN OF COMMON CARRIAGE (1901-1910)

The weak tradition of common carriage placed information flows under the command of those who controlled the bottlenecks through which information had to flow before entering the broader political culture. Yet, it was not until such problems impinged on powerful segments of the social hierarchy—the press—and a large swath of other groups in society that the legal/regulatory regime of "electronic publishing" was abolished.[17] Relations between the telegraph industry and press had deteriorated so badly that in 1901 the Canadian Press Association called on government to nationalise the industry. This dramatic call was no doubt related to the history and perception of abuses stemming from the duopolistic nature of the telegraph industry shared, by this time, between Canadian Pacific (CP) and Great North Western Telegraphs (GNWT) (the latter under the control of Western Union) and that CP had exclusive rights to distribute the Associated Press services in Canada. In contrast to this state of affairs, the fact that the government-sponsored "All Red" route was nearing completion and that the nationalised telegraph system in England had lavished benefits on the press, as well as the public generally,[18] demonstrated that the state could play a key role in developing a national telecoms system, especially if generous press subsidies were included (Fleming, 1902, p. 1). Yet, despite this confluence of factors, another decade had to pass before strategic rivalry between the press and telecoms industry, combined with regulatory decisions by the recently formed Board of Railway Commissioners (BRC) (1903), led to GNWT and CP abandoning news wire services and reinstating of the common-carrier principle (Babe, 1990, pp. 57-59; Nichols, 1948; Rens, 1993, p. 50).

From the initial relationship between telegraphy and news services forged in the late 1840s, news services were seen as having a "public service" dimension and this, coupled with the fact that the volume of news flows helped fill vacant network capacity, resulted in the promotion of special telegraph rates for the press—although this concession in Canada was incomparable with the lavish system of press subsidies in England. For an economically weak press incapable of supporting the production and distribution of national and international news, such subsidies allowed them to supplement local news with information they might otherwise not obtain. It also allowed local newspapers and journalists to become independent news agencies of sorts, distributing information by wire to others. At least in theory, press subsidies gave the hinterland press access to the same information as their cosmopolitan counterparts and favoured the decentralisation of information production. However, such subventions also tended to reinforce information monopolies, accentuating the hold of information produced and disseminated from centralised "information hubs" such as New York, Montreal, and Toronto, over the political-cultural space of the country as whole. Similar patterns prevailed at the local level, as access to the wire service was according to a "first-come first-serve" policy, and latecomers needed to show that competition did not threaten the viability of existing newspapers (Nichols, 1948, pp. 51-52). In combination, then, the press subsidy and the "first-come first-serve" policy buttressed an integrated information monopoly between the news wire service (AP), the carrier (CP), and local newspapers.

Despite the neat and convenient appearance of these arrangements, they were not sturdy and durable. As mentioned earlier, already by 1901 relations between newspaper publishers and CP were severely frayed. A year later, the Canadian Press Association invited Sandford Fleming to discuss the details and benefits of government ownership, distance insensitive tariffs, and greater press subsidies, and how similar arrangements might be implemented in Canada. Fleming (1902) painted a compelling (but lopsided and biased) picture for his audience, arguing that

> Canada is the only country in the British Empire where the telegraph service is not state-owned; [that besides] Canada and the United States, the telegraph service of every civilised nation on the face of the globe is controlled by the state; and [that it was because there was no state-ownership] in Canada and the United States that the charges for the transmission of telegraph messages are practically double the rates charged in . . . other . . . countries. (p. 7)

The potential for a radical transformation of telecoms in Canada notwithstanding, it was not until actions by CP between the years 1907 and 1910 that conflicts between telecoms and the press were brought to a head. The crisis was precipitated by CP's announcement, in 1907, that it would no longer provide western newspapers with its combined AP/Canadian news service directly from Montreal. It would continue offering such services to the press in Ontario and Quebec, but for those in Winnipeg and further west, the new plan meant that (a) the composite service would be abandoned; (b) the AP service would be brought up through a private line from St. Paul, Minnesota; and (c) the western press would have to bring the Canadian news service "in from the east at their own expense" (Nichols, 1948, p. 20). Obviously, the proposal created disparities between the western and eastern press, adding considerably to the cost of news production for the western press.

The western press responded by devoting substantial efforts to develop an alternative news service and distribution system. Even though the presence of the competing telegraph systems of Great North Western and the more marginal Canadian Northern suggested that it might be possible to break the CP/AP news monopoly, these two companies' networks did not extend beyond Manitoba. As a result, rival news services could not avoid dependence on the CP system, a factor the company exploited by charging commercial rates for would-be rivals, refusing to carry reproduced news stories despite an absence of copyright law governing news, and by raising rates between 65% and 233%, among other actions.[19]

On the one hand, such efforts rendered attempts to establish alternative wire services futile. On the other, though, this abuse of network dominance intensified and broadened the calls for nationalisation, or at least for stronger regulation of tariffs and telegraph companies' ability to control the flow of news and information. Perhaps more importantly, CP's efforts to control the flow of information turned the issues into a far-ranging debate over "freedom of the press." Freedom of communication issues thus became tightly tied to telecoms matters—something that seems to have been forgotten in much present-day literature—as well as to a strong critique of the deleterious influence of corporate control of information. Welding together themes of economic dominance, public ownership, telecoms, and media freedom, the tenacious critic of concentrated corporate power, W. F. Maclean, wrote an article in the *Toronto World* criticising "attempts on the part of public service companies to muzzle free expression of opinion by withholding privileges that are of general right cannot be too strongly condemned" (quoted in Nichols, 1948, p. 41).

CP responded by threatening to cut back services even further to those publishers offering news space to such malcontents and by continuing to offer different terms for members of the press depending on whether they were subscribers to the AP service or one of the rival services, arguing that such differences were legitimate because of the financial burden imposed by "press subsidies" on the company and, furthermore, that the rates charged for its news services were beyond the purview of the new regulatory agency, the Board of Railway Commissioners. The scope of these differences were not minor, as indicated in Table 3.3, nor were they beyond the scope of regulatory intervention, as will be seen later.

These differences stemmed from the fact that CP was charging its "subscribers for the commodity, viz., the news, delivered at a flat rate; . . . while in the case of [Western Associated Press] the payment . . . was for the transmission, and not for the commodity" (BRC, 1910, p. 274). Although CP argued that the BRC had no regulatory powers to compel telegraph companies to separate costs for news services and for transmission, the BRC rejected this. The BRC responded that the *Railway Act*[20] compelled it to ensure that rates were "just and reasonable" and that unless transmission rates were separate, explicit, and equitable, "telegraph companies could put out of business every newsgathering agency that dared to enter the field of competition with them" (BRC, 1910, p. 275). Consequently, *all* telegraph companies were required to submit separate tariffs for distributing news services, and all newspapers,

intervention, not technological imperatives (Babe, 1990). Three things defined this period (1840-1910) of telecoms history: passage of the telegraph industry through phases of innovation, methodless enthusiasm, and consolidation. Although particulars and exact times differed, the general trajectory was paralleled in Canada, the United States, and England, although bypassed in France and Germany where state monopoly was imposed from the outset. A second notable feature was the shift from regulation based on analogies to railways and use of the common-carrier principle, toward a regime of "electronic publishing" (or a hybrid electronic publishing/common-carrier "model") as relations between telegraphs and the press strengthened and links with railways became less salient, and finally back to the common-carrier model by way of government ownership (England),[22] threats of state intervention (the United States), or regulatory intervention (Canada). Finally, the analysis of shifts in industrial organisation and modes of regulation suggests that boundaries now drawn between different means of telecoms (telegraphy and telephony), broadcasting, and publishing do not have a solid anchor in history (or technology). Historically, attempts to divide media into separate areas have been induced by the interests of power. They have been transitory and, as seen from legal points of view, superfluous, or even silly.

The role of the Canadian State in telecoms policy has always been a unique one, neither conforming to the model of "regulatory neglect" in the United States or that of "direct and active intervention" in Europe. The image of the Canadian State that emerges is of a state whose first allegiance was to promoting economic accumulation, second to maintaining political legitimacy, and only residually to promoting a "public service" orientation toward new means of electronic communication. Although the close proximity between telecoms and "electronic publishers," and a nascent critical discourse connecting the two to issues of media freedom, suggested that the era might end as one noted for its democratising impulse, it was not. Despite regulatory decisions by the BRC truncating CP's cross-media exercise of monopoly power, little was done to check the growth of industrial monopolies/oligopolies within telecoms and publishing. In fact, one might argue that media regulation became governed by an interest in limiting control across the media but only meekly considered the influence of economic concentration within segments of the communications field. This point is considered in detail in the following two chapters.

As the next chapter indicates, the situation between 1900 and 1910, and perhaps for the next decade as the organisational framework for telephony was worked out, did suggest that the entire institutional framework for Canadian telecoms was up for grabs. However, this was only possible if the natural monopoly concept could be contained and cross-media boundaries left open to negotiation rather than removed from the grasp of broader public discussions by strategic interests bent on maintaining positions of dominance, eliminating "chaos," and restoring order, control, and predictability to the communication industries.

ENDNOTES

1. The fact that the Montreal Telegraph Company had just acquired the British North American Telegraph Company from Gisborne also suggests that this may have been another link between the Montreal company, Associated Press, and the American and British telegraph interests.

2. According to the cartel's arrangements, the six members divided North America up into exclusive zones. The companies agreed not to compete with one another in their respective territories and did their best to ensure that no others could sustain a viable competitive threat. They also agreed to interconnect and share traffic with one another and not with those outside the Treaty. Where their networks did overlap, they shared and distributed traffic and revenues between themselves on a pro-rated basis (Thompson, 1947, pp. 310-330).

3. Parallels to phase one of "media divergence" in the United States occurred when Western Union refused an offer to acquire Bell's telephone patents for $100,000. The corollary in England is more complex and inextricable from the policy of government ownership of telegraphy instituted in 1870 (explained further later). Several factors are key to understanding "media divergence" between the telephone and telegraph in Britain. First, the *Telegraph Act* authorising public ownership defined telegraphy as "*any apparatus* for transmitting messages or other *communications* by means of *electric signals*" (United Kingdom, 1869, sec. 3; emphasis added). In the decisive case confirming government control over telephony, the courts claimed that this definition was broad enough to include telephony. The court argued that it was pointless, even a bit silly, to suggest that the entire organisation of telecoms could turn on minor distinctions between the electronic communication of the printed word or the spoken voice (*The Attorney General v. The Edison Telephone Company of London*, 1880, pp. 248-249). The thrust of the court's argument was that telephony was only a minor modification to existing technique. As such, it could easily be accommodated by the existing institutional framework (e.g., government ownership). However, government did not assume ownership but licensed private companies to develop telephony. This was not due to the altruistic feelings of the Post Office (PO) or the conviction that the private sector would do a better job developing the telephone. Instead, it reflected the following: (a) the PO was labouring under the cost of acquiring the telegraph system and was thus without sufficient resources to develop local telephone exchanges; (b) restraints imposed on the PO budget by the Treasury; (c) a squeeze on PO revenues by subsidies given the press,

railways, and other users (see later); (d) political/ideological concerns within the government about the expanding scope of the public sector and a desire to put the brakes on further incursions into capitalist market space; and (e) a relatively strong and persistent view that the "telephone must be and remain a luxury of the rich" and not worthy of specific policies to make it available among the "ordinary labouring classes" (Baldwin, 1925/1938, p. 214; Hills, 1993b, pp. 189-196; Perry, 1977, p. 76; Post Office, 1898, paragraphs 4314-4344). Given this latter view, it followed that the public's telecoms needs could be satisfied through the telegraph system, or if need be, a periodic visit to a public call box, whereas private companies could be licensed to extend the local telephone network to meet the more exacting needs of commerce, administrative agencies, and the well off. Thus, technological considerations were rather insignificant determinants of telecoms, as it was rather more the perceptions of social needs and the details of British capitalism that drove the evolution and organisation of telecoms. To underscore this point, the two systems—telegraphy and telephony—were reunited in 1912.

4.   The concern with "overcapitalisation" here is that the bulk of efforts were now aimed at organising capital for the sake of expanding it rather than telecoms networks. It illustrated perfectly Marx's critique of the fetishisation of money, as economic activity turned from the production of things toward the production of money for its own sake, as represented in the M-C-M formula. As Veblen's (1924) quote introduced in the last chapter noted, the "corporation is . . . not an industrial appliance, . . . [but] a means of making money" (p. 85). As the non-marxist analyst of telegraphy Robert Thompson (1947) pointed out, the fact that capitalisation had no relation to productive property was evident in the wide variation in the capitalisation to revenue ratios between Western Union (9.2:1), United States Telegraph Co. (6:1), and the American Telegraph Co. (1.4:1). Also, investors typically received two or three times the value of their investment in stock, that is, $1 immediately produced stock valued at $3. Western Union's own books showed the network as capitalised by at least two times its actual book cost (pp. 408-409). That this was a new way of organising capital was confirmed by the fact that governments continued to collect taxes only on the value of productive property (assets) not the value of capitalisation (Kieve, 1973, p. 47). While the new world of "semiotic capitalism" took its place, governments continued to live in a world where economic value resided in land, labour, gold, or some other tangible *thing*. One of the strongest powers reserved for governments in later telecoms policies was the right to review (and restrict) capitalisation levels—although it was a power left quite dormant (see Chapter 4). The were two further effects of overcapitalisation: First, the interests of patent holders was subsumed to financiers—a fact complained about bitterly by some of the most creative minds in electronic communications such as Morse, Wheatstone, Marconi, and Deforest—as patent holders received payments as a percentage of profits, that residue left over after paying out dividends on inflated stock. This furthered the symbolic annihilation of links between economic values and productivity, let alone individual creativity. Second, overcapitalisation obscured the existence of "monopoly rents/profits." For

example, a "normal" 5% profit on capitalisation of $22,000,000 (e.g., that of Western Union in 1864) would yield about $1 million and likely be considered acceptable within parameters of a competitive, capitalist economy. However, if the rate of capitalisation for the company was calculated at the more modest level of, for example, the American Telegraph Company (e.g., 1.4: 1, not 9.2:1), and similar rates of profit allowed, the corresponding amount of profit would be about $167,400 on a rate base of about $3.35 million. Profits of $1 million on a $3 million investment look a lot more like monopoly rents than they do on the much higher levels of capitalisation. Basically, lower rates of profit look more legitimate alongside an enormous sum of money than do lots of profits alongside smaller amounts of capital invested. Reasonable conjecture suggests that the former method was less likely to draw the attention of antimonopoly and regulatory forces than the latter, hence the ideological/political function of overcapitalisation.

5. It appears that the Atlantic and Pacific Telegraph and Transit Company never began operations in Canada. The anticipated company seems to have been envisioned as a joint venture among Great North Western, the Montreal Telegraph Co., and the United States Telegraph Company. It seems to have been finally nixed in 1864 due to persistent problems in securing the cooperation of the Hudsons Bay Company, over whose land the system would have to pass, and the government's less than enthusiastic embrace of the subsidies called for (Innis, 1923/1972, p. 42).

6. This development was somewhat peculiar because, as introduced earlier, the English government had been subsidising the Anglo-American trans-Atlantic network to the tune of £14,000 annually, perhaps out of an interest to avoid overdependence on Reuters's control over the flow of international news into Britain.

7. Whether Bell's charter did or did not exclude it from operating in telegraphy is a contested point. The arguments are presented in detail in the next chapter, but looking ahead somewhat, the conclusion I draw is that Bell was not excluded from telegraphy and any restrictions that were in place were merely "window dressing." For other companies, the answer is unequivocal: there were no such restrictions.

8. The date refers to the news services of Great North Western's predecessors, who merged together to form the Great North Western Company, first chartered in 1859. The company was also affiliated with the Grand Trunk Pacific Telegraph Company (identified in the previous quote) via the parent company of Grand Trunk Railways (Innis, 1923/1972, p. 40; Nichols, 1948, pp. 10-11).

9. The Post Office allowed licencees to broadcast information services to subscribers over the telegraph network. Information could be sent simultaneously from one person to many subscribers, and this was encouraged by the fact that the cost fell dramatically after the "first-off" cost was incurred. According to the tariff schedule, during "off-peak" charging periods the cost of the first message sent was 1 shilling for 100 words, whereas each additional address was charged at only 2 pence, or 1/6 of 1 shilling, for the same number of words. The same economics are present in more recent media, such as radio, film, and so on.

10. Not everyone supported the press subsidy. Some critiqued it for aggravating the Post Office deficit (Fleming, 1902, pp. 5-6; Kieve, 1973, pp. 201-216; Post Office, 1876, pp. 180-181). Second, it was argued that the subsidy increased the provincial press' dependence on the London press. The subsidy helped flatten the "informational space" and culture of the country and bolstered the hegemony of a London-based political culture. It was also claimed that the subsidy favoured the provincial press because they relied more on the telegraph, and that it also encouraged "information piracy," as news produced in London was loaded onto the wires as soon as it hit the streets and then simply reproduced locally throughout the rest of the country. This point gave urgency to efforts to transform the copyright regime to recognise a new property right in news/information (Post Office, 1876, pp. 179-186). Finally, it was argued that those depending on the subsidy did so at the cost of media freedoms—their own and that of others more generally.

11. The amount of the subsidy was indeed considerable. Press rates were at least 12 times cheaper than charges to regular users and up to 72 times less expensive when the "broadcast" rates were applied. As a consequence, although the press accounted for half of all the communications carried across the telegraph system, it accounted for less than 6% of the Telegraph Department's annual receipts in 1901 (Fleming, 1902, p. 6).

12. Licensing of "online" services and private networks was not a transitory practice but was retained well into this century. The Post Office regularly renewed Extel's license and continued to license other "online" service providers "broadcasting" information and entertainment services over the telephone network such as Electrophone, who offered services to over 600 subscribers in the London area. A provocative thesis might even be developed that this was the framework adopted for regulating relations between the Post Office and the private telephone companies between 1880 and 1912, especially given that the backbone of the public telecoms network (PTN) was considered to be the telegraph and the telephone system was seen mainly as a local extension of the PTN. Telephone exchanges were to be developed under license by private companies to meet the more exacting demands of large, specialised users, without subsidising them from the Treasury or at the expense of the general public, who were seen as not desirous of such a system. That the first telephone exchanges were usually set up around financial districts or the stock exchange adds weight to such speculation (Baldwin, 1925/1938, pp. 265-267; Post Office, 1898). Looking ahead a bit, those who argue that new "online" and media services such as Internet bring telecoms policy into uncharted territories might ponder this era as an example of how online services and private networks have been regulated in the past. This is not an argument for regulation of new media services, but a claim that we are not as devoid of a compass for the future as is often suggested by the new wave of "electronic frontier" cowboys.

13. There were even some attempts in the 1880s, and again in 1893, to exclude Extel from the London Stock Exchange. Many Stock Exchange members complained that the electronic distribution of market information was responsible for their declining fortunes and for turning over the stock

market to rogue operators without a vested interest in the general good of the Exchange. All of this was a very thinly veiled attempt by the small club of Exchange insiders (about 3,400 brokers were members in the 1890s) to maintain their "information monopoly" and to prevent outsiders from getting at the spoils of finance capitalism (see a host of articles, for example, in the *Financial Times*, November 20-23, 1893). Although Extel was temporarily kicked out of the Stock Exchange, it eventually was allowed reentry, whereas other service providers remained excluded (as discussed next).

14. Others tried to circumvent Extel's monopoly over information emanating from the London Stock Exchange, but they were unsuccessful, and were either found guilty for information piracy or had their connections cut to the Extel services for "reselling information," and so on (*Exchange Telegraph Company v. Gregory & Co.*, 1895; *Cochrane v. the Exchange Telegraph Company*, 1895-1896; *Exchange Telegraph Company v. Howard et al.*, 1906). These cases were instrumental in pushing news into the net of copyright. The courts were unequivocal about the fact that telegraph news agents "had a common law right of property in information" (*Exchange Telegraph Company Limited v. Gregory & Co.*, 1895, p. 155), a conclusion that stood in vast contrast to conditions less than 20 years earlier when editorial staff from the *London Times* stated before a Select Committee that they hoped that even a qualified notion of copyright (e.g., lasting 24 hours) could be secured for news, while admitting how difficult this would be to achieve (Post Office, 1876, pp. 183-186). It seems that as the telegraph erased the possibilities for the arbitrage of time differences, economic value had to be derived from information directly, hence the need to turn information into a commodity. Unlike 20 years before, it was no longer true that time was money; now information was, or at least was in the throes of becoming so.

15. For example, in Britain the courts stated explicitly that it was "immaterial" in terms of the issues at hand—in this case, mainly copyright and subscriber contracts for the Extel news service—"whether [information] was produced . . . by means of a telegraphic machine . . . or by writing the information down" (*Exchange Telegraph Company Limited v. Gregory & Co.*, 1895, p. 156).

16. The parallels between these distinctions in late 19th-century telecoms and media law and their resuscitation—albeit unknowingly—by U.S. courts in the recent Prodigy and Compuserve cases are striking. In these recent cases, the question of whether or not Prodigy or Compuserve network services could be prosecuted for libelous content turned on whether they had an active editorial policy vis-à-vis the services they offered (*Stratton Oakmonth, Inc and Daniel Prush vs. Prodigy Services Company*, 1995). These cases are taken up again in Chapter 7.

17. The following chapter indicates that government ownership of telephones was also being raised at about this time by a wide range of groups, including municipal and provincial governments, civic organisations, labour unions, independent telephone providers, and so on. There was also a group of British telecoms experts, including Francis Daggar, Sandford Fleming, William Mulock, and William Preece, among others, who played an active role on the Canadian "telecoms scene." Their "technical knowledge,"

gleaned from British experience with public ownership, plus their positions as government advisors to the federal and some provincial governments, committee chairs, public spokespersons, and so on, helped underpin and legitimate the efforts of the broader social forces, as well as the more-or-less self-interested groups, pushing for a quite substantial transformation of the Canadian telecoms policy and organisational regime.

18.   Of course, this is only meant to refer to the public's increased access to the telegraph system and not the broader issues raised by the long-term burden placed on the public coffers by government ownership.

19.   This and the following paragraphs are derived mainly from Nichols (1948, pp. 38-41). Other background is derived from Babe (1990) and Rens (1993).

20.   The *Railway Act (1903)* and the mandate of the BRC were extended to encompass the regulation of telecoms in 1906, a matter covered in some detail in the following chapter.

21.   The telegraph companies' continued control over the "bottleneck facilities" meant that the BRC would be regularly called on to settle conflicts between them and news service distributors. For example, in 1914 the BRC squashed CP, GNWT, and Western Union's attempt to double their rates for "Press Specials" in the Maritime Provinces but not in Central or Western Canada. However, the BRC had little to say about the collusive, cartel-like relations between telecoms providers, who were obviously practicing a form of price fixing, thus suggesting that regulation was of prices and not of monopolistic behaviour (BRC, 1914b, p. 35).

22.   The English "model" is the most difficult and complex of these three models. On the one hand, government ownership more clearly separated carriage from content than was previously the case, especially as the Post Office was not allowed to become a content provider and emphasised principles such as first come first serve, universal access and reasonable pricing, a nondiscriminatory and transparent licensing and access regime for content providers, and so on. At the same time, it was through this adherence to such principles and a broader government policy framework that the telegraph was brought into closer contact with content providers as (a) a host of new content providers sprung to life, (b) generous press subsidies favoured the press and were legitimated as part of more ubiquitous political and cultural policies linked with ideas about universality and nation building, and finally (c) a view within legal circles that distinctions between various means of electronic communication, and between these and print media, were for the most part irrelevant.

4 FROM ELECTRONIC COMMUNICATION TO TELEPHONY: A SOCIAL HISTORY OF TELECOMMUNICATIONS IN CANADA

As with the telegraph, the early history of the telephone cannot be disconnected from an initial period of "methodless enthusiasm." In this period, one searches for the factors that defined telephony as a distinctly new technology, or the institutional characteristics and social uses that set it apart from innovations in electronic media that came before and after it. From the point of view of technique, functions, organisation, and law, there appeared to be precious little distinguishing telegraphy and telephony. In fact, the two techniques were so alike that Bell's U.S. patent (1876) referred to a "talking machine . . . [that] transmitt[ed] vocal or other sounds telegraphically" (cited in Danielian, 1939, p. 7). In the United States during 1875, Bell's long-distance telephony experiments used Western Union's telegraph system; a year later, and then in Canada, ongoing experiments relied on Dominion Telegraph facilities. Nonetheless, the two arts did eventually develop, for the most part, along separate lines, an account of which offers insights into the political, economic, and social forces shaping the historical evolution of Canadian telecoms along the lines of natural monopoly and as a distinct sector of the communication industries.

TELEPHONY AND ELECTRONIC COMMUNICATION: A CRISIS OF IDENTITY

Although invention of the telephone is often assigned to Alexander Graham Bell or to Thomas Edison, the attribution depends on the features used to demarcate telephony from telegraphy. As noted previously, the English courts argued that the former merely entailed inconsequential

115

revisions to the latter. Other arguments, however, were made, and common-sense seems to continue with the idea that the difference lay in the fact that telegraphy was, as its etymology suggests, the long-distance electronic communication of writing, whereas telephony was the long-distance communication of sound. Yet, it seems unlikely that separate institutional frameworks and investments could be organised solely on content-based demarcations between written and verbal messages. Moreover, the explanation cannot account for the transmission of music, speech, and other sounds by a German inventor (Reiss) in 1860-61 (*Attorney General vs. Edison Telephone Company,* 1880, p. 252; Brooks, 1977, p. 209).

Other distinctions, for example, between telegraphy as a one-way, point-to-point medium versus the simultaneous and two-way nature of telephony also fail to offer a satisfactory account of how separate organisational structures evolved. Although transformations in the social relations of telegraphy stretched it into new content services and toward "broadcasting," there are parallels in the history of the telephone but in the opposite direction, that is, from broadcasting toward point to point communication. From its first commercial moments, the telephone was used in Montreal, Kingston, and Ottawa to broadcast information and entertainment services. A "telephonically reported" story in the *Ottawa Citizen* offers a flavour of this history:

> Pursuant to an invitation from . . . the Bell Telephone Company, a *Citizen* reporter found himself, with a number of ladies and gentlemen, seated in a gentleman's private office. The occasion was the rare and rather novel experiment of enjoying a concert by telephone. . . . A telephone-transmitter had been placed upon the front of the Grand Opera House stage, and connected by wire with the Telephone Exchange. A number of telephone receivers were then attached at convenient intervals . . . , each one of the audience being furnished with a telephone and programme of the concert . . . . If any doubts existed as to the capabilities of the telephone, last nights test has almost completely dissipated them. (The choral union, 1881, p. 2)

Such events were not unique to Canada. In Hungary, the Telephone Hirmondo company "broadcast" to over 6,000 subscribers as early as 1893, bringing in music, political speeches, lectures, and even a "telephone newspaper" as Stentors read out the news at scheduled intervals. Not surprisingly, Hungarian telecoms policy dealt primarily with content and cultural issues, especially those issues concerning the balance among the entertainment, information, and instructional aspects of the service (Briggs, 1977, pp. 44-51). In France, the telephone had to break through perceptions among Parisian and local political elites to ensure that it did not become just another media for amplifying the existing state-lead monologue with civil society (Attali & Stourdze, 1977, p. 97).

Similarly in Britain, telecoms and broadcasting came together with the establishment and licensing of the Electrophone company in 1894. For more than a decade, the company was partially financed by, and leased network capacity from, the National Telephone Company and compiled a service from over 30 content sources—churches, music halls, clubs, political organisations, and so on. The services were delivered to over 600 London subscribers, who chose either a basic service, an extended service, or certain programs on a pay-per basis. For five pounds a year, subscribers got "music . . . on demand . . . [but] had no power of selection"; this was essentially a one-way flow of music into the home. For an additional £3, subscribers were given a "private line" over which they could select from a wider range of "on-demand" theatre, concerts, and opera performances, or from a range of sermons from any of the 13 churches available "online." In addition, subscribers could access special events such as the Royal Opera on a pay-per basis (Baldwin, 1925/1938, p. 267; Electrophone, n.d.; Post Office, 1899, 1902).

Commercial practice, social perceptions' and uses of the telephone showed that the "new" means of communication had yet to be "fixed." Even engineers saw the new media as highly malleable well into the 20th century. As Frank Gill, International Westinghouse engineer and past president of the Institution of Electrical Engineers, wrote in a foreword to *The History of the Telephone in the United Kingdom* (the then-authoritative text on British telephony [Baldwin, 1925/1938]), "Telephony has some of the properties of the letter and of the newspaper; it can be clothed with privacy, given to one individual only, or it can be broadcast to millions simultaneously" (p. v).

However, despite the persistent perception that the potential uses of telephony were many and the technology inherently malleable, these perceptions were epiphenomenal. Beneath the fluid surface of perceptions and the belief that "new" media technology could flexibly adapt to shifts in social demand, urgent and persistent efforts were exerted to consolidate the institutional framework for the new means of communication.

STATE LEGALISATION OF COMPETITION VERSUS THE MONOPOLISTIC DEMANDS OF INDUSTRY

As was noted in the preceding chapter, the telephone was initially developed in Canada by the Dominion and Montreal telegraph companies in Ontario, Quebec and, along with brief incursions by the Western Union Telegraph Company between about 1878 and 1880, in parts of the Maritimes. In 1877, Western Union spurned Bell's offer of exclusive rights to his patent for $100,000.[1] However, a year later the company briefly reentered the field through its affiliate, the Gold and Stock Telegraph Company. Gold and Stock purchased the rights to use the Edison patents and began the American Speaking Telephone Service (Danielian, 1939, p. 10). Western Union's associate, the Montreal Telegraph Company also used the Edison system, whereas the Dominion Telegraph Company controlled the Bell patents in Canada.

From its commercialisation in 1878, Canadian telephony featured duopolistic rivalry in several local exchanges between the Dominion and Montreal telegraph companies. Although this may have produced short-term benefits (1878-1880), the price wars and efforts to secure monopoly did not offer a sustainable model of media development. Both companies exited the field after ruinous duopolistic competition drained them of the capacity to develop local networks. The Bell Telephone Company of Canada gained control over the patents shortly afterward through its parent company in the United States, the National Bell Telephone Company—the predecessor to AT&T. Although the relationship between Western Union and its Canadian associate, the Montreal Telegraph Company, suggested the potential for a sustainable duopoly in Canadian telecoms between the two and Bell, this did not transpire. Instead, in 1879, Western Union and the US National Bell Telephone Company agreed to stay out of one another's operations for the next 17 years. Western Union also received a portion of National Bell's revenues during this time. A year later similar arrangements were made in Canada between Bell and Western Union, a factor that allowed each a momentary monopoly in their respective field (Babe, 1995, pp. 188-189; Danielian, 1939, p. 10; Rens, 1993, pp. 53-55).

The proximity of the Bell Telephone Company to systemic forces originating in the United States was not coincidental. In fact, the company was closely aligned with the U.S.-based National Bell Telephone Company, first and foremost, and second with Canadian commercial, financial, and mercantile elites (Babe, 1990, p. 68; FCC, 1938, p. 19). The failed forays of the Montreal and Dominion telegraph companies into telephony tightened these ties, as National Bell acquired both their patents. Moreover, the unanticipated reluctance of Western Union to finance the Bell system forced its innovators—Alexander Bell, Charles Hubbard, Thomas Watson, and a few others—to relinquish some of their control over the company in return for closer ties with some of the leading U.S. banks and finance capitalists such as William Forbes, Alexander Cochrane, Richard Fay, and George Silsby, among others. This group of a dozen or so people, representing both the innovatory forces of Bell et al. and finance capitalists of Forbes et al., owned half the shares of the new company and set out to secure its position across North America (Danielian, 1939, p. 11).

Some of these individuals were among the American contingency appointed to the Bell Telephone Company of Canada's board of directors. Bell's board included William Forbes, then president of National Bell; Theodore Vail, National Bell's general manager; and Charles F. Sise, National Bell's representative to Canada. Sise was also charged with obtaining a favourable legal mandate allowing Bell to extend services across Canada—a point returned to momentarily. However, given the nationalist sentiments expressed by the MacDonald government at the time, decisions were also made to include several Canadian representatives on the board. The appointments that followed established tight connections between the company and key Canadian financial, industrial, and political institutions such as Royal Trust, Bank of Montreal, Banque Canadienne Nationale, La Caisse d'Economique du Québec, Continental Life Insurance Co., Sun Life Insurance Co., Molson Breweries, Canadian Industries Ltd., Canadian Pacific Railways, and the Liberal Party, among a few others (Huyek, 1978, p. 32). As a result of the Canadian and U.S. appointments, the company was extremely well connected with the authoritative centres of political and financial power across the continent.

However, any semblance of Canadian control of the company was purely cosmetic. The Canadian telephone system was integrated into the U.S. network from the outset through patent licenses, manufacturing subsidiaries, and cross-border purchasing arrangements with U.S. National Bell (Smythe, 1981, p. 143). The largest block of voting stock (43%) in Bell's manufacturing arm, Northern Electric, for instance, belonged to U.S.-based Western Electric (Danielian, 1939, p. 26). However, U.S. National Bell's ownership in the Bell Telephone Company changed considerably over time, ranging from 50% at the outset to 40% in 1905, 30% at the end of the 1920s, and near zero by the mid-1970s.[2] One conclusion that Babe (1990) draws from this history is that "telephony has hardly been an instrument of national unity and sovereignty" (p. 89)—popular political rhetoric aside. Indeed, the Act enabling the new company contained no restrictions on foreign ownership whatsoever (Canada, Committee of the Whole, 1880, Art. 9).

An accommodating legal framework for these economic arrangements was achieved in 1880 with the passage of the *Bell Telephone Company of Canada Act*. The passage of the Act was not novel. For the most part, the new legislation merely extended what government had been doing since it began granting charters to the Montreal Telegraph Company (and many others) since 1847, including the *Electric Telegraph Act* (1852). It was, however, the first time that government authority explicitly embraced telephony.[3] As with measures adopted in telegraphy, Bell secured extensive rights to develop telephone systems across the country. The charter was introduced in Parliament on February 3, 1880, and was passed by the House and Senate less than a month later. The only substantive debate was whether the Bill usurped too much power from the provinces and municipalities, as it stripped them of any power to influence the company and prohibited them from appropriating its system (Canada, House of Commons, 1880a, pp. 151, 264-267; Mavor, 1917). Although the Charter did not countenance monopoly, it did little to preempt the problem either, because it offered no guidance for dealing with the issue should it arise.

According to the *Bell Telephone Company of Canada Act* (1880),[4] the new company had the right to:

- manufacture telephone and other apparatus used in connection with the business of a telegraph or telephone company (Art. 2).
- construct, purchase, acquire or lease, and maintain and operate . . . any . . . telephone [system] in Canada and elsewhere (Art. 2 and 4).
- make connection, for the purpose of telephone business, with other telephone and telegraph companies in Canada and elsewhere (Art. 2).
- freely access public rights of way in order "to construct, erect and maintain . . . lines of telephone" (Art. 3).
- amalgamate with, lease, become a shareholder in, or establish a partnership with any company offering telegraph or telephone services in Canada or elsewhere (Art. 4) (Canada, House of Commons, 1880a).

Two years later the Act was amended to allow Bell to manufacture communications technology and to make it clear that Bell could "extend its telephone lines from any one to any other of the several Provinces, . . . for the general advantage of Canada" (Canada, House of Commons, 1882, Arts. 3 and 4). Yet, despite the wide scope and generosity of the Bell charter, Babe (1990, p. 68) and Surtees (1994a, p. 11) claim the company was precluded from operating in telegraphy. They argue that telegraph companies—Dominion Telegraph Company, Montreal Telegraph Company, Western Union, Great North Western Telegraphs, and a few others on the competitive remnants of the sector—successfully pressed Parliament to protect them from the monopolistic threat posed by the Bell Telephone Company.

However, such an interpretation stands at odds with the overall tenor of the legislation, a political climate more supportive of legitimating monopolies than preventing them, and the meaning of the Act taken at face value. It is unclear how a company permitted to build, interconnect with, and acquire telegraph systems can at the same time be restricted from the area. It is more likely that the constraining sections of the Act were meant to mollify the telegraph interests rather than block Bell. Perhaps a better interpretation is that by not specifically authorising Bell to "operate telegraphs", the company was required to enter telegraphy through a separate subsidiary. This is consistent with Bell's acquisition of the Kingston-based North American Telegraph Company around 1900 (Babe, 1995, p. 189),[5] the legal context of the time, the future history of the "separate subsidiary" device in telecoms, agreements between telegraph and telephone companies not to compete with one another, and other forms of collusive behaviour.

With respect to the general legal context, it is important to note— as indicated in the last chapter—that jurisprudence at the time did not distinguish between various media, let alone electronic communication. This was clear in the *Electric Telegraph Act* (1852) and most, if not all, of the charters granted between 1847 and 1910. A typical exemplar of this trend is the *Northern Commercial Telegraph Act*, renewed in 1906, which permitted the company to "operate lines of electric telegraph and telephone" (Canada, 1906b, p. 223). Likewise, the Grand Trunk Pacific Telegraph Company's Act of the same period is broader yet, allowing it to control any means of electronic communication available or invented in the future (Canada, 1906a, p. 129). Similar wording was used to establish Canadian Pacific's (CP) presence in telecoms in 1880,[6] 10 months after the Bell Act. Thus, in contrast to Surtees' (1994a) claim, the fact that government legislation allowed CP to provide telegraph and telephone services was not unique (p. 12). This had little, if anything, to do with whether Parliament saw CP as a check against a possible Bell monopoly in telephony, and was a more mundane example of the Canadian state's subservience to capital, in general, rather than any industrial corporation, in particular. Given the terms of each of these other charters, and the manifest meaning of key provisions in the Bell Act, it would be surprising if the Canadian government actively singled out the new company for overly restrictive, special treatment in this respect.

Another factor that suggests that Bell was not strictly precluded from telegraphy is the presence of enduring collusive behaviour between it and telegraph concerns. If Bell could not act in telegraphy, why the 1881 agreement with Western Union with respect to telephony and telegraphy? Furthermore, because competition was a legal possibility across the entirety of telecoms, why did CP limit its forays into telephony to a brief and feeble effort in Montreal between 1889 and 1890 (Babe, 1990, pp. 76-78; Surtees, 1994a, pp. 20-21)? The Canadian Electrical Association, an organisation dominated by Bell and Great North Western Telegraphs, offered a glimpse of an answer when it reminded its members "of the wisdom of rubbing off little aspirities of rivalry and banding together for mutual protection" (*Canadian Electrical News*, 1892, p. 1).[7] Thus, although there were few legal or technical impediments, if any, to a competitive telecoms system or media convergence, private industry actively opposed both possibilities.

Perhaps the clearest examples of collusive behaviour were the exclusive agreements between Bell Canada and the railways, and CP in particular. Bell's network expansion to the west paralleled that of the railroad, and a key element in this simultaneous expansion was the exclusive contracts obligating the Telephone Company and CP (or whichever railway was involved, as the agreements were rather standard) to:

> furnish the Railway Company at all points in the Dominion of Canada connection between the offices and stations of the Railway Company and the exchanges of the Telephone Company, long distance passes free of charge. [In return] the Telephone Company shall have the exclusive right of placing telephone[s] . . . in the stations, offices and premises of the Railway Company throughout the Dominion of Canada . . . . [E]ach company . . . grants to the other company facilities for carrying its wires and lines . . . [a]nd the Railway Company will not grant similar facilities to any other company. (sample Bell contract cited in Canada, Mulock Committee, 1905, pp. 183-184)

These agreements excluded competitive telephone companies from railway premises, including those of CP and other railways increasingly active in telecoms. Such restraints on competitive telephone companies were particularly onerous at this time, as railway stations often constituted the commercial hub of local communities. Furthermore, under these agreements, Bell and the railways, some of which were beginning to operate extensive telegraph systems, shared their facilities while denying competitors access to the nascent national information grid. (Again, if CP wanted to compete with Bell in telephony, and had not signed away this possibility in a *quid pro quo*, why did it exclude itself from its own premises?)

THE CRITIQUE OF MEDIA MONOPOLY AND THE TRANSFORMATION OF CANADIAN TELECOMS

Rather than an immutable march toward consolidation, however, several counter-currents to corporate monopolisation of electronic media were visible in the formative years of telephony in Canada (approximately 1880-1920): the nullification and/or expiration of Bell patents in 1885 and 1893-94, the emergence of independent and competitive telephone systems (post-1893), and a broad-based and intensive politics of telecoms (circa 1898-1920). These are discussed next.

At the turn of the century, the value of telephones for home, business, and community life was widely appreciated. Canadians were among the world's most avid telephone users, and in some sparsely populated provinces like Manitoba and Saskatchewan, they lead the world in the number of calls per telephone by a large margin. As commentators and government inquiries regularly noted, the telephone was "a great . . . factor binding people together in scattered communities" (Canada, Senate of Canada, 1928, p. 3990).

However, the telephone was first used "primarily as a business tool" (Pike & Mosco, 1986, p. 20). Telephony provided a local extension to the long-distance telegraph. In some ways, the telephone also "privatised" social communication, as public telegraph facilities were displaced by telephones put in personal offices. The telephone allowed business to more easily coordinate their activities with train schedules and to access metropolitan distributing and producing centres. The simultaneity, and local, private, and oral qualities of the telephone complemented the long-distance, public, and written record features of the telegraph to produce a valuable, powerful, and integrated information system. Whereas the press had been the largest initial user of the telegraph in Canada, the earliest and most intense users of the telephone were "banks and leading business men" (Canada, Mulock Committee, 1905, p. 623).

These trends in who used and what uses were made of the telephone tended to push the "pleasure view" of telephones spoken about earlier this chapter to the margins of public perception, as telephones came to be seen as an extension and engineering improvement on the telegraph and mainly used to serve administrative and commercial needs (Briggs, 1977; Flichy, 1995). Differing views of the telephone did not, of course, disappear. Instead, they continuously surfaced in innumerable permutations. Divergent social conceptions of telecommunications were evident, for instance, in the *Ottawa Citizen* story introduced earlier that contrasted the *aesthetically-orientated clamour of women listening* to a "telephone concert" with "the gentlemen, *more sedate, and probably thinking more of the marvellous feat the telephone was performing, than of the music*" (The choral union . . ., 1881, p. 2).[8] Beside the manifold socially constructed dichotomies between telegraphs and telephones, men and women, engineering and aesthetics, an even broader range of sociopolitical cleavages had opened up as the telephone network was put into place. It was soon clear that rifts had opened between business and residential users; urban and rural areas; large and small communities; capital and labour; federal, provincial and municipal governments; corporate versus independent telephone service providers; and so on (Telecommunication Workers Union [TWU], 1988, pp. 2-5). These dynamics in the realm of "ideas," society, and culture, in conjunction with

Figure 4.1. Electrophone ad

the political economy of how telecoms were organised in the country, pressed the Canadian telecoms system into its more enduring and familiar shape.

Some of these tensions reached deep into the institutional core of Canadian society, especially in 1885, 1893, and 1894, when Bell's control over certain technical patents were either nullified by the courts or expired, in accord with requirements of patent law. Nullification and expiration of Bell patents combined with widespread public discontent to fuel the growth of a vibrant independent telephone company movement (Babe, 1990, p. 79; TWU, 1988, p. 2). Furthermore, in 1893, the government amended Bell's charter requiring the company to obtain the approval of the Governor-in-Council to raise its rates (BRC, 1914a), although this arguably only mediated distortions of an imperfect market through the equally distorted pressures of "backroom politics."[9] More substantially, by 1898, municipalities began "agitating" for government control over Bell. A year later Manitoba amended its laws to permit municipal and provincial ownership (Mavor, 1917, p. 15), a move that suggested the province might challenge the federal government and Bell over the most basic structural issue of telecoms policy: ownership. Discontent with Bell's operations in soon-to-be Alberta intensified in the early 1900s. Elsewhere, Trades and Labour Councils[10] were encouraging municipal ownership. In some northern communities, miners tried to take control over the local telephone service as part of their efforts to construct institutions outside the control of mine owners and their company towns (personal correspondence with N. Morrison, vice-president, TWU, September 9, 1992).

While during the early to mid-1880s all appearances suggested that telephony and telegraphy were settling down into mutually exclusive areas of dominance and monopoly, for a short period thereafter competing perceptions of telephony, expiration of Bell patents and the broader political context converged to suggest that the fundamental structure of the telecoms industry in Canada was again up for grabs. As patents were eliminated, especially in the United States, technology became more available and as a result many independent telephone companies were established. These independents were often monitored and made accountable to municipal governments by limited and renewable franchises. One such franchise was granted for 10 years in 1893 by the Edmonton town council to the privately owned Edmonton District Telephone Company (Cashman, 1972, p. 69). By the turn of the century, several cities had even put the question of municipal ownership of telephones before their citizens. The results of these plebiscites were mixed, supporting municipal ownership in Edmonton, Fort Williams, and Port Arthur, but not in Brantford or Ottawa (Babe, 1990, pp. 84-85; Canada, Mulock Committee, 1905, pp. 77-88). These measures stood in stark contrast to the Bell Charter, which removed formal links between the development of local telephony and civic accountability. Nonetheless, despite the expiration of its patents and proclaimed disinterest in unprofitable areas, Bell continued to threaten independents with expensive litigation (Canada, Mulock Committee, 1905, p. 646).

In 1905, the government of Manitoba studied the feasibility of public ownership and lobbied the federal government to amend Bell's charter to allow provincial appropriation of Bell's property within the province (Mavor, 1917, p. 16). Manitoba's inquiries were joined by petitions from the Trades and Labour Councils, the Union of Canadian Municipalities, the Montreal Chamber of Commerce, and independent telephone companies. All alleged inadequate service and anticompetitive actions by Bell; most called for public ownership of telephones. Three frequently mentioned targets of these critiques were Bell's refusal to interconnect with independent telephone companies, its constant threats of litigation, and the exclusive agreements between Bell, the railways, and telegraph companies, especially that of Canadian Pacific (these three practices are discussed further later) (Canada, House of Commons, 1909, p. 1763; Canada, Mulock Committee, 1905, pp. 101, 170).

As in England during the 1860s, from the mid-1890s onward, opinion and a broad range of social, political, and economic forces emerged in Canada to challenge how the telecoms system in the country had been organised. The similarities extended beyond local forces pressing for change in telecoms to include, among other things, an alternative body of "technical knowledge" introduced by British telecoms experts—Francis Dagger, Sanford Fleming, William Mulock, William Preece, and H. L. Webb. Each played a key role in public debates, government inquiries, and the policymaking process. As well, British and U.S. traditions of political radicalism were called on, with the aim of opening leading institutions to wider participation by all members of society across lines of class, and later gender and race. The telecoms debates were also couched in the context of debates about people, power, and information generally, and second, about relationships between the telegraph and the press.

Key social and political changes defining the era included the uncoupling of voting rights from property requirements for men in 1885, the introduction of universal public schooling between the 1870s and 1880s, and the initiation of public libraries between 1883 and 1903. Although the exact links between this context and the particulars of telecoms politics cannot be precisely specified, efforts to democratise society and politics no doubt called forth similar energies with respect to electronic media. That this was the case was also evident—recalling the discussion from last chapter—in the Canadian Press Association's call for nationalisation of all telegraph systems in 1901, its strident criticism of CP telegraph system's negative impact on freedom of the press, and the press' early and enthusiastic use of the regulatory system that emerged from this intensely political period in Canadian telecoms. In short, an impressive range of social forces opposed the whole organisational set up for telecoms, and the government that had sanctioned the arrangements and turned a blind eye to corporate collusion and the callous disregard for people displayed by Bell, CP, and a few others. Three things followed: a government inquiry, federal regulation, and public ownership of telephones in the prairie provinces. These are discussed next.

GOVERNMENT TELEPHONE INQUIRY (1905): VINDICATION OR FRAGMENTATION OF TELECOMS POLITICS

Even though many of the leading forces in the telecoms politics of this era called on the federal government to assume ownership of the telecoms infrastructure, this course of action was not adopted. Instead, the government convened a committee to investigate the telephone system in Canada and elsewhere. The Mulock Committee, named after its chairman, William Mulock, sat 43 times during 1905 and received interventions from members of the public, cooperatively run telephone companies, municipal governments, foreign telephone system administrators and experts, and Bell management personnel, among others. The proceedings testified to the importance of the telephone, set an example for achieving some measure of public influence over national telecoms policy (in contrast to ad hoc dispute settlement through the courts), and suggested that basic questions about electronic communication in Canada were still within the realm of public debate.

Once again, the form of ownership and control in Canadian telecoms became unsettled questions. Throughout the hearings, references were made to municipal ownership, conditional municipal franchises, ownership and regulation by the Postmaster General, private ownership of local networks and state-owned long-distance networks, state ownership, and privately owned cooperatives, as well as government-chartered private companies. Bell was criticised for its excessive long-distance rates, high urban rates, almost complete lack of rural service, neglect of small towns and villages, anti-competitive practices by establishing restrictive covenants with public places such as railways, refusal to interconnect with independent telephone companies, and higher costs and lower availability in comparison to Denmark, Norway, Sweden, and, with respect to some services, Britain (Canada, Mulock Committee, 1905, pp. 8-17, 400).

With respect to independents' ability to interconnect with Bell's system, one rural telephone company representative spoke of ill-fated plans to develop

> a cooperative farmer's concern[.] [B]ut the Bell . . took it over . . .
> [and] raised the rates. Now it is really better . . . because they have a
> railway connection . . . . The Bell . . . brought pressure to bear, you
> see . . . they insinuated they would put us out of business. (Canada,
> Mulock Committee, 1905, pp. 59-61)

Another spoke of

> the unanimous opinion of the business men that it is against their
> interests and a great public inconvenience that the Canadian Pacific
> Railway should make such . . . agreements[s] with the Bell Telephone
> Company of Canada. There have been protests by the dozens, and
> the council protested about their difficulties, and presented their
> demands to the railway commission and brought the telephone
> company into court. (Canada, Mulock Committee, 1905, p. 100)

Bell did agree to interconnect with some of the independent telcos, but only if they were not seen as a competitive threat *and* if they purchased equipment solely from Bell (Canada, Mulock Committee, 1905, pp. 249-254). Bell countered that the charges of collusive practices, restraint of trade, and poor quality ignored its need for technical standards to maintain network integrity and the need to adhere to basic economic principles.[11] The basic economic principles in question were stated as follows:

> If it is a question of erecting an exchange in one large place and of
> giving a service needed by 1,000 people we certainly . . . give preference
> to the needs of a large number rather than to a lot of farmers . . . . [I]f
> a line is required to give a service to the . . . mercantile community of
> Montreal and Toronto, and on the other hand the same amount of
> money is required for farmers' lines . . . *on any proper business principle*
> *anyone would say,* build the long line, and give the service to the greatest
> number of people to whom it is of the greatest value. (Canada, Mulock
> Committee, 1905, p. 622; emphasis added)

Essentially, Bell wanted to engage in cream skimming, serving areas of substantial economic development that were easily accessible by major waterways or railways, rather than undeveloped and less lucrative areas. However, this conveniently ignored the fact that its charter to develop a nation-wide telephone system was premised on the idea that the company's operations would be "of general benefit to Canada."

The committee's invited expert, Francis Dagger, advocated that the government spend $3,300,000 to assume ownership over long-distance facilities, while allowing local municipalities to construct their own systems or to grant conditional franchises to others willing to establish local networks. These proposals envisioned a government-owned long-distance monopoly and a duopoly, or more competitive arrangements, in the local network. The proposals did not seek to remove Bell from telephony but to foster local competition, public accountability at the local level, and a government-owned long-distance monopoly. It was also suggested that legislation be introduced covering technical standards to allow interconnection between competing and noncompeting systems (Canada, Mulock Committee, 1905, pp. 16-20). The framework advocated was one of regulated local competition, and the use of telecoms policy to mediate market distortions and to secure ideas of social responsibility and the public interest.

THE BEGINNING OF FEDERAL TELECOMS REGULATION: FROM REGULATED MONOPOLY TO REGULATED COMPETITION AND BACK AGAIN

Regulation: The Basics

Although Mulock's retirement from the committee under dubious circumstances and his replacement by Bell's legal counsel, A. B. Aylesworth, suggested that nothing would come of the committee's efforts, important consequences slowly emerged. First, in 1906, two years after its inception, the mandate of the Board of Railway Commissioners (BRC) was enlarged to include the regulation of telephone systems (BRC, 1908, pp. 1-3). The delegation of telephone matters to the BRC suggested an analogous relationship of the telephone to the railroad in terms of infrastructural importance, and a further move away from the "electronic publishing" model of regulation that had characterised much of the history of the telegraph. Yet, even though the telephone was moving closer to railways in regulatory terms, the key parallels were not based on functional similarities. Instead, both shared a propensity to abuse positions of market dominance and, thus, to confront regulators with similar sorts of antitrust considerations. It was through these kinds of considerations that telephones and railways were brought within the framework of regulated monopoly doctrines (although the idea that telephones were a "natural monopoly" was not yet universally accepted; (Benidickson, 1991, p. 1245).

The BRC was not the only government actor involved in regulating telecoms. Despite the semi-autonomous status of the BRC, Parliament retained control over it and telecoms policy in several ways. Every 10 years or so, companies such as Bell, BC Tel, and CP came before Parliament to amend their charters, usually to increase their rates of capitalisation. Because capitalisation rates affected the rate base, the cost of telephone services, and companies' construction plans (and because of the history of abuses in telegraphy noted in the last chapter), Parliament decided to retain authority over this matter. Most companies requesting charter amendments claimed this was needed so they could develop new technologies and expand their service areas. In this way, the private interest of the company and technological progress were presented as coequal with the public interest: more money equaled more telephones was the picture offered. (However, as the last chapter argued, it was also the case that more money begot more money. This was even truer under a "regulated rate base" regime.) On every occasion politicians refused to second guess the companies' capitalisation proposals, despite the protests of labour groups, provinces, municipalities, and various public interest groups (see, e.g., Canada, House of Commons, 1906, pp. 5995-5998, 1928, 1948).

The government also retained power over the BRC by allowing those affected by the regulator's decisions to petition the government. The government could overturn the regulator's decision, send it back to the BRC, or dismiss the petition altogether. It appears that government was reluctant to second guess or preempt the decision-making process, and those appealing agency decisions were largely unsuccessful (e.g., see Canada, House of Commons, 1922, p. 227).[12] This process inoculated the government from criticism, avoided over(tly) politicising telecoms, isolated telephone problems to a specific area of the bureaucracy, and legitimated the regulatory process as a proper institution within the political legal system.

From Unregulated Monopoly to Regulated Competition

The major issues before the BRC, and all subsequent regulatory agencies, have been about telephone rates, as regulators defined their mandate as primarily, if not only, about ensuring that telephone prices are "just and reasonable" and "not unjustly discriminatory or unduly preferential" (*Railway Act*, 1979, c. R-2).[13] The BRC's remit was enlarged in 1908 to cover interconnection between local and long-distance networks, technical standards for network interconnection, and with respect to new measures requiring the telephone companies to file tariffs (BRC, 1908, pp. 1-3; Canada, House of Commons, 1908, p. 10654). Although Bell had required government consent for rate increases for a brief period between 1893 and 1897, the new terms obligated all telecoms providers—telephony and telegraphy—to have their rates approved, a measure that took one of the key policy issues out of the backrooms of Parliament and into the BRC's more open regulatory arena. It was in this context that Western Associated Press obtained redress against CP's abusive rates—an evident improvement over having to find a friendly ear with enough political clout to change things (Nichols, 1948, pp. 34-65). This obviously expanded the "social space" available for telecoms politics, although certain constraints were imposed. Afterward, issues were mainly considered to be technical and limited in nature, as the telcos needed to periodically submit requests for interconnection and tariff arrangements. In return for regulation of rates, the assumption seemed to be that challenges to the overall structure of telecoms in Canada would be abandoned. This was wishful thinking.

The BRC began to use its powers rather cautiously. Between 1909 and 1911 it established an annual telephone company survey to collect data to inform its policies and regulatory decisions, and adjudicated individual challenges to Bell local and toll rates (BRC, 1912, p. 8). An action with greater implications was the agency's announcement that it was favourably predisposed to allow independents to connect their systems to local railway stations (BRC, 1911, 302). This suggested that intercorporate, restrictive covenants were becoming intolerable and might be removed to further a competitive telephone industry. In 1912, the BRC prohibited restrictive covenants between Bell and other companies that denied interconnection to third parties (BRC, 1912, pp. 218-220). In the same year Bell was ordered to reduce rates in Montreal; develop more equitable rates for large and small, urban and suburban users; and extend its flat-rate calling areas so that they were coterminus with civic boundaries. The regulator also expended great effort trying to achieve adequate accounting methods so that a fair distribution of costs between local and long-distance services could be calculated (BRC, 1914a, pp. 19-35).[14] In their entirety, these actions indicated that the concept of natural monopoly had yet to be accepted and that regulation would have some influence on whether the 1,700 telcos in Canada at the time would thrive or disappear in the future.

Just as elimination of Bell patents in 1885 and 1893-94 propelled the development of a large number of independent and competitive telcos, regulatory initiatives taken between 1908 and 1912 caused a second wave of growth in telcos to follow, especially between 1911 and 1916. The positive influence of regulation and competition during this period was unequivocal. In the ten years preceding the Mulock Commission, Bell laggardly increased the number of telephones in service by about 5,000 per year. With the spur of regulation after 1906, Bell expanded the number of telephones in service by, on average, 18,500 per year over the next decade. Just as importantly, independent and competitive telcos were expanding their subscriber base at about the same rate. During the period between 1911 and 1916, the independent and competitive telcos consistently split the total number of subscribers equally with Bell (BRC, 1918, p. 11; Bell, 1893-1916). Figure 4.2 indicates this explosive growth and the alternative organisational structures employed by the numerous new telcos.

The independent telcos competed with Bell in local exchanges or extended telephone service to many areas unattended by Bell. In the decade after 1905, the total number of telephone companies offering services across Canada tripled, a factor that contributed to a seven-fold increase in the availability of telephone service during this period.[15] The most intensive period of competition was between about 1911 and 1916, as the number of telcos went from about 600 to 1,695, and access to telephone service rose from 4.2 telephones to 7.5 telephones per 100 people, an increase of over 50%. Altogether, at their high point in 1916, the independents served just over one half of all telephone subscribers in the country (BRC, 1918, pp. 10-11; Bell, 1916). Throughout the period, independent telcos were praised for "effectively providing telephone service" (BRC, 1918, p. 8), and for the "great and growing value" of the service they provided (BRC, 1913, p. 8).

The independents developed local networks that built on existing patterns of social, economic, and communicative interaction. Much of their success was due to the fact that they provided services where Bell would not and at rates considerably lower for local telephone service. In contrast to the independents, Bell charged high rates for local service and used this to subsidise long-distance service. Obviously the latter practice turns today's telecoms policy myths about long-distance service subsidising universal, low-cost local service on their head (also see Babe, 1990, pp. 121-126; 1995, pp. 190-191). By 1916, however, policymakers took it for granted that control of the long-distance network meant local subscribers would pay for having access to that service, whether they used it or not, with higher rates. For Bell, and the many policymakers that were coming to see the world through its eyes, long distance was a "loss" that had to be "borne by the local . . . exchanges" (*Ingersoll Telephone Co. vs. Bell*, 1917, pp. 55, 63).

This was a novel departure from the views expressed at the 1905 Telephone Inquiry, at which it was claimed that *usual practice* was for the cost of the long-distance network, network maintenance, and depreciation to be assigned to business subscribers through general rates because they used the service most, and then to others on the basis of actual use. This was not a unique Canadian practice, but one that prevailed in other countries surveyed during the Telephone Inquiry (Canada, Mulock Committee, 1905, pp. 249-254).[16] However, what had

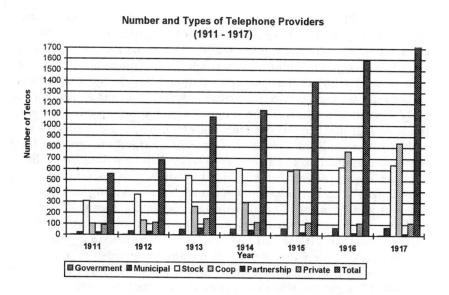

Figure 4.2. Number and types of telephone providers (1911-1917).
Source: BRC (1913, p. 8; 1918, p. 7)

typically been charged against business users in 1905 had, a decade later, become an expense for *all* local subscribers. At least this was the case in Bell's system, although most independents rejected, indeed, challenged attempts by Bell to universalise its pricing strategy. Yet, regardless of who subsidised who in the overall system of telecoms charges, it appears that "rate rebalancing" and the chimera of "cost-based pricing" have been durable features in the politics of Canadian telecoms policy from the outset—an interesting point worth bearing in mind for when contemporary "rate rebalancing" and "cost-based pricing" strategies are discussed in Chapters 5 and 6.

From Regulated Competition to Regulated Monopoly

The challenges over who paid what for telephone service were resolved in a series of bouts before the BRC and, ultimately, the Supreme Court and Parliament, between 1911 and 1917. Two decisions, both involving interconnection issues, were of decisive importance, as their resolution marked a shift from regulated competition toward regulated monopoly—

the framework that prevailed for the next 60 to 70 years in Canadian telecoms.

The first instance raised crucial issues for Bell because it had a virtual monopoly over long distance, but was required by the BRC to allow interconnection with other telephone companies, and because of the far-reaching implications for how telephone companies could price their services. The problem for Bell was that it was charging subscribers higher rates for local service than most independents *and* applying a 15¢ charge to access the long distance network each time subscribers wanted to use it. This practice was not universally followed, as some systems such as the Ernesttown Rural Telephone Company, charged a flat rate for local service and applied no extra charges to access Bell long-distance facilities. This confronted Bell with the choice of reducing its charges, ignoring competitors' alternative pricing schemes, or attempting to eliminate diversity and harmonise tariffs through regulatory means. The latter option was chosen. Through a most peculiar interpretation of the "discrimination clause" of the *Railway Act* and interconnection agreements designed to constrain Bell's anticompetitive practices, the BRC decided that all subscribers should pay their local telephone company for accessing Bell's local network. Although Bell did not receive one penny from the new line charge, the regulator's decision protected its pricing policy, raised rates for everyone, and, by eliminating pricing alternatives, wiped out one of the reasons for the existence of competition (BRC, 1915b).[17]

If the "line charge" decision was not bad enough news, another set of events that had been unfolding since 1911 was about to end with even more dire consequences for the future of regulated competitive telephony in Canada. The key issue once again dealt with interconnection. The main protagonists in this struggle with the Bell Telephone Company were the Ingersoll Telephone Company and eight other independents operating throughout southwestern Ontario. The BRC was headed by Chief Commissioner Judge Mabee. The issues before Commissioner Mabee and his colleagues required that they decide whether their new interconnection policy meant that independent telcos had to pay only for the engineering and service costs of interconnecting with the Bell network or if they should consider "the effect of such connection upon the local service of the Bell company" (BRC, 1916b, p. 180). In a remarkable decision, the BRC chose the latter option, declaring that Bell should be compensated for any lost business as a result of competition and interconnection. To achieve this incredible feat, the BRC had to (a) invent several new regulatory principles, (b) declare its commitment to the "natural monopoly" view of telephony (despite the existence of between 600 and 1,700 telcos during the period when the decision was made), and (c) embark on a 5-year process of reviews, revisions, rejections, and finally a Supreme Court challenge of the decision.

The agency introduced the idea that it should distinguish between competing and noncompeting companies when deciding interconnection issues, although this flew in the face of the nondiscriminatory clauses in the *Railway Act* and the nascent common-carrier doctrine. However, when principles confronted power, the former had to yield. The BRC then concluded that companies posing a competitive threat to Bell's system should pay a surcharge to compensate Bell for business losses that might follow from interconnection.

Shortly after delivering the initial decision, Mabee died, thereby leaving others to deal with the 6-year long effort to save competitive telephony in Canada from the devastating effects certain to prevail if the decision was allowed to stand. One of the most strident critics of the decision was Mabee's successor, Commissioner H. L. Drayton. During one of the many subsequent reviews of the decision, Drayton paid polite tribute to his predecessor and colleagues, then lambasted them for "creating a new and novel law of compensation covering the business losses suffered by one public service corporation as the result of competition with another public service corporation" (BRC, 1916b, p. 166). Two weeks later, as the board was considering an application to appeal its decision to the Supreme Court, Drayton declared flatly: "The Board's Order is illegal" (BRC, 1916b, p. 260). However, this was an age of invention, and as such, reality could be rapidly transformed. A year later, the Supreme Court declared that the BRC had "absolute power to regulate . . . [and] the widest discretion." If the agency wished to introduce new principles of regulation, so be it (*Ingersoll Telephone Co. v. Bell Telephone Co.*, 1917, p. 53).[18] Although a Parliamentary bill was introduced the next year to rectify this situation, it was defeated (Canada, House of Commons, 1917, pp. 3543-3548). Herein lies the creation of the regulated natural monopoly[19] concept in telephony that came to guide Canadian telecoms for so many years to come. As Babe (1990, p. 121) notes, the last competitive telco disappeared in 1925.

Afterward the remaining discordant pieces that did not conform to the new "natural monopoly" picture were quickly brought into line. Companies that had not done so already quickly pushed to be regulated by the BRC to escape the reach of local regulation and conditions of earlier agreements made with lower levels of government (BRC, 1919, p. 19; 1922, p. 124). As Bernard (1982) claims, for example, the transfer of BCTel to federal jurisdiction was calculated to avoid "demands for nationalisation and local regulation, accountability and control" being raised in the west coast province (p. 74). The BRC's refusal to recognise earlier agreements involving the municipalities and provinces was beyond challenge because the courts had confirmed the supremacy of the agency's authority over that of local governments—although this authority was conveniently ignored and left dormant when expedient (discussed later) (*Toronto vs. Bell*, 1905).

Two other events confirmed the arrival of a telecoms policy framework based on regulated monopoly. First, the BRC increasingly viewed telecoms policy as a system of decision making and rule by experts and technical knowledge, thereby truncating the more expansive discourse on communication, society, and democracy evident between about 1895 and 1906. Although "technical knowledge" always had a special status in regulatory affairs, afterward telecoms policy became the exclusive preserve of BRC commissioners, company accountants, engineers, and lawyers, and rarely had much to do with people and communication in a direct way. Of course, there were exceptions, as in 1921 when a large, varied group came before the BRC to oppose Bell's request for an across-the-board rate increase of 12%. This exception, however, proved the rule, as the BRC accepted Bell's request, instituted a "new service connection charge," and increased the speed at which the company could write off its investments. All were justified as necessary measures to extend the telephone system and maintain the company's 8% return on investment, an integral part of the rate of profit regulatory scheme adopted by the agency (BRC, 1922, p. 247; Canada, Senate of Canada,1928, p. 3133). The dubious outcomes of the case lend support to the idea that the regulatory processes now did little more than fragment public energies.

Finally, in the early 1920s the BRC declared that Parliament had not given it authority to regulate or inquire into companies controlled by Bell (Babe, 1990, pp. 178-179; Canada, House of Commons, 1928, pp. 3134-3137). Although bills were introduced in 1928 and 1929 to increase the BRC's power to investigate Bell's affiliates, they were never passed into legislation. Even the BRC appears to have been divided on the issue: "some members of the board were anxious to get further information as to the affairs of the Northern Electric Company," whereas the Chief Commissioner was quite apathetic about the matter (Canada, House of Commons, 1928, p. 3986; 1929, p. 118).[20] As a result, the relations of Bell to its subsidiary, Northern Electric, and to AT&T (which still controlled 32% of Bell's stock and 43% of Northern Electric's stock)[21] remained outside the scope of regulatory control and public scrutiny. One consequence of this set up was that National Bell/AT&T continued to receive royalties "for . . . patents which had long expired" (Canada, Mulock Committee, 1905, p. 9; also Canada, House of Commons, 1928, p. 3135; Canada, Standing Committee on Transport and Communications, 1976, p. 7). This inflated the capital base on which rate cases were adjudicated, hampered development of telecoms-related technology in Canada, and crippled the potential of meaningful public participation in the regulatory process as information remained sequestered behind obscure and closed corporate relationships. Finally, the decision indicated acceptance of vertical integration, another dimension of natural monopoly.

On the basis of these observations it seems that Bell had considerable grounds for accepting regulation rather than rejecting it. However, although Bell may have been content, calls for state ownership continued until 1917, suggesting that the regulatory regime did not have widespread legitimacy (Canada, House of Commons, 1906, 1908, 1909, 1917). Thereafter, the original impulse of regulation seems to have been transformed into minimal "expert-based" regulation of private natural monopolies. As the *Toronto Globe and Mail* editorialised, "There are few corporations in the country but would welcome . . . guaranteed profits such as the Bell Company obtains" (cited in Canada, House of Commons, 1928, p. 3135).

PUBLIC OWNERSHIP AND CONTROL IN THE PRAIRIES

Natural or not, the three prairie provinces of Manitoba, Saskatchewan, and Alberta established telephone monopolies between 1906 and 1909. Shortly before the 1905 Telephone Inquiry, the Manitoba government announced that the

> telephone is . . . one of the natural monopolies, and yet is one of the most . . . necessary facilities for the despatch of business and for the convenience and pleasure of the people . . . . [T]he price . . . should be so low that laboring men and artisans can have convenience and advantage of the telephone, as well as the merchant, the professional man and the gentleman of wealth and leisure. (quoted in Mavor, 1917, pp. 17-18)

The references to pleasure and to social classes suggested that the province was not only adopting an alternative organisational framework for telephony but new ways of thinking about communication. Three years later in 1908, Manitoba acquired Bell's system for $3.3 million. At the time of purchase there were about 700 workers employed by the company and 14,042 subscribers. The original plan envisioned the municipalities operating local exchanges, while the province would manage the long-distance network. However, many municipalities balked at the undertaking and the province had to go it alone (Manitoba Telephone System [MTS], 1991, p. 7).

Early on the government established a commission to oversee the administration and advancement of the telephone system. Although directed to behave in a nonpartisan manner, the Commission's expansion policies greatly favoured farmers, despite the lack of economic return involved with such service (MTS, 1991, p. 2). As a result, rural subscribers paid about half of what it cost the government system to provide the service (Manitoba telephone surplus, 1946, p. C1). As an early *Annual Report* noted,

> the system was obligated to some extent to extend the value of its service even at a loss, to points that have no other means of direct communication, as telephone service is one of the greatest factors in the development of the province. (cited in MTS, 1991, p. 7)

To achieve this policy the government rebalanced rates in 1909 so that businesses assumed more costs while residential fees fell. At other times, proposals for competition in the largest urban area, Winnipeg, were rejected as uneconomic entry and a threat to the social policy built into the Manitoban system. Because of this policy, Manitobans enjoyed some of the lowest rates in the world, despite the fact that the "number of calls per subscriber [was] more than double that in the cities of Great Britain, Germany, Australia, and the US." By 1910, the number of subscribers had doubled. The number doubled again to 56,000 by 1914 (Mavor, 1917, pp. 91-94; MTS, 1991).

Alberta followed Manitoba's lead in 1906, allocating $225,000 of its $2 million budget "for preliminary work in establishing a government telephone system" (Cashman, 1972, p. 130). In 1907, the Alberta Government Telephone system began with the purchase of several independent systems followed by outright purchase of the Bell system for $1.9 million in the following year (Babe, 1990, p. 110).

In 1909 Saskatchewan joined the prairie-wide movement by buying out Bell for $369,000 and the independent Saskatchewan Telephone Company for $150,000 (Babe, 1990, p. 107; Cashman, 1972, p. 188). As in Manitoba, a policy was adopted of allowing municipal development and control over local exchanges, government provision of long-distance facilities, and government supply of local exchanges in areas where municipal control was declined (Saskatchewan, 1908, p. 9; 1915, p. 43). This policy of joint development by different levels of government and the "private sector" was most successful in Saskatchewan; even as late as 1917 some 700 independent telcos continued to provide telephone service in the province (BRC, 1918, p. 8). Moreover, as Bernard (1982) has pointed out, these efforts provided greater access to telephone services across the province. The levels of telephone "saturation" in the province after 12 years of service were "the highest . . . in Canada" (p. 75). Although public ownership had been proposed in Ontario, it never occurred outside of smaller municipal and independently owned telcos.

After establishing public ownership, the Prairie telcos were often criticised for faulty bookkeeping. It was alleged that questionable accounting practices were hiding the fact that, for instance, the Manitoba Telephone System was being run at a loss. The principal criticism was that the provinces were not setting aside a depreciation fund, but funding expansion, maintenance, and repairs out of general revenue, consequently showing a profit where normally there would be none (Babe, 1990, p. 104; Mavor, 1917). A later publication by MTS concedes the point, acknowledging that the government system "lost money every year" up to 1912, whereas annual reports of the time showed a surplus (MTS, 1991, p. 8). However, it should be noted that even Bell did not establish a depreciation reserve until it became advantageous to do so after regulation was introduced in 1908, that is, at the point at which Bell could build the costs into, and thereby raise, the rate base from which regulated levels of profit were calculated (Canada, House of Commons, 1928, p. 3136).

Besides academic and Bell-sponsored criticism of the Prairie telcos, there was also discontent within the provinces themselves, such as when the Manitoban government tried to introduce local measured service in 1912. So strong was the protest that a provincial Royal Commission was called, the measure rescinded, and the Public Utilities Commission (PUC) created. The creation of the PUC was mainly intended "to regulate rate changes and serve as a nonpolitical regulatory body between MGT and the government" (MTS, 1991, p. 9). This mirrored the set up in areas regulated by the BRC, albeit with the key difference that the PUC regulated a state monopoly and the BRC, eventually, a private monopoly. Despite the overture to public accountability, Babe (1990) asks if it was not mostly an effort "to depoliticise telephones in the midst of a controversy" (p. 105)?

A similar regulatory framework prevailed in Alberta. There the Public Utilities Board encouraged public interventions and undertook an explicit policy of maintaining low local and rural rates through a series of cross-subsidies. The Saskatchewan system was regulated through ministerial oversight, the provincial legislature, and a board of directors. Thus, there was no attempt to separate regulatory authority from political and operating authority, as had been done in other provinces, and, indeed, under the federal government. Citizens wishing to press claims on the system did so directly through the company or through local political representatives and the provincial legislature. This system still prevails in Saskatchewan, although will come to an end by 1998 (personal correspondence, J. Meldrum, vice-president, SaskTel, September 3, 1992).

REGULATING MONOPOLY: TELECOMS IN BROADER SOCIAL AND HISTORICAL CONTEXT

The formalisation of organisational and regulatory structures throughout Canada were part and parcel of the beginning of regulated capitalism, the bureaucratic state, and social welfare democracy. Canadian telecoms not only bore the imprint of such trends but contributed to their articulation.

The BRC signaled the birth of a federal regulatory bureaucracy. It was the first independent regulatory agency created by the Canadian parliament, and there was much hesitation expressed over whether Parliament had the power to delegate its powers to such an institution (Benidickson, 1991, p. 1224).[22] Even accepting that Parliament possessed such power, it was asked on many occasions if the creation and expansion of the BRC had not improperly altered the balance of power among the federal government, provinces, and municipalities (Canada, House of Commons, 1908, pp. 10632-10655). The federal government recognized the sensitivity of its position and refused to regulate the provincial telcos, despite the confirmation of its constitutional powers in telephone matters (*Toronto v. Bell,* 1905, p. 371). In the prairies, government control over the telephone system greatly increased the scope of government activities and obligations, while at the same time offering a concrete alternative to private ownership and pure capitalism. With the ascendancy of public ownership of the telephone systems in Manitoba and Alberta, total public expenditure immediately increased by 100% (Mavor, 1917, p. 9). The moves also expanded government payrolls. By 1915, 1,130 employees were added to the Manitoba government system, 574 to the AGT system, and about 500 to Sasktel (BRC, 1916a).

Some members of Parliament called these developments socialistic or characterised them as an abdication of government responsibilities to unaccountable officials (Canada, House of Commons, 1906, pp. 6213-6216). On the other hand, the unwillingness of the federal government to exercise public ownership reinforced the ascendancy of capitalist democracy by legitimating the efficacy of private ownership and by refusing to enhance the position of Canadian labour in general, and in the telephone industry in particular. In countries like England, France, Germany, and Switzerland, where the telephone system was under public ownership and regulation, pressure was brought to bear on the state to augment labour's position in terms of working conditions, the formation of public policy, and in relation to capital in general. This was consistent with the Hegelian notion that the state is the highest expression of sociopolitical rationality and, therefore, must lead capitalist industry by example (Holcombe, 1911, pp. 256-351). By refusing public ownership, the Canadian State reaffirmed the social relations of power between labour and capital in the telephone industry. The federal government's "conclusion that private ownership with government control" was the best solution in the populous provinces of Quebec, Ontario, and later, British Columbia, allowed private ownership and minimal regulatory control to prevail over outright nationalization and a dramatic realignment of class-based political power (Canada, House of Commons, 1908, p. 10635). Thus, federal regulation was a system of control not only on unbridled capitalism but also on labour and the political process in general, rather than the beginning of socialism.

These measures promoted the emergence of large corporate forms in the telephone industry and the advent of a large and organized workforce. After the brief period of respite from monopoly between 1893 and 1915, the Bell system once again began to assert its dominance. Whereas patent laws and government regulation had previously fractured industrial consolidation, after 1915 government regulation, the legal system, and economic power combined to reverse this trend. The industry was already concentrated by 1915 when Bell and six other large telcos controlled 76% of all telephone service and employed 82% of all telephone workers. Thereafter, the trend toward concentration became more pronounced, as almost all competition was eliminated (despite the fact that the number of independent telcos continued to grow), and even fewer companies came to account for over 82% or more of all telephone subscribers within a few years—a figure that has stayed relatively constant ever since.[23] The trends were even more evident at Bell, as it went from serving 45% of all telephones subscribers in the country and employing 54% of the work force (1915) to account for 60% of all subscribers, 66% of all revenues, and about the same percentage of workers by 1955 (BRC, 1916a; Dominion Bureau of Statistics, 1957, p. 7).

As the number of companies in the field increased, and the large corporate form of organization in the field of telephony took hold, the number of people employed in the telephone industry grew steadily. Between 1911 and 1915, the number of workers increased almost 50%, from 10,425 to 15,072 (BRC, 1916a, p. 11). In the prairies, part of this rapid growth was due to the integration of the publicly owned telcos into a broad program of economic development, job creation, and skills training designed to attract settlement and offset the centrifugal force of central Canada's political, commercial, and cultural domination.

As the structure of the industry stabilized, labour organisations developed, indicating a change over previous practice in which work had been parceled out on a daily basis to people who had come out of the telegraph system or who had no experience at all. As Bernard (1982) points out, in the early years of telephony, "men . . . were hired for a particular construction project and laid off when it was completed" (p. 15).[24] Under such conditions it was next to impossible for workers to assert their rights in an organized fashion. The assertion of collective rights only occurred once work became regularized and institutionalised.

The organization of unions took hold first in the western Canadian provinces. British Columbia Telephone Company (BCTel) workers established the trend by joining the International Brotherhood of Electrical Workers (IBEW) in 1901 and 1902 (Bernard, 1982, p. 17). By 1907 the IBEW organized the line-workers at the Alberta Government Telephone system (AGT; Cashman, 1972, p. 184). The union represented plant workers at Manitoba Government Telephones (MGT) seven years later and operators by 1917 (MTS, 1991, p. 11).

The institutional nature of work also developed at other large telephone companies, most notably Bell, albeit without the benefit of union representation for workers. Indeed, Bell imported the methods of Henry Ford, employing vertical integration to control all aspects affecting the price, quality, and supply of material used in its production process (Canada, House of Commons, 1928, p. 3134). This also meant employing engineers and "scientific methods" to control the work force and vigorously resisting unionisation.

In 1906 Bell retained an AT&T consultant to report on the working processes of operators in the busy Toronto exchange. The consultant suggested that the operators should work harder and longer with only marginal increases in wages.[25] Within a year the company duly extended the operators' hours without consultation or an increase in pay. The operators walked off the job. To underscore its aggressive management style, Bell refused to try to resolve the problem with the aid of a government mediator and brought in strikebreakers from Montreal to avoid disrupting service at the commercially important exchange (Canada, Department of Labour, 1907, pp. 4-25; Sangster, 1978, p. 112). Sangster (1978) claims "that the Bell management was determined to avoid setting the precedent of discussing and negotiating working conditions with their employees" (p. 115).

With no official union representation the operators mainly found their way into the labour movement through Labour Temples (Canada, Department of Labour, 1907). Labour Temples were found in cities across Canada. They offered the Trades and Labour Councils, people without a union, and those already unionised a place to meet, talk politics, and organise strategy in labour's battles with employers and employer associations. In this particular instance the Toronto Labour Temples brought together 400 operators with a wide group of individuals united by the causes of economic democracy, public ownership of the telephone system, and concern for the welfare of the *women* working for Bell (Sangster, 1978, p. 113).

At the behest of Toronto's mayor a Royal Commission was convened to adjudicate between the striking operators and Bell.[26] Most interestingly, the mediator, William Lyon Mackenzie King, linked the welfare of the operators and their wages to Bell's telephone monopoly in the city. As King wrote in the final report, the two were linked because

> there is one company carrying on the telephone service for the entire city, and whether they like it or not the public generally of the city . . . is obliged to pay the Bell. . . . Viewed in this light . . . an element is introduced which justifies . . . due regard for the welfare of employees which might be urged with less reason in the case of competitive industries. To the extent to which the citizens of Toronto have parted . . . with their right to choose between competing concerns . . . [they] have parted also with their power to extend their patronage in the direction in which they believe the interests of justice and fair play may best be served, to that extent it is . . . not only their right, but their duty . . . to insist upon a company. . . treating its employees in a manner which is equitable and fair, . . . whether they be men or women . . . . To the extent to which the Bell Telephone Company has . . . secured services at a rate which would not have enabled those who rendered them to have lived, but for the support received from members of their own families, or in ways other than those provided by the company, . . . the profits of the company have been derived by a species of sweating, or by the levying of a tax upon homes and individuals for which no compensation has been made. (Canada, Department of Labour, 1907, p. 37)

King's critical interpretation of the circumstances is extremely interesting, especially as it comes from someone well within the mainstream of political thought and power at the time. Essentially, he accepts classical economics propositions about free markets and, crucially, insists on maintaining the ethical link between competition and human interests. The absence of competition, in this view, robs people of means for deriving ethical measures of economic behavior; thus the need, indeed the moral justification for, state intervention. In less prosaic terms, just as public policy had been used to secure an adequate relationship between telcos and the communities they served, principals were now applied to the labour relations of private monopolies. Henceforth government would not shy away from securing minimal standards of equitable relations between capital, the labouring classes, and the public. Bell capitulated to the new "capitalism with a human face," if only to avoid further public attention, labour militancy, and the possibility of even more government intervention.

Later that year an *Industrial Disputes Investigation Act* (1907) was passed, echoing many of the principals outlined in the previous case (Canada, 1920). The new law secured basic standards of labour relations, but also prohibited labour's right to strike without first going through the new Labour Board's grievance and arbitration procedures. In the first appearance of telephone workers before the new Industrial Dispute Investigation Board in 1911, the BC Telephone workers, represented by the IBEW, brought forward a wide range of grievances, including the right to a closed union shop, the length of the work day, job classification, and wages. Although the board ruled in the union's favour on the issue of wages, it did not consider the other issues raised. Because of the constrained focus of the inquiry process, the BCTel workers took an ambivalent attitude toward the board. Appearing before the board in 1917, the union had a similar experience. Once again, the board adjudicated in favor of the union on the issue of wages, but refused to consider demands for a "closed shop" and the use of unskilled labour (Bernard, 1982, pp. 37-46).

During World War I the loose strands guiding labour militancy gained clarity and focus in some areas of Canada, as an acute shortage of skilled labour occurred, the demand for economic supplies put a premium on productivity, inflation raged alongside low wages, and the government invoked an unpopular policy of conscription (Penner, 1973, p. xiii). Discontent came to a head in the Winnipeg General Strike of 1919. From the outset Manitoba telephone workers joined other labourers in the 2-month strike (MTS, 1991, p. 11). The conflagration was triggered by the Winnipeg municipal council's efforts to legislate "no strike" provisions for all civic employees. The day after an amendment was passed rescinding unions' right to strike telephone workers and 95 other unions engaged in a general city-wide work stoppage. Shortly afterward, most unions of the city and nearby areas of the province followed suit (Bercuson, 1990, pp. 60-65; Canada, House of Commons, 1921, p. 3359; Penner, 1973, p. xxvi).

CP telegraph operators in Winnipeg, Calgary, Edmonton, Vancouver, and smaller cities in between took control of the telegraph news-wire service and actively edited the country's news about the strike for several days before the network was shut down and rerouted through a private line connected with Associated Press facilities in the United States (Nichols, 1948, pp. 204-208). In BC, another general strike was called in sympathy for workers in Winnipeg and against the government's use of the militia and other state powers to quell the unrest there. Telephone operators in BC were among the last to stop their strike action. But more than just striking in sympathy for workers in Manitoba, BC Telephone workers became part and parcel of the broad-based opposition to efforts to restrain labour's power, the industrial organization of work processes, and, in general, high rates of inflation (Bercusson, 1990; Bernard, 1982, p. 79).

The effects of the general strike were mixed. Despite the temporary expression of labour solidarity, the strike divided the labour movement. In BC it caused a significant division within the telephone workers that, by 1926, contributed to the emasculation of their union and benefits won in earlier struggles. The strike also opened tension between labour on an east-west dimension, the western labour organizations feeling that there was a lack of support coming from their counterparts in central and eastern Canada. The division still permeates the organization of telecoms labour (Bernard, 1982, p. 70; personal correspondence, J. Kincaid, regulatory affairs advisor to the CWC, Ottawa, July 7-10, 1992). The strike also revealed the extent to which government could marshall a variety of powers against perceived antagonistic forces, such as the use of violence, the enactment of repressive legislation, and suspension of civil liberties.

The strike brought the debates about capitalism, communism, and socialism to the fore of public and parliamentary discussion for the next 10 years (Canada, House of Commons, 1919, pp. 12-13; 1921, pp. 3359-3361; 1927, pp. 2236-2237; 1929, 2367-2369). The debates indicated the seriousness given to the crisis and the possibility of radical social transformation. The General Strike had brought about "condition[s] . . . so serious that revolution was threatened and the future of Canada was imperiled" (Canada, House of Commons, 1921, p. 3359). Nonetheless, the opportunity does not appear to have brought forth serious public discussion of the merits and philosophical principles of alternative economic arrangements and systems of political governance. Instead, they were constrained to utilitarian considerations of how freedom of speech, education, labour organizing, and state funding of industry could be used to diffuse dissent and channel energies toward the support of capitalism and limited, representative democracy.

More positive outcomes of the strike for labour were its subsequent successful efforts to achieve representation at all three levels of government, a pattern of political representation that persists to the present in some prairie provinces (Penner, 1973, pp. xxii-iii). Some political parties also increased their efforts to incorporate labour in their platforms. Shortly after the strike, the Liberal party, by then under the leadership of MacKenzie King, won national elections. Part of the electoral victory reflected King's efforts to include labour into "corporatist style" political and economic policies. The final consequences of the General Strike were not the eradication of labour strife or the end of capitalism, but the inclusion of labour groups into policy planning and an expansion in the politics of limited democracy.

Yet, the emerging trend toward pragmatic democracy did not mean enhanced political participation for the public, redistribution of wealth and economic control, or an increase in unionism, but mainly the integration of capital, state, community, and labour into formal structures of problem resolution and "class harmonization." Political structures and the policy process were used to eradicate the radical edge of dissent as common interests were invoked, for instance, around the need to raise productivity for the betterment of society rather than asking how the fruits of these efforts should be distributed (Whitaker, 1977, pp. 138-169). The ascendancy of corporatism meant that notions of irreconcilable class antagonism and direct mass democracy would be jettisoned in favor of technocratic planning of economic processes and pragmatic democracy. The effort of the corporatist prototypes, the BRC and IDIA board—both articulated in close proximity to the dynamics of the telecoms industry—to limit their concerns to prices and wages ably illustrated how "economics as science" coincided with a broader political desire to use the policy process as an objective exercise in economic development, technical planning, and social control.

In the telephone industry corporatist relations were evident in numerous attempts to enhance the regulatory framework, acceptance of the natural monopoly regulatory regime, and company-sponsored employee associations (Canada, House of Commons, 1929, pp. 118-122; 1938, p. 937; Canada, Senate of Canada, 1928, pp. 3132-3139, 3986-3994). By the 1920s and 1930s the regulatory bureaucracy was no longer a contested feature among contemporary political and economic institutions. As the imperatives of large industries superseded market considerations, uniform administrative systems for clerical, accounting, and other functions were created; so, too, was a large body of clerical workers. One important outgrowth of these changes was the development of employees' associations. Bell, taking heed of its earlier experience in labour relations, committed to avoiding unions, and cognizant of the emerging political climate, made the employee association an adjunct to its management practices (Sangster, 1978, p. 125). This augmented the company's aim to replace the operators' union that had formed under the auspices of the IBEW in 1918 and remain union free.[27]

Even though the operators had pursued unionisation for some years after the lock out in Toronto, their experience with unionisation only lasted three years. By 1921, a number of factors, not least of which was the chauvinistic disposition of the IBEW toward women members, conspired to bring about a replacement of the union with a company-sponsored employee's association (Sangster, 1978, pp. 126-127). In the United States, AT&T had used the employee association in "hope . . . [that] . . . the employees of the Bell System throughout the country will have no affiliation with any labor organizations and will cooperate thoroughly for the good of the business" (Schact, 1985, p. 15). Like its American counterpart the Canadian Bell organised employee consultative committees, raised wages, and instituted stock ownership plans to advance amicable labour relations within the company (Canada, House of Commons, 1928, p. 3133). By the early 1920s a combination of elite political consensus around "pragmatic democracy," organisational imperatives, company desires, and union conservatism spelled the demise of unionism and militant labour relations. This pattern of labour relations prevailed in the prairies into the 1940s and for over 50 years at Bell.

With their dominant position secured, the large, federally regulated telcos avoided rate increases for better than 20 years, while their continuing efforts to consolidate control over the industry proceeded unencumbered (Babe, 1990, p. 123; Bernard, 1982, p. 77; Canada, House of Commons, 1948, p. 4263). In 1948, Bell representatives boasted that "by reason of economies and technological improvements in telephony we have been able to maintain our present rate structure since . . . 1926" (Canada, House of Commons, 1948, p. 4263). Again technology assumed historical agency, obscuring the relationship of regulatory constraints and political pressure to the company's "willingness" to exercise restraint. Moreover, it has been often noted that there are many ways in which the company could "milk" excess profits from the regulatory arrangements, despite the intent of regulation to reconcile capital accumulation and organisational prerogatives with public interest considerations (Babe, 1990, pp. 170, 190; Canada, House of Commons, 1928, p. 3991).

In large part, this latter phenomenon was an attribute of the regulatory regime's tolerance for vertical integration. Although vertical integration escaped regulatory attention for much of the early history of telecoms, it did occasionally get attention and criticism in Parliament from labour unions, academics, municipalities, and would-be competitors (Canada, House of Commons, 1928, p. 3991; 1939, p. 937; 1951, p. 4176; Congress asks postponement, 1952, p. 19). It was only much later, for example in 1976 and 1983, that vertical integration became subject to inspection under the *Combines Investigation Act*, although nothing substantive ever came of the investigations (Babe, 1990; Restrictive Trade Practices Commission [RTPC], 1982).

Ironically, the Depression seems to have solidified the emerging consensus at the same time that it brought forth criticism of the telcos. The telephone companies were chastised for laying off some 16,000 workers during the recession. Bell laid off 4,000 employees and exacted concessions from others, all the while improving its business prospects and profits (Canada, House of Commons, 1938, p. 941; 1939, p. 3139).[28] BCTel was also admonished for using the Depression to roll back benefits. It instituted a series of layoffs, implemented pay reductions, and used job reorganization as a way to undermine the gains made earlier in the century by workers (Bernard, 1982, pp. 80-85).

That even the publicly owned prairie telcos laid people off and cutback on plans to extend their networks indicates that the telcos were universally faced with hard times. The point, nonetheless, is that some of the private companies used the occasion to reclaim power earlier lost to labour unions and to maintain profits at the expense of labour. This latter feature was not present in the prairie telcos where layoffs were accompanied by fewer subscribers and a precipitous drop in profits (MTS, 1991, p. 16; Saskatchewan, 1934, p. 14). Thus, it appears that part of the regulated monopoly regime assumed that companies would conscientiously attempt to maintain employment stability. This was indicated more than once, as some politicians took Parliamentary opportunities to remind the companies to

> remember that these men who work for you have hearts and souls, have wives and families who have to be looked after. Spread work out among your employees; see to it that every possible bit of work is given to your employees, and forget during this time of stress and strain in Canada that yearly dividend or yearly balance sheet with its big profit. (Canada, House of Commons, 1938, p. 941)

Such appeals to human interests appear almost quaint, even naïve, when considered against the context of "savage capitalism" prevailing today. Yet, the fact that even this—by today's standards quite radical critique from within the mainstream of political institutions—appealed only to ethical considerations and did not critique how the economy, and more narrowly, telecoms in Canada, was organised, suggested that the framework of monopoly capitalism was beyond challenge, or even consideration. Monopoly capitalism was now accepted as natural, not only in telephony, but in many areas of the economy (Canada, House of Commons, 1948, pp. 4266, 4519).[29] In contrast to classical economic theory, the new economy consisted of three sectors: a monopoly core, a public sector, and competitive fringe.[30]

Despite the end of the Depression around 1937, World War II extended stagnant patterns of telephone growth for another decade. Besides the implementation of automated direct dialing and development of the Trans Canada Telephone System in 1932, other activity in the telephone system stood still. From the beginning of the 1930s until after the war the domestic network underwent only enough growth to maintain parity with pre-Depression rates of availability (DBS, 1962, p. 15). Attention to developing the public network during the war was obviously preempted by military needs and the diversion of supplies to the armaments industry. The most visible development during this time was the length of the waiting list for a telephone in all areas of the country.

SUMMARY COMMENTS

Before telephony passed from infancy to maturity, key questions about which uses would predominate, whose interests would be served in the first instance, and what organisational framework would prevail, had to be resolved.

After an early period, perceptions of telephony as an instrument of pleasure and an extension of public communication broadcasting information into homes and offices gave way to a view of telephony as a means of private communication mainly used to meet commercial and administrative needs. However, even this changed, as the telephone became appreciated across a broad strata of social classes and needs—a factor that gave rise to the politics of, and enduring concern with, universal service.

Transformations in the uses and organisation of telecoms did not occur primarily in the realm of ideas, however. The new means of communication were shaped in several distinct phases and by several key events. Telephony was first commercialised as a local adjunct of telegraph networks and as a competitive local duopoly in Ontario, Quebec, and the Maritimes. However, neither the complementary technical affinity between telegraphs and telephones nor conditions of duopoly prevailed. These possibilities were put to rest during the formative years of telecoms in Canada (1878-1920), as telecoms passed through phases of unregulated monopoly, regulated competition, and, most enduringly, regulated monopoly. Transition from one phase to another had little to do with technological change, and everything to do with the dynamic interplay of legal, economic, political, and governmental forces.

Unregulated monopoly occurred through a combination of market failure, patent monopolies, and collusive agreements between Bell, CP, Western Union, and a few others, and was strongest between 1881 and 1893. It was also facilitated by weak state regulation of media boundaries, a factor that left corporate interests free to divvy up the communication industries among themselves.

The shift toward *regulated competition* unfolded with the nullification of Bell patents, notably in 1893, the rise of an intense politics of telecoms between 1895 and 1906, the *Telephone Inquiry* of 1905, and the birth of the BRC and the expansion of its regulatory mandate between 1906 and 1908. Western Associated Press' successful challenge of CP's monopoly over telegraph-news services; new policies curtailing the collusive arrangements between Bell, CP, and others; and decisions mandating that Bell interconnect with independent and competitive telcos suggested that the BRC might vigorously take on the forces of monopoly. In this period, the number of competitive and independent telephone companies, based on every kind of organisation, proliferated.

This did not endure. By 1916, the BRC had opted for *regulated monopoly*, as it invented new regulatory principles, helped Bell to impose its tariff structures on the rest of the industry, and committed itself to the view that telephony was a natural monopoly. Despite the existence of 1,700 telephone companies, an absense of price-setting capacity by Bell at the local level, and the acknowledged contribution of independent telcos to increasing access to telephone service, the BRC, Bell, members of the Supreme Court, and others whose opinions could change society *believed* that telephony was a natural monopoly. In several acts of unparalleled "judicial activism," reasonably stable and clear principles of telecoms law were jettisoned and the world made to conform to what regulators and Bell believed to be true rather then what they saw before their eyes. Afterward, telecoms was a "natural monopoly," a particularly flexible, port manteau concept into which almost anything could be made to fit.

The survival of telecoms as a natural monopoly until the 1970s, and its demise thereafter with the unleashing of regulatory liberalisation, changes in ownership, and the legalisation of competition—first in peripheral areas, then gradually into services, and finally into the core of the telecoms network—is covered in the next two chapters.

ENDNOTES

1. There are probably two reasons why Western Union passed on the Bell offer: first, its overly liquid capital had precipitated a crisis among U.S. financiers, stockholders, and stock markets (Thompson, 1947, pp. 408-409), thereby rendering further expansion difficult. Second, Briggs (1977) suggests that the decision was due to the misperception that because telephones did not leave a record of transactions, they were ill-suited to administrative and commercial purposes. The company only saw the instrumental uses of the new technology and downplayed its contributions for social intercourse or just pure pleasure.

2. The other most historically significant U.S. owner of Canadian telephone companies has been GTE, although it did not extend its activities into Canada until 1916 and did not completely engulf its predecessor, the Okanagan Telephone Company, until 1966. Through its holding company, Anglo-Canadian Telephones, set up in 1926, it has owned the vast majority of the stock in British Columbia Telephones and Quebec Telephones (Smythe, 1981, p. 151).

3. It must be recognised, however, that prevailing definitions of electronic communication meant that government authority already applied to telephony by default, even if only implicitly. The Montreal and Dominion telegraph companies did not need to revise their charters to extend their operations from telegraphy to telephony. They did so merely as a *natural extension* of existing operations, an unobjectionable process given the accepted understanding of electronic communication/telecoms. The point is covered in more detail later in this chapter.

4. Also see Babe (1990, p. 68).

5. This paragraph has benefited from discussions with R. E. Babe. Although I am not sure that he would agree with the conclusion that I come to here, he has been helpful in keeping the issues clear and for suggesting the

relevance of the "corporate veil" to thinking about how Bell may have been excluded from telegraphy but not prevented from doing so through a separate subsidiary.

Another point to bear in mind is that when companies were licensed to offer telecommunications services, those which *they were not allowed to provide* were specifically enumerated. This is evident in British law of the time (Post Office, 1881, p. 10) and in later legislation governing Bell Canada (Canada, 1968) that spelled out with absolute clarity those areas (e.g., broadcasting), in which the company could not operate, even through separate subsidiary.

6.   The key section of the *Canadian Pacific Railway Act* (1880) is section 16:

> The Company may construct, maintain and work a continuous telegraph
> line and telephone line . . . , to construct or acquire . . . any other line or
> lines of telegraph . . . and may undertake the transmission of messages
> for the public by . . . telegraph or telephone . . . [or] any . . . other
> means of communication . . . that may hereafter be invented. (Canada,
> House of Commons, 1880b, p. 16)

7.   The CEA was formed in 1891. It aimed to "conserve the commercial and scientific . . . interests of the industry, . . . protect . . . capital and . . . keep in touch . . . with legislation affecting electrical interests" (*Canadian Electrical News*, 1892, p. 1). Although it represented the electronics industry as a whole, evidence from the membership list published in the Canadian Electrical News, and a survey of those attending the first annual conference in 1892, indicate that it was dominated by Bell and the Great North Western Telegraph Company. twenty of 64 members at the conference were from Bell, and another three were from the Great North Western Telegraph Company (also recall from the last chapter that by this time this company was under the control of Western Union). Given these relationships, it appears that the CEA was one more "loop" in which agreements segregating the communication industries were reproduced.

8.   Note the contrast between women, aesthetics and orality (listening) and the character of men's involvement as rational (thinking) and concerned mainly with the instrumental/engineering ("marvellous feat") qualities of the telephone. The advertisements of the Electrophone company also contained similar assumptions. Their advertisements stressed the system's aesthetic appeal, the lack of "physical exertion" needed to operate it, and its value as 'home entertainment' (Electrophone, n.d., see Figure 4.1). In the promotional material that I've seen, the only people pictured are women, and some of them in quite sexually suggestive attire, suggesting, perhaps, an early link between electronic media and sex.

9.   This early attempt at rate regulation was overturned by the courts in 1897, and once again reinstated in 1902 (Babe, 1990, p. 91).

10. Trade and Labour Councils (TLCs) were early coordinating and representative organisations for unions and employee organisations. There tended to be TLCs in each city or town that would act as a coordinating agency among various labour groups. TLCs had national affiliation through the Trades and Labour Congress (Bernard, 1982, p. 50).

11. It was during this hearing that Bell appears to have first trotted out the "end-to-end" or "systems integrity" argument to prevent interconnection on "objective technical grounds" that had nothing to do with economic considerations. Lack of interconnection with other local exchanges or a long-distance network seriously constrained the long-term viability of would-be competitors. The "systems integrity" theme eventually became a standard feature of Bell's arguments, brought out each time regulators, competitors, or new services threatened its monopoly. Yet, committee members were already wise enough to note that even given technically compatible equipment, Bell still refused interconnection on competitive grounds (Canada, Mulock Committee, 1905, pp. 622-623).

12. Another avenue of appeal was the courts—a point returned to and illustrated later.

13. These provisions were contained in section 320 of the *Railway Act* and have been incorporated into the new *Telecommunications Act* (1993). They have been the primary sources of regulatory power in telecoms, although the terms are considered much more expansively than probably thought possible by the BRC (Babe, 1990, p. 168; Janisch, 1986, p. 586)—although aspects of regulatory liberalisation might be thought of as attempting to reconstruct the conservative, historical rendering of these terms.

14. Surprisingly the "unscientific" quality of the process did not undermine the belief in the technical, "objective" nature of regulation. That the process remained laden with politics is evident in the frequency with which telephone issues were raised in Parliament, and by the number of appeals/petitions to Parliament attempting to overturn regulatory decisions (for one example among many, see Canada, House of Commons, 1922, p. 227).

15. Access to telephone service increased from a rate of about 1 telephone for every 110 people, to 1 telephone for every 15 people (BRC, 1916a; Canada, Mulock Committee, 1905, p. 8).

16. This was also different from conditions that followed in years to come, as rates were once again rebalanced so that more revenues were obtained from long-distance services (again, see Babe, 1990). It is this latter episode in "rate rebalancing" that has fueled contemporary cross-subsidy myths, although it is likely that none of the myths are right, as who pays what for telephone service is essentially a political question, not one inhering in the technology of telecoms, economic imperatives, and so on (also see Gabel, 1995, p. 453).

17. Only three years earlier, the annual *Telephone Statistics* report by the BRC commented on the enormous range of pricing practices, an indication interpreted in classical economical theory as at least one, albeit inconclusive, indication that an industry displays some features of competition (BRC, 1913, p. 13).

18. Interestingly, the same key words that helped to wipe out competition in Canadian telecoms were later relied on by the Federal Court of Appeals in a 1992 decision to confirm the CRTC's wide discretion with respect to reintroducing regulated competition back into Canadian telecoms.

19. Even though one judge (Idlington) on the Supreme Court was scathing about the liberties his colleagues were taking with the law, it is also interesting to note that neither he nor Drayton rejected the idea that telephony was a natural monopoly, despite all the evidence to the contrary. Thus, at this more abstract level, there was almost hegemonic agreement, although opinion seemed to differ as to whether this end should be brought about by state coercion (i.e., by the BRC's decision) or "naturally" (see Idlington's remarks in *Ingersoll Telephone Co. v. Bell Telephone Co.*, 1917, pp. 58-60).

20. It was not until 1987, after numerous intervening inquiries, that legislation was passed to enhance the regulator's power to investigate the intracorporate relations of Bell (Babe, 1990, pp. 194-195).

21. AT&T availed itself of increased revenue each time the regulator granted rate increases. Between 1923 and 1927 rate increases escalated the flow of revenue from Canada to AT&T from $330,000 to $510,000 (Canada, House of Commons, 1928, p. 3135).

22. This probably offers one of the reasons why the government retained the prerogative of reviewing regulatory decisions through the Petition of The Governor in Council process.

23. The situation in Canada had parallels in the United States, where a period of competition existed between 1893 and 1914, after which the Bell system began to again assert its dominance (FCC, 1938, 138-139). Babe (1990) explains that the Canadian development was most certainly the outcome of a regulatory policy amenable to the interests of Bell. However, he periodises the development later than is being done here.

24. This observation is confirmed by statistical evidence gathered by the BRC in 1915 showing that most independent telcos still had no permanent employees (BRC, 1916b). It was also observed during the Telephone Inquiry that the independents relied primarily on volunteer work or contracted temporarily with the large telephone system providers who would install the system and be called in for repairs on an "as needed" basis (Canada, Mulock Committee, 1905)

25. "Performance" was measured on the basis of the number of calls handled in an hour, percentage of errors on incoming calls, and time taken to respond to incoming calls. The consultant suggested that operators answer between 210 and 225 calls per hour, each within four seconds of coming in. Other measures restricted the amount of information to be proffered by operators in the course of their duties and the range of movements that could be undertaken (Canada, Department of Labour, 1907, pp. 9-19; personal correspondence, L. Renaud, president, Windsor and area operators of CWC local, July 20, 1992).

26. The commission was headed by William Lyon MacKenzie King, then Deputy Minister of Labour and later head of the liberal party and Prime Minister.

27. Huyek (1978) suggests that the IBEW was trying to extend its representation to other Bell workers in the period just prior to the establishment of a employees' association. This was also the case in the United States, where AT&T devised employee associations to eradicate unions that had taken root, especially during and after the period of nationalisation in 1918 (Schact, 1985).

28.   Huyek (1978) cites Bell annual reports from 1929 to 1936 to show that the reduction in staff was even greater, somewhere around 8,500 people. She also claims that effects of the Depression were aggravated by the implementation of automated dialing equipment. Perhaps the difference between the number she cites and the number reported in Parliament is the difference between the layoffs attributable to the Depression and those to technological displacement associated with the implementation of automated dialing equipment.

29.   That criticism and discussion of Bell or the telephone system temporarily drops off altogether from the record of Parliament and the Senate during the Depression in the 1930s suggests that it had become an accepted institution and its contribution to economic and social stability in immiserating times thought to offset any perceived evils of concentrated capital and political power.

30.   Despite the acceptance of natural monopoly, there continued to be many independent telcos, and some federal and municipally owned telcos on the periphery, as well as the telecoms networks of CN and CP railways, a point discussed in the next chapter.

5 TELEPHONES, NATURAL MONOPOLY, AND ENFORCING THE BOUNDARIES OF ELECTRONIC COMMUNICATION

The natural monopoly regime for telecoms gained widespread assent between 1916 and the 1930s, a fact in itself reflecting a broad shift in principles of interaction between the key actors of Canadian society. The shift was away from the allocative efficiency of "free markets" toward dynamic innovation by monopolistic corporations and bureaucratised politics that mediated relations among capital, labour, government, new technology, and civil society. Such a system was legitimated through the "promise" that regulated economic efficiency would translate into improved economic well-being and new technologies that served the public interest. At the most general level, natural monopoly in telecoms and certain sectors of the economy were mirrored by corporatist politics that involved government, labour unions, and industrial corporations, and a mass mediated culture of consumption. In Canadian political theorist C. B. Macpherson's (1985) words, politics was no longer about competing versions of the good life but about making sure that a broader strata of consumers got the goods.

The promise of dynamic innovation in communication technology contained a certain amount of truth. Regulated monopoly led to rapid expansion in the telecoms network, especially after World War II, intense investment in network modernisation, and a host of technological innovations that vastly improved long-distance communication for most members of Canadian society. However, the system also contained the seeds of its own destruction. It did so by propelling further consolidation of economic power across the Canadian landscape as those in certain areas of the communication industries began to try and reach into and control other areas of the media. Such attempts were actively resisted by a broad array of social, economic, and political actors, ultimately at the

155

expense of the natural monopoly regime altogether. Finally, though, it also needs to be recognised that the inclusive politics of corporatism was also a politics of exclusion, civil passivity, and "systems maintenance" at the expense of the idea that democratic societies should be open to criticism by citizens and, if need be, fundamental change (Habermas, 1984/1987, p. 260).

EXTENDING TELEPHONE SERVICE (1930-1970)

The existence of regulated monopoly did not mean that there were no other telecoms operators offering telephone, telegraph, and other telecom services across Canada. Quite to the contrary, there were many telephone systems, and the number continued to climb until 1954 to a total of almost 2,800 systems (DBS, 1957, p. 7). Numerous independent telcos and some federal and municipally owned telcos operated in the peripheral regions of Canada. Canadian Pacific (CP) and the government-owned Canadian National Telecommunications (CN) also operated extensive telecoms networks. The government became more deeply involved in ownership of telecom facilities after its takeover of the railway and telegraph networks of the Grand Trunk Railway Company in 1921 (Surtees, 1994a, p. 28). Although the government-owned system competed with CP in telegraphy for about a decade, the two companies largely served different areas. Moreover, after an initial 10-year period of competition, the two telegraph-based companies began cooperating to offer long-distance carriage to the national broadcaster (later known as the Canadian Broadcasting Corporation), to provide private line services and eventually to develop a microwave system in duopolistic competition with the Trans Canada Telephone System (TCTS).

CP provided long-distance carriage for the telephone companies from 1926. The telephone companies established a national consortium, TCTS, in 1932, and developed a long-distance network at the same time, although they still relied on CP and CN facilities for many years afterward in some areas of Newfoundland, Northern Ontario, the Northwest Territories, and the Yukon. Even after 1953, and until 1965, when CN and CP were engaged in duopolistic competition in microwave communication with TCTS, they still cooperated with the telephone companies in order that the latter could complete its national long-distance network (Babe, 1990, pp. 128-129; DBS, 1967, p. 6; Surtees, 1994a, pp. 28-32).

In addition to cooperating with CP and the telephone companies, CN was used as an instrument of federal policy to extend "telephone services where . . . the investment of private capital would not be warranted and would not be compensated . . ." (Canada, House of Commons, 1931, p. 2830). Through CN, the government developed telephone networks in peripheral regions of Canada until they became profitable, then sold them for nominal amounts, usually to Bell (Canada, House of Commons, 1921, p. 3088; 1922, p. 2012). Although Bell, BCTel, and about 40 other relatively large companies provided 90% of telephone service across the country, independents and government systems broadened access to the telephone for the remaining large number of people scattered across the country (DBS, 1957, pp. 9, 20). As repeatedly noted in the annual government report on the telephone system, "[o]utlying districts . . . are served principally by provincial and federal systems" (DBS, 1957, p. 7). As such, neither the competitive era, natural monopoly, or government policy single handedly brought about universal telephone service.

The most rapid development of the Canadian telecoms network occurred after World War II. Much of this was a result of massive amounts of research funding during the war being translated into technological innovations and given civil applications after the cessation of hostilities. Within 10 years of the end of the war, the number of telephones per capita increased by 50%. Between 1945 and 1960, the percentage of people with residential phone services doubled (DBS, 1962, pp. 9). By the end of the 1960s, 93% of homes across the country subscribed to telephone service (Pike & Mosco, 1986, pp. 19-21). The Manitoba Telephone System (MTS) noted that from 1945 until 1955, the number of telephone lines doubled, "the biggest boom in Manitoba telephone history" (MTS, 1991, p. 23). Saskatchewan Telephone's (SaskTel) *Annual Reports* during the period also mention remarkable advances in service to urban and rural areas of the province using new technologies. The number of SaskTel subscribers increased by 50% in four years (Saskatchewan, 1948, p. 1; 1952, p. 1). Whereas only 1 in 8 people had access to telephone service prior to the war, by 1960 this increased to almost 1 telephone line per every 3 people— a level of access surpassed only in the United States and Sweden (DBS, 1962, p. 1). The availability of telephone service between 1940 and 1970 is shown in Table 5.1.

NETWORK MODERNISATION

The rapid expansion in the telephone network was partially attributable to massive investments in network modernisation and government regulatory policies that aimed, among other things, to enhance universal service. Regarding the first point, it can be noted that although network investment in the competitive period prior to 1916 was usually under 20% of annual

Table 5.1. Availability of Telephone Service (1939-1970).

Year	Number of Telephones per 100 population
1939	12.35
1945	15.26
1950	21.07
1955	26.61
1960	32.16
1965	38.00
1970	45.00

Source: Dominion Bureau of Statistics (1967), Statistics Canada (1972).

revenues (BRC, 1918), investment exploded under the "natural monopoly" regime. Between 1955 and 1970, investment in network modernisation programs swallowed between 53% and 62% of annual revenues. Throughout this period, the rate of investment in the network steadily increased by 5% to 15% over the previous year.[1] As a result, references were continually made to the implementation of extended area service, teletype services, Direct Distance Dialing, and development of the microwave relay network after 1953—a factor vital to the emergence of television on a nationwide basis. Year after year, the government's annual report on telecoms remarked on the "large programmes of new construction" (DBS, 1957, p. 1); "expenditures on new plant and equipment . . . that were the largest on record" (DBS, 1962, p. 7); the "unprecedented . . . growth in the number of telephones . . . [and] microwave . . . relay systems [that] provide hundreds of additional telephone circuits[,] . . . carry television programmes and other types of electronic communication" (DBS, 1967, pp. 1, 11). Unlike regulatory liberalisation in the 1980s and 1990s, however, nobody claimed that investments were contingent on changes in media law, the introduction of competition and a miserly approach to social programs. These unparalleled levels of investment focused on the efficiencies and dynamic innovation associated with the pooling of resources, long-range planning, and "technology-push" programs instead of stressing measures of allocative efficiency favoured by competition, regulatory liberalisation and attention to the needs of specialised users in the short term.

      Improvements in the means of communication were experienced by all subscribers, although the expanding range of services met the more exacting demands of some users more than others. It was widely acknowledged that network modernisation was particularly directed at expanding the capacity and functionality of the telecoms system in commercial centres along the Montreal, Toronto and Vancouver corridors, especially in anticipation of an economic boom in North America in the early 1950s ("Nation-wide busy signal," 1953, pp. 33-34; "So you can't," 1953, p. 25).

More broadly felt were the conversions of party lines common in rural areas to individual line service, and the replacement of manual switching in the local and long-distance exchanges with direct dialing facilities. With increased availability, the use of the telephone rose dramatically. In 1955 there were 7 billion local telephone calls, 154 million long-distance calls, and about 7.3 million international calls. Fifteen years later, usage was even more intensive, as local calls doubled, long-distance calls tripled, and international calls quadrupled. From the view of social uses of the telephone, the bias of telecoms toward local communicative interaction was now complemented by a more distant orientation (DBS, 1957; Statistics Canada, 1972a).

TELEPHONE PRICES, UNIVERSAL SERVICE, AND CROSS-SUBSIDIES (?)

Of course, people's increased access to the telephone was not merely a consequence of telephone companies' investments or new technology. Crucially, it reflected flat-rate pricing schemes, rising incomes, service availability on demand, and regulatory policies and telephone company practices that favoured affordable telephone services. Pike and Mosco's (1986) research shows that after the 1940s, telephone service costs declined in relation to household incomes. It has also been commonly thought that affordable local telephone service stemmed from various cross-subsidies between different users, for example, between long-distance and local service and between business users and residential service; individual telephone companies subsidising different areas within their jurisdiction, for example, heavy routes within and between urban areas subsidised low traffic routes in rural areas;[2] and the "revenue settlement plan" of TCTS (now Stentor), which cross-subsidised on a national basis. Presumably the latter involved transferring revenue from Quebec, Ontario, and BC to the prairies, northern territories, and Atlantic regions.

However, debates about cross-subsidies and universal service are complicated by several factors. The first point, as indicated earlier, is that people use the long-distance network much less than they use the telephone for local communication. For example, between 1939 and 1975, the number of long-distance calls accounted for less than 2.5% and 4% of total telephone use, respectively (BRC, 1957, p. 11; Statistics Canada, 1977a, p. 11). As recognised prior to the first phase of rate rebalancing (1905-1915), long-distance service is of most value to business users and those with distributed operations. Therefore, the cost of long-distance service should be attributed mainly to them. Although long distance service continues to be of most value to a small number of users even today,[3] the nature of who pays for it has changed. As was shown in Chapter 4, more costs were assigned to local subscribers during the phase of regulated competition between 1911 and 1916. Gabel (1995) argues that "long-distance standards [have] dictated the design of the local network from approximately 1892 to 1983" (p. 454). Although the costs of building long-distance capabilities are borne by all users, not everybody derives equal benefits from long-distance service. To the extent that long-distance services don't cover "stand-alone" production costs, they are subsidised by users of the local exchange. Likewise, Melody (1982) has argued that the greater use of the network by business, the need to build networks to the demanding needs of business equipment, and maintenance of excess capacity for business purposes means that it is likely that residential users subsidise business users (cited in NAPO, 1987). As Roman (1990) argues, the key question is not which services subsidise other services, but who defines costs and thus determines who pays what for telephone service.

The politics of cost allocation is treated in greater detail in the next chapter. For now it will be suggested that it is more fruitful to consider where telephone companies obtained most of their revenues. Considered from the perspective of the prairie provinces from the late 1950s, and from the late 1970s in central Canada, it can be seen that long-distance revenues accounted for a greater percentage of total revenues. Arguably, this relieved pressure on local and rural services to generate revenue and thus helped to reduce the cost of telephone service. Although such conditions applied across the country, they were most pronounced in the prairie and maritime systems. Consequently, telephone costs for local service in the prairies have consistently been among the lowest in the world and contributed to universal service, despite small, dispersed populations (personal communication, B. Gowenlock, Regulatory Affairs Advisor, MTS, Winnipeg, September 1, 1992; personal correspondence, D. Beresh, Senior Business Planner, SaskTel, Regina, September 2, 1992). Changes in revenues sources for SaskTel and all telcos is illustrated in Figures 5.1 and 5.2, respectively.

BROADENING THE POLITICS OF TELECOMS

In addition to the vast network modernisation projects introduced earlier and the increasing social ubiquity of the telephone, several other trends defined the post-war period in Canadian telecoms: first, the unionisation of the telephone labour force; and second, tension between corporate

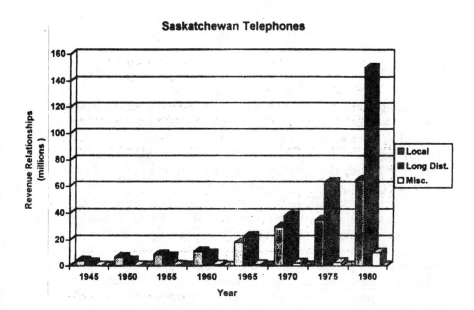

Figure 5.1. Revenue Sources at Saskatchewan Telephones (1945-1980)
Source: Saskatchewan, Dept. of Telephones (1945-1980).

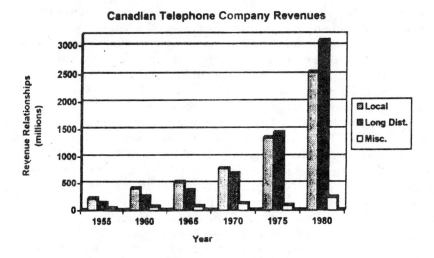

Figure 5.2. Revenue Sources for Telephone Service Providers (1955-1980)
Source: DBS (1957-1967), Statistics Canada 19702-1980).

expansion across the telecoms landscape, on the one hand, and ambiguous attempts to constrain this expansion, on the other, through regulatory policy, the introduction of competition, and a more intense politics of telecoms in general. These are considered next.

Unionisation

The elimination of competition and the relatively rapid extension of the telecoms network, as well as the intensive modernisation of the system, resulted in a dramatic increase in the number of telephone workers. The development of a monopolistic industry structure also led to formalised work relations in the telephone industry and to structured patterns of interaction among industry, unions, and government (Bernard, 1982).

In 1946, Bell alone hired an additional "10,000 employees, eighty percent of whom were women" (Huyek, 1978, p. 45). In Saskatchewan, the workforce doubled in the 10-year period after the war (Saskatchewan, 1958, pp. 22-23). In addition, abundant work in the telephone industry combined with the passage of crucial government legislation to make it easier to organise labour unions (personal correspondence, H. Raper, National representative of the Communications Workers of Canada (CWC), Winnipeg, September 1, 1992). The legislative trend was occurring at provincial and federal levels of government, suggesting that there was relatively widespread political support for such initiatives, and perhaps adherence to the sentiments expressed much earlier by Mackenzie King about the compelling moral need for the state to ensure ethical relations between labour and industry within the context of a monopoly.

Early unionisation initiatives spread from Saskatchewan, where the socialist-oriented Cooperative Commonwealth Federation government implemented the Trade Union Act in 1945 and directed the publicly owned provincial telephone company, Saskatchewan Telephones, to establish model labour relations (CWC, 1984, p. 1). The legislation immediately led to creation of the United Telephone Workers of Canada (UTW). Despite the UTW's independent roots, shortly afterward it aligned itself with the Communication Workers of America (CWA). Thus, by the early 1950s, there were two strong telecommunications-based unions in Canada, the long-standing Telecommunications Workers Union of BC and the recent entry of the CWA by way of Saskatchewan. Yet, just as there were efforts to spread the influence of labour unions in the telephone industry, so, too, were there attempts to block their emergence. This was true of the Manitoba Telephone System, and especially Bell, as each tried to thwart unionisation efforts by establishing employee associations.

During the early 1950s, the CWA expanded from its Canadian base in Saskatchewan to organise workers at the Manitoba Telephone System, the Toronto Northern Electric plant, and then to the Northern Telephone Company located in the upper reaches of Ontario and Quebec (personal correspondence, B. Mather, past Director of the CWA in Canada, Toronto, August 11, 1992; Shact, 1985, p. 180; "Union leader hopeful," 1950, p. 11).

The Communication Workers of Canada formed at the beginning of the 1970s, when several members left the CWA to protest the close links between that organisation and U.S.-government sponsored anti-Communist initiatives and efforts to set up docile labour unions in the volatile political regions of South America (CWC, 1984, p. 3; personal correspondence, B. Mather, Toronto, August 11, 1992). Supported by the BC-based TWU, the Communications Workers of Canada began pressing harder to secure the unionisation of Bell during the 1970s, ultimately with a large degree of success in the mid-1970s, and after resolute attempts by Bell to stymie unionisation efforts were stopped by the courts. Other workers in Alberta and certain areas of Manitoba, Ontario, and Quebec, as well as in the maritime provinces, also came to be represented by the International Brotherhood of Electrical Workers (IBEW) and the Atlantic Canadian Telecommunications Workers Union (ACTWU) at about the same time ("Court rejects appeal," 1975, p. 13; personal correspondence, T. Blackstaffe, Research Director at CWC, Ottawa, August 10, 1992; personal correspondence, J. Hanafin, National Representative, CWC, Ottawa, August 4, 1992).

Almost from the inception of labour unions, there were indications that ensuing relations between unionised workers and the telephone industry would be antagonistic. Again, Bell led the way in this respect, steadfastly resisting unionisation attempts well into the 1970s. Of course, the labour unions' primary interest was with wage and workplace issues, points in and of themselves not always welcome (Saywell, 1960). Yet, it was commonly understood that in monopolistic sectors of the economy, wages could no longer be set in the "free market." Instead, wage bargaining took place through a triumvirate bureaucratic structure of corporations, labour unions, and government. In contrast to disorganised workers in the remaining competitive fringes of the economy, unionised workers in concentrated industries such as telecoms were, in part, wage makers not just wage takers (Galbraith, 1967/1977, p. 202; Habermas, 1975, pp. 36-39; Offe, 1984, pp. 43-44).

As the noted institutional economist John Kenneth Galbraith (1967/1977) stated at the time, "[l]abour had won limited authority over its pay and working conditions but none over the enterprise" (p. 202). This was only partially true, however, in the Canadian context, because labour unions actively sought to expand the range of issues beyond wages and working conditions. As eluded to earlier, the CWC was partially born out of a politics of resentment against the United States' strident anti-communism and efforts to establish token unions in South America with the help of the CWA. The Canadian-based CWC also set itself apart from its American counterpart with its broader view of issues relating to apartheid in South Africa and of economic aid to third world countries (CWC, 1984, p. 3; personal correspondence, B. Mather, Toronto, August 11, 1992). The more pertinent matters impacting on telecoms politics involved labour unions in Parliamentary proceedings that dealt with the telephone companies' rates of capitalisation as well as regulatory hearings dealing with requests by the telephone companies for rate increases — issues that are discussed in the next section.

Corporate Consolidation: Eliminating the Independent Margins of Telephony

Once the natural monopoly regime was stabilised, and in the midst of the massive network modernisation programs referred to in the preceding pages, federally chartered companies such as BCTel and Bell approached Parliament for vast increases in their levels of capitalisation. Bell, for instance, increased its capitalisation from $75 million in 1928, to $500 million in 1948 and $750 million two decades later (Canada, House of Commons, 1928, 1948; Canada, Standing Committee on Transport and Communications, 1967). Coinciding with these increases in capitalisation rates, Bell approached the Canadian Transport Committee (CTC, the regulatory authority superseding the BRC) for substantial rate increases in 1951 and again in 1952. Labour unions and the national Trades and Labour Congress intervened against both attempts and called for an inquiry into the effects of vertical integration within the telecoms industry ("Congress asks postponement," 1952, p. 19). Of course, it was not only labour organisations that intervened on such issues, but a relatively broad body of subscribers, would-be competitors, government agencies, and so on (Babe, 1990, p. 336).

It soon became clear that increased capitalisation and higher rates were being used to finance network modernisation programmes and to fuel an aggressive bid to absorb the independent telephone providers. For the first time in Canadian telephone history, the number of telephone companies declined in 1955, from a high of 2,788 systems to 2,739, absorbed mainly by Bell, BCTel, MTS, SaskTel, or Alberta Government Telephones (AGT). Only half the telephone systems existing in 1955 prevailed in 1970 (DBS, 1957, p. 7; Statistics Canada, 1972a, p. 9). Today, only 61 companies remain throughout Canada.

Acquisitions were not limited to any particular area. In Western Canada, BCTel purchased the North West Telephone Company in 1960 and the Okanagan Telephone Company in 1966 (DBS, 1962, p. 6; Smythe, 1981, p. 161). BCTel's parent company, General Telephones and Electronic Corporation (GTE), also bought one of the largest independents in Quebec—Quebec Tel—in the same summer (Surtees, 1994a, pp. 47-48). Babe (1990) indicates that Bell took over some 160 Ontario-based independents between 1950 and 1959, and a further 218 between 1960 and 1975. In a spate of acquisitions between 1962 and 1966, Bell gained control of the maritime-based Avalon Telephone Company (now Newfoundland Tel), New Brunswick Tel, and Maritime Telephone and Telephone Company (MT&T), moves Bell legitimated as protecting the Canadian telecoms industry from being absorbed by GTE—the second largest telephone company in the United States.

However, Bell's bid to buy MT&T in 1966 met strong opposition. Bell's move was seen to threaten local ownership and regulation by the Nova Scotian government and was steadfastly resisted. Although ownership eventually passed to Bell, provincial legislation was enacted to restrict Bell's ability to control the company or avoid provincial regulation (Saywell, 1966, p. 121).

By the early to mid-1960s it was obvious that there were widespread fractures in the natural monopoly telecoms regime. Although the trends toward consolidation would seem to be an expected outcome of the natural monopoly doctrine, such trends encountered a political context more sensitive to issues of abuse of economic power. Within the overall contours of the natural monopoly regime, the support of labour unions was at best highly conditional and pragmatic. The rapid introduction of new technologies was transforming work in the industry, a fact that was heavily contested by unions from the mid-1950s onward (Bernard, 1982, p. 159; "Walkout won't hit," 1958, p. 19). Elsewhere, independent telephone companies were usually bought off rather than won over to the idea that bigger is better for telecoms in Canada. As Babe (1990) notes, owners of acquired companies were given handsome premiums for selling. Remaining independents were squeezed further to the margins of telephone history, and subscribers saddled with the costs of achieving unassailable dominance as local rates typically doubled after takeover. It was also clear that the unfolding structure of ownership would increase pressure to eliminate the 'balkanised' regulation of telecoms in Canada, a characteristic that had developed out of deference to provincial sensitivities rather than from any firm constitutional or legal basis. Constitutional battles for control of electronic media have been a perennial feature of media politics in Canada for the last century. Essentially, as will be seen, ownership changes that strengthened economic power in the 1950s and 1960s helped shift political power over telecoms toward Ottawa in the 1980s and 1990s.

The cleavages were broader yet. Certain government agencies became interested in investigating the effects of vertical integration in the telephone industry. As such, in 1965, the CTC inspected the relationship between Bell and Northern Electric, and several years later inquired into the links between BCTel, its U.S.-based parent GTE, and its manufacturing arm, Lenkurt Electric (Babe, 1990, pp. 181-182; Smythe, 1981, pp. 151-153). Further investigations took place in the 1970s and early 1980s. Reflecting the increasing intensity of the politics of telecoms, some parties rejuvenated long-dormant calls for government ownership of the telephone industry (Bernard, 1982, p. 138; Canada, House of Commons, 1966, p. 10810). Yet, there was no coherent alternative view of "how things should be," a fact reflected in some politicians' calls for the privatisation of the publicly owned prairie telephone companies as early as 1956 ("Willis calls for," 1956, p. 15). However, such calls were feeble and unable to find a receptive audience. That had to wait until the 1980s and 1990s. In the meantime, government telecoms policy was, to say the least, confused, variously upholding a monopolistic industry structure and regulatory barriers to entry, while at other times, as in microwave communications, favourable to allowing duopolistic competition (Babe, 1990, pp. 128-129; Surtees, 1994a, pp. 36-39). Despite the dispersed points at which the natural monopoly regime was being challenged from the mid-1950s onward, it remained, for the most part, intact well into the 1970s.

However, beneath the disparate forces chipping away at aspects of the telecoms system, shifting alliances between industrial power, government, regulation, courts, and new technologies were undermining the entire foundation on which the concept of natural monopoly was based—a point covered in the following section.

DISSOLVING THE FOUNDATIONS OF NATURAL MONOPOLY IN TELEPHONY

The natural monopoly regime was predicated on consolidating control within the telephone industry. However, there were also extensive pressures fomenting *across* the electronic communication industries that would render the idea of natural monopoly unsustainable.

The natural monopoly regime and boundaries between various electronic media were anchored in the capricious vagaries of strategic rivalry and legal frameworks adopted in the 1880s to regulate the boundaries between telegraphy and telephones; at the turn of the century for telecoms and publishing; and again in the 1920s to embrace telecoms and broadcasting. In the following pages, it is suggested that such foundations were too feeble to address altered circumstances. This became evident during struggles to control microwave communication in the 1950s among the telephone companies (champions of the *monopoly view*), telegraph companies (proponents of the *duopoly view*), and cable broadcasters (advocates of an *anything goes* view), and government policy that eventually adopted duopolistic competition. The subsequent advent of broadcast facsimile, cable television, satellites, and computer communication further confounded an industrial and regulatory structure based on artificial foundations.

To establish the background to these recent efforts, the following pages retrace the origins of the split between telephony and broadcasting in the 1920s that have recently returned to perplex the organisational and regulatory frameworks for electronic media. The crux of the argument is not that new media technologies *cause* institutional arrangements to change, but that institutional arrangements born of strategic rivalry and instrumental convenience lack legitimacy and durability over the long run.

TELEPHONES, WIRELESS COMMUNICATION, AND THE MASS MEDIA

Broadcasting and Film

From the origins of wireless telegraphy at the turn of the century, telecoms and broadcasting have been inextricable. In previous chapters it was shown that media law during the period did not distinguish among available means of electronic communication, whether wire or wireless. Although the *Wireless Telegraph Act* of 1905 set out special requirements for radio receiver manufacturers, these were of only minor importance in practice. Moreover, such fine distinctions were conveniently ignored by the courts and Privy Council in 1932, as Ottawa's authority over telegraphs was used to assert its control over broadcasting (Re Radio Communication in Canada, 1932).

Given this legislative context, it is not surprising that the history of CP and Bell is intertwined with wired, wireless, and broadcast communication. CP broadcast Canadian programs to travelers on its transcontinental train route. It also, in conjunction with CN, distributed signals for the CBC between 1932 and 1952. However, CP's parochial view of Marconi's experiments in wireless communication led it to spurn closer connections with the evolution of radio broadcasting (Surtees, 1994a, p. 30). Marconi moved from point-to-point wireless telegraphy to establish an experimental broadcasting station in 1918. Within a year or two he was broadcasting programs on a regular basis. The Bell Telephone

Company was also interested in radio from at least 1910 until just prior to the establishment of the predominantly publicly owned Canadian broadcast system, around 1932 (Nichols, 1948, pp. 258-259).[4] As Bell's manufacturing arm, Northern Electric declared, it "entered the . . . Radio business . . . as a natural result of its position in the Wireless Telephone field . . . [then] emerging from what might be termed the 'novelty' stage . . . into an industry of considerable importance and *stability*" (Northern Electric, 1923; emphasis added). Babe (1990) traces Bell's radio interests to 1910, when AT&T purchased patent rights in wireless communication, "the rights for Canada reverting of course to Bell . . . , thanks to the Bell-AT&T service agreement" (p. 201). Media convergence was tightened even further by the patent pooling arrangements formed among the electronics and communications industry in World War I.

It is necessary to briefly review the situation south of the border just after the war and during the formative years of broadcasting to grasp the context within which events in Canadian electronic media were unfolding. The first thing to be noted is that the patent pools formed during the war obliterated any lingering ideas about radio and telephony and other electronic media being separate arts. Reflecting the complete disrespect for any remaining boundaries amid various media, AT&T began incursions into radio broadcasting in 1922, first with WEAF in New York and a year later with WCAP in Washington. The company also licensed others to use its equipment to set up similar stations, all along the lines of what it called "toll broadcasting." The model employed common-carriage principles, allowing one and all to buy access to air time, thus establishing a counterpoint to the advertising model later to take hold of the US broadcasting system (Barnouw, 1982, p. 48).

However, between 1924 and 1926 machinations among AT&T, GE, RCA, United Fruit, Westinghouse, and Zenith were afoot that led to the evacuation of AT&T from broadcasting in return for promises from the other parties to stay out of telephony. On July 7, 1926, as Barnouw (1982) recounts, "twelve documents were signed" that led to AT&T selling WEAF to RCA for $1,000,000, closing WCAP, and, overall, "a new division of empire" (p. 53). As Danielian (1939) describes the situation, AT&T was "anxious to protect . . . its investment in wire telephone plant," and to this end secured from GE et al.

> promises not to cross this line, either over the land by wire telephony or through the air by wireless telephony. . . . Agreeing not to cross each other's boundaries, the Radio-Bell System groups pooled their resources in an assault upon the telegraph industry; . . . through wireless telegraphy, . . . telephone, radio transmission, teletype exchange, and private line telegraph services. (p. 165)

Aspects of the agreements were quite illegal, as often noted during the numerous radio conferences held during 1925 and 1926 as a prelude to formalising a legal framework for electronic media in the United States (Barnouw, 1982, p. 51; U.S. Senate, 1926, p. 548). However, faced with a choice of enforcing anti-trust laws, ignoring them or changing them, law makers wrote the *Radio Act* (1927) and the *Communications Act* (1934). The new laws, among other things, sanctioned the arrangements drawn up among the major communication industry interests.

Events in Canada paralleled those in the United States, but were brought to a head earlier and settled with fewer legal machinations. Events were tied to those in the United States through the organisational relationships between Bell Canada and AT&T and decisions that led to telephone carriers offering long-distance distribution of broadcast programming on a commercial basis from 1923. A. B. Clark (1929/1930), an AT&T engineer, described the North American system at a conference in Tokyo as follows: "wire telephone systems are employed almost exclusively for the national distribution of broadcasts . . . [and] radio broadcasting stations are essentially local distribution centres" (p. 1). A map of the system accompanying Clark's presentation showed the Canadian system hardwired into the U.S. network at several points, including London, Montreal, Niagara Falls, and Toronto (see figure 5.3). Although it is difficult to make definitive statements about this period given the paucity of available information (see footnote 4), it appears that Bell fit into this system quite well. In 1922, Bell obtained licenses for stations at Montreal (CKCS) and Toronto (CFTC) (Babe, 1990, p. 202)— just as AT&T had done with WEAF and WCAP at the same time. However, and likely due to the circumstances unfolding in the United States, one year later Bell withdrew from the field of local broadcasting.

Details of Bell's withdrawal from radio broadcasting were announced in the company's *Annual Report* of 1923 and also printed nearly verbatim in several leading Canadian newspapers. On August 14th, the *Toronto Star*[5] contained a story entitled, "Canadian Interests Pool Patents for Good of Radio: Six Great Companies Agree to License Each other on Plan Similarly Inaugurated in States Recently to Avoid Litigation and to Improve Radio." The account of the agreements divvying up the field of electronic media was as follows:

> An important step has recently been taken in Canada. The Canadian General Electric Co., the Marconi Wireless Telegraph Co. of Canada, the Canadian Westinghouse Co., the Bell Telephone Co., the Northern Electric Co., and the International Electric Co., have now agreed to pool all their patents *for the common good*. Under the terms of the agreement each party agrees to license the other parties within their natural fields, that is, the Marconi Co. will have the use of all the

Figure 5.3. Routes of Bell system program network chains

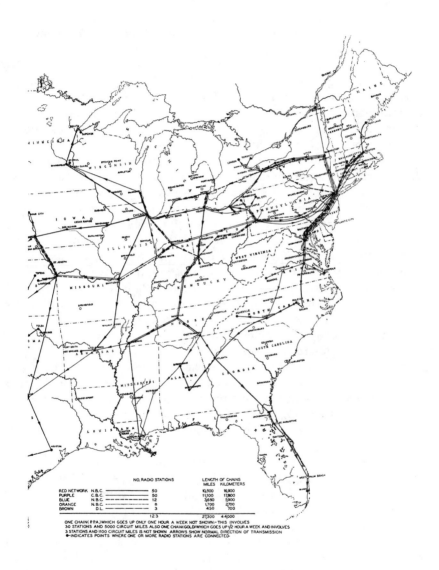

in the United States as of September 1, 1929

patents derived under the agreement for the purpose of wireless telegraphy, the Telephone company in the field of public telephone communication, and the manufacturing companies, which includes the Marconi Co., have the rights to make and sell . . . .

The Canadian agreement just announced is for the life of all existing patents *and also covers future patents or applications for patents.* (emphasis added)

Although the agreement divided the field among the major corporate players—and illustrated the subservience of the Canadian communication system to events in the United States—it did not mean that telephone companies would have no role in radio broadcasting, or the whole of electronic media, for that matter. The agreement, however, reiterated in no uncertain terms that cross-media excursions would occur through consent and cooperation, not competition. In the United States, AT&T distributed NBC, CBS, and a few other networks' programming under preferential terms in return for long-term, exclusive commitments by the broadcasters to use its facilities (Barnouw, 1982, p. 53; Clark, 1929/1930, p. 2). In Canada, owing to the under-development of a national long-distance network, carriage of broadcast signals did not fall to Bell and the other telephone companies, but, in 1932, to a partnership between the telegraph companies CN and CP. Who connected local broadcasting stations in the intervening, formative years of broadcasting (e.g., between Bell's exit in 1923 and the formation of the CBC in 1932) remains somewhat of a mystery, mainly due to a lack of cross-media scholarship in the area. The map of AT&T's network, however, suggests that broadcasting in Canada was closely aligned with AT&T and the U.S. networks. A somewhat cryptic remark by Nichols (1948, p. 259) suggests that the telephone companies continued to pay attention to broadcasting policy up until the 1930s, mostly opposing public ownership.

The participation of the telephone companies in other forms of mass media did not end at these points, either. From 1929 onward, AT&T played a key role in developing co-axial cable for the distribution of broadcasting programs, and later television (Clarke, 1929/1930, pp. 1-5; Danielian, 1939, p. 307). The company also fought with RCA for control of key areas of the film industry, most notably sound and projection equipment. Even though, in 1921, the U.S. government restricted AT&T's forays into the film industry by forcing it to divest the movie theatres it owned (U.S. Senate Committee, 1991, p. 2), the company moved aggressively into all other aspects of the film industry. As the licensing agreements of 1926 did not cover the film industry, AT&T and RCA fought one another, and a few unfortunate others on the competitive fringes of the electronics industry, for a monopoly over the supply of projection and recording equipment to the industry.

Danielian's (1939, pp. 139-143) account is replete with details of collusive agreements between AT&T and the Hollywood majors, attempts to maintain cartel-like agreements and to import the "systems integrity" argument from telephone policy infamy by insisting that only film recorded on AT&T/Western Electric equipment could be shown on its projectors, unless additional royalties were paid. AT&T's participation in the film industry was so great, that by 1932 an AT&T division president, John Otterson, boasted that it was "the second largest financial interest in the motion picture industry . . . next to that of the Chase Bank" (cited in Danielian, 1939, p. 152). It achieved this status by financing Hollywood studios, funding independent producers and advancing money to theatre chains. The company was also intensely interested in the content of film, as it financed films such as *Crime Without Passion, Once in a Blue Moon, Emperor Jones,* and others, and actively intervened editorially. AT&T started to leave the film business in the mid-1930s, after litigation began to chip away at its collusive practices and, perhaps, in response to the Federal Communication Commission's (FCC) *Telephone Inquiry,* convened in 1934 (Danielian, 1939, pp. 154-162; FCC, 1938). As just another submarket in the U.S. film industry, such arrangements no doubt extended into Canada—even if only indirectly.

At the same time as Bell Canada and AT&T were moving out of broadcasting, and the latter into film, a smaller, publicly owned Canadian telephone company was moving into radio. In 1923, the Manitoba Telephone System (MTS) opened station CKY in Winnipeg and five years later another station in Brandon, Manitoba. The telephone company's foray into broadcasting was a consequence of the prairie government's attempt to save the broadcasting licenses of two newspaper-owned stations in Winnipeg that had become financially insolvent (Government of Manitoba, 1974, p. 28). Babe (1990, p. 203) also reports that the head of MTS, John Lowry, believed that public broadcasting could better serve the public interest than private ownership and competition. He was also concerned that agreements struck among the major players in the communication industries would lock the province out of future developments in electronic media.

The MTS-run broadcasting stations continued until the 1940s. Confirmation of the federal government's authority over broadcasting in 1932, however, led to pressure being put on the Manitoba government to abandon radio broadcasting. Although public ownership and media convergence in Manitoba encouraged Alberta, Saskatchewan, and Quebec to initiate similar operations, Ottawa became more resolute in its efforts to assert authority over broadcasting. In 1946, the powerful Member of Parliament, C. D. Howe, in response to a query from J. G. Diefenbaker, stated the following:

> broadcasting is the sole responsibility of the dominion government. B]roadcasting licenses shall not be issued to other governments or corporations owned by other governments. In regard to the two stations in Manitoba, discussions are taking place . . . which we hope will lead to the purchase of these two stations by the dominion government. (reported in Government of Manitoba, 1974, p. 28)

Two years later the stations were sold, one to the CBC and the other to private interests (Babe, 1990, p. 204; Government of Manitoba, 1974, p. 28). Ottawa's policy of separating provincially owned telephone companies from broadcasting was further reinforced through several Orders-in-Council between 1946 until the present (see, e.g., Governor General in Council, 1985, P.C. 1985-2108). Thus, it is clear that the division of electronic media had nearly nothing to do with the underlying technologies involved but developed in response to corporate collusion in central Canada during the 1920s and to Constitutional skirmishes in the prairies from the 1940s on.

Broadcast Facsimile

Organisational relations across the electronic media that had settled into place over the first four decades of the 20th century have been challenged in the latter half of this century by broadcast facsimile, microwave communications, satellite technology, and cable television. In each case, existing press, broadcasting, or telecoms interests struggled to either absorb, squash, or mitigate the impact of new technologies and new potentials.

One of the lesser known but more potent technologies that threatened to undo the arrangements among broadcasting, telecoms, and the press was broadcast facsimile. The technology had been developed between the 1920s and 1950s and perfected during World War II as a means of distributing maps, plans, and other information to allied navies. After the war, it was generally thought that the new technology would lead to the development of broadcast facsimile newspapers, as production costs were exceedingly cheap in comparison to conventional newspapers,[6] receiving equipment was inexpensive, and because the promise of cities with a plethora of newspapers and diverse sources of information seemed to coincide with democratic political theory (Royal Commission on National Development in the Arts, Letters and Sciences, 1951, p. 63; Smythe, 1981, p. 83). However, this was not to be.

The Royal Commission on National Development in the Arts, Letters and Sciences (1951) eloquently summarised the potentials of the new media, and is thus worth quoting at length:

The vigorous brief of the Canadian Daily Newspapers Association was *devoted entirely to a discussion of the consequences to the present newspaper business* if the new device of facsimile broadcasting should become, *as seems possible,* an effective and popular rival to newspapers as we know them . . . . In brief, as we understand it, this process can deliver directly into the home a printed newspaper as readily and by essentially the same means as radio and television are now received. No printing machinery or delivery services are needed, and any radio station could go into the newspaper business for a small fraction of the investment required to establish a normal newspaper. The Canadian Daily Newspaper Association states that this development will attract newcomers to the newspaper field, and that the facsimile reader will be able in his home to dial any one of several newspapers just as now he tunes his receiving set to radio programmes. . . .

We are sympathetic to the anxiety which newspaper publishers feel toward the possibilities of this new medium. We also readily understand the apprehension of newspaper men at that thought that this new means of newspaper publication should be subject to the legislation and to the regulations now governing radio broadcasting which . . . might not be reconcilable with our traditional views on the freedom of the press. (p. 63; emphasis added)

Broadcast facsimile never saw the light of day, at least in any popular way.[7] Reference to concerns about freedom of the press were gratuitous, masking the fact that vested interests lie behind the monopolisation of existing and new media. Although it was common to deplore the rise of media monopolies and the decline of media diversity—as the Royal Commission itself did on several occasions—such occurrences were usually explained away as inevitable, a result of the technological base of the industry, certain ill-defined economic imperatives, or, as with de Sola Pool (1983), the nebulous but inexorable changes wrought by the industrial revolution. Yet, the quote introduced above suggests that matters differed from these typical refrains. In short, the press were scared stiff of full-blown competition entering their one- or two-paper towns,[8] advertisers feared a threat to the mass media and thus to mass consumption, the public broadcaster remained wary of treading on the private press,[9] policymakers believed that promoting concentrated economic resources would invigorate cultural production, and the exit of the telephone companies from broadcasting a short time earlier strengthened the separation between carriers and content—a trend unlikely to be reversed in the short term. As Smythe (1981) surmised, broadcast facsimile threatened the role of mass media in the production of consumer capitalism. As such, it could never obtain a well-endowed sponsor willing to transform the new medium into an organised system in the service of human communication.

Microwave Communications

Microwave communication—innovated at the same time as efforts were taking place to implement broadcast facsimile—proved a more formidable and resilient technology, no doubt due to the fact that it had powerful sponsors in the Canadian government, the U.S. and Canadian military, and the telecoms providers, in particular CNCP, who was eager to make up for its blunderous earlier failure to cooperate more closely with Marconi. Microwave communications came to Canada through military contracts given by the U.S. government to Canadian firms, and developed first and foremost to serve continental defense needs. In the name of continental protection, the Defense Early Warning System (DEW), ADCOM, and Mid-Canada Line projects were implemented. Hefty contracts were given to Bell, Northern Electric, and other Canadian electronics firms (Communications Canada, 1992b; Huyek, 1978, p. 47; Smythe, 1981, p. 101; also see Surtees, 1994a, pp. 32-34). TCTS also integrated microwave technology into the public telecoms network, a move that allowed it to renew and complete its cross-country network, transfer huge volumes of data, and to distribute programs for the CBC and other broadcasters—a particularly important task given the introduction of television (Babe, 1990, pp. 128-129; Canada, House of Commons, 1966, p. 462).

TCTS argued that microwave should develop as an adjunct of the natural monopoly regime. However, from the outset, it was clear that this would not happen. The real question was whether microwave communication would develop as a monopoly, duopoly, or as full-blown competition. Each had its proponents. The tilt toward duopoly began in 1952 when the national broadcaster, the CBC, called on CNCP and TCTS to submit bids to serve its national distribution needs. Further inclination toward duopolistic rivalry between the telegraph and telephone groups occurred a year later when the Cabinet announced that microwave communications would not develop as a monopoly. Subsequent attempts in the 1960s by TCTS to thwart the development of a second microwave network were also spurned (Babe, 1990, p. 128; Surtees, 1994a, p. 34).

Some current Industry Canada (formerly Department of Communication) staff claim that these moves indicated an early preference for competition within government circles (personal correspondence, D. Mozes, Telecommunications Policy Branch, Ottawa, July 30, 1992). However, a duopoly in telecoms services is not competition. The most likely area to support more competitive provision of microwave systems during the late 1950s and into the 1960s was cable television. Cable systems were proliferating, often under American ownership.[10] There was also burgeoning demand among these systems for the Department of Transport to issue more microwave licenses so they could import distant signals, meaning American programming. However, such demands were rejected, and a clear preference established to issue licenses only if it could be shown that this was in the public interest, that there was a demonstrable need for additional facilities and that this need could not be met by existing common carriers (Government of Manitoba, 1974, pp. 28-37).[11] This hardly constituted a competitive communication policy, although it dovetailed with broader cultural policy aims and a desire to promote traffic on the existing public telecoms network as a way of driving further modernisation and expansion of the public network.

Of course there was some rivalry between TCTS members and CNCP. However, this was not in the core of the public telecoms network, but in a number of niche-based services. There is no doubt that some of these were quite important, as CNCP was the first carrier to introduce a new telex service, to compete in private lines, to offer data communications to large users, and to make available broadband network facilities. It is also without doubt that such services had an impact on the pricing practices and service offerings of the telephone companies and even facilitated, from the late 1960s, the emergence of the first computer-generated service providers in Canada such as Systems Division Ltd., SHL System house, Alphatext and Infomart (Surtees, 1994a, pp. 43-51), although this resurrected issues that seemed to have been alleviated so many years earlier when CP was pushed to leave "electronic publishing."

Yet, although leased private lines for data communications constituted upward of 75% of CNCP revenues by 1968, it is also true that this amount was a pittance compared to the overall revenues of the telephone companies. Moreover, CNCP could only offer its services over private networks, lacking, as it did, either its own local exchanges or the right to connect with those of the major telephone companies—a point discussed near the end of the chapter. Perhaps most importantly, CNCP soon learned that the members of TCTS would match its prices for private line and data communication services, or even undercut them when necessary. The deep pockets of monopolists can be used just as easily to drive prices below costs in an economic war of attrition, as they can be refilled at other times by monopoly prices. Studies conducted for the CRTC and the U.S. regulator, the FCC, showed that Bell, AT&T, and other monopoly telephone providers willingly received far lower rates of return on services where there was a competitive threat, and attempted to cross-subsidise these from monopoly services (Babe, 1990, pp. 151-152; Smythe, 1981, p. 146). Throughout the 1970s, the telcos regularly lined up for rate increases for monopoly telephone services, although "their competitive services . . . such as Datapac and Dataroute were generally exempted from the increases . . . sought" (CRTC, 1978, p. 349).

The role of government regulators between the 1950s and 1970s within this complex mix of abuses and strategic rivalry was dubious, at best. Although the role of the CRTC during the 1970s and beyond will be returned to at the end of the chapter and in the next, I want to conclude this section with the following points. First, in the period just discussed, there was a definite change in the mode of economic regulation between CNCP and TCTS, and in government policy. Although relations between the telegraph and telephone groups had been, for the most part, based on cooperation and collusion from the 1880s, starting in the 1950s they turned decisively toward regulated duopolistic competition in services. Second, the pinnacle of the "natural monopoly" telecoms regime was between 1916 when the Supreme Court confirmed the BRC decision in the Ingersoll case and started to wane in 1955 with the sanctioning of a duopolistic regime in services. The veneer of political legitimacy that had built up for the natural monopoly regime was also wearing thin at about the same time. Of course, these boundaries only reflect the regime at its most stable point in time and recognises that TCTS members strove to revive the natural monopoly regime for a far longer period—but to no avail.

One of the more decisive testing grounds in the battle for control over the future of electronic media in Canada was that of cable systems and visions of "wired cities" that were maturing in the late 1960s. This is the topic of the following section.

WIRED CITIES AND POLICING THE BOUNDARIES BETWEEN ELECTRONIC MEDIA

Early Development of Cable

Vast investments in network modernisation, the advent of microwave communications, and integration of computer services into the public telecoms network, as well as the spread of cable systems from the periphery to the core of the Canadian electronic media system, underwrote broad visions of wired cities and information societies from the mid-1960s onward. These developments posed numerous choices with respect to the implementation, organisation, and uses for new and existing electronic media. The system of flux generated by those choices remains today, although there is now a sense of urgency attached to efforts to decisively settle the organisational parameters for "new media" that was not as intense several decades earlier.

As in the United States, cable systems grew in Canada to extend television to rural areas beyond the reach of over-the-air broadcast signals. Early systems developed in the late 1940s, but expanded quickly in the 1950s with the introduction of television. The latter development also saw the cable systems spread into urban areas as a solution to the problem of "ghosting" caused when broadcast signals were obstructed by tall buildings.

At first, the regulatory framework—if it can be called that—did little to prevent, nor directly to promote the new medium. Until 1964 the Department of Transport (DOT) issued licenses freely, including licenses to wire the same area. As such, cable spread without many government restraints imposed on cultural or competition policy grounds. By 1971, more than one in five homes in Canada subscribed to cable (Government of Manitoba, 1974, p. 28; Report of the Task Force on Broadcasting Policy, 1985, p. 553).

Despite, or perhaps because, of this reasonably quick rate of growth, policy shifted abruptly in the mid-1960s. The DOT instituted a freeze on new licenses, began a new Canadian ownership policy, and required that all new license applications be referred to the Board of Broadcast Governors, who would consider the impact of a new cable service on existing broadcasters (Government of Manitoba, 1974, p. 28).

In 1968, jurisdiction over cable passed to the new-borne CRTC. The regulator neither prevented nor promoted cable systems, but took a cautiously permissive approach to licensing them. However, within a few years, the CRTC abandoned its cautiously permissive view of cable as a Trojan horse likely to undo the economic viability of broadcasting in Canada, in favour of cautiously promoting the new media as a vehicle for expanding the distribution of Canadian content across Canada, increasing the diversity of programming, offering a channel for local expression, and allowing U.S. programming into the country in controlled amounts. The commission noted that it could either promote cable, squash it as a threat to Canadian broadcasters, or enable the new media in such a way as to complement the existing media system. Choosing the latter option, the CRTC (1971) announced that it would

> develop a policy which would integrate cable television into the Canadian broadcasting system, avoid disrupting the system, enhance the capacity of the system to produce programmes, and finally to *permit a vigorous development of cable television and of the whole Canadian broadcasting system.* (p. 5; emphasis added)

Radical Potentials for New Media Institutional Structures

Despite the emphasis on the potential impact of cable on the broadcasting system, evolution of the "new media" was also affected by, and affecting, what was happening in telecoms. Recognising this, Babe (1975) offered an economic and political analysis of cable systems that showed how two key attributes of this new means of communication had radical implications for the structure of the communication industries in Canada, *tout court*.

First, Babe's analysis showed that economies of scale for cable were quite minor and quickly dissipated after a comparatively small size. Although local monopoly was likely, according to Babe (1975), "small CATV systems tend to be more efficient than large systems, although a minimum system length of 150 to 200 miles appears to be necessary. . . . There do not appear to be any *technological* imperatives leading to concentrated ownership in the CATV industry" (pp. 56-58).[12] Essentially, cable communications did not require gargantuan media conglomerates to efficiently offer services. Because of this, it followed that cable systems did not have to mimic the development trajectory of either the telephone companies or the mass media toward large, concentrated industrial structures, if proper communication policies fostered this potential. Cities such as Calgary, London, Montreal or Windsor could sustain several small cable systems, each with a "natural monopoly" in a relatively small area, but competing through the example of "best practices" across a city or region as a whole.

The second point was that cable technology was flexible enough to carry all forms of communication. This included television programming, as well as telemetric services, data communication, information retrieval, interactive services on demand, and, of course, local telephone service (Babe, 1975, pp. 83-84). With several hundred times the carrying capacity and the potential to include two-way, interactive communications, cable was widely heralded throughout North America as ready and able to usher in "wired cities." Broadband cable and interurban links of microwave communication, satellite distribution, or carriage by the traditional telephone companies offered a chance to rebuild modern systems of human communication from scratch. Such claims were commonly found in most analyses of cable in Canada, the United States, and elsewhere (see e.g., Government of Manitoba, 1974, pp. 12-14; Sloan Foundation, 1971; Smith, 1972; Streeter, 1987, pp. 174-200). Babe's analysis differed from most, however, in its insistence on the compelling arguments and evidence against large monopolies *and*, as will be seen shortly, his focus on how the role of regulating cable had been usurped by the telephone companies.

Although the study was not born of starry-eyed, wishful thinking, its ramifications were in tune with some of the more politically charged projects of harnessing cable to efforts to invigorate people's access to the media and, generally, to democratise the new means of electronic communication. Throughout the 1960s and early 1970s, media politics in

Canada demonstrated a renewed sensitivity to the link between democracy and communication. The new *Broadcast Act* (1968) reflected this, as it incorporated for the first time explicit reference to electronic media freedoms. Certain CBC documentary program-makers began taking a more engaged approach to the relationship between their work, social issues, and the broader political culture, a move the CBC and CRTC seemed to tolerate, if not advocate (Morris, 1972, p. 45).[13] Moreover, recognising that media freedom and media production did not occur in an economic vacuum, from 1970 until 1981 there were three inquiries into the potential impact of concentrated ownership on freedom of expression, ideological diversity, and cultural production (Canada, House of Commons, 1978, 1981; Canada, Special Senate Committee on Mass Media, 1970). All were guardedly critical of the effects of the trend toward media concentration on the media, culture, and democratic politics.

There was also a strong "media access" movement, much of which pinned high hopes on the community-access channels promoted by media activists and being incorporated into CRTC cable policy (CRTC, 1971a, pp. 16-18). Even universities at which media law was taught appeared to have been busy studying cable access, rather than how to "get government off the back of private enterprise." Although some legal scholars asked if the CRTC's dedication to community programming and cable access was just "paper tiger rhetoric," the general belief was that it was not. The key issues were how communities could use media resources at their disposal and how to prevent concentration of cable ownership. At least one nongovernmental group, Intercom, brokered relationships between dispersed community programming organisations and even proposed trying to thwart cable buyouts by Maclean-Hunter, Rogers and other budding cable empire builders with community-based, cooperative buy-outs of private cable systems. Although Intercom was later accused of becoming "part of the establishment," or a front for the New Democratic Party (NDP), there were other groups such as the on-again, off-again McGill University Group, consisting of students, faculty, native Americans, and others, who pushed for a radical reform of Canadian media institutions (Berry, Garton, Parkinson, Pyne, & Wallace, 1970, pp. 59-63).

Eliminating the Economic Threat of "New Media"

Against this backdrop, however, several other developments were leading toward a small number of large cable systems: a view that cities—of whatever size—were co-terminus with the natural monopoly characteristics of cable; the prevention of media convergence; and regulation by government *and* the telephone company monopolies.

Part of the shift lay in the rethinking of cable policy that had been underway since the late-1960s. This contained two elements. First, in response to high levels of foreign ownership of cable and over-the-air broadcasters, in 1968 the Cabinet introduced a directive limiting foreign ownership in each of these areas to a 20%, noncontrolling interest. Within four years this served to "repatriate" $125 million worth of broadcast undertakings out of a total of $150 million. However, it did so at the expense of fueling higher levels of corporate concentration in cable and broadcasting, as only those with deep pockets could marshal the requisite resources to acquire the U.S.-owned systems in such a short period of time (CRTC, 1971b, 1972a; Government of Manitoba, 1974, pp. 30-34). Although the policy strengthened a small number of Canadian capitalists at the expense of U.S. capitalists, it did little to serve—and perhaps even hindered—the goals of media politics mentioned previously or, as will be seen, cultural production.

By the early 1970s, the CRTC also concluded that consolidation of cable ownership could help fund cultural production. The DOT's earlier policy to liberally issue licenses, even for competing or adjacent systems in a single city, was abandoned and a policy of one license per city instituted. Shortly after Canadian Cablesystems took over Famous Players, and Premier Cablevision the operations of CBS Systems, they were, in turn, swallowed by Rogers and Videotron, respectively. These latter companies, as well as a few others such as Cablenet, Maclean-Hunter, Selkirk, Shaw Cablesystems, and so on, went on a buying spree for the rest of the decade (CRTC, 1971b, 1972a; Report of the Task Force on Broadcasting, 1985, p. 629). By 1973, three companies—Rogers/Premier, Maclean-Hunter and Videotron/Canadian Cablesystems—accounted for over 40% of cable subscribers and revenues (Babe, 1975, pp. 89-90). By 1985, five companies controlled 53% of the cable industry. A decade later the trend had progressed even further.[14] Rounding things off, government policy dogma stuck to the fiction that "concentration of cable ownership . . . may well be desirable" (Report of the Task Force on Broadcasting, 1985, p. 629), despite contrary findings produced during the course of several media ownership inquiries. The inquiries concluded that large, multiple-systems owners put less money into program production than smaller, independent providers[15] (Canada, House of Commons, 1978; Canada, Special Senate Committee on Mass Media, 1970). The two major thrusts to regain control of cultural production and to foster the development of cable systems in Canada not only missed their target, but decimated the potentials expressed by scholarly analysis and the more popularly oriented media politics of the day.

Demise of the Technological Threat of "New Media"

Despite the technological potential of media convergence throughout the 1960s and 1970s, cable television and telecoms carriers continued to develop independently. This was a result of government policy, content regulation of cable services by the telephone companies, and a tacit understanding between the common carriers and cable systems that it would be mutually advantageous to stay out of one anothers' business. The issues are discussed next.

Paradoxically, the reason cable systems and telecoms advanced separately was because they were so alike. Cable providers depended on the telecoms carriers for their technical, economic, and functional survival from their humble origins. Telephone companies either built complete systems that they then leased to cable providers, or partial systems that cable providers leased while adding their own head-end, amplifiers, and subscriber drops.[16] At the very least, cable system operators needed permission from the telephone companies to get pole attachments for their network.

Due to this dependence and the relatively lackadaisical approach to cable regulation until the late 1960s, the telephone companies employed practices designed to squash any possibility of cable systems becoming the local broadband infrastructure envisioned by the "wired city" scenarios. They continued this until the CRTC regained control over cable policy from the telephone companies in 1977.

In the meantime, the agreements imposed by Bell and the other major telephone providers allowed cable communications in Canada to develop only so long as they restricted themselves to

> the distribution of signals conveying television and/or radio programmes. Such signals may be disseminated to the complete network, a limited network or on a point-to-point basis. Nothing in this contract shall be construed as permitting the transmission of data which is not part of or ancillary to a broadcast or cablecast, radio or television programme. The signals conveying television and/or radio programmes may flow either direction on the Bell facilities provided only that the Customer shall not utilise the two-way capability of the cable for any inquiry or any interactive type of communication. Customer shall not use in any installation with or connect to the Bell facilities any device capable of performing automatic or manual exchange switching. (Article IV, para. 3, Bell Partial System Agreement, reprinted in CRTC, 1977a, pp. 71-72)

Restrictions were even more starkly stated for New Brunswick Tel, a Bell subsidiary. A typical clause in New Brunswick Tel's cable contracts read as follows:

> The Licensee . . . will . . . carry only television signals whose *program content is intended solely for entertainment purposes* and . . . only such content is hereby made a condition of this agreement . . . . The Customer shall not *under any circumstances whatsoever provide point-to-point and/or limited network services over the cable facilities . . . for industrial, commercial and educational purposes* . . . (cited in Harris, 1969, p. 98; emphasis added)

In other words, to lease a cable system from the telephone companies, or to even attach a cable to their poles, one had to agree to neuter the technological potentials of cable media. Recalling that Bell had expanded vigorously throughout Ontario, Quebec, and the maritime provinces, and that BCTel had similarly done so in British Columbia, the two companies preempted the possibility across much of the country that the new media might develop into local broadband systems that could even remotely threaten their dominance in telecoms. Failure to abide by the terms of the contracts, as Quebec-based Transvision found out, could lead to cable system wires being cut and left dangling from telephone poles (Babe, 1990, p. 217; CRTC, 1977, p. 72).

The telephone companies supplied most of the hardware involved, regulated the content, and effectively lorded over the distribution of cable licenses, as they decided which companies could have pole attachment rights, what sectors of metropolitan areas could be wired, and how large the systems could be (Babe, 1975, pp. 120-124).[17] From this they reaped a handsome reward, charging excessive rates for constructing systems and receiving upward of 80% of a cable providers' profits without the hassle of programme scheduling or otherwise servicing cable subscribers (Babe, 1975, pp. 125-128). Similar practices were carried out by MTS and SaskTel, albeit with different aims in mind—as discussed later (Government of Manitoba, 1974, p. 20). Quasi-clandestine, unlegislated regulation by private authority was thus national in scope and a key factor turning the new media into just another form of broadcasting.[18]

Somewhat peculiarly, regulation of cable through the backroom politics of private corporate interests did not gather much regulatory attention until late in the 1970s. In the meantime, a full-blown conflagration between new and old media was postponed by a tacit understanding between the two systems about where boundaries between them ought to be drawn. Inklings of a mutual understanding began to surface during hearings of the Standing Committee on Transport and Communications in 1967. In response to a question by the chairperson of the hearings, Bell's vice-president, A. J. deGrandpré, stated emphatically that the company did not want to be broadcasters, that we did not want to be community antenna operators, that we did not want to be publishers, and that we did not want to control in way the contents of the message or the impact of the message. We want to be common carriers, purely and simply. (Canada, Standing Committee on Transport and Communications 1967, p. 65)[19]

The Canadian Cable Television Association (CCTA) also appears to have been of like mind. Around the same time that Bell was relinquishing any formal, active role in broadcasting or cable television, the CCTA was claiming before Quebec government officials that

[c]able television operators have no intention of competing with the telephone companies in their *traditional services*. At the same time, domestic broadband coaxial communications should not be turned over to the telephone companies. (cited in Government of Manitoba, 1974, p. 20; emphasis added)

These concessions are nothing less than amazing in the context of current discussions regarding media (re)convergence and because they preceded any legislative measures preventing cross-ownership or convergence between telephone companies and cable communications. How can they be explained? There are several conjectures that help illuminate some of the factors that may have led to such outcomes.

To begin, recall that telcos, especially Bell in Ontario, Quebec, and the Maritimes, and BCTel in the west, had gorged themselves on takeovers within the telephone industry from the mid-1950s onward. There were few reasons to feed such voracious appetites across the media industries, though, as this could have led to an extension of universal service mandates to cable, regulation under the *Broadcast Act,* and perhaps raised eyebrows among the few government ministries concerned with concentration within the media and across the whole economy.[20] Moreover, there was no point risking entry into the lush telephone industry, with its revenues of $1.57 billion in 1970, for the sake of obtaining even a dominant position in an industry with pithy annual revenues of $132 million. Likewise, given the pygmy to giant nature of the relationship, it was unlikely the cable industry would press for more competitive space, out of fear of being swallowed alive. In the early 1970s, after completing the takeover the American-owned system, the largest cable provider, Premier/Rogers, had revenues of between $17-18 million—hardly a competitive rival to Bell, whose annual take was around $900 million in 1970 (Babe, 1975, p. 89; Report of the Task Force on Broadcasting, 1985, p. 554; Statistics Canada, 1972a, p. 11). Moreover, cable television had enough enemies among broadcasters and the new regulator, the CRTC, that it did not need to raise the ire of the telcos.

Finally, telephone companies were making monopoly profits from the lease of cable systems, and cable companies enjoyed profits from exclusive local franchises, especially as they were regulated under the *Broadcasting Act* and therefore not subject to rate-of-return regulation. Cable systems averaged profits[21] between 14% and 30% from 1968 to 1975, a high level that can mainly be attributed to their local monopoly position and the fact that rates and profits are not regulated under the broadcast regime (Babe, 1975, p. 92; Government of Manitoba, 1974, p. 19; Report of the Task Force on Broadcasting, 1985, pp. 556-567). Thus, in return for maintaining the fiction of common carriage[22] and separate media boundaries, telephone companies postponed having to fight in their own lush field for the potential of meager profits elsewhere; for their part, cable companies could carry on with their own little fiefdoms, so long as they could tolerate the constant din of hollow admonitions from the CRTC to foster Canadian culture as well as avoid the hassles of universal service obligations or rate-of-return regulation. A CCTA statement before the federal regulator in August 1973 captured the tradeoff well: "The *association accepts federal authority beneath the Broadcasting Act of 1968* . . . . [However,] the association seeks support from the CRTC to raise rates at an incremental amount . . . *without public hearings*" (cited in Government of Manitoba, 1974, p. 41; emphasis added).

Of course, things were not always so pristine that there were never conflicts of interest among the parties privy to these arrangements. Although the telephone companies and cable system operators seemed quite satisfied to divvy up the field in each of their traditional services, there was friction among them and the federal and provincial governments regarding new communication services, especially computer-generated services. The cable companies argued that there should be monopoly in the core traditional services, but competition in new services (Government, of Manitoba, 1974, p. 20). At other times they advocated regulated duopoly, although this looked more like a plea for government to use regulation to split new services into monopolistic subregions of a two-carrier communications system (Babe, 1975, pp. 111-112). According to this latter proposal, a regulated duopoly in the local exchange would match the arrangements found between the telephone and telegraph groups in long-distance private line and data communication services.

The telephone companies retorted that cable companies should not be able to enjoy both the fruits of broadcast and common-carriage regulatory regimes, while avoiding the obligations of either. The telcos argued that they were the only proper common carriers and that distribution of all nonbroadcast (read, anything that was not television or radio) services should fall to them. Government policy was fragmented and a mess, a fact the telephone companies used to move swiftly into computer-generated services beginning in 1971. Refusing to wait for government agencies—the CRTC, Canadian Transport Commission (CTC), Department of Communications (DOC), and various ministries struggling to coordinate federal/provincial positions on the issues—to get their regulatory houses in order, the telephone companies, led by Bell, began moving into computer services. Bell set up the Computer Communications Group in 1971. A year later it acquired, through its maritime-based subsidiary, MT&T, the time-sharing computer company, Consolidated Computers. BCTel's Quebec Telephone began offering computer time-sharing in the same year. Two years earlier CNCP had moved in the same direction by acquiring a 51% share in Computer Sciences (Canada) Ltd., a data processing company (Babe, 1975, pp. 105-106; Surtees, 1994a, pp. 50-58). Herein lies the beginning of the end of the common-carrier principle in Canadian telecoms, and the rapid thrust of the telecoms carriers into a variety of electronic publishing services—developments that will be more fully recounted in the following two chapters.

The CRTC's Struggle to Regain Control Of Communication Policy

For now, it is important to note two other intertwined developments: namely, new initiatives by the CRTC to regulate telco/cable cross-ownership and convergence as well as to regain control over cable policy; and second, the ambitious broadband projects launched by the publicly owned prairie telcos in the mid-1970s.

With the broad contours of relations between the telcos and cablecos in place and competition limited to new information services, the CRTC and other agencies moved in to ratify what had already been accomplished. The first step indicating the new direction in communication policy has already been introduced: the revisions to the Bell charter in 1968 preventing the company from holding a broadcast or CATV license, directly or by way of its subsidiaries. Section 5(2) of the Act was explicit and is worth repeating given recent developments discussed in later chapters. According to the new section, Bell

> and its subsidiaries do not . . . directly or indirectly or by any other means, have the power to apply for or to be the holder of a broadcasting license . . . or of a license to operate a commercial Community Antenna Television service . . . and shall neither control the contents nor influence the meaning or purpose of [any] message emitted, transmitted or received. (Canada, 1968, sec. 5(2)(3))

The following year the CRTC issued its "Licensing Policy in Relation to Common Carriers," announcing that

> it would not be in the public interest to encourage common carriers to hold licenses for CATV systems [, except] . . . under certain circumstances [when] smaller common carrier companies may be the only entities capable of providing a CATV service . . . in certain of Canada's smaller population centres. (CRTC, 1969, p. 1)

Again, this had nothing to do with whether or not media convergence was technically possible. That possibility was demonstrated in the same year when the CRTC licensed the Amtel Group to offer cable and telephone service in the small southern Ontario town of Elgin (CRTC, 1991a, pp. 3-4). Instead, the policy was motivated by a range of interests that had much to do with broader cultural policy objectives, politics, and power. The CRTC was motivated by the fear that regulating cable as a common carrier would result in faster growth of the system and even more U.S. content distributed throughout the country. As the head of the CRTC, Pierre Juneau, commented, "Every time you talk about developing cable as if it were a utility, like telephone . . . , what you are saying in fact is, 'Let's make sure we get those four American networks into Canada as fast as we can'" (cited in Government of Manitoba, 1974, p. 20).

Although it is tempting to read laudable goals back into the CRTC's policy, as well as into revisions of the Bell Act, the discussion to this point cautions against this. The crucial point is that by 1970, government policy, the telecoms providers and cable operators all seemed to agree that cable and telephony systems should develop in separate solitudes. Essentially, the new policy regime, enforced by private interests and buttressed by government, ensured that there would be, at least in the short term, neither competition between the two, nor the potential for anyone to develop a broadband platform to support a panoply of new communication services.

Government policy continued to legislate media divergence throughout the 1970s, 1980s and 1990s. In 1971, the CRTC did so with its "minimal facilities ownership" policy, which required cable companies to own at least the head-end, amplifiers, and subscriber drops of a cable system. The new policy was said to give cable operators greater control over their systems and, therefore, their ability to implement the government's broadcasting policy. However, this is questionable, as the new policy merely formalised the status quo negotiated privately between cable and telco interests up to that point (e.g., the partial systems lease) and did nothing with respect to the telcos regulating the content of cable systems (CRTC, 1977a, p. 74; Government of Manitoba, 1974, p. 34).

The private sector usurpation of Canadian cable policy was finally put to an end in 1977, when the CRTC, in one of its first acts after replacing the CTC as the federal telecoms regulatory authority, announced its "pole attachment" decision. Henceforth, the telephone companies had to submit their tariffs and contracts for CRTC approval, meaning they could no longer unilaterally set prices nor determine the content carried by cable operators. Although it seemed that the CRTC had, for the most part, regained control of the country's communication policy from the private sector, this did not mean anything would change with respect to the long-standing potential for either competition between telcos and cablecos or the removal of policies hindering the emergence of broadband communication systems (CRTC, 1977a, p. 75).

Constitutional Politics and the Potential for Media Reconvergence

The decision of federal communication policymakers to continue driving a wedge between various electronic media put them on a collision course with the publicly owned telcos in Saskatchewan and Manitoba, who had decidedly different ideas about how to develop public telecoms networks and new communication services. According to these plans, the prairie telecoms providers would develop broadband, digital networks, whereas program packagers would lease MTS and SaskTel facilities to deliver cable television service to subscribers' homes. Cable television was to be the mass market anchor used to underwrite a broader project of rapidly unrolling digital broadband networks capable of carrying every kind of communication services—data services, information retrieval, telephony, television and so on—throughout their territories (Government of Manitoba, 1974, pp. 73-77; SaskTel, 1977, pp. 8-9).

Although MTS and SaskTel would provide network facilities on a common-carrier basis, according to the provinces' view of things, the CRTC would license cable companies and other online content providers to deliver their services over MTS and SaskTel facilities. As such, the prairie provinces would control the network infrastructure and the federal government the content, especially broadcasting content services which were most firmly under federal jurisdiction ("Manitoba to be," 1979, p. 12; SaskTel, 1977, p. 7).

This directly contravened CRTC policy on cable ownership requirements—head-end, amplifiers, and subscriber drops—and raised issues about the Constitutional authority of the provinces to regulate telecoms, an issue that had remained dormant on political grounds rather than any affirmation of such provincial authority. The CRTC rejected these plans and, in 1975, called for applications to develop cable systems in Brandon, Dauphin, Portage la Prairie, Selkirk, and Winnipeg, all in Manitoba. Similar intentions were announced for Saskatchewan. The CRTC was also backed by cable operators, who challenged the provinces' authority to usurp control over cable services, arguing that broadcasting was undisputedly within the purview of the federal government. Yet, although the CRTC appeared to be regaining control of cable policy with gusto, SaskTel was adamant that "[t]he hardware ownership conditions imposed by the CRTC were not acceptable . . . [and] an erosion of its role . . . to deliver telecommunication signals in Saskatchewan. At year end the issue had not been resolved" (SaskTel, 1976, p. 7).

The issues, however, were solved that year in Manitoba, and in the following year in Saskatchewan. The CRTC was forced to back down from its policy after the federal government intervened, first to set aside the CRTC's newly issued licenses and then to sign agreements with the two provinces allowing them to pursuit their plans (Governor General in Council, 1976, P.C. 1976-2761). According to the agreement between the federal government and Manitoba signed on November 10, 1976,

> [T]he Province has responsibility for regulating and supervising common carrier services provided through . . . the Manitoba Telephone System . . . [While] the regulation and supervision of programming services distributed in Manitoba . . . are exclusive responsibilities of Canada. (CRTC, 1976a, pp. 136-137)[23]

Thereafter, MTS and SaskTel began unfolding their fibre optic-based broadband network initiatives. By the early 1980s, they had the most digitalised networks in the world, while maintaining telephone rates among the lowest in Canada or, indeed, the world. The projects also laid the ground for work during the mid-1980s to universalise individual line service and extend local calling areas. Moreover, the network modernisation projects undertaken in the prairie provinces created jobs, not decimated them. SaskTel's workforce, for example, expanded from 2,500 in the mid-1970s to 4,500 a decade later (AGT, 1988; MTS, 1991; Saskatchewan, 1985a, pp. 257-274).

Although Manitoba and Saskatchewan proceeded toward media convergence from the late 1970s, communication policies made in Ottawa continued to divide the electronic media until the mid-1990s. Table 5.2 summarises the legal and policy instruments developed over the last half century in Canada to restrict cross-media convergence and/or competition.

Table 5.2. Legislating Media Divergence.

Date	Source/Agency	Summary of Instrument
1946	Ministerial Statement by C.D. Howe	Prohibit provincial government ownership of broadcasting undertakings.
1968	Bell Canada Act	Section 5. Prevent Bell from obtaining broadcast or CATV license, or controlling content in any way.
1969	CRTC	Licensing Policy for Common Carriers preventing ownership of CATV, except exceptional circumstances.
1971	CRTC	Cable basic facilities ownership policy.
1971	CRTC	Cable microwave facilities governed by Broadcast Act and not eligible to provide telecoms services (CRTC Cable Policy Statement).
1977	CRTC	Pole attachment decision prevents telcos from regulating CATV, but reaffirms complementary role of telcos and cablecos.
1985	Order-in-Council	Provincial telcos—AGT, MTS and SaskTel—ineligible to hold broadcast licenses.
1986	Cable Television Regulations	Basic facilities ownership policy reaffirmed.
1987	Bell Canada Act	Renewal (sec. 7 and 8) of restrictions on holding broadcasting/CATV licenses.
1990	Broadcasting Act	Ineligibility of common carriers to hold broadcasting license.
1993	Telecommunications Act	Ineligibility of common carriers to hold broadcasting license.

CRISIS OF COMMUNICATION POLICY: FRAGMENTATION, DEMOCRATISATION, OR CONCENTRATION OF STATE AUTHORITY IN COMMUNICATION POLICY?

The corporate takeover of key aspects of Canadian communication policy from, say, 1965 through 1977, betrayed a larger crisis in government. In communication such a crisis was experienced as internecine rivalry between different agencies within the state for supreme command over the future direction of media development in Canada, and as turf wars between the provinces and Ottawa for control of the means of communication. Even broader yet, fragmentation, dissension, and the people-oriented media politics discussed earlier, according to some influential commentators, reflected nothing less than a crisis of democracy. In the section on Canada entered into *The Crisis of Democracy: Report on the Governability of Democracies to the Trilateral Commission*, Crozier, Huntington, and Watanuki (1975) argued that colloquia held in Canada indicated

> a general consensus . . . that Canada's Governability problems . . . — various democratic dysfunctions, the delegitimisation of authority, systems overload, the disaggregation of interests, [among other things]— . . . while not insoluble are real and deserve urgent attention and remedial action. (pp. 203, 209)[24]

Elsewhere, Crozier et al. argued that the problem lies in the fact that

> the democratic spirit is egalitarian, individualistic, populist and impatient with the distinctions of class and rank . . . . [Yet,] a pervasive spirit of democracy may pose an intrinsic threat . . . . Every social organisation requires . . . inequalities in authority and distinctions in function. To the extent that the spread of the *democratic distemper corrodes . . . authority throughout society [it] contributes to the weakening of the authority of government.* (pp. 162-163; emphasis added)

Until changes in 1968 with respect to broadcast regulation, and 1976 for telecoms, media policy in Canada avoided the "corrosive influence of democracy" by being made outside the public arena. Until 1968 broadcast policy remained tucked away behind the closed doors of the Board of Broadcast Governors, and only achieved a modicum of autonomy from the CBC and government thereafter when the CRTC took over regulating the CBC and private sector media. Yet, the CRTC did not stray far from existing practices until some years later. Even Pierre Juneau, first director of the new agency, candidly admitted that the CRTC dealt with "mainly vested interests" (quoted in Dawson, 1972, p. 20).

CTC regulation of telecoms was a similar affair. The agency argued that only it and the telephone industry understood the highly specialised body of technical knowledge needed to regulate telecoms, a claim both parties wielded with impunity to eviscerate public discourse about how telecoms could best be developed, organised, and used to serve society. CTC head, John Gray, dismissed the idea that 'public interest groups' could contribute to hearings, arguing that they and their hired experts "tend not to be helpful" (CTC, 1975, p. 65). Although some, such as Michael Trebilock, University of Toronto law professor, were scathing of such arrogance, the CTC's view of telecoms politics prevailed until regulation was transferred to the CRTC in 1976 (Trebilock, 1977/8, pp. 101-113).

Expanding the CRTC's mandate to embrace telecoms responded to the crisis of communication policy in at least two ways: first, it appeared to reduce fragmentation within the Canadian State on communication policy issues because the CRTC received a broad and integrated mandate over the field of electronic media as a whole. Second, the newly invigorated CRTC promised to put communication policy squarely in the public domain. The CRTC's initial statements were emphatic with respect to how it saw its role vis-à-vis the public. In one of its first statements after assuming authority for telecoms, the CRTC (1976b) announced:

> [i]n a country where essential telecommunications services are provided largely by private enterprise with some degree of protection from competition, the public interest requires that those services should be responsive to *public demand over as wide a range as possible, and equally responsive to social and technological change.*
>
> The principle of "just and reasonable" rates is neither narrow nor a static concept. As our society has evolved, the idea of what is just and reasonable has also changed, and now takes into account many considerations that would have been thought irrelevant 70 years ago, when regulatory review was first instituted. Indeed, *the Commission views this principle in the widest possible terms,* and considers itself obliged to continually review the level and structure of carrier rates to ensure that telecommunications services are fully responsive to the public interest. (p. 3; emphasis added)

The CRTC's pronouncement was not idle talk. Immediately, it went on to change everything from the language it used, to greater public participation in regulatory proceedings; the quality of data and forthrightness expected from telephone companies; and even to reverse the onus of the natural monopoly regime against new providers, to the burden being put on the telephone companies to show why the public interest would not be served by allowing competition in telecoms services.

The language formerly used to disparage people's potential contribution to public policy proceedings disappeared, and the language of self-interest, consumption, and information markets (temporarily) kept at bay. The discourses of technical experts and/or market ideologues was pushed aside by a stress on people, citizens, publics, and the relationship among communication, technology, and society. The CRTC even decided that the value of public knowledge to communication policy could be so great as to merit funding when and where such contributions by interveners was made (see, e.g., CRTC, 1976b, pp. 4-15; 1978b, pp. 4-6, 37-42).

Whereas the CRTC dealt with the crisis of communication policy in Canada by broadening the basis of political legitimacy, public participation, and interveners' sense of efficacy, others steadfastly advocated the Trilateral Commission's preferred approach to the "excesses of democracy"; namely, trying to eliminate the basis of citizenship and democracy. Bell, for instance, tried to circumvent CRTC efforts by arguing that the regulator needed to realise that certain areas were out of bounds, or exclusive "management prerogatives," although this was rebuffed (CRTC, 1978b, p. 5). Bell also attempted to withhold information or to file studies the CRTC was forced to dismiss as "inadequate and disappointing" (CRTC, 1978a, p. 323). Essentially the telephone companies tried to scupper the potential for a democratic politics of telecoms, or failing that, to turn the new experience into just another game to be approached strategically and "won." Above all else, Bell et al., were determined to insure that CRTC efforts did not set an example of how corporate interests, public policy, and people might peacefully coexist.

Perhaps just as important was a pervasive sense among many of the "communication policy elite" that regulatory changes required a strong State. The CRTC's expansive interpretation of the concept of "just and reasonable" was lamented (Janisch, 1986, p. 586), and efforts to get a tighter reign on telecoms politics advocated. To counter the perception of government losing control over communication policy, those well-placed in the policymaking elite advocated greater reliance on ministerial directives to preempt CRTC decisions and Orders-in-Council and overturn the agency's decisions when need be. In 1978, Ottawa proposed a new telecoms law (Bill C-16) that, among other things, would allow the Minister of Communications to issue directives prior to CRTC decisions, in addition to maintaining the long-standing power to review, vary, and rescind agency decisions after they were made. Other proposals advocated eliminating the "balkanised regulatory authority" between the federal and provincial governments (Canada, Consultative Committee on the Implications of Telecommunications, 1979).[25] By 1982, even John Meisel, new chair of the CRTC, had endorsed cabinet directives (Bartley,

1988, p. 52), an intriguing turn of events given that Meisel was among the key participants in the *Crisis of Democracy*[26] proceedings held in Canada several years earlier.

Although Meisel may or may not have been a "crisis of democracy" prophet, the crucial point is that the CRTC's short-term foray into a more democratic-oriented politics of telecoms was running into a brick wall just after getting off the ground. Moreover, the discourse of new media and democracy certainly sat oddly alongside the cacophony of voices calling for a strong state. By the late 1970s, the CRTC's effort to open communication policy to people appeared to be hemmed in on one side by attempts to postpone the collapse of the natural monopoly regime and on the other side by a range of interests bent on creating a strong state. With only narrow space to maneuver, the CRTC cautiously steered toward regulated competition in the public interest. The next and final section of this chapter looks at this development.

REGULATED COMPETITION IN THE PUBLIC INTEREST?

As noted earlier, competition was first reintroduced into Canada in the 1950s through regulated duopolistic competition in services. In the late 1960s, "end-to-end" monopoly was relaxed further, with decisions by the CTC that allowed customers to attach equipment to the telephone network, so long as it met Bell-defined technical standards. Those unsatisfied with the reasonableness of Bell standards could appeal to the CTC, and later the CRTC. The CTC took a meek view of its review powers. Consequently, conflicts between equipment manufacturers and Bell often fell to the courts for adjudication. Bell's reign over communications equipment manufacturers was first weakened through the courts with respect to an electronic credit card processing system and later via the CRTC with respect to mobile communications (Babe, 1990, pp. 145-147).

The latter case demonstrated the extent to which the CRTC was highly circumspect of "system integrity" arguments used by Bell to maintain the natural monopoly regime. In the Challenge Communications Ltd. decision, the CRTC rejected Bell's attempt to employ the "systems integrity = natural monopoly = universal service" strategy, noting that in the present instant Bell was the cream-skimmer, as it developed mobile communications exclusively in the well-traveled Hamilton to Montreal corridor and refused network connectivity purely on competitive grounds, not by genuine technical considerations. In addition to banishing the "systems integrity" argument to the annals of telecoms history, the CRTC abandoned presumptions against competition, found Bell's actions unjust and discriminatory, and used its new funding mechanism to award costs to Challenge representatives for contributing valuable information/knowledge to the proceedings (CRTC, 1977b, pp. 499-597).

Two other decisions between 1979 and 1982 drove the natural monopoly concept further into retreat; one dealt with customer premise equipment (cpe), the other an application by CNCP to interconnect with Bell's local exchanges to provide competitive data and private line services. With respect to the first issue, Bell moved in 1979 to have all regulatory restrictions on cpe, except minimal technical standards, removed. Bell claimed that it no longer wanted to be responsible for establishing and policing industry standards, preferring to transfer these tasks to the DOC. It appeared that even Bell was now moving toward ending the end-to-end monopoly set up, arguing that any equipment certified by the DOC should be allowed network connectivity (Babe, 1990, pp. 145-148).

Several labour unions, including the TWU and CWC, along with the National Anti-Poverty Organisation (NAPO) and a few other public interest groups, opposed efforts to "deregulate" cpe. They argued this would be the thin edge of the deregulatory wedge and were opposed to the initiative because Bell and BCTel had tied it to "basic local exchange service becoming more fully compensatory" (CRTC, 1982a, p. 20). The CRTC argued that a liberalised cpe attachment regime would serve the public interest and that it could sever the link between competition and any subsequent drive toward "rate rebalancing." The commission also noted that another consideration had entered its decision: international competitiveness. As the decision stated, Bell and BCTel were eager for a favourable decision because of its expected beneficial impact on their ability to secure "full reciprocity in the international telecommunications market" (CRTC, 1982a, p. 27). The telephone companies—at least the privately owned ones under federal regulation—appeared to be abandoning natural monopoly arguments on their own accord and thus driving the shift to a competitive-oriented telecoms regime.

A more significant shift from competition in a few peripheral areas to substantive competition in an expanding area of telecoms network services was signaled by the CNCP application for interconnection with the Bell network. The move completely repudiated the historical practice whereby the "telegraph" and "telephone" groups negotiated access to one anothers' facilities on an ad hoc basis and signaled CNCP's thrust into the nascent telecoms and computer services "markets." The decision also revealed that an array of powerful forces, including the largest domestic and transnational users and suppliers of telecoms services, were now intimately interested in communications policy and would henceforth play a key role in trying to shape it to their ends. Finally, because the decision applied only to telephone companies under federal jurisdiction, it suggested that more intense pressure would follow to bring the provinces into line with the increasingly competitive-oriented federal telecoms regulatory regime (CRTC, 1979, p. 74). The fact that the federal government was part-owner of CNCP also demonstrated that the push against the provinces had Ottawa's blessing. Thus, what the government could not do through federal/provincial negotiations and legislation, it would attempt to do through the market; a novel twist to the political economy of telecoms, indeed.

Some of the prairie and maritime provinces were alarmed by events unfolding in Ottawa, as they were in the midst of their broadband initiatives ("Manitoba to be," 1979, p. 12; "Phone devices," 1977, p. 7; SaskTel, 1980, p. 2). Although the provinces were not directly regulated by the CRTC, they realised that national policies could "alter . . . fundamental aspects of the delivery of telecommunications services . . ., impacting service levels and rates throughout Canada" (CRTC, 1979, p. 75). It must be recognised that the provinces were not arguing to retain the status quo, because that would have prevented the projects being unfolded in Manitoba and Saskatchewan, but actively taking a different route to telecoms than being pursued nationally. The provinces wanted to retain strict monopoly over the core network, while allowing competition/diversity in the provision of services. The CRTC was moving toward competition in services as well as scope for infrastructure-based competition. It was the latter part that was abhorrent to the provinces. Labour unions preferred the prairie approach and were especially concerned that competition would occur at the expense of jobs, in particular, unionised work in telecoms (personal correspondence, Sid Shniad, Regulatory Affairs Advisor, TWU, Burnaby, BC September 8, 1992; Verschelden, 1980, pp. 9-15).

The idea that regulated competition could serve the public interest was based on several premises. One premise is that which concerns the impact of regulatory changes on labour within the telecoms industry. As has been seen several times in this and previous chapters, there were broad grounds for considering the interests of telecoms workers under monopolistic conditions within the telephone industry. This had been evident since the Bell telephone operators' strike in 1907, repeated appearances of telecoms-based labour unions before the Industrial Disputes Investigation Board, comments in Parliament and so on. Even the CRTC (1982a) admitted that it had to consider the impact of its decisions on labour, arguing in the cpe decision that its decision would not result in a net loss of jobs, but "a transfer of jobs from the telephone companies to terminal equipment companies" (p. 25). Yet, the CRTC failed to realise that working conditions and wages are better under monopolistic conditions in which there are higher levels of unionisation, than in the competitive fringes of the industry characterised by lower rates of pay, greater instability, and less unionised workforces. Further discussion of this will be briefly considered again in the next chapter.

Beyond the interest of labour unions, the second premise on which the CRTC tried to lay claim to regulated competition being in the public interest is that it could sever any attempts by the telephone companies to forge links between competition and "rate rebalancing." In some senses, the CRTC did try to enforce its commitment to preventing competition being linked with massive increases in basic services. Nonetheless, as soon as it was clear that competition was moving out of the periphery and more centrally into services, the telcos began lining up for quite massive rate hikes, always in monopolistic services and almost never in competitive services. In the first of this long run of rate increase applications, Bell reached out for rate increases of 20% for residential basic service and 28% for business services. Unimpressed, the CRTC grudgingly allowed increases of 5% and 10%, respectively, and turned a circumspect eye to the fact that Bell had not approached the agency for any hikes in its competitive services such as Data Route or Telpak. With respect to the latter, Bell was admonished to refrain from using revenues from its monopoly services to cross-subsidise competitive services (CRTC, 1978a, pp. 349-353).

A torrent of rate increase applications poured forth from telephone companies across the country. In 1978, the government-owned CN systems in Newfoundland and, under the name of NorthWesTel (before being acquired by BCE in 1988) in the Yukon, Northwest Territories, and Northern British Columbia, proposed rate increases of 50% for residential services and 100% for business services (CRTC, 1978c, 1981a). Similar applications were also made by Terra Nova (also acquired by BCE in 1988), for areas in Newfoundland (CRTC, 1981c). Bell was back again in 1981, cup in hand, seeking to raise rates 30%, 40%, and between 9% and 28% for residential, business and long-distance services, respectively (CRTC, 1981b). Bell's competitive services were, again, either excluded, or price increases sought that were far less than in its monopolistic services. Even competitive services, though, were not exempt from rate hikes, as CNCP also strode forward, seeking rate increases for its Broadband Exchange, Telenet, Infoswitch, and other services, a move that, reminiscent of matters before the BRC some 70 years earlier, brought forth the press, news wire services, broadcasters and other content providers to oppose CNCP's attempt to feed at the trough of regulated competition. In each case, the CRTC's response was the same: proposals were scaled down to between one-third and one-half their original amounts, companies sent back in light of CRTC directions with instructions to redraw and resubmit their tariffs, and, perhaps most amazingly, each and every decision just mentioned was overturned by Cabinet order (see Governor General in Council, 1982b, 1982c, 1982d, 1982e). Each time the CRTC was directed to allow greater rate increases.

Whenever the CRTC tried to push forward regulated competition in the public interest, the Cabinet squashed its initiatives. When the CRTC directed Bell to go back and resubmit higher tariffs for its competitive services in line with the increases sought for its monopolistic services, an Order-in-Council swiftly followed overturning the CRTC's instructions (Governor General in Council, 1983). Perhaps most egregious of all was the Cabinet's actions with respect to the Telesat arrangements. Broke and faced with an imminent need to replace aging satellites, the federal government, DOC, and TCTS/Stentor members cooked up a plan to bring Telesat—already jointly owned by TCTS/Stentor, the federal government, and a phantom "public" in equal one-third shares—closer under the control of TCTS/Stentor. According to the new plan, Telesat would be a carriers' carrier, meaning that no one could use the national satellite system (developed with public funds, of course—$110 million between 1969 and 1971, and another $95.7 million in 1978/79) without going through the telephone companies. Throughout hearings on the wisdom of these arrangements convened by the CRTC, the telephone companies hindered the commission's and public's access to information, and otherwise squandered an opportunity to investigate how the Canadian government and telephone companies had decided to organise this relatively new and powerful means of communication on behalf of Canadian citizens. Of course, when the CRTC concluded that the arrangements did not meet any sane test of the public interest, the Minister of Communication, Jeane Sauve, stepped in and overturned the agency (Babe, 1990, pp. 222-226). Several years later when the CRTC—still not beaten completely into submission—again refused to raise rates for Telesat services, "His Excellency the Governor General in Council determined that it was in the public interest to . . . increase rates 6% [for certain services], . . . a further 5%" for other services, and so on (Governor General in Council, 1982a, P.C. 1982-2558).

Politely put, regulated competition was increasing rates. More stridently stated, the federal government was ramming through regulated competition in the corporate interest and Canadian citizens were going to pay for it. The strong state had come to Canadian communication policy, and, as is shown in subsequent chapters, the recalcitrant sectors of Canadian society unwilling to bend to the new wisdom would be bypassed, ignored, or overruled.

Before closing out this chapter, it is important to look briefly at a few things the CRTC had in mind with respect to the possibility of regulated competition in the public interest. First, as just noted, it refused a straightforward link between rate rebalancing and competition. Second, it interpreted universal service in an expansive light. Recall that in one of its first public announcements regarding its new mandate, the Commission stated that universal service was not a static concept but had to adjust to new technological potentials and social change (CRTC, 1976b, p. 3). In light of this anticipated expansion in what constituted universal service, the CRTC was loath to accept telephone company proposals for "budget service . . . for low income groups." The CRTC dismissed Bell plans for a measured service scheme or telephone welfare program paid for by government, as well as its proposal for some "form of test to determine eligibility," arguing that such tests are "anathema to many people . . . and accordingly an unacceptable feature of telephone service" (CRTC, 1978a, p. 323). The point, it seems, was that people should not have to abandon their dignity to get a basic necessity of life. Charity still reached some areas of the Canadian state. Third, the CRTC put aside self-serving accolades about how universal service had been achieved in Canada and focused on the remaining groups of people and areas of the country without adequate service.

Finally, and this is crucial, the CRTC raised critical questions about Bell's plan to spend $6 billion on a network modernisation project. Although I will not spend a lot of time on the issues right now (they are one of the main themes covered in Chapter 7), I do want to point out the following. First, we need to compare, even if just superficially for a moment, the fanfare accorded Stentor's recent Beacon Proposal to spend $8.5 billion over 10 years on broadband network development in Canada, as a quid pro quo for massive regulatory changes, with Bell proposals to spend $6 billion over five years (1978-1982). Just doubling Bell's 1978 proposal so that it coincides in length (e.g., 10 years) suggests that the Beacon proposal may not be such a windfall after all. If we adjust the figures to account for changes in the value of money over time,[27] the increase in revenues, and so on, the Beacon Proposals begin to look a bit lame. Since this will be covered in detail in Chapter 7, we can move to other points not covered there.

The first thing to note is that the CRTC, rather than committing itself to radically transforming the entire body of electronic media law in the country in return for massive investments, actually looked at Bell's proposal with somewhat jaundiced eyes. Although the figures represented only slightly over 41% of estimated revenues for the period, and thus were not high by historical terms (e.g., between 53% and 62% of annual revenues plowed back into network construction between 1955 and 1970, as indicated earlier), the CRTC seemed to be adhering to the widely held assumption that regulated monopolies had produced massively gold-plated public telecoms networks. With regulated competition in the public interest, it seemed the underlying economic dynamic was supposed to shift from government-sponsored dynamic efficiencies to greater emphasis on the allocative efficiency of market-led investment and distribution of goods. The CRTC, therefore, pressed the company to justify its proposed investment levels, to indicate a link between investment and demand, and to demonstrate how it would avoid burdening average subscribers with the cost of network functions, capacity and so on that they would never need. Although the Commission expressed its dissatisfaction with Bell's answers on each one of these points, it nonetheless allowed the proposal to go ahead, warning that future proposals would bear a heavier burden of proof before gaining the assent of the "little regulator that thought it could" (CRTC, 1978a, pp. 325-330).

SUMMARY COMMENTS

The concept of natural monopoly in telecoms has never been inevitable, stable, or complete. Its most unnatural origins as a construct of "judicial activism" within the telephone industry (of course preceded by an extensive history of corporate abuses), and corporate collusion across the entire field of electronic media, robbed it of any intrinsic merit. Thus, it was inevitable that the same sources that gave life to and sustained natural monopoly in the short term would bury it over the long run: strategic rivalry, power, and marriages of convenience.

The natural monopoly was at its strongest, least vulnerable between the 1916 Supreme Court ruling affirming the BRC's turn toward regulated monopoly, at the one end, and the advent of microwave communication and introduction of duopolistic competition in private lines and data services in the early 1950s, at the other end. Although attempts to resuscitate natural monopoly persisted into the 1970s and 1980s, they were unsustainable. Attempts to prop-up internal boundaries between telephony and cable communications were also unsustainable due to the illegitimate usurpation of media regulation by the telephone companies, and regulatory policies by the federal government that defied the trajectory of technological and economic imperatives, and most importantly, strategic interests.

Choices facing policymakers have never been limited only to selecting between monopoly and/or competition. Considered outside the blinkers of dichotomous thinking, it is clear that there were at least three or four paths the natural monopoly regime could take. One was to reject alternatives and insist on maintaining the status quo—artificial divides between telephony and cable and all (the natural monopoly forever scenario). A second approach, as advocated by MTS and SaskTel, was to expand broadband networks as a monopoly but allow many content service providers (the prairie scenario). A third approach, and one that seems to constantly recur in Canadian telecoms (e.g., recall Dominion Telegraph and Montreal Telegraph [1875-1881]; Bell and CP [1880-1932]; the telephone group versus the telegraph group [1932+]), is that of duopolistic competition. This again has been a strong feature (or potential) in Canadian telecoms since the 1950s, with the telegraph group and telephone group engaged in strategic rivalry within certain long-distance services. Duopoly has also presented itself in the local exchange, mainly between the telcos and cablecos. A fourth potential, and one that regulatory policy has sought from the late 1970s is regulated competition, although questions remained until quite recently as to whether this would apply only to niche areas, services, or to the network core.

As indicated earlier, the big question after 1976 became whether regulated competition was going to be in the public interest or the corporate interest. A tilt toward the latter seems to have strengthened the role of the Canadian state vis-à-vis the CRTC and the provinces. Paralleling this, regulated competition truncated the public policy process and raised telephone rates. The following chapter considers the transition from competition in fringe areas of Canadian telecoms to strategic rivalry in the network core.

ENDNOTES

1. The point of this section is to illuminate how rapid rates of network modernisation corresponded with an extensive commitment of resource—financial, labour, and otherwise. Arguments about how plowing such vast quantities of capital and other resources resulted in "gold-plated" networks to the disadvantage of residential users are crucial, but are temporarily put aside to overview the intensity of the modernisation programmes implemented in the post-War period. The point of the exercise is to anticipate discussion in the next two chapters regarding competition, network investment, and so-called Information Superhighway proposals. To look ahead slightly, it will be argued that, from a historical perspective, so-called "information highway" proposals and all the regulatory changes that have ensued pale alongside the resources committed to developing the telecoms network after the war.

2. Despite this claim of rural subsidies, as well as government ownership in sparsely populated regions, disparities continued to persist with respect to the availability of telephone service in rural and urban areas. Thus, the Dominion Bureau of Statistics' (1967) report for 1965 notes that almost 70% of all telephones were located in urban centres with populations of over 25,000 each, although such centres only accounted for 58% of the population.

3. For example, an OECD study in 1988 indicated that between 50% and 60% of all long-distance and international revenues came from about 4% of all users (OECD, 1988, p. 28).

4. The origins, extent, and detail of Bell's participation in broadcasting are sketchy at best. Repeated attempts by myself, Babe (1990, p. 202, fn. 20), and others have turned up little on the subject. What follows is derived from source material that is available—as referenced—and from discussions with staff at the Bell Archives who helped me to the best of their ability.

5. The story was also printed in the *Financial Post* on August 20, 1923.

6. About $10,000 compared to between $1 million and $10 million to establish a daily newspaper in a medium to large North American city in the late 1940s (Liebling, 1961, p. 32; Smythe, 1981, p. 83).

7. A more docile approximation of broadcast facsimile, videotext, was introduced in the 1970s in many countries, most notably the United Kingdom, albeit without the print capability originally intended for broadcast facsimile (a sop to the press?).

8. Recall the discussion in Chapter 3 regarding the press' attempts to monopolise access in any given city to the telegraph by limiting membership to the CP news-wire service to the first subscriber.

9. So fearful was the Canadian Press of alternative media sources, that during the first 10 years of the CBC's service the Canadian Press news-wire service gave its service to the CBC free of charge. The "free lunch" helped stave off committed CBC action in news gathering, production, and distribution. After 1943, Canadian Press began to charge the CBC a nominal fee for its service. Similar, albeit more commercially oriented, arrangements were also made with private broadcasters, although in each case the news-wire service and newspapers supplying radio broadcasters with news were restrained by the proviso that all news had to appear in newspapers first before being broadcast by radio (Nichols, 1948, pp. 264-268).

10. In the early 1960s, the U.S.-based Famous Players (subsidiary of Paramount Pictures) and CBS either owned or had significant ownership interests in cable systems in Ontario, Quebec, and British Columbia that served 51% of all subscribers (Report of the Task Force on Broadcasting Policy, 1985, p. 629). This changed after the introduction of new federal legislation in 1968 promoting Canadian ownership of all broadcasting facilities.

11. The CRTC relaxed the predisposition against additional microwave systems in 1971 in relation to its cable television policy (CRTC, 1971a, pp. 33-5). In the decision, the agency allowed cable providers to use/share microwave systems to import distant signals, restricted to three the number of signals that could be imported, and stated that any licenses given for such purposes would be governed by the *Broadcast Act,* a move preventing competition in the supply of private and/or public telecoms services. More broadly, the policy indicated that the CRTC did not prevent cable television growth in Canada. Neither did it promote its development. Instead, as will be seen further, it permitted cable television development while actively trying to mediate its evolutionary trajectory with the broader goals of Canadian cultural policy.

12. Although Babe does not state the exact numbers of subscribers associated with an "optimally-sized" cable system, from figures elsewhere in the book it appears that the size he has in mind is probably around 10,000 households.

13. For example, see the CRTC's public announcements regarding the *Air of Death* program (issued July 9, 1970), the *Miles for Millions* (issued March 28, 1972), and another public announcement issued on February 24, 1977, regarding programming balance by licensees.

14. By 1996, just under 50% of all cable subscribers and revenues were controlled by three companies—Rogers (23.3%), Videotron (14.6%), and Shaw (10.4%) (total = 48.3%; data from CRTC sources).

15. Babe (1975) notes that despite the existence of high profits coexisting with the CRTC's policy – for example, in the order of between 17% and 20% return on net assets—commitments by cable systems to program production remained a pithy 2% to 4% of gross revenues (pp. 53-54).

16. The *head-end* is the central antennae used to receive the broadcast signals that are distributed throughout the system. *Amplifiers* are located throughout the distribution network and function to strengthen and repair signals on their way from the head-end to subscribers' homes. *Customer drops* are the wires running from the local distribution network to people's houses. The most common agreements were of the "partial system" type, an arrangement that became, in the 1970s, part of CRTC cable policy.

17. This point is crucial, indicating the extent to which Bell had become a government unto itself. Whereas DOT policy had been to grant nonexclusive licenses, Bell practice was to grant permission to only one cable system per area. As Babe (1975, pp. 120-121) relates, several small cable providers had obtained licenses from the DOT to establish cable systems in Toronto, but were thwarted in their efforts due to a $5 million deal made between Bell and five cable companies—Maclean-Hunter, Rogers, Metro Cable, York Cablevision, and Coaxial Colourview—to wire the city in mutually exclusive zones.

18. Private regulation of new media was made even sturdier by government policy in 1968 that licensed the new domestic satellite carrier, Telesat, to a consortium consisting of TCTS members, CNCP, and the federal government (McNulty, 1988, pp. 1-15; Report of the Task Force on Broadcasting, 1985, pp. 589-601). While TCTS members were eliminating the possibility of cable as an alternate, competitive local network, Telesat wiped out the potential of satellites offering cable systems with an alternative interurban carrier. Locally and nationally, the development of cable communications in Canada was hemmed in by the unlegislated regulatory authority of the telecoms industry. Thus, in a few short years, it appears that potential threats to concentration across the media industries were emasculated.

19. The Department of Communication (1971b, p. 103) also reported that the telephone companies by and large did not seek broadcasting licenses. Babe (1975, pp. 97-98) provides reference for a few other quotes from Bell regarding its lack of interest in cable and broadcasting, although they need not be repeated here.

20.   Private sector broadcasters also stated that they opposed telcos entering into broadcasting. In their presentation before the DOC-sponsored Telecommission, the Canadian Association of Broadcasters argued that telcos' deep pockets would allow them to "monopolise the private sector of broadcasting. Because the carriers would also be handling all other telecommunications, the broadcasters feel that such monopoly trends would result in a reduction of variety . . . (DOC, 1971b, p. 103). Thus, the merits of continued segregation were being argued on diversity and monopoly grounds, not on technological concerns. The substitution of the latter for the former in current debates is, as will be argued in subsequent chapters, crucial to the massive regulatory changes now taking place in Canadian media.

21.   As a percentage of revenues and of net assets.

22.   Based on the interpretation offered here, it can be seen that the "common-carrier" doctrine was becoming "strategised." Essentially, this diminished its future prospects considerably, as its support was no longer based on intrinsic merits but on its ability to function in the service of power.

23.   Also see the CRTC's *Annual Report* for 1976/1977 (CRTC, 1976/1977).

24.   It is important to note that even Crozier, Huntington, and Watunuki were forced to admit on numerous occasions throughout the book, and especially in the Canadian section, that their claims and premises were rejected by many of those attending its meetings. Nonetheless, the three chiefs of the Trilateral Commission Report insisted that the biggest threat to democracy was, oddly enough, democracy. Either the authors were too highly steeped in the narrative of tragedy found in the literature of "high culture," or they simply confused democracy with leadership (e.g., just another means of picking leaders), who thereafter had free reign to lord over the populace until the next time the people exercised their democratic right to vote.

25.   Such proposals to concentrate state power were not unique to Canada. In the United States, Eugene Rostow headed up the President's Task Force on Communications Policy (1968), and proposed "a new centralised government agency . . . to advise the President and to coordinate activities of strategic military and economic importance in telecommunications" (cited in Streeter, 1987, p. 185). Although the proposed Office of Telecommunications Policy never saw the light of day, a close cousin was born shortly thereafter with the National Telecommunications and Information Agency, as part of the U.S. Department of Commerce.

26.   In fact, Meisel is singled out by the report's authors, among 12 others, for the special contribution he made to the analysis and conclusions found in the final report (Crozier, Huntington, & Watanuki, 1975, introductory note, unnumbered).

27.   Adjusting for inflation, the real term value today of the proposal would be about $9.63 billion—a figure just over the amount proposed for the Beacon Plan, but spread only over 5 years, not 10. The calculations are based on a conservative estimate of 3% annual inflation over the 16-year period between the announcement of the 1978 Bell Construction Programme and the 1994 Beacon announcement.

6 POWER SHIFT?
A POLITICAL ECONOMY OF THE "NEW" TELECOMS IN CANADA

Choice manifests itself in society in small increments and moment-to-
moment decisions as well as in loud dramatic struggles; and he who
does not see choice in the development of the machine merely
betrays his incapacity to observe cumulative effects until they are
bunched together so closely that they seem completely external and
impersonal. No matter how completely technics relies upon the
objective procedures of the sciences . . . it exists as an element of
human culture. (Mumford, 1934/1963, p. 6)

To those living in North American societies the slow, barely perceptible
changes that Mumford refers to were quite typical for much of the history
of electronic media. In recent years, however, the dull calm surrounding
electronic media systems whose "big questions" were all but removed
from the social and political agenda after the 1930s have burst back onto
the scene. According to information age prophets, basic issues about
media, politics, and society are once again up for grabs. Within the realm
of public culture, the threshold between "old" and "new" media societies
was symbolically crossed during the mid-1980s, when coverage of new
media technology by national news magazines such as *Macleans*, *Newsweek*,
and *Time* peaked, and the passage toward an information-intensive future
lubricated with abundant references to the magical, spiritual, even
religious, qualities of new media machines (Stahl, 1995, p. 243). The
quasi-religious-like aura built around information technology was also
accompanied by frequent pronouncements from policy circles, analysts,
industry, and academia regarding the imminent potential for a renewed
democratic ethos forged on the link between innovations in
communication technology and the profusion of information.
Information abundance now complements the historical link between

communication and democracy founded on arguments from theology, natural rights, utilitarian ethics, and pragmatic concerns with truth (Keane, 1991).

Whereas the state in democratic theory has always straddled competing demands to, on the one hand, protect the supremacy of property rights versus, on the other, obligations to promote the conditions supportive of equality, liberty, and general well-being (Keane, 1991, pp. 165-170), many see new communication media negating dualistic thinking by offering ubiquitous networks of communication, competitive markets, and withdrawal of government from public life. According to such commentators, the increased scope of private transactions, the reduced range of state intervention in public life, and enhanced networks of communication among people, are bringing about societies fundamentally different from today. Crucial to this view of change are communication infrastructures that enhance the flow of information within society and among its major constituents.

Invoking the privileged relationship between communication and democracy and the radical language of social critique and political movements of the 1960s, the advertising messages, images, and writing of popular culture suggest that emerging technologies will democratise society by dispersing power from its traditional institutional manifestations. Representative of such modes of thinking in popular culture are advertisements in the computer magazine *Wired*, that promise technologies that deliver "Power to the People." Replete with peace symbols, references to major events in the emergence of a radical culture of the 1960s and frustrated hippies unable to translate their visions of the Good Life into reality, the language of critique is now being pressed into service to promote the diffusion of technology and secure technologically determined visions of the future (see Figure 6.1). According to popular culture discourses, information societies will be spiritually meaningful places in which to live, effortlessly co-mingling religiosity, magic, peace, and democracy.

Such visions are not confined to the images of popular culture. In the more staid context of academia similar visions abound. Canadian communication and legal scholars Richard Schultz and Hudson Janisch suggest that authority is being transferred away from politicised regulatory arenas and concentrated monopolies as "technological change increasingly offers the . . . possibility that all markets will be competitive in the not-too-distant future" (1993, p. 7). Reflecting on the new *Telecommunications Act* and the long-distance competition decision (CRTC 92-12), they claim that these decisions will produce

a massive power shift in . . . telecommunications . . . from a hierarchical, centralized, carrier-driven system . . . [towards] freedom

Figure 6.1. Gateway 2000 ad. © 1994 Gateway 2000, Inc.
Reprinted with permission

of user choice . . . [that] elevates the user from telecommunications subject to equal partner with carriers and other service providers. Freedom to compete requires no less massive power shift in the regulatory system. (Schultz & Janisch, 1993, p. 7)

Similarly, the former Director of Investigation and Research under the *Competition Act,* and now director of the recently privatised

Telus Corp. in Alberta, George Addy, states, "[T]echnology is clearly the agent of change in global telecommunications markets. The . . . structural and economic assumptions" of telecoms regulation "are rapidly being undermined by technological change—not only in Canada, but around the world" (1994, p. 2). To facilitate these potentials, regulation must change from "the regulation of individual rates and services" to ensuring that competition works (p. 3).

I agree that a fundamental shift in communication is underway. However, given the analysis developed in this book, I find it impossible to subscribe to the imputed origins of change in telecoms. Instead of looking for causal relationships between technology and social change, we need to ask how social forces shape the innovation, architecture, and uses of new technology. The analysis in this book is intended to demonstrate that regulatory and industry structures are not inscribed in technological infrastructures. They are born of strategic rivalry, social imperatives, competing views of communication and society, and the historical context from which they emerge. This way of seeing is not based on a negative theory of technology, but offers a way of thinking about how technological potentials are shaped by sociological realities. As Schiller (1986) notes,

> Viewed exclusively as a technological capability, it is hardly unrealistic to regard the present situation as one of . . . unprecedented abundance and richness of information. It seems all the more shocking therefore, to acknowledge at the same time, the deepening division of the society into informationally-privileged and informationally-impoverished sectors. What accounts for this? (p. 102)

From a political economy of communication perspective, information technologies are embedded in the historical process of extending commercial relations to greater areas of social life. This is the purpose of new technologies, not the result. For instance, Smythe (1981) showed how mass media recast leisure time and domestic space in its quest for the audience commodity, Garnham (1990) similarly points to the extension of commercial relations to public spheres of communication, and Schiller (1986) writes of pressures to commercialise public-domain, government information.

This commodification of time, space, and communication also affects the image of the state found in democratic theory, in favour of an instrumental role in the formation of national industrial policy. As Addy candidly acknowledged in the earlier quote, regulation does not disappear but changes focus; at one time to stress certain aims and now to ensure that competition works. Although the coupling of state and economic interests may promote economic accumulation and reduce uncertainty in a complex international economy, it does so at the cost of democratic politics, communication, and citizenship. Rather than politics being about competing conceptions of the "good life," efforts are directed to legitimating the state/economy relationship with promises about global competitiveness and higher levels of material comfort for the population at large. Citizenship is defined by choice in consumption, economic progress, and periodic post-hoc ratification of government policies through the vote. Finally, democracy as industrial policy changes society by transferring the tensions of the market to the political sphere, as particular capitalists battle for control of the state and policy agenda (Habermas, 1975).

This chapter argues that the driving forces of technological and social change in Canada are linked to the embedding of telecoms and network services into global trading regimes, privatisation, the commoditisation of information, industry concentration, commercialisation of the policy sphere, and consolidation of the strong state. I marshal evidence to show that these developments extend control along the three dominant axes of power within Canadian telecoms: carriers, the federal government, and major user groups. Recent developments indicate a shift from regulation as social policy to regulation as industrial policy. Regulatory policy as industrial strategy promotes the economic value of telecoms firms and large users of information services. Reconciling the sometimes contradictory interests of these groups is the objective of contemporary telecoms policy, as concerns with democratic communication wane.

REGULATORY LIBERALISATION IN CANADIAN TELECOMS

As noted in the previous chapter, regulatory liberalization originated in the late 1970s with the transfer of regulatory authority from the CTC to the CRTC. At the time, the CRTC undertook a program of regulatory liberalisation that applied as much to the politics of telecoms as it did to the economics of telecoms. Just as monopolistic control over markets was to be challenged, so, too, were the cloistered backrooms of telecoms politics to be opened to citizens. Regulation, it appeared, was to be used to balance competing claims, with at least a strong eye cocked toward realising the public interest. Almost immediately after assuming its new mandate, the CRTC began to chip away at the telephone companies' monopoly over almost all areas of telecoms. As indicated in the last chapter, decisions in 1979 and 1982 allowed CNCP to interconnect with the federally regulated telcos to provide competitive data services and for the complete liberalisation of cpe. Crucially, the CRTC believed a competitive telecoms policy could still be in the public interest. This covenant soon attenuated, however, probably because of insistent government intervention and the appointments of those more ideologically in-tune with the government's telecoms policy thinking, such as John Meisel in 1980.

The decisions revealed that the CRTC considered the natural monopoly argument as circumspect and that telecoms companies themselves were willing to allow competition on the gamble that they could force through rate increases and use liberalisation at home as a quid pro quo for access to markets abroad. The connection to foreign markets was said to turn on the reciprocal treatment that would be bestowed on Canadian firms in markets that were home to providers given access to Canadian markets—a point confirmed by the heavy presence of foreign equipment and service providers in both decisions. Thus, the decisions introduced the principle that domestic policy would now be, at least partially, determined in relation to questions of global competitiveness and as a weapon in international trade policy. The decision also signaled government's support for the introduction of competition because CNCP was a joint venture between the private and public sector. Finally, competition in federally regulated regions aligned Ottawa and the private sector in a pursuit of liberalised telecoms policies across the country. This was an extraordinary development given that the federal regulator had been granted jurisdictional authority over all telecoms systems almost 80 years earlier but had refused to exercise this option given its sensitivity to provincial interests.

Why was the federal government at this particular point in history suddenly emboldened to do what it had previously avoided? This question will be taken up next. First, however, a list of key decisions that have substantially altered the Canadian telecoms industry, the regulatory system, and the types of public policy goals that can be pursued is introduced.

1976   CRTC authority broadened, allowing it to regulate telecoms in addition to broadcasting (Canadian Radio-television and Telecommunications Act, 1976).

1979   Private line interconnect allowed for competitive data services (CRTC 79-11).

1982   Complete liberalisation of customer provided equipment (82-14).

1984   The CRTC adopts U.S. definitions of basic and enhanced services that map out where the natural monopoly concept is to be maintained and where competition will be allowed, that is, natural monopoly in public local and long-distance voice services and competition in enhanced services (84-18). CNCP challenges AGT to provide interconnection for competitive data services, beginning the constitutional challenge to provincial authority in telecoms.

1985   Concept of competition in public long distance is accepted by the CRTC but not implemented because of CNCP's inability to maintain the principle of universal service. Bell proposes rate restructuring. Reselling and private line access for the purpose of providing enhanced services is approved (85-19).

1986   A Federal Provincial Task Force considers long-distance competition.

1987   Reselling basic carriage capacity granted for enhanced services (87-1). CRTC exempts certain carriers and services from filing rate tariffs (87-12). Policy is challenged by the TWU in the courts and overturned. The reseller Call-Net offers basic services in violation of CRTC policy. Cabinet and DOC help Call-Net achieve compliance with CRTC policy.

1988   Another task force considers implications of long-distance competition.

1989   Supreme Court confirms federal authority in telecoms but exempts provincial, publicly owned telecoms agencies.

1990   CRTC allows private line sharing and resale for public local and long-distance services (90-3). AGT is privatised.

1991   The Federal government and Manitoba sign a memorandum of understanding (MOU) transferring regulatory authority to the CRTC.

1992   CRTC allows facilities-based, long-distance competition (92-12). The Federal government introduces the *Telecommunications Act* (Bill C-62), seeking a fully liberalised telecoms regulatory environment and federal authority over the remaining provincial and municipal telecoms authorities. The Bill does not receive passage. CRTC calls inquiry into development of new regulatory methods (92-78).

1993   *Telecommunications Act* becomes law. The DOC is shifted to Industry Canada.

1994   Canada becomes signatory to World Trade Organisation (WTO) agreement on telecoms services.

1994   CRTC releases the *Review of Regulatory Framework* (Dec. 94-19) decision, outlining a new approach to regulating telecoms, interconnection, and utility services, as well as its intention to introduce price cap regulation.

1995   CRTC begins *Implementation of Regulatory Framework* (Dec. 95-21) based on results of the regulatory review carried out the previous year.

1995   CRTC publishes *Competition and Culture on Canada's Information Highway*

1996   Federal Government publishes policy document, *Building the Information Society: Moving Canada into the 21st Century*, based on the CRTC's *Competition and Culture* statement and the Information Highway Advisory Council's findings.

1996   Minister of Communications introduces Convergence Policy Statement outlining the conditions under which full-scale (re)convergence between telecoms, broadcasting, and cable can occur.

The result of these regulatory changes in Canada is one of the most "liberalised" telecoms regulatory regimes in the world. Table 6.1 illustrates this point in comparison to the United States, Germany, the United Kingdom, and France.

CANADIAN TELECOMS IN GLOBAL CONTEXT

Three factors drive regulatory liberalisation in Canada: linkages between domestic communication law and international trade agreements, the relationship of telecoms to economic development strategies, and a desire for Integrated Broadband Networks (IBNs). Crossing these themes is an urge, especially in light of the long-term decline in economic growth in Canada, the United States, and elsewhere, to use regulatory liberalisation as a means to realise the economic value of telecoms and information. As representatives of the former DOC stated, "the economic infrastructure provided by telecoms services and networks is essential to local, regional, and national economic growth and international competitiveness" (Racine, Mozes, & Kennedy, 1992, p. 1).

During the 1980s, telecoms policy became tightly tied to efforts to liberalise financial trading, investment, and energy regulations. Given the importance of telecoms to international securities trading, and that Canada has the world's fourth largest securities market, relaxed financial trading and investment rules during the 1980s intensified pressure to adapt the telecoms system to the needs of the transnational finance community (Smith, 1991, p. 41). At the beginning of the decade, over US$650 billion in electronic funds flowed through global telecoms networks, meshing together the world's regional financial hubs—Frankfurt, Japan, London, New York, Paris, Shanghai, Singapore, and Toronto—into a web of global speculation (Frieden, 1991, p. 428). By 1995, the sum surpassed US$1 trillion per day. Whereas global finance used to facilitate trade in things (e.g., 1960s ratio: 10% finance to 90% trade in things), by the early 1990s the ratio of trade to finance had reversed (Magdoff, 1992, p. 56). As Cox (1992) notes,

> Global finance has achieved a virtually unregulated and electronically connected 24-hour-a-day network. The collective decision making of global finance is centred in world cities rather than states . . . and extends by computer terminals to the rest of the world. (p. 30)

The impact of these changes has rippled across the fabric of a highly informatised global capitalism. Impacts are observable in the recomposition of journalists' efforts away from political and general news

Table 6.1. Liberalisation Indicators for Select OECD Countries.

Country	Canada	France	Germany	U.K.	U.S.
VANS/Enhanced Services[a]	3	3	3	3	3
>1 Int'l Carrier	1	1	1	2	3
Foreign Ownership[b]	2	2	2	3	3
Local Exchange Competition	2	1.5	1	2	2
L. D. Competition	2.5	2	2	2.5	3
CPE	4	4	4	4	4
PTO Managerial Independence[c]	4	3	3	4	4
Separate Regulator[d]	2	2	2	2	3
Private/Public Interconnect	4	2	2	3	4
Market Pricing[e]	2	2	2	3	3.5
Total	26.5	22.5	22	28.5	32.5
Lines/100 People	57.5	49.8	47.4	44.2	45.3
Basket of Bus. Services ($US)(1990)[f]	1,023	896.4	1062.6	896	1075
Basket of Res. Services ($US) (1990)	287.3	307.5	358.4	343.9	434.9
Network Investment	23% ▼ (1995)	24.6% ▼	51.8% ▲	14.4% ▼	15% ▼
(3 to 5 year trend prior to 1992 ▲▼)	34.4% (1989/91)	27.6%	41.8%	19%	18.6%
+/- Labour	-33%	+18%	+9%	-29.1%	-25%

Source: OECD. (1995a, 1995b). Other sources cited elsewhere in this book on each of the measures included in Table 6.1.

[a]*Unless otherwise noted, scores are 1 = legal monopoly; 2 = competition legal/contestible markets/weal competition/duopoly; 3 = oligopolistic/ imperfect market; 4 = perfect/near perfect competition.* [b]*1 = no foreign ownership; 2 = limited to noncontrolling amount; 3 = residual limits; 4 = open.* [c]*1 = government department; 2 = public, not state run; 3 = corporatised; 4 = private.* [d]*1 = ministerial dept.; 2 = semi-autonomous, but regular government interference; 3 = autonomous; 4 = no telecoms-specific regulator reliance on general legislative tools.* [e]*1 = tariffs required for all rates and rate of return regulation; 2 = mixed tariffs, price caps, and forbearance; 3 = price caps; 4 = prices set entirely by market.* [f]*Sources for rows below also include: OECD (1990) and Statistics Canada (1972, 1995a).*

toward business and financial news reporting, to a host of global financial news services such as AP/Dow Jones, Bisnews, Bloombergs, CNN, and Reuters Financial Television, among others.[1] Global trade regimes that embrace telecoms and computer-generated services for the first time are cut from the same cloth. It is in this context that we need to situate Canada's assent to the 1987 Canada-U.S. Free Trade Agreement (CUFTA), the 1992 North American Free Trade Agreements (NAFTA) (1992) and the recent World Trade Organisation (WTO) (1993/94) pact covering telecoms and computer-generated information services, among other matters.

Although regulatory liberalisation predates free trade, there are basic links between changes in Canadian communication law and the CUFTA, NAFTA, WTO trilogy. These agreements harmonise communication and investment policies by diminishing constraints on transborder data flows, restricting the scope of public sector activity, and limiting the range of telecoms services that can be publicly regulated (Canada, 1987, 1992; Mosco, 1990b). Moreover, the subsequent General Agreement on Trade in Services (GATS) organised under the auspices of the new World Trade Organisation contains a *Annex on Telecommunications* that is a carbon copy of the NAFTA's chapter 13, albeit with a few minor changes in syntax and the addition of two additional clauses dealing with developing countries and international organisations such as the ITU. Although many realised that the earlier CUFTA and NAFTA agreements would provide a model for the WTO, few predicted that NAFTA would be *the* model subsequently adopted by the WTO negotiators (Canada, 1992; Trade Negotiation Committee, 1993).

The liberalisation of telecoms across North America has thus been connected to regulatory change in Canada and served as a model for the organisation of telecoms worldwide. In addition to the CRTC's computer data services decision in 1979 that strengthened the focus of Canadian telecoms policy on global competitiveness, several other events prefigured the march toward free trade in telecoms unleashed in 1987 by the CUFTA. Crucial was the breakup of AT&T and provisions in the Modified Final Judgement (MFJ) that prevented the Regional Bell Operating Companies (RBOCs) from engaging in equipment manufacturing. One result was vast new opportunities for Northern Telecom—Bell Canada Enterprises' (BCE) manufacturing arm—to supply equipment to the U.S. telecoms industry. The company's sales of equipment in the United States rose from US$108 million in 1981 to over US$4 billion in 1991 (BCE, 1991; Melody, 1994; US Subcommittee on Communications of the Committee of Commerce, Science and Transportation, 1988, pp. 77-78). By 1991, Northern Telecom operated in Canada, the United States, the United Kingdom, France, Malaysia, Singapore, Brazil, and Turkey, among several other countries. The strong transnational profile of the company placed it firmly among the biggest five or six global telecoms equipment manufacturers (Mansell, 1993).

Northern Telecom's global expansion was complemented by similar moves by BCE, MTS, AGT, and in satellite communication, by the DOC and Telesat. BCE acquired interests in New Zealand's Clear Communications and in the largest cable provider in the United Kingdom, Videotron, through which it is connected into a dense web of ties with several of the U.S. Regional Bell Operating Companies (RBOCs), the second-largest U.K. telecoms provider, Cable and Wireless, and finally back to Quebec-based Videon, the second largest cable provider in Canada (BCE, 1991). Increasing poverty and the debt crisis in developing countries, and the emasculation of the public sector throughout the world, also beckoned Canadian telecoms providers. Despite failing to obtain Mexico's telecoms provider (TelMex), BCE's efforts revealed a stronger global focus, a factor that would underpin efforts in Canada to transform the regulatory environment (Benitez, 1992, p. 8; Department of External Affairs, 1992, p. 6).

Support for the "globalisation" of domestic telecoms policy was widely diffused throughout the power centres of Canada. In 1988, the head of Anglo-Canadian Telephones (BCTel and QuebecTel), Theodore Brophy, chaired the U.S. delegation to the ITU's Radio Conference and World Telecommunications Conference, at which the United States, with the help of Canada, Australia, Japan and the United Kingdom, insistently pushed for telecoms liberalisation—a point returned to later. Also, despite popular opposition, editorial opinion in leading newspapers such as *Toronto Globe & Mail* leaned in on the side of free trade, as did the Canadian Business Telecommunications Alliance (CBTA), the Information Technology Association of Canada (ITAC), and the Computer and Telecommunications Alliance. Several commissioned reports urged government to "proceed with deregulation, to unleash . . . companies to compete both at home and abroad . . . [and] to press international regulatory bodies, such as the ITU . . . to deregulate . . . markets to the maximum . . ." (Science Council of Canada, 1991, p. 24).

A new conception of the state was also in the making. Unlike the focus of democratic theories on the links between people and government formed by communicative interaction, political legitimacy, and guaranteed rights of citizenship (e.g., voting, assembly, and so on), the role of the "new State" became, as Robert Cox (1992) argues, "adjusting national economic . . . policies to the perceived exigencies of the global political economy. The state became a transmission belt from the global to the national economy. (pp. 30-31).

In this "new" global political economy, trade regimes structure and formalise the rules of trade and unite decision makers around a "shared view of the world," as well as deepen information flows about particular policy practices and issues of importance. Moreover, consistent with the Trilateral Commission reports of the late 1970s, the unfolding global trade regime insulates transnational economic transactions and new political institutions from public interference (Gill, 1992, p. 165). As Galtung (1994) recently noted, democratic theories presuppose communicative relations and political interaction between the state and civil society, although there are no formal channels of political and communicative interaction available for people within a context of supranational, state-led organisations. Again, Cox (1992) is instructive, stating that the emerging global political economy seeks to ensure that "key aspects of economic management are . . . shielded from politics, that is to say, from popular pressures" (p. 32). He and Gill call this "limited democracy."

Origins of CUFTA/NAFTA/GATS Basic/Enhanced Services Distinctions

This analysis fits well with contemporary changes in telecoms policy and regulatory liberalisation that remove certain issues and new media technologies from the public policy agenda. Of course, there have always been attempts to remove telecoms policy issues from the political agenda, as the last chapter showed with respect to collusive agreements dividing electronic media in Canada (and the United States) in the 1920s, the telephone companies' usurpation of cable policy in the 1960s and 1970s, and again at the end of that decade as the strong state began stifling an overzealous CRTC from pursuing its remit. Perhaps it is not surprising, then, that the CRTC's (1976b) early ambitions to ensure that new media were implemented in a socially responsive manner gave way, in 1984, to distinctions between basic and enhanced services—a framework for new online content services that had developed over the preceding decade in the United States.[2]

The *Enhanced Services* (84-18) decision defined basic services as limited "to the offering of transmission capacity for the movement of information, while an enhanced service is an offering utilising the telecommunications network which is more than a basic service" (CRTC, 1984, p. 6). As a result, new content services such as data retrieval, computer networking, voice mail, and so on, were placed beyond the reach of public service obligations. Universal services were capped at local and long-distance voice service, and new services deemed enhanced. This refusal to expand conventional basic and universal service concepts was opposed by labour unions and various public interest groups who proposed competition in enhanced services and enlarging the array of content services delivered on a "public service" basis (CRTC, 1984, p. 25).

Although the Commission refused to expand the nascent "electronic public sphere" in favour of deepening new information markets, it also showed that competition had not yet become the end-all and be-all of regulatory policy. This was evident in two respects.

First, although the decision allowed the federally regulated members of Stentor to offer enhanced services, they could not offer services requiring editorial intervention (CRTC, 1984, p. 35). As Wilson (1993) states, most enhanced information service providers would be unregulated, but distinctions between carriage and content were preserved. The PTOs could offer database "access" and "gateway" services but could not exercise editorial control over content services (p. 207). In the scheme of things, telephone companies were not yet electronic publishers, a factor that, at least in theory, bode well for the potential of distributed, small- scale electronic publishers. The view of computer communications implied by the decision reflected experiments then taking place among the PTOs and government with the early e-mail system, Envoy, as well as the idea that computer services would evolve mainly as computer utilities, a view reflected in the Telidon projects. It did not anticipate the "distributed intelligence" model of computer networking now associated with the Internet, and thus only weakly foresaw the types of regulatory questions posed by, for example, the Internet, with respect to access regulation, telco/Internet Service Provider (ISP) relations, universal service, Canadian content, pornography, and so on.

However, the decision did reveal the contours of a consensus amid the CRTC, the DOC, the telcos, and electronic content providers that competition would be in services, not facilities (CRTC, 1984, pp. 15-22). This partially vindicated the path embarked on by the prairie provinces several years earlier (yet, not with respect to cable television). Reflecting the budding consensus, in 1987 the DOC announced a new policy that it had imported from Japan. The policy envisioned two types of service providers; Type I would be network providers, and monopolistic in nature. Such licenses would be handed out begrudgingly, continuing the long-standing practice among federal telecoms licensing authorities. Type II licenses applied to service provision and would be dispensed more liberally and competition fostered (Communications Canada, 1987).

The changes in Canada mirrored those in the United States, as well as events taking place in Europe, Japan, and elsewhere. Each region, however, contained specific qualities. Consistent with historical trends in telecoms policy, the Canadian model lay somewhere between those of Europe, the United States, and now Japan. In the United States, the MFJ prevented the RBOCs from engaging in all content services, including "gateway services," although the RBOCs resisted the restrictions even before the ink on the consent decree dried. Within three years, they filed

over 160 petitions with the courts seeking to overturn these restrictions
(US Senate Subcommittee on Commerce, Science and Transportation,
1991, p. 6). Some success was obtained in 1988 when Judge Greene, the
person responsible for overseeing compliance with the MFJ, allowed the
RBOCs to offer database "access" and "gateway" services but not to
generate their own information services. Arguing that the companies'
financial clout and historical record made it probable that they would
cross-subsidise content services and use anticompetitive practices
detrimental to the nascent electronic online services and the possibility of
media freedoms in "electronic space," Judge Greene prevented them from
becoming "electronic publishers" (US v. Western Electric, 1988, p. 1).

The battle for control of electronic public space was on. The
continuation of these restrictions collided head-on with the position
adopted by the Bush Administration, the FCC, NTIA, Department of
Justice, and, of course, the RBOCs (US, 1990, pp. 37-43; "White House's
Blue", 1991, p. 27). The redubitable Judge Bork (infamous Reagan
nomination for the Supreme Court) of the Court of Appeals "reversed
and remanded" the decision. Bork instructed Greene to ignore history
and irrelevant considerations such as "the impact of removing the
restrictions on various public policies, the welfare of local ratepayers,
innovation . . ., universal telephone service, first amendment values," and
so on (US v. Western Electric, et. al, 1990, pp. 293-99). With nothing left
to consider, Greene admitted the RBOCs into electronic information
services in 1991, but complained bitterly about being "a `rubber stamp' for
the Department of Justice" (US v. Western Electric et. al., 1991, p. 309).

As a consequence of the decision, the U.S. position had become
somewhat similar to that prevailing in Europe: No restrictions impeded
the dominant PTOs from participating in burgeoning enhanced services
markets. In Europe, national and European-wide telecoms policies
distinguished between reserved and nonreserved services. The
distinctions were prompted mainly in response to attempts throughout
the 1980s by the United States to forcefully introduce the basic/enhanced
distinctions into Europe through trade initiatives, the "globalisation" of
the FCC's regulatory remit, and bilateral agreements between the United
States and several other countries, including Germany, the United
Kingdom, and a few others between 1984 and 1988 (FCC, 1988, pp. 993-
996; OECD, 1988, pp. 25-44; US, 1988, pp. 24-55). Rather than passively
adopting the basic/enhanced method, however, the European
Commission initiated a series of decisions between 1987 and 1991, most
notably the 1987 *Green Paper*, that adopted distinctions between monopoly
telecoms services (reserved) and competitive services (nonreserved)
(Commission of the European Communities, 1987).

As in the United States after 1990, European distinctions between
reserved and nonreserved services did not preclude traditional PTOs

from any area of telecoms services, nor did they constrain editorial intervention into electronic services. As such, the European and U.S. contexts were distinctly different from the Canadian position. The European policy framework was different from the U.S. model and closer to that prevailing in Canada, however, by the fact that it drew a line around those services reserved exclusively for national PTOs and those that were open to competition. In 1990 the EC issued a directive that drew the lines even more starkly, as it tightly circumscribed monopoly services to public local and long-distance voice services (Commission of the European Communities, 1990). All other areas were to be contestible, except the infrastructure.

Although telecoms policies in Europe, Canada, and the United States appeared to be similar, there was an enormous factor distinguishing events in Europe: national telecoms policies could require even nonreserved services to be delivered in accordance with a limited range of public policy objectives. European countries could insist that enhanced services be made universally available, that such services conform to data protection and privacy policies,[3] and other policies that could be demonstrated to be in the public interest, narrowly tailored and not unnecessarily conflicting with competition policy (Bauer & Steinfield, 1994, pp. 55-65; Commission of the European Communities, 1990). Leading edge initiatives by the CRTC over a decade earlier that struggled to reconcile competition with public service objectives in communication policy (not industrial/competition policy)—only to be squashed by Ottawa's intrusive hand—were now being implemented in Europe.

New Thinking About Network Services or Protecting Old Monopolies?

Inspiration for attempts to reconcile new potentials in telecoms and content services with the history of monopoly and the prospects of competition, however, probably did not come to Europe by way of Canada but from the experience of France and Germany with telecoms reform beginning in the 1970s. With Britain on the sidelines of Europe, France and Germany had a strong hand in shaping the evolution of CEC initiatives.

The German experience is particularly interesting given the Constitutional status of telecoms in the country. According to the German Constitution, the federal government has responsibility for "organising telecommunications, ensuring that this organisation is maintained and supplying and performing the telecommunications services *as one of the necessities of life*" (cited in OECD, 1988, p. 38; emphasis added). This is generally accepted as meaning that government has a powerful mandate to ensure universal service throughout the country and to provide citizens with access to services commensurate with technological potentials. At least Deutsche Telecom has interpreted its mandate in this regard, with the blessing of citizens, labour unions, and communication ministers (at least until the conservative Kohl government began to enforce changes after its election in 1986). Up to that point, though, Deutsche Telecom began to unroll a universal Integrated Services Digital Network (ISDN) that it used as a platform for a wide range of new content services including videotext, data packet switching, e-mail, voice mail, and cable television (OECD, 1988, p. 44; 1991, p. 51). Unlike similar developments in Saskatchewan and Manitoba that had taken place a decade earlier, Deutsche Bundepost extended its monopoly to include content services. However, CEC initiatives and regulatory changes at home in 1989 forced it to restructure tariffs and allow competition in enhanced services, private lines, and cpe (Duch, 1991, p. 159). Nonetheless, new services were to remain consistent with the Constitutional obligation regarding the need to equitably provide service to all citizens and at a level commensurate with the state of technology (Goodhart, 1988, p. x).

Perhaps the strongest illustration of what it means to develop the new telecoms in line with an expanded public service concept is provided by France. Over a 20-year period, France went from being the laughing stock of European telecoms and an example of the evils of government-owned telephones—a dubious honour held from the turn of the century (Holcombe, 1911)—to having one of the best telecoms systems in the world. Levels of universal service (97%) are among the highest in the world and greater than in the United States (94%) and the United Kingdom (88%). This public service mandate has been achieved while also providing for the universal provision of a wide range of telecoms network-based services (OECD, 1990, p. 95; 1995, p. 29).

Inklings of big changes afoot in French telecoms first appeared between 1966-1970, when the Director General of Telephones' (DGT) budget was substantially enriched. Between 1976 and 1980, yearly appropriations were 10 times as great as they had been in the previous five years. Such patterns continued throughout the 1980s (Duch, 1991, p. 173). The second prong in the project to revitalise telecoms in the country was unleashed with the publication of Nora and Minc's (1978) famous *The Computerisation of Society*. Although French intellectuals and communication ministers quickly turned the terminology into a call to democratise computers (rather than to "computerise society"), the outlines of the project were clear (Mattelart & Stourdze, 1985, p. 41). Mind-numbing oppositions between state and market, concentration and competition, and the global and the local were studiously avoided in a rigorous effort to reconcile basic tensions posed by new communication technologies, content services, and all that attends the "information age."

Money was not only poured into research and network modernisation, but policies implemented to decentralise and invigorate local economies, politics, and culture, while at the same time fostering a universal digital telecoms network that served a broad cross-section of public and business needs. "Synergies between telecommunications and information processing" (Voge, 1986, p. 111) were promoted, while at the same time a commitment was made to lessening the hegemony of Paris and the global political economy over the "local social fabric" (Mattelart & Stourdze, 1985, p. 119).

Two aspects of the project were crucial to the overall program: the Audio Visual Law and Plan Cable, on the one hand, and the Minitel/Teletel plan, on the other. As in Manitoba and Saskatchewan, France Telecom would "build, own and operate" a fibre optic, interactive broadband network, while local authorities and private business would cooperate to develop information services, data banks, interactive services, and cable television. Paris would underwrite the cost of network development and contribute 2 billion francs to support content production, whereas local governments were required to provide 1-1/2 billion francs (OECD, 1988, pp. 16-17; Voge, 1986, pp. 115-125). This part of the project, however, met with little success, as local governments did not rise to the task, private capital refused to combine at the local level to develop content services, and as the newly elected conservative Chirac government in 1986 sanctioned private cable systems without any commitments to the earlier political and cultural goals of the Plan Cable (Duch, 1991, p. 198).

More successful and politically durable, however, was the Minitel/Teletel project. Citizens were given, free of charge, Minitel terminals through which they could access "over 8000 information services, ranging from electronic mail, banking and other financial services, travel reservations, . . . property and stock market information, access to manifold data banks and a host of other on-line services. In addition, numerous local authorities and public agencies established their own services" (Humphreys, 1990, p. 219). The program was taken up rapidly. In 1983, citizens requested over 90,000 of the Minitel terminals. By 1990, there were over 6 million terminals being used, on average, about 15 hours per year (Humphreys, 1990, p. 219; Duch, 1991, pp. 180-181). Public use of Minitel/Teletel services accounted for more than half of all use of the new digital network, a vast difference to the more commercially skewed profile of digital communications in other countries. Not only were individuals "being digital," to steal American media guru Nicholas Negroponte's (1995) terminology, so, too, was the public culture at large embracing digital communications in a big way.

Two problems, however, plagued the Minitel. The first was that public use was so intense that it overburdened the network, a feature now common in North America, especially around "high-tech parks" and universities as use of the Internet spreads. Essentially, universal public access and government social policies outstripped technical capacity and commercial criteria. Rather than accommodating this higher than expected usage, however, the government imposed stricter commercial operating procedures on use of the network to limit systems overload. Systems overload, then, was resolved by drawing on the regulatory functions of the market, not the state which, as the *Crisis of Democracy* pundits had noted, tended to proliferate excess participation and demands. The French state did not face a crisis of legitimacy, though, because the whole project was directed precisely at creating more information-intensive markets. Tensions between the needs of people, technological potential, and economic constraints did not vanish, either (nor could they be expected to). However, rather than following the proscriptions of free market ideologues or crisis theorists, problems raised by the informatisation of public life were dealt with through relatively transparent interactions between state, capital, and civil society.

A second problem was that the Minitel terminal was rather "dumb," as most of the intelligence resided in the network or in remote computers. Although this facilitated cheap access to the system and served as the basis for a "mass market" for the new system, it also put limits on the uses to which the technology could be put. From a political and cultural perspective, dumb Minitel terminals constrained people's capacity as media producers, and thus the potential contribution of the system to "media freedom." The more common critique, however, is that the system hindered development of enhanced services for business (Humphreys, 1990, pp. 220-221). Some recommended moving away from the "public technology" model of the system to greater use of proprietorial protocols and private supply of computer terminals to enhance the quality of business services available over the network (Duch, 1991). Each of these criticisms reveals that there are fundamental contradictions between public and commercial imperatives in "electronic space" yet to be reconciled and which, in fact, may be insoluble. However, the French pursued a policy of reconciliation further than anyone else and have been quite successful from a balanced consideration of public and commercial criteria.

Bell Canada tried to implement a scaled-down version of the French Mintel/Teletel project in Ontario and Quebec between 1988 and 1993 but without much success. Although the service provided a gateway to some 650 enhanced service providers, and claimed 27,087 users at one point (although some claimed the number of active users was only about half that), it never really got off the ground (Wilson, 1993, pp. 198-200). Although it has been suggested that part of the problem lay in the absence of a "mass market" anchor such as free terminals, and that Bell failed to properly promote the service, the problems were more deeply political, economic, and cultural than that.

A major source of the problem likely lay in the fact that there was no authority with as clear cut a mandate as the French DGT to implement the service; not Bell, because of the regulatory constraints imposed by the Enhanced Services decision (and CUFTA, as discussed next), nor the CRTC. In the first instance, as indicated earlier, the universality of enhanced services envisioned by the Minitel/Teletel project was explicitly abandoned in the enhanced services decision. As has also been seen, the CRTC has consistently been at logger-heads with the federal government, the provinces, and sometimes the DOC. Moreover, CRTC attempts to develop a regulatory culture that dealt sensitively with contradictions between competition and commerce, on the one hand, and communication, culture, and citizenship, on the other, were scuppered by the intrusive hand of the strong state. More generally, the direction of political culture in Canada was at odds with the localising objectives of the Minitel/Teletel project, as Ottawa forcefully extended its hold over the provinces, especially with respect to communication, information, and culture.

CUFTA, NAFTA and GATS as Constraints on Communication and Public Life

The CUFTA and NAFTA obliterated any possibility of a viable Minitel/Teletel in Canada. First of all, these agreements strengthened the centralising tendencies in the Canadian political culture because, as the legal scholar Krommenacker (1991) notes, it is "inconceivable that service sectors falling under local jurisdiction . . . could be excluded . . . on that account alone" (p. 468). As such, the new trade regimes created greater pressure to harmonise legal, regulatory, and economic practices within Canada, as well as across the continent (Mosco, 1990b, p. 48). The provinces' years of control over telecoms were now numbered and would soon be extinguished—a point discussed at length in later sections of this chapter—and with it a strong basis for implementing one of the key political and cultural goals of the Minitel/Teletel project: communication as a basis for rejuvenating local culture. This trend was also reinforced at the level of people and politics because, as Gill (1992) states, the global trade regimes served first and foremost to protect "the interests of transnational capital from domestic interference" (p. 173), also known as democratic politics.

Employing the North America basic/enhanced distinctions, CUFTA, NAFTA, and GATS provisions covering telecoms shield online content services from government regulation. Although this may contribute to the emergence of a transnational "electronic free press" by constraining repressive regimes' capacity to restrict free flows of information (Samarajiva & Hadley, 1996), it also removes the new "technologies of freedom" from the political/public policy agenda. Defining basic communication services very narrowly, the new trade-in-services regimes prevent media policies from expanding the range of publicly regulated services commensurate with the emerging technologies and felt needs of some citizens as we enter the "information age" (TNC, 1993, Articles 3 & 5(4)(6)).

This state of affairs did not come about uncontested. The Europeans had fought just a few years earlier at the ITU to allow public service regulation of the new media and network-based content services. Although backed by many from the "developing" regions of the world, the Europeans' proposal to globalise the reserved/nonreserved framework was opposed by Canada, the United States, the United Kingdom, Japan, Australia, and a few others, who preferred the basic/enhanced services dichotomy (Mansell, Holmes, & Morgan, 1990, pp. 50-66). The compromise outcome of this contest has ambivalent implications for future attempts to expand the historical links between communication, citizenship, and democracy at the global level: on the one hand, a public service-oriented regulatory framework for enhanced services was adopted. On the other hand, those wishing to sign bilateral and multilateral agreements covering enhanced services could exempt themselves from ITU regulations.

As events proceeded even this compromise faded, as the basic/enhanced framework set the norm for subsequent NAFTA and GATS agreements. NAFTA (Canada, 1992) very clearly declares that governments cannot require a person providing enhanced or value-added services to:

(a) provide . . . services to the public generally;
(b) cost-justify its rates;
(c) file a tariff;
(d) interconnect its networks with any particular customer or network; or
(e) conform to any particular standard or technical regulation for interconnection other than for interconnection to a public telecommunications . . . network. (Article 1303(2))

Without any remaining capacity to foster universal access to new information services such as, for example, the Internet, or a Minitel/Teletel-type project, regulate rates for "enhanced services," establish public technology programs, and so on, it is hard to imagine what purpose future government regulation of new media could possibly serve.

Although these agreements pretend that their distinctions between basic and enhanced services are based on objective technical criteria, they are arbitrary exercises in drawing lines between, on the one hand, information markets and, on the other hand, legitimate areas of public intervention (OECD, 1988, p. 44). As Mansell (1988) emphatically states, there is no "category of services that use telecommunication networks which represent 'value added' and another which does not' (p. 245).[4] The new "global trade regimes" simply insist on expanding the information commodity rather than electronic public spheres of communication. As such, they are deeply political. All three regional/ global trade regimes would prevent any new efforts to develop public communication systems along Teletel/Minitel lines. Thus, even if Bell, the CRTC, and Canadian citizens agreed to implement a full-scale Alex project, they could not. That is "limited democracy"!

A U.S. negotiator of the NAFTA agreement, Ivan Shefrin (1993), recalls that Canada sought to retain control over its telecoms policy to promote cultural objectives. Yet, as he claims, this had to be rejected because it "was too far-reaching and would undermine the liberalising provisions of the NAFTA" (p. 19). Another advocate, Hudson Janisch (1989, p. 100), notes that the new trade regimes define basic services very narrowly. Two other Canadian commentators, Stephen Globerman and Peter Booth (1989), also acknowledge "that the Canadian regulator will be constrained to move closer to the American position" (p. 325). The same point now applies to the 30 other signatories of the GATS *Annex on Telecommunications*.[5]

TELECOMS, ECONOMIC VALUE, AND COMMUNICATIONS LAW: PRIVATISATION, THE STRONG STATE, AND THE CONSTITUTION

Although analytically distinct, regulatory liberalisation and global "free trade" cannot be separated from the privatisation of communication resources. Privatisation is the act of selling public assets to the private sector, mainly as a means of opening new areas for investment and appropriation of economic value. The general policy of privatisation has been central to the economy and a key plank in the former Conservative Government's agenda since the early 1980s. The centrality of privatisation to the Canadian political economy during these years was emphasised by the creation of a Minister of State in 1986 to manage privatisation and restructuring programs. In eight years 15 Crown corporations were sold, including Air Canada, Petro Canada, de Havilland Aircraft, and Canadair, and public sector employment cut by 50% (Pugliese, 1992, p. A5).

Privatising Information

Privatisation targets three areas: government information, resources held in common under national and global communication law, such as the radio spectrum, and PTOs. Trends toward privatisation are only beginning in the first area, as commercialisation of information by government agencies, greater public sector reliance on private vendors for data about Canadian society, and discussions about allowing commercial firms to resell government information indicate a trend toward the commoditisation of public information (Industry Canada, 1994b, p. 7). Although the federal government extols new information technologies as a means of providing people with access to government, it increasingly levies user fees for public information. This not only contrasts with its own stated aims, but also with efforts, for example, by the Open Government Campaign, to promote free access to government information, perhaps via the Internet (McMahon, 1996).

The privatisation of public data affects people in several other ways as well. When public agencies buy commercial information services they sign contracts that limit users to those associated with the institution. As a consequence, "outsiders" cannot access these resources. Public institutions and personnel are changed as a result, as they no longer encourage access to information but are contractually forced to restrict it. This becomes eminently perverse when universities buying Statistics Canada's electronic data services sign a contract that prevents people outside the university from using the electronic media resources. The role of the university is thus further impoverished and delegitimated. It is clear that although new technologies can enhance people's access to information, economic relations, government policies, and legal restrictions conspire to subvert this potential.

Privatising Telecoms Providers

A prominent form of privatisation applies to the sale of PTOs, a process pursued by both levels of government. In 1987, Teleglobe, Canada's signatory to INTELSAT, was sold. The government claimed this would allow Teleglobe to pursue commercial goals and "contribut[e] to deficit reduction," despite the fact that the company's "annual profits averaged some $50 million, on an asset base before privatisation of . . . $300 million" (Communications Canada, 1992, p. 3; Department of Finance, 1987, p. 1). Despite these aims, the sale increased corporate concentration as BCE obtained a dominant interest in the company and Teleglobe's monopoly over global telecoms traffic was extended for another 10 years (BCE, 1991, p. 46). In 1988, Terra Nova

Telecommunications and NorthwesTel were also sold to BCE (Babe, 1990, p. 30). A year later, government shares in CNCP were sold and eventually acquired by Rogers Communication/Unitel (third largest communications conglomerate in Canada) and AT&T (world's second largest telecoms company) (Communications Canada, 1992, p. 18). During 1995 and 1996, three of the largest banks in Canada—Bank of Nova Scotia, Royal Bank, and Toronto Dominion—and AT&T acquired the hemorrhaging Unitel, ending AT&T's hiatus from Canadian telecoms. The government obliged this reentry a short time earlier by rewriting sections of the *Telecommunications Act* (1993) to abolish requirements that common carriers be 80% Canadian-owned and controlled (Governor General in Council, 1994, P.C. 1994-1772).[6]

In 1992, the privatisation spree continued as Ottawa sold "the public's" 53% interest in Telesat, the national satellite system (Dept. of Finance, 1992, p. 2; Telesat, 1991). The privatisation of Telesat further concentrated the telecoms industry, as it was bought by a consortia including the telcos[7] and Canadian satellite builder, Spar Aerospace. Once again, the bargain was sweetened as government extended Telesat's monopoly in satellite communication for another 10 years (Dept. of Finance, 1991, p. 1).

In the prairies, AGT was sold between 1990 and 1991 (Telus, 1991). A few years later (renamed as the Telus Corporation), it acquired Edmonton Telephones—the municipally owned PTO that had stood as a reminder of the early years of corporate abuses and public communication needs since 1893. In 1996, plans to sell off MTS were announced (Demont, 1996, p. 1)—although unsolicited bids for the company had been routinely rejected for years. The cost of providing telephone service was suddenly too expensive, Premier Gary Filmon explained, a point backed up by the new political forces of telecoms—CIBC Wood Gundy, RBC Dominion Securities, and Richardson Greenshields. It seems that the memory of Francis Dagger, William Mulock, Sir Sandford Fleming, William Preece, and H. L. Webb, and the other forces in Canadian telecoms history, have thus vanished from public memory, replaced by bankers and investment houses eager to "linguistically liberate" the politics of telecoms from the constraints of the "old" public service language in favour of the exclusive language of the stock market: shares, debt/equity ratios, share swaps, financial reports, and so on.

Although privatisation has not significantly affected government spending,[8] it has shifted control over telecoms from the public sector to the private sector. In 1981 the private sector accounted for 68% of industry revenues, in 1992 about 81%, and once MTS is sold it will equal 96%.[9]

Such unprecedented dominance of the private sector over the public sector is paralleled by high levels of *concentration*. Although the presence of 61 companies providing telecoms services creates the image of competition and diversity, the fact that 13 firms account for 98% of all revenues, and nine carriers for 83%, suggests otherwise. Just two carriers, Anglo Canadian Telephones and BCE, supply service to 78.3% of subscribers and control 73% of all network and service revenues, as opposed to 63% 15 years earlier. The largest provider is Bell, with well over half of all subscribers (58%), revenues (55%), and employees (50%), as well as a subsidiary of BCE, one of the largest corporate entities in Canada. It is clear, then, that regulatory liberalisation and privatisation have not diffused control in telecoms, but created the highest levels of concentration since the expiration of Bell patents in 1893.

Although alternative carriers such as Telesat, Teleglobe, AT&T, Sprint, wireless personal communication services (pcs), two cellular networks, and some 150 resellers compete in certain areas—data and mobile communications, long distance, network management—they comprise an estimated 10% to 15% of the industry (Mozes & Sciadas, 1995, p. 75).[10] Even alternative networks are dominated by Stentor members and other entrenched behemoths such as Rogers, AT&T, and Sprint. Potential rival networks have been swiftly swallowed by such interests, a recent example being the four pcs licenses issued in December 1995 to Mobility (the Stentor Group), Cantel (Rogers/ AT&T), Microcell (Call Net/Sprint Canada), and Clearnet (Motorola, Nextel, and ComDev). Of course, Ottawa is lauded for "creating a viable market"—not too much competition—"and for holding some frequencies back for future use" (Surtees, 1995a, p. A2). Historical patterns of vertical integration are now being supplemented by horizontal integration, as telcos conquer new media, consolidate their position through amalgamation, and jockey for position in the global telecoms market.[11]

Current trends might have been understandable 10 years ago when there was some consensus that competition should be in services, not the infrastructure. At present, however, these trends deviate from stated commitments to competition and broadband communication systems based on a "network of networks." Acquisitions of alternative networks by dominant PTOs illustrates that new network technologies do not substitute for, but complement the existing infrastructure. The emerging communication network and industry structure suggests that contradictory principles in the *Telecommunications Act* and the *Competition Act* are being resolved in favour of global competitiveness rather than more local concerns. The result is displacement of regional monopolies in favour of national and global oligopolies. The folly of this strategy is already obvious as regulated oligopoly in long distance brings forth a "non-choice" among reinstating a Stentor-led "Canadian monopoly," swapping that for an AT&T-led "American monopoly," or a regulated truce between them with competition sprawled across the remaining fringes. As the clarion cries of competition continue to screen government from the "excesses of democracy," the Canadian State steadfastly continues to bolster oligopolistic rivalry and monopolies at about the same rate that it helps tear them down.

Privatising Telecoms Policy

> The new telecommunications policy could be considered as favorable to big business. The . . . government must develop a strategy to dissipate the formation of a common front. (confidential DOC document to Minister of Communication, May 1985)

Rather than furthering the radical decentralization of economic and political power or contributing to the diffusion of information production, contemporary regulatory policies promote the "competitiveness of the economy as a whole" (Racine et. al., 1992, p. 6). Reconciling the sometimes contradictory interests between PTOs and large users who incorporate communications services as intermediary inputs into their primary products is the key aim of contemporary industrial policy in the telecoms sector, whereas concerns with democratic communication and universal service wane.

For the most part, the differences between network operators and large users are minimal. Telecoms carriers see regulatory liberalisation as increasing access to new communication markets, and endusers hope changes will reduce telecoms costs. As the DOC (now adjunct of Industry Canada) notes, a convergence of thought is occurring as the importance of the communications dependent, service sector of the economy is recognised. According to Industry Canada officials, up to 5% of "large business' total expenditures are on telecommunications services" (personal communication, D. Mozes, DOC/Industry Canada, Ottawa, July 30, 1992). As Mozes and Sciadas (1995) note, a study of business use of telecoms services in Canada during 1994 revealed that about half of all large business firms[12] spend over $10,000 per month on such services and a significant number (13%) of large computer firms "have monthly bills in excess of $50,000" (p. 75). Canada's six largest banks spend $470 million annually on telecoms services, about 3% of the carriers' $16 billion in revenues (Communications Canada, 1992, p. 14). The Royal Bank has $100 million in annual telecoms expenses (Mosco, 1990, p. 10), the Toronto Dominion Bank $50 million (Gates, 1992a, p. S5), and Manulife, a large insurance and financial institution, spends $5.2 million per year on long distance services (Gates, 1992b, p. T1). According to these firms, Canada must import U.S.-style deregulation. Representatives from the Royal Bank note that,

AT&T has introduced more new services in the past five years than during the entire century. Many of these services are new export products, both goods and services. Prices for long distance services are about one-half of what Canadian carriers charge our businesses. And in the case of high speed data lines the cost differential is an incredible seven to one! All this has occurred without jeopardizing Americans' access to affordable basic telephone service. (Grant, 1991, p. 45)

The banks have been so enamored with competition that the Royal Bank, Toronto Dominion, and the Bank of Nova Scotia continuously bailed Unitel out of financial difficulty throughout its short life and have now even assumed joint ownership of the company with AT&T (Daglish with Fulton, 1995, pp. 44-45; Munk, 1995, pp. 43-44).[13] With their deep pockets, the banks have promoted changes in telecoms policy, subsidised unsustainable competition, and even assumed the role of active midwives in a process that otherwise might have fallen to the "invisible hand" of the market. The visible hand of banks in Canadian telecoms is not unique but reflects a resurgence in the role of finance institutions in telecoms globally. Although this role had lessened after the telegraph era and early days of the National Bell Telephone Company, today Canadian banks and those in the United States—such as J.P. Morgan, Citicorp, Bond Co., and so on—and elsewhere are propelling liberalisation and privatisation, even owning PTOs in Argentina, Canada, Chile, and the United Kingdom[14] (Benitez, 1992, pp. 10-13; Mustafa, 1993, p. 348).

As telecoms and regulation become inextricably linked with banks and the so-called debt crisis,[15] it is not surprising that the forces of change in telecoms are concerned with realising the economic value of communication. Obviously, such an agenda challenges conventional political and legal frameworks for telecoms and impinges on questions about the future of democratic communication in "electronic space." These institutions' influx into the heartland of the new telecoms also impedes measures to secure data privacy, and so on, because it is such institutions that are the nexus of consumer credit and financial transactions to begin with. Unfortunately, the clamour of convergence seldom considers convergence of consumer capitalism, banks, and the control of network space. As will be seen, these thrusts back and forth across the lines separating media and finance have also coincided with the weakening of the consensus on telephone companies' entry into content services and cable television since the beginning of the current decade. The death of the common-carrier model of communication is thus symbolised by more than just "media reconvergence" and legislative shifts (points to be discussed in greater detail in the next chapter).

The privatisation of Canadian telecoms policy is not greased solely by money and access to the corridors of political power, however. Instead, shifts in telecoms policy are also accompanied by more subtle redefinitions of what the main policy issues are and what counts and does not count as valid knowledge. The "cognitive framework" girding telecoms policy has undergone a massive transformation over the last two decades, as new groups have organised and been called on to address telecoms issues. Of course, knowledge is not distributed evenly across social classes and groups, as it tends to gravitate to centres of economic, political, and technical power—just like every resource of power in modern societies. This can be observed, for instance, as private sector consultants are called on more often to study the potential implications of regulatory changes, assist in the privatisation of public property, and help companies strategically important to the Canadian telecoms industry.

The production of knowledge about telecoms in Canada has devolved to prominent industry groups such as the Canadian Business Telecommunications Alliance (CBTA), the Canadian Banking Association (CBA), the Communications Competition Coalition (CCC), and the Information Technology Association of Canada (ITAC). The CBTA represents 340 private and public sector interests with annual telecoms expenditures of $4 billion, or about 25% of all industry revenues (CBTA, 1992, p. 1). ITAC lobbies on behalf of 300 members from the high technology industry whose combined revenues are about $15 billion per year, or about 2% of the GNP (ITAC, 1992, p. 2; Mosco, 1990a, p. 10). The CCC is even smaller, but consists of 40 of the largest corporations in Canada, including the Canadian Imperial Bank of Commerce, General Motors, and Sears (Crockett, 1991, p. 27). The CBA represents the six largest banking institutions in Canada, with combined annual expenditures on telecoms services and equipment in the order of $470 million. Overall, the telcos receive about 40% of their long distance revenues from 300 of the largest corporations in Canada (Gates, 1992a, p. 25). Similar patterns prevail in the Prairie and Atlantic Regions (personal communication, D. Beresh, Senior Business Planner, SaskTel, Regina, September 2, 1992; personal communication, B. Gowenlock, Regulatory Affairs Advisor, MTS, Winnipeg, September 1, 1992).

A steady process of consultation through industry associations, attendance at annual conferences, and participation on government boards helps to reaffirm the "new coalition's" status as a community and to define solutions to current and anticipated regulatory issues. In addition, these meetings contribute to the "revolving door" between the CRTC, DOC/Industry Canada, and private sector corporations such as BCE, Call Net, Unitel, Telus, and the resellers. As public officials put their knowledge of regulatory processes and experience in drafting legislation out for hire the demarcation between private and public interests is obscured, as is the claimed impartiality of government agencies' advisory role.[16]

Of course, low income people, workers, and average Canadians are represented by groups such as the NAPO, CWC, TWU, Atlantic Canada TWU, Public Interest Advocacy Centre, and Consumers Association of Canada. However, these groups' limited resources and unheard of appointments to the corporate board of directors of Canada's major telecoms carriers tends to mitigate their effectiveness. Instead of being at the centre of policy initiatives and defining telecoms policy issues through conferences, coordinating boards, and so on, they mainly react in the margins afforded by strategic skirmishes and tactical dissent among the telecoms policy "power elite." Nonetheless, such groups persist, maintaining offices, analysing and publishing position papers on Canadian media policy and policy options, and staying abreast of issues by being on the mailing list of the CRTC, Industry Canada, and Minister of Communications. A crucial role has been played by the CWC, the largest telecoms union in Canada, in creating and maintaining the Action Canada Network (ACN), a focal point for a range of social and political action groups. The ACN maintains an office, supports the Centre for Policy Alternatives—which regularly publishes analyses of government policy—and was instrumental in distributing leaked copies of the NAFTA and GATS agreements, thus helping to break the secrecy imposed on trade negotiations by Canadian, U.S., and other governments worldwide.

REGULATED CONTESTIBLE "MARKETS" AND THE STRONG STATE

Consolidation of ownership and control within the telecoms industry, the web of connections between telecoms and the apex of Canadian capitalism, and alterations in the "knowledge frames" underlying telecoms policy are mirrored by political and legal centralisation. This is evidenced by changes in relations among administrative agencies with a hand in telecoms policy, unrelenting intrusions of the Cabinet into regulatory affairs, and the strengthening of political authority brought about by the new ministerial powers of the *Telecommunications Act* (1993).

Changes in administrative relationships can be seen from the ascendancy of the DOC/Industry Canada over the CRTC as a source of policy inspiration. DOC officials played key roles in negotiating the CUFTA, NAFTA, and GATS agreements, briefing foreign governments and industry officials about Canadian telecoms, and selling the virtues of competitive telecoms and global trade to provincial agencies (personal communication, L. Kincaid, CWC, Ottawa, July 10, 1992; personal communication, D. Mozes, Industry Canada, Ottawa, July 30, 1992). New agencies have also ascended in importance to displace the CRTC's authority over telecoms, including the Department of Finance, the

Ministry of State, and Consumer and Corporate Affairs.[17] These commercially oriented agencies' solutions tend to be conceptualized in economic, accounting, and finance terms. The Ministry of Consumer and Corporate Affairs regularly sends representatives to CRTC proceedings to promote competitive policy positions. The Ministers of State, Communications, and Consumer and Corporate Affairs also took the unusual measure of invoking the *Competition Act* to guide the privatisation of Teleglobe and Telesat (Dept. of Finance, 1992). In contrast to the ideological constructions that saturate common sense, then, telecoms policy changes expand the state bureaucracy and create more, not less, regulation. What needs to be seen is that the state plays a crucial role in constructing the "new" political economy and is certainly not a neutral arbiter among competing interests.

These points are evident in the formidable alliance that was forged between Industry Canada and Cabinet from the mid-1980s onward, although this transgresses arms-length arrangements designed to inoculate telecoms and legal process from political pressures. The politicisation of telecoms was illuminated in 1985 when a confidential memo from the DOC to Cabinet was leaked to the telecoms unions. Instead of introducing legislation to replace the antiquated *Railway Act*, the DOC recommended that:

> [t]he government should undertake a public consultation process, publishing a consultation document in autumn 1985 and possibly a white paper at a later date . . .
>
> Release a speech in June, to be followed by consultations with interested parties and lobbying groups, and continuing discussions with the provinces.
>
> The government would authorize the Minister to spend $1 million from the economic envelope for public information, studies and consultation.

The DOC envisioned the proceedings, concluding that:

> Canada should move to cost-based pricing . . .
>
> Canada should introduce competition gradually . . .
>
> If Canada's policies don't change, international bypass and higher costs for Canadian industry could have severe consequences. (DOC, 1985, p. 1)

This is only one of numerous instances in which CRTC authority has been usurped or superseded. For instance, in 1987, after finding that Call Net, the largest reseller, violated regulatory policy by offering basic, public, long-distance services, the CRTC allowed the telcos to refuse network access to the company. Call Net, however, petitioned Cabinet twice for a reprieve from the decision and secured DOC help to bring it into compliance with CRTC regulations (Call Net, 1987, 1988; CRTC, 1987b, p. 15; Communications Canada, 1988, pp. 1-2). Ultimately, rather than Call Net changing its practices, the CRTC altered its policies to correspond with the operations of Call Net and the desires of the government. It was in this way that resale of basic services and private line sharing for public telephone services was introduced to Canada (CRTC, 1990, p. 37). In the interim, the Conservative government commandeered the regulatory framework from the CRTC for about 1-1/2 years, as they rammed through their "competitive policy" using no less than five directives from "Her Excellency the Governor General in Council" (Governor General in Council, 1988, P.C. 1988-265; 1990, P.C. 1990-620).[18]

In the end, the CRTC executed the government's policy absent a legislative mandate. Similar actions were apparent in matters concerning Telesat and in dubious activities on the part of the Communications Minister in a rate case involving Bell (Telesat, 1991, p. 2). In response to these episodes, an article in the *Financial Post* scolded the Minister for intervening in regulatory affairs more times "in 20 months than all her predecessors in the past 20 years" ("MacDonald's record," 1988, p. 1). The article was factually wrong, but not in spirit: the crucial point was that the politics of telecoms had left the CRTC and was taken over by the government of the day. In an *Ottawa Citizen* article in 1996, resigning CRTC head, Keith Spicer, lambasted Chretien's Liberal government for ruling telecoms from the inner sanctums of Cabinet instead of through the more open CRTC processes (Cobb, 1996). Rule by government fiat is represented in Figure 6.2.

Although Spicer may have complained about government intrusions that fell outside the normal bounds of good practice, such practices are not unknown to the CRTC, either. Perhaps realising the futility of resistance, in late 1987 the CRTC began adhering more closely to the government's defacto competitive telecoms policy as it agreed to allow CNCP (Unitel's predecessor) to offer competitive data communication services without filing tariffs. According to the CRTC's (1987b) decision, competition could ensure "just and reasonable" rates. However, the TWU and the Federal Anti-Poverty Group challenged this ruling in the Courts, arguing the *Railway Act* did not allow the CRTC to forbear from regulation. As the case proceeded, Bell, BCTel, and others filed similar requests, although to no avail. The Courts declared that Parliament had not authorised "the regulatory regime . . . to be dismantled by the CRTC" (TWU v. CRTC et. al., 1988a, p. 328; 1988b, p. 7). Tariffs were once again filed, as they had been since 1908. Immediately afterward, however, the CRTC appealed for the Minister of Communication to amend the *Railway Act* to specifically give the Commission the discretionary power of forbearance. This change would enable the Commission to relieve carriers from burdensome, cost-bearing regulatory requirements, such as the filing of tariffs, in circumstances where they have been rendered unnecessary, for example, by reason of market forces, such as competition. (cited in Bird, 1992, p. 86)

In between this appeal and the introduction of new legislation in 1993, the TWU made several attempts to get the CRTC to defer from introducing more competitive-oriented decisions until Parliament introduced a new telecoms law. The TWU also tried to engage the Commission in a explicit debate about the merits of competition but was rebuffed. The CRTC insisted that administrative practices required the TWU to argue on specific points of law and individual cases (CRTC, 1991b, p. 21). However, the point was, as the TWU noted, that "in

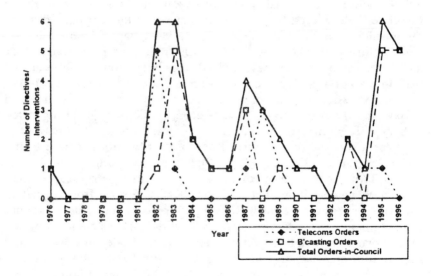

Figure 6.2. Government intervention in the regulation of electronic media (1976-1996)

Note: Data is derived from a review of Governor General in Council notices published in the *Canada Gazette, Part II*. Decisions refusing to vary/rescind/or refer back to the CRTC have not been included.

isolation, each one of these decisions appears innocuous. Taken together, however, they will create ever increasing competition and deregulation" (TWU, 1989, p. 1).

In 1993, the new *Telecommunications Act* was passed (Canada, 1993a). Among other things, the new law raised "increased reliance on market forces for the provision of telecommunications services" to the status of a policy objective (section 7(f)). It also formalised links among this goal, regulatory liberalisation, and the strong state. With respect to the latter point, the law retains the *Railway Act*'s powers for ministers to "vary or rescind" CRTC decisions, while also giving the Communications Minister exceptional new powers regarding consultations with the provinces, regulatory forbearance, interventions in CRTC matters, and the issuing of policy directives (see sections 8 through 14). The Cabinet can now intervene before, during, and after CRTC hearings, an unprecedented usurpation of regulatory authority in the history of Canadian telecoms.

The CRTC (1992b) argued that the new law would undermine its status as "an expert, quasi-judicial tribunal, accessible, public, . . . independent and non-partisan" (p. 3). It warned the government that it would be "beleaguered by . . . petitioners who no longer believed in the Commission's public proceedings" (p. 4). The Atlantic Communication and Technical Workers (ACTWU) (1992) put the point even more forcefully, arguing the law would "lead to politicisation of the industry," "rule with an iron fist," and regulatory deals made in "secrecy" (pp. 1-4).

Excessive discretionary powers undermine public policy and support the thesis that competitive telecoms policies beget strong states. Others note similar trends, arguing that changing telecoms policy requires a state willing to push liberalisation without fear of losing political legitimacy (Duch, 1991, p. 243; Pettrazzini, 1993).[19]

Two other sections of the new telecoms law reinforce these tendencies, namely, those that allow the CRTC to forbear from regulation and another that gives the CRTC new powers to exclude interest groups from regulatory proceedings (sections 34 and 9(3)). As competition has never been clearly defined within the context of telecoms policy (and such definitions that do exist are riddled with "loopholes"), the new forbearance powers appear to give the CRTC carte blanche to do whatever it wants. Submissions made by trade unions during the Senate Hearings focused on these ambiguities and how, when combined with the the greater range of Ministerial powers and the CRTC's new right to exclude would-be interveners,[20] the new telecoms law could remove telecoms politics from the public arena (Canadian Labour Congress, 1992, p. 11; TWU, 1992, p. 11). Given that unions have been a considerable thorn in the side of the government over the last decade, such concerns may not be ill-placed. The Canadian Labour Congress

(1992) proposed that the new law allow for "strong public regulation involving a more open process in which the public has influence on the policy agenda" (p. 13).

ECONOMIC EFFICIENCY, TECHNOLOGY, AND CONSTITUTIONAL CHANGE

The centralisation of political authority can also be observed in provincial/federal relations. Traditionally, jurisdiction over telecoms has been divided between Ottawa and the provinces, despite the fact that the Constitution always provided Ottawa with clear authority over telecoms. However, the federal government had turned a blind eye to the provinces' forays into telecoms, as long as they did not step into broadcasting. This led to what some called a "balkanised" regulatory regime. As a result, for instance, reselling and private line interconnection prevailed in BC, Ontario, and Quebec, but not Manitoba, Newfoundland, or Saskatchewan. Likewise, media (re)convergence developed in the prairies but not in federally regulated areas. As such, there was not *a* Canadian telecoms system, but a collection of companies loosely unified through Stentor. However, this diffuse constitutional ordering of political power encountered the wrath of the ITAC, CCC, and CBTA. According to the "new coalition," "inter-provincial trade barriers . . . weaken competitiveness and effectiveness"(Canada, 1991, p. 18), especially as the economy feels the pressures of free trade (Communications Canada, 1987, p. 61).

As a result, 80 years after its powers were affirmed over telecoms matters, the federal government attempted to assume authority over the provincially regulated telcos (*Toronto v. Bell*, 1905). The Supreme Court reconfirmed this authority in 1989 (*AGT v. CRTC and CNCP*, 1989).[21] The decision brought the privately owned, provincially regulated, Atlantic region telcos under CRTC jurisdiction, but left AGT, SaskTel, and MTS as Crown Corporations, and several independent telcos across Canada, outside of federal jurisdiction. Shortly before and after the AGT ruling the government tried to obtain control through negotiations dubbed the "Edmonton Accord," and subsequently through legislation. Both efforts were rebuffed. Playing on historical tension between the prairies and Ottawa, the *Winnipeg Free Press* ran a series of articles disparaging the attempt as an unparalleled "federal raid on the jurisdiction and regulatory authority of the provinces" ("PCs put move," 1989, p. A3).

However, the election of a Conservative government in Manitoba to match the one in Ottawa led to a more sympathetic relationship between the two previous rivals. An example of the improved relationship was the 1991 Memorandum of Understanding (MOU) between Manitoba and the federal government. The MOU transferred authority to the CRTC, instituted local representation on the CRTC, assured that policy issues would be considered with great "sensitiv[ity] to regional interests," and set competition and "regulatory forbearance" as priority policy goals (Canada/Manitoba, 1991, p. 2). However, it is important to note that the MOU was achieved only after business lobby groups bypassed the Manitoba legislature and regulatory board, and the Manitoba government centralised regulatory power in the hands of the newly unified, provincial Minister of Telecommunications and Policy, much to the consternation of the unions (CWC and IBEW), the Public Utility Board, and other social interests (personal communication, D. Birdwise, Policy Analyst, Manitoba Government, Winnipeg, August 31, 1992).

The "prairie alliance" further deteriorated in 1990 when the Alberta government issued the first shares in the privatisation of AGT. As a consequence, AGT lost its Crown immunity and came within the purview of the CRTC. The government may have privatised AGT to escape the contradictory pressures generated through local political structures by labour unions and residential and rural users, on the one hand, and the CRTC's competitive initiatives, the federal government's display of resolve on the jurisdictional matter, and the pressure of local, national and transnational business' efforts to commercialise the company's operations, on the other (personal communication, P. Desrochers, Director of Regulatory Affairs, AGT, Calgary, September 3, 1992). Others suggest that privatisation reflected the Conservative government's belief that the public sector should not compete with the private sector for limited economic resources, an observation that accords well with the fact that AGT was a very profitable company when sold (personal communication, T. Panelli, Business Manager, IBEW, Calgary, Sept. 3, 1992).[22]

Late in the 1980s, Constitutional proposals began to flow from Ottawa. Although most people honed in on sections dealing with acutely sensitive issues involving political and cultural differences among Canadians—French Canadians, English Canadians, First Nations, women, and ethnic minorities—just as important were proposals to reform the Constitution to give business new rights to challenge government economic, social, or cultural policies if they impeded the vaguely defined but sacrosanct goal of "economic efficiency." Other proposals buried in these initiatives urged the adoption of a national competitive telecoms policy to help diffuse enhanced services, reselling, alternative networks, and private lines (Canada, 1991, pp. 13-22; Communications Canada, 1987, p. 61). These proposals were nothing less than an attempt to write the proscriptions of "crisis of democracy" theorists into the Canadian Constitution. As such, they were a bid to constitutionalise the subordination of social objectives to economic imperatives and to inscribe the centralising pressures of "global trade" agreements into the highest law of the land.[23] Some of the aims were achieved by provisions in the new telecoms law that gave the federal government absolute jurisdiction over telecoms in Canada. The CBTA and other large user groups lauded the initiative, stressing "how important it was to have just one regulator for the sector . . . and that jurisdiction . . . be held inviolate from provincial encroachment in the future" (CBTA, 1992, p. 4). SaskTel continued to oppose this, arguing that

> the needs of the customer in Metro Toronto are not identical to those of a farmer in northern Saskatchewan . . . . [T]here are regional sensitivities and geographic realities which the individual telcos are the best ones to address in order to satisfy the unique requirements of their own customers. (Teichrob, 1992, p. 2)

The new telecoms law brought all the telephone companies, except SaskTel, under CRTC's supervision. A 1994 Supreme Court ruling removed any lingering possibility that the independent telcos might be beyond the CRTC's reach. From 1980 to 1993 the number of PTOs under federal authority rose from 70% to 95%. While at the start of the 1980s, 7 of the 19 largest telcos were under federal jurisdiction, by 1993, 12 of the 14 biggest telcos were federally regulated. The last vestige of the prairie's battles to establish their own telecoms systems will disappear in 1998, when SaskTel becomes regulated by the CRTC (*Telecommunications Act*, section 133).

COMPETITION IN THE CORE NETWORK INFRASTRUCTURE

Competition Rejected? The First CNCP Application

As political and economic power were being consolidated, there was increasing fragmentation in the fragile consensus that competition should be limited to enhanced services. In 1984, CNCP filed the first application to compete in public long distance. However, at that time, there had only been a short-term commitment to competition in services, and even this had been achieved through a protracted process of "regulatory incrementalism." Marking the tenuous commitment to competition, the application was rejected. Nonetheless, it established the direction for subsequent events in Canadian telecoms policy and is thus worth reviewing in some detail.

Reminiscent of the Mulock Inquiry 80 years earlier, the CRTC received 1,700 written comments and heard presentations from 43 delegations during 36 days of public hearings (CRTC, 1985, pp. 3-5). Most interveners worried about the negative impact of competition on universal telephone service. As MTS noted, the issue was not "whether customers would be required to pay a dollar or two a month more, but rather whether these users, in toto, will . . . pay the millions, if not billions, necessary to allow a new entrant into this market, from which they will not derive a benefit" (MTS, n.d., p. 2). CNCP, of course, rejected this, but argued that the crux of the issue was not universal service but whether or not the *Railway Act* required the incumbent PTOs to interconnect with their networks to provide a competing public long-distance service (CRTC, 1985, p. 17). CNCP was correct, on legal and historical terms, but even so, said the TWU and the Federal Anti-Poverty Organisation, the Commission might have to go beyond "narrow" legal issues to "protect the public interest" (CRTC, 1985, p. 18). In a bold move, the CRTC dismissed all of these arguments. Although it rejected CNCP's application, it did not do so because of concern about the effects of competition on the public interest, nor because competition would have nefarious impacts on the national telecoms system. In fact, the CRTC embraced the principle of competition but rejected CNCP's application on the grounds that it could not achieve the price discounts it promised while at the same time offering universal service (CRTC, 1985, p. 43). Indicating a remarkably pragmatic, nondogmatic view of the world, the principle of competition was accepted, but only as a means to achieve social objectives, of which universality was a priority. In the balance of things, competition remained subordinate to social policy.

Indicating the overall direction of the decision in favour of competition, the CRTC also allowed reselling and private networks to interconnect with those of the PTN, with the only restriction being that these could not be used to provide local or long-distance voice services (CRTC, 1985, pp. 86-88, 100-101). Also reflecting some independence of thought was the Commission's attempt to bring about one of the perceived benefits of the application that it had just rejected—lower long distance rates—without drastic hikes in local rates. To do so meant accepting certain aspects of Bell's audacious proposal to "rebalance rates," but just as importantly, it meant rejecting other aspects. Bell proposed a 150% increase in local rates and a cut of about 70% in long-distance prices. In essence, Bell and other Stentor members were trying to remove the rationale for competition and thus maintain their monopolistic position (CRTC, 1985, p. 53). A key aspect of the proposal was who would pay for the "network access costs" (estimated by Bell at $1.76 billion), those costs assigned to the gateway between the local exchange and the long-distance network. Bell argued that "access costs should be recovered from local service charges" (CRTC, 1985, p. 50).

Incredibly, this brazen proposal was accepted. However, at the same time, the Commission capped long-distance rates at their current levels and stated that it would look warily at applications to further raise local rates. Under the unfolding strategy, long-distance prices would fall, local prices would not be permitted to rise significantly, and the CRTC would look favourably on future applications for network-based, long-distance competition so long as it contributed to the realisation of social policy aims, or until the CRTC changed its evaluative criteria.

In some ways, the CRTC was committed to an independent path, neither conforming to the unbridled "competition" found south of the border (or advocated by the business groups now so prominent in its proceedings), nor to the expansionist conception of regulated competition in the public interest pursued in Europe. The CRTC's agreement to allow network access charges to be assigned to local users was, however, a carbon copy of practices adopted by the FCC. The new approach to network access charges began to emerge in the United States after a 1983 decision by the FCC to reapportion network access charges over a 5-year period, as represented in Table 6.2.

Table 6.2. Redistribution of Network Access Charges in the United States

Year	Carrier Contribution to Network Access Charge (%)	Local Subscriber Funding of Network Access Charge (%)
1984	100	0
1985	80	20
1986	60	40
1987	40	60
1988	20	80
1989	0	100

Source: Federal Communications Commission (1983, p. 285).

In the United States, the amount of the network access charge was US$8.5 billion, and as Table 6.2 indicates, the general body of subscribers would go from a position of paying none of these charges out of local basic service rates to paying for all of them. Even the FCC remarked that the "end user charges constituted a substantial departure from the historic means of cost recovery" (FCC, 1983, pp. 285). It was, as Mosco (1990a) notes, an incredible "redistribution in the burden of paying for the national . . . network" (p. 40). Recognising the opposition that was raised by many of the state regulators, public interest groups, and others, the FCC was forced to spread the costs across a longer period of time. However, it noted that in the future it would "preempt the States from applying . . . safeguards inconsistent with [FCC] orders" (FCC, 1986, p. 714).

Although the CRTC decision resembled that of FCC two years earlier, a key difference was that Canadian policy refused to accept rate increases on the same magnitude as those approved in the United States. In the United States, rates increased between 61% in urban areas to 95% in rural areas between 1980 and 1987 (Crandall, 1990, p. 65). Whereas rates typically fell between 5 and 10 percentage points below the annual consumer price index average before the introduction of competition in basic telephone services in 1980, afterward all telephone prices declined at the negligible rate of only 1.5% per year, and local rates increased, when measured against the consumer price index (OECD, 1995a, p. 36). In contrast to the American situation, the CRTC still held open the possibility that regulated competition might yet be in the public interest and lead to reduced telephone rates.

A Time for Reflection or a Chance to Change the Terms of the Debate?

Immediately after the CNCP application was rejected, a flurry of initiatives were launched to consider the wisdom of long-distance competition. It was by no means an easy decision. Of course, the business community held to the unqualified notion that competition would be a good thing. The CRTC was not far behind, either, agreeing that long-distance competition would bring "lower MTS/WATS rates, greater customer choice, supplier responsiveness and accelerated rate of diffusion of new technology," although it admitted that evidence to support these claims was inconclusive (CRTC, 1985, pp. 44-49).

Yet, more nuanced data demonstrated that things were not so simple. First, even CNCP could not produce evidence showing that telephone service was not a natural monopoly, a considerable weakening of its case because the existence of natural monopoly would suggest that the introduction of competition would be inefficient (CRTC, 1985, p. 30). In addition, the OECD (1990) released a study comparing the cost of telecoms services around the world. The study revealed the bias of the business lobby's evidence that focused on cost differences between Canada and the United States for one or two services. The OECD study presented prices for a basket of business services and showed that although costs in Canada were above the OECD average, they were below those in the United States, Japan, and Germany. In relation to mobile communications and leased, high-speed digital lines, costs in Canada were below the OECD average and those of key trading partners, except for the United Kingdom, for high-speed digital lines. Such data was especially impressive given that Canada had one of the highest levels of universal service, and among the lowest costs, for residential users. In contrast, where competition had proceeded furthest, costs were highest (OECD, 1990, pp. 50-67).

The same study and others also showed that competitive-oriented telecoms policies were associated with considerable disinvestment. If regulated monopolies contributed to "gold-plated" networks, liberalisation began a trend toward under-investment. In countries where competition was weakest, network investment remained the highest as a percentage of annual revenues: Germany (42%), France (28%), Canada (26%), the United Kingdom (20%) and the United States (19%). Whereas OECD member countries' average investment was US$197 per subscriber line, in the United States it was $US110, a rate less than one-third of that in Singapore and half the rate in France and the United Kingdom (Davidson, 1991, sec. 4, p. 6; OECD, 1990, p. 151). These findings reflected a deeper change in the underlying mode of telecoms regulation, economics, and technical innovation from an emphasis on dynamic efficiency in the long term to allocative efficiency in the short run. These are discussed in detail in the next chapter in relation to information highway initiatives.

Of course, the production of knowledge about telecoms has not been one-sided against, or in favour of, competition. A recent study by the OECD (1995a) reveals that competition has not eroded extension of basic telephone services, even if services are provided at higher prices than before. It has become common to note that more people now have telephone service (94%) in the United States than before telecoms reform began (93%). This shows that competition, higher prices for basic services, and more people with telephones can coexist. From a critical perspective, however, this simply means that people value access to telephone service so much that they are willing to pay dearly for it. In economists' terms, it means that demand for telephones is inelastic—demand is not very sensitive to price changes. This should underscore perceptions of telephone service as a basic necessity of life, rather than give license to charge "what the market will bear."

While the OECD and others were busy producing crucial evidence, several studies were conducted within Canada, most notably the two Federal Provincial Task Force Inquiries into Long Distance. They came up with several crucial conclusions: first, after comparing regulated monopoly against competitive regulatory regimes on five measures—costs, productivity, economies of scale/scope, technological and services innovation, and responsiveness to users—the Task Force found that, theoretically, competition should increase the telcos' responsiveness to user needs; second, most users would not see significant, if any, cost benefits from competition; and finally, evidence for each of the other measures was inconclusive (Federal Provincial Task Force on Telecommunications, 1988, pp. 84-104).

Another key finding was that telecoms costs as business expenses were overstated. The 1986 Task Force Report concluded that despite some differences between U.S. and Canadian costs, changes in the rate structure would "have only small impacts on the overall cost structure and the performance of Canadian business . . ., even for large price changes" (Federal Provincial Task Force on Telecommunications, 1986, p. 51). It found that telecoms costs, on average, represented only 0.7% of business costs. Bank and financial institutions' balance sheets support this finding. Recent data shows that although Canada's six largest banks have over $470 million in annual expenditures on telecoms services, this is a paltry sum alongside total annual operating expenses of $58.1 billion. It also pales alongside annual profits of $5.2 billion (*Globe and Mail Report on Business*, 1996, p. 155), an amount calculated a few years earlier to be slightly more than half of all profits reported on the Toronto Stock Exchange (Marotte, 1991, B12). Even ardent supporters of competition have not been able to produce data showing that telecoms costs make up an exceptionally high portion of even large business users' expenses, and readily admit that this is certainly not the case for the vast majority of small to mid-size firms (Mozes & Sciadas, 1995, p. 77). In simple terms, the cost of telecoms services as a business expense have been exaggerated.

The fact that the largest corporations allocate between .7% and 2.4% of their disbursements on telecoms services is similar to the levels made by citizens for telephone service. On average, Canadians allocate about 1.2% of their family income on basic telecoms services, an amount similar to what they spend on electricity bills, education, health care, and recreational pursuits. In relation to income, the poorest among us spend as much on telecoms services as the richest, most intensive telecoms-using businesses. For people living below or near the poverty line, the cost of basic service equals about 2.7% of their income. That people are willing to allocate such a sizeable portion of their income to telephone costs signifies the social importance attributed to telephone service. A reasonable conclusion drawn from these comparative measures, and from the perspective of social justice, is that the traditional pricing regime resulted in a rough level of equality between business and residential users. If anyone needed adjustments to offset the disadvantages of the old pricing structure, it was low income users. This is especially true because telephone penetration as a whole is 98.7%, whereas for low income families it falls to around 86% (NAPO, 1987, pp. 9-11; Statistics Canada, 1994c, Table 3). There are no persuasive reasons to require citizens to spend more of their budgets on telephone costs than is required of business.[24]

Historically, the "just and reasonable" test applied to all requests to increase the cost of telephone prices, something that helped the price of telephone service to fall faster than the rise of the consumer price index (Pike & Mosco, 1986; Stats Can, 1970-1992a). Despite the benefits of this historical approach, two important points need to be raised. First, given that labour unions and groups such as NAPO, FAPG, and so on have been the most erstwhile defenders of affordable, universal services, provisions in the new telecoms law allowing them to be excluded from regulatory affairs could allow all-too-frequent rate rebalancing proposals to be implemented. Second, although full rate rebalancing was resisted prior to the CRTC's 1992 long-distance competition decision, things have changed dramatically since. These issues are considered after the review of the CRTC decision to introduce competition in long distance that follows.

BELIEVING IN COMPETITION

Although the evidence regarding competition remained pretty much the same between 1985 and 1992, the means-end relation between competition and social policy changed. Competition became an end in itself, marking the transformation of regulation from social policy to industrial policy. Nowhere is the industrialisation of telecoms policy more evident than in the CRTC's *Competition in the Provision of Public Long Distance Voice Telephone Services and Related Resale and Sharing Issues (CRTC 92-12)* decision. The decision introduced facilities-based competition and demonstrated the extent to which competition has achieved ideological status within the CRTC. Even with the benefit of elaborate methodological slights of hand that collapsed analysis of economies of scale into narrowly conceived "toll specific scale economies",[25] the CRTC could not produce any conclusive evidence supporting the inherent competitiveness of long distance services (CRTC, 1992a, pp. 18-19). On each of the measures on which the decision was supposed to turn, the CRTC had to admit the "inconclusive nature of the evidence" (CRTC, 1992a, pp. 36-40).

During interviews, some members who participated in the decision acknowledged that evidence for and against competition had not changed between 1985 and 1992. The crucial difference, they said, was that they had come to believe in competition. Although this would be fine if the issue was individual religious preferences, it is less compelling as a basis for policy in an area that is supposed to be crucial to the future of the country.

Under the "new religion" the CRTC could dispense with meddlesome problems such as a lack of evidence, and even change the criteria by which it judged things. The first criteria to be jettisoned was universal service. Recall that CNCP was not permitted to enter long-distance competition in 1985 because it could not ensure discounted tariffs and universal service at the same time. In the 1992 application, though, the renamed company, Unitel, proposed discounted long-distance services and universal service availability after six years. Unitel's new plan followed the 1985 criteria closely, if not perfectly. In the "new world," however, advised the CRTC, "competitors" were not "required . . . to provide universal service as a condition of entry" (CRTC, 1992a, pp. 62-63). According to the "new" CRTC, service allocation according to market principles was preferable to route averaging or the goal of universality. Other competitors such as British Columbia Light Rail (BCLR) proposed to serve only large cities in BC, Ontario, and Quebec. The CRTC agreed, acknowledging that this could increase regional disparities in network development, access, and costs. It also accepted that the telcos would continue to route average their tariffs intra-regionally but not on a cross-Canada basis, as previously done through Stentor's Revenue Settlement Plan.

By overturning its commitment to universality, the CRTC signalled a decisive shift in the means/ends relationship between competition and social policy. This negated the concerns of those who had consistently opposed long-distance competition. At the forefront of the opposition were MTS and SaskTel, who contended that new entrants would concentrate on the 150 to 200 corporate customers in Winnipeg, Regina, and Saskatoon that provided around 20% of their revenues (MTS, n.d., p. 2; personal communication, B. Gowenlock, Regulatory Affairs Consultant, MTS, September 1, 1992; personal communication, D. Beresh, Senior Business Planner, SaskTel, September 2, 1992). The Manitoba government also claimed that there were at least 50 groups representing business, farmers, labour, municipalities, and social and religious organisations opposed to CNCP's bid. Likewise, and perhaps anticipating the CRTC's decision-making methods, AGT's 1988 *Annual Report* stated "that competition must be *conclusively* determined to be in the best interests of Canadians, prior to introduction of major legislative or regulatory changes" (p. 12; emphasis added). In British Columbia, 52 city councils, including Vancouver, passed resolutions opposing the Unitel decision. The Ontario and Quebec governments held similar positions. The telecoms unions—TWU, CWC and ACTWU—also led cross-country campaigns against the application, but to no avail.

The CRTC did not abandon universal service aims altogether, of course. Such aims became the preserve of incumbent PTOs. According to the regulator, the conventional telcos were obligated to preserve universal service, whereas new competitors would be given expedited regulatory consideration. Through this move the CRTC introduced yet another new feature into Canadian telecoms policy: a two-tier regulatory regime. The two-tiered regulatory structure reflected a decision to use regulation to help new entrants overcome the historically entrenched position of the telcos and to actively use regulation to influence the shape of the emerging market (CRTC, 1992a, p. 14).

The incumbent companies, not surprisingly, vehemently opposed responsibility for universal service. Instead, they suggested that this be transitory as new methods to achieve social policy aims are considered such as direct subsidies, local measured services, "incentive regulations, price caps or other variations" (Stentor, 1992, p. 2). As Schultz and Janish (1993) correctly argue, specific sections of the private sector cannot be made responsible for government social policies. As such, something had to change. Either affordable universal service would be abandoned altogether, all "market" participants made to contribute to some kind of universal service fund, or government would socialise market failures through direct subsidies. These issues have been taken up in two subsequent CRTC initiatives, its *Review of Regulatory Framework* (Dec. 94-19) (1994a) and its *Implementation of Regulatory Framework-Splitting of the Rate Base and Related Issues* (Dec. 95-21) (1995b), whereas other proceedings remain underway at the time of writing. A review of the post-long-distance telecoms decision environment follows in the next and last section of this chapter.

IT AIN'T COMPETITION, AND IT'S NOT A MONOPOLY, EITHER: WHAT HATH GOVERNMENT AND THE CRTC CREATED?

Any benefits accruing to citizens in their everyday use of telecoms services from competition has occurred despite the new telecoms policy and regulatory initiatives taken by the CRTC and other government agencies, whereas any benefits for business or new telecoms providers have been because of regulation, not a lack of it. From these embryonic years of regulated infrastructure competition, three casualties have already emerged: Unitel; the potential for an independent, "made in Canada" telecoms policy; and people. These are considered in the next section.

Unsustainable "Competition"

The first indications that the new "competitive" telecoms in Canada was in big trouble came in 1994-95, if not earlier, when it was announced that Unitel was hemorrhaging badly. It was losing more than $500,000 daily.

Indications were that it might not survive. However, Unitel was not exactly a David among Goliaths, either. It was the progeny of Rogers Communication, the third largest media conglomerate in Canada, with revenues of $2.6 billion in 1995, and Canadian Pacific, an entity whose history was synonymous with telecoms and Canadian corporate capitalism, with revenues of $8.7 billion in 1995. The latter's revenues and reach across the country's economic landscape surpassed that of even the largest telco, Bell (*Globe and Mail Report on Business*, 1996, pp. 80, 164). Despite such parentage, Unitel was still unable to defy the "invisible hand" of the market. At first it was propped up by the banks, although this proved to be a transitory step. Between 1995 and 1996, the Bank of Nova Scotia, Royal Bank, and Toronto Dominion, in tandem with AT&T, took complete control of the faltering company. The deep pockets of all the parties, as well as AT&T's excess network capacity in the United States and tentacles stretching across the globe, ensured that a new bout of duopolistic rivalry was ready to once again engulf telecoms in Canada. At the time of writing, it is still too early to tell if this will be durable, complemented by even greater sustainable competition, or end in familiar ruinous strategic rivalry.

Although this turn of events dramatically illustrated that something was very wrong in the "new competitive" environment, there were earlier indications as well. First, recall that competition was only installed after staff at the CRTC changed their minds, although the available evidence still, at best, only tepidly supported the potential for viable competition in Canada. Second, the CRTC had introduced regulated contestible markets,[26] and this has entailed a panopoly of new activities deeply involving it in ensuring that competition works. As the Commission announced in a 1995 decision, the *Telecommunications Act* (sec. 7) required it "to ensure the competitiveness of Canadian telecommunication" (CRTC, 1995a, p. 21).[27] To this end, Unitel and the other new entrants were relieved of the "burden" of universal service and given a regulated discount on what they paid to interconnect with the incumbents' networks. Whereas in 1916 the BRC wiped out competition by imposing a surcharge on competitors, in the new regime incumbent monopolists had to give the newcomers a discount. Divine justice, perhaps, but not competition!

Whatever has been created, it is not competition. The favourite terms in the new lexicon of psuedo-competition include: "competitive in the future," "sufficient competition," "sustainable competition," "workable competition," "workably competitive," and so on.

Buried in its reports, the CRTC readily admits that competition is pretty well nowhere to be found in Canadian telecoms. Even MTS's claim that newcomers might chip away at 14% of its long-distance "market" in 1995 was dismissed by the CRTC (1995b) "to be an over-estimation" (p.

74). In an incredible deference to reality, the Commission "acknowledge[d] *Stentor's* argument that competition occurs at the margin, and . . . that the simple threat of entry may be enough to cause incumbents to behave competitively" (CRTC, 1994a, p. 69; emphasis added). Elsewhere, the CRTC acknowledged that long-distance competition was meagre and agreed with the "new coalition" that the "market" for enhanced services was a duopoly with "persisten[tly] . . . high market shares [held] by the Stentor companies" (CRTC, 1994a, p. 75). The evidence introduced showed that, despite "competition" being introduced a decade earlier in enhanced services, the Stentor group retained over 67% of telecoms network-based/enhanced services, Unitel had 25%, while resellers/competitors struggled for the leftover 6% to 8% (CRTC, 1994a, p. 74). A year after local exchanges became contestable, the CRTC (1995b, p. 58) admitted that competition would be even less in this area than in long distance, although it hoped this would change over the long run.

The problem with such candid breaths of fresh air is that they do not prevent the CRTC from slipping back and forth across different levels of analysis. The basic problem is that wedded to an unshakable belief in competition, the regulator can abuse binary oppositions between monopoly and not monopoly and thus ignore that there are least five options to consider: legal monopoly, legally permissible competition, contestible market theory, imperfect competition (market dominance, duopoly, oligopoly, etc.), or perfect competition. Without such distinctions the CRTC can, basically, abuse its position as the overseer of the public's interest through capricious determinations of when and where to regulate (see, e.g., the discussion of market power and use of the *Merger Enforcement Guidelines*, especially pages 64-67 in the *Framework* decision). There are two points to be made in respect to the present discussion.

Instead of adhering to any normal measures of industry dominance (Trebing, 1995, pp. 315-318), government policymakers have insisted on substituting new measures that make it next to impossible to find market power and thus to enforce strict regulation across the board, and not just in those areas most susceptible to the power and influence of dominant user groups. The CRTC (1994a) noted that although the *Mergers and Enforcement Guidelines* offer a measure of market dominance based on market share (35%), it would not adhere to this (pp. 67-68). Clearly, if it did so, it would have problems with the entire industry on its hands. The evidence introduced thus far clearly indicates that on this measure, there are definite inklings of something askew. Other accepted measures of market power, such as excess profits and exploitative pricing practices have been studiously avoided. Although definitions of what constitutes excess profits are no doubt subjective, profits in the range of 8% to 10%, even 12%, are usually considered within the norm of

competitive markets. Profits of between 15% and 20%, such as has been
the case for Stentor members, on average, over the last four to five years,
are usually considered abnormal (*Globe and Mail Report on Business*, 1996,
p. 162; Industry Canada, 1995, p. 4). Allegations of price setting are
perennial features of telecoms policy proceedings (Babe, 1990; Smythe,
1981) and have not gone away under regulated competition.

Developments in Canadian telecoms are not unique. In fact, they
are typically found wherever "competition" has been introduced. Even
after 16 years of contestible long-distance services in the United States,
and a dozen years since the implementation of the AT&T "break-up,"
long distance is still characterised by an oligopoly shared among AT&T
(68.5%), MCI (18.6%), and Sprint (8.3%) (total = 95.4%). This has only
tightened over the last few years, not weakened (Jackson, 1995, p. 13;
Trebing, 1995, pp. 317-318). Approximately 400 to 600 other entities
licensed by the FCC scramble for the remaining 4.5%. Despite an
ideological commitment to "deregulation" and "competition" that is
second to none, U.S. law makers recently passed the new
Telecommunications Act of 1996 (United States, 1996). As anticipated, this
has reinforced the trends just described, as BT and MCI amalgamate and
the RBOCs swallow one another as well as others across the electronic
mediascape.[28] Commenting on recent mergers between SBC and Pacific
Telesis on the west coast and Bell Atlantic's "cannibalisation" of Nynex in
the East, Noll (1996) provocatively asks if USWest is ready to mate with
SBC to form a Bell West, if Bell South will unite with the Bell
Atlantic/Nynex group to form a Bell East, and, if stuck in the middle,
Ameritech will "join the West or the East, or . . . act as the glue containing
all into a single maxi Bell" (p. B-9).

Adding to this speculation, we can ask if trends in Canada,
combined with the CRTC's tolerance of monopoly, could lead to
consolidation among the Stentor members to form a Bell North?
Together, the four companies, plus AT&T and the BT/MCI[29] group,
could devise a cartel modeled along the lines of the North American
Telegraph Association, which divided the field of electronic media among
the giants of telegraphy (and the press) almost 140 years ago (see
Chapter 3). The moves to release telecoms providers into the provision of
online content services, some of the arrangements made between
BT/MCI and Murdoch's News Corp., and similar initiatives afoot in
Canada contain compelling and interesting historical parallels.

Regulated Competition Could Still Be A Good Thing, Couldn't It?

With competition elevated to the ultimate goal of telecoms policy, the
regulator has now focused first and foremost on ensuring that its

decisions foster that goal. Whereas Bell, AGT/Telus, BCTel, and other Stentor members have implored the regulator to forebear from regulating each and every service, the "new coalition" has pleaded with the CRTC to continue regulating telecoms (see, e.g., CRTC, 1994a, pp. 74-75). With no conceptual space remaining to consider options, even the public interest groups such as the Public Interest Advocacy Centre, NAPO, the BC Old Age Pensioners Organisation, and labour unions, have had to form strategic alliances with either the "new coalition" or the incumbent telcos depending on the issue at hand.

The CRTC has accepted that competition in telecoms is weak, that long-distance prices "have not declined significantly since Decision 92-12," and that local rates have risen considerably (CRTC, 1994a, pp. 21-22; 1995a, p. 24). The Commission has committed itself to letting rates rise as much as possible, in essence to the point at which universal service is put in jeopardy. Prices will no longer be pushed to decline faster than the consumer price index, or in line with the falling cost brought about by the economics of the new media. Instead of reflecting "embedded costs," telephone prices will reflect "economic costs"; in other words, what people will pay just to stay connected to the PTN (CRTC, 1995a, p. 22). To this end, in 1995, price hikes of $2 per month for the next three years (total = $72) were approved. Indicating, however, that it was going to at least try to salvage something of the anticipated benefits of regulated competition, the CRTC refused telco requests for even larger increases and required that decreases of the same magnitude just granted in local service be applied to long-distance rates for typical subscribers (CRTC, 1995a, p. 24). Even such meagre efforts, however, to secure a modicum of benefits for people were squashed by the Governor General in Council (Liberal Minister of Industry, John Manley). At Stentor's behest, Manley eliminated sections of the decision requiring long-distance price cuts (Governor General in Council, 1995, P.C. 1995-2196). Afterward, Manley announced that his adjustments to the CRTC decision better reflected the need "to ensure a . . . globally competitive Canadian telephone industry in the international marketplace" (quoted in Surtees, 1995a, p. A2). Apparently, the Commission had not yet grasped the idea that citizens had to pay for competition at home as well as, according to the redubitable logic of Manley, subsidise it abroad.

The CRTC had not forgotten about "global competitiveness" but was busy instituting what it, the "new coalition," and telcos call "rate rebalancing" and "cost-based pricing." According to proponents of rate rebalancing, people have paid too little for local telephone service in the past because it was cross-subsidised by lush revenues from long-distance markets. However, in the new context, the price of telecoms services must come down because, as seen earlier, they are such a big "cost of production." Such "subsidies" can no longer be afforded. Moreover, this is one of those unjust "forms of taxation" saddling business, claim leaders of the "new coalition" such as the CBTA (CRTC, 1994a, p. 17).

However, not everybody agrees with this analysis. Instead, some argue that the price of local telephone service only looks low because too many costs have been loaded into the "local service" category. Evidence of this was introduced earlier, in relation to the 1985 decision to transfer $1.76 billion in costs (network access service charges) from the long-distance account to the local account. Yet, even that transfer of who pays what for different services did not meet the CRTC's "rate rebalancing" demands because in the latest round of hearings it has allowed any remaining network access service charges to be carried over and charged against local telephone rates, and even added a few more costs that used to be buried in the "long-distance" account. It did draw the line, however, at the point at which the telcos tried to charge the costs of collecting long-distance revenues against local subscribers.

Some argued it was wrong to charge all these things to people who might never even use long-distance services, or use them very little. The CRTC disagreed. They were "common-costs," it argued, and should be paid for by everyone. The CRTC (1995b) argued that trying to isolate those costs associated only with the supply of local telephone service ignored "economies of scale and scope that could arise when services are supplied on an integrated basis" (p. 20). Absolutely, but why resuscitate this concern now, as it was exactly this point that the CRTC conveniently ignored to create regulated competition in the first place? Committed to "competition," however, the CRTC either no longer cares about coherence or is willing to use whatever methods confirm its beliefs.

Despite the herculean efforts to make the world fit new theoretical concepts, certain critics still persisted. Even Unitel and other new competitors complained that the incumbents were inflating the cost of the local exchange, something of pecuniary interest to them because the cost of the local exchange agreed on between CRTC and Stentor determines what newcomers pay in interconnection fees. Unitel introduced data showing that Bell attributed more costs to the local exchange than is usual practice in the United States. Unitel also claimed that Bell underestimated what it cost to produce long-distance services, a claim it buttressed by showing that Bell's costs were lower than AT&T's costs for the United States. The upshot of the Unitel/AT&T claim was that people were paying too much for local phone service and that Bell might be using local rates to cross-subsidise long-distance services in a bid to retain its monopoly.[30]

In support of such claims, the public interest group NAPO also introduced a model that identified the stand-alone cost of producing local telephone services, competitive services, optional services, and long distance. According to this model, the only reason the cost of local service appeared so high was because too many costs (e.g., common costs) had been assigned to the local exchange. If these were properly attributed, then there was, in fact, no cross-subsidy. The conclusion to be drawn was that local telephone service, if "cost-based" pricing was really followed, might be more affordable than ever before. Of course, this supported the public interest groups. It also suited new competitors, as it buttressed their efforts to establish a regulated price floor beneath which long-distance prices could not drop, and thus opened the road to greater profits. This was hardly the outcome expected by the "new coalition," government, or the CRTC, however. They had not spent the 15 years dismantling the monopoly regime just to get competition and lower prices for the vast majority of subscribers.

The Commission dismissed the findings as "academic" and not sensitive to factors that made long distance in Canada inherently cheaper than in the United States (CRTC, 1995b, p. 17). This was astounding because up to that point it was always claimed that geographical factors and lower population densities conspired to make long-distance charges more expensive in Canada. Rather than explaining the "new wisdom," however, the Commission just mumbled about how all these things were quite subjective no matter how you cut them, and then returned to repeating the old mantra about how long distance cross-subsidised local service and that this would have to change to create competition in telecoms (see the CRTC's [1994a] *Regulatory Framework* decision or the subsequent CRTC [1995b] *Implementation of the Regulatory Framework* decision (especially pp. 16-21).

Just as regulated competition raised rates before the creation of natural monopoly, it looks like it is repeating this again in the 1990s. Of course, this is not true for those large businesses who pick and choose among the 150 "competitors" scrambling to get hold of their lush accounts (Mozes & Sciadas, 1995), nor for those who want to call between Toronto, Montreal, and Vancouver, and a few other places in between. The link between regulated competition and higher costs for telephone service just apply to most people. Historical trends in telephone pricing are presented in Figure 6.3.

Universal Service?

Indicative of the trend toward higher rates is the greater attention now given to efforts to ensure that people at least have access to basic telephone services. As the CRTC (1995b) states,

> the prospect of further local rate increases, particularly for residential subscribers, warrants an examination of how best to ensure that local

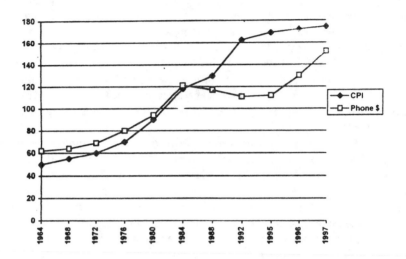

Figure 6.3. Telephone charges and the consumer price index (1964-1997)
Source: DBS (1965-69) and Statistics Canada. (1995, 1972-1996).
Note: Rates for 1996 and 1997 extrapolate from trends in the cpi over the last four years. Telephone price increases have been estimated on the basis of rate increases announced by the Canadian Radio-television and Telecommunications Commission (CRTC, 1995c).

> service remains universally accessible at affordable rates. The Commission notes that approaches for addressing local service affordability have generally taken one of two forms: budget service or targeted subsidy programmes. (p. 3)

According to AGT's proposed budget service—which the CRTC has mentioned as particularly impressive—affordable, universal telephone service could be maintained by "reducing levels of service" such as preventing access to long-distance capabilities, or imposing a surcharge for the use of such facilities. Perhaps this scheme interests industry and regulators, but universal service used to include long distance. Why the narrowing of the concept? If competition is to be in the public interest, it should expand, not contract, access to the PTN and the concept of universal service. Other programs suggest that government administer a universal service fund. In others, there are targeted subsidies for those who can demonstrate that they are poor. Apparently, and again in contrast to CRTC policy not so long ago, concern about people's dignity is just one more casualty in the stalwart march to the information economy.

This erosion of the concept of universal service cannot be severed from earlier decisions (84-18) and the CUFTA/NAFTA/GATS trilogy that tightly constrains what services can be governed by universal service policies. Cumulatively, these measures enforce a narrow definition of universal service and ensure that new communication technologies and services remain beyond the reach of public policy. Altogether, universal service has been diluted in terms of geographical coverage, the range of services covered, the definition of basic telephone service, and agents responsible for achieving social policy goals.

This is not to say that competition must erode universal service. Universal service can be improved under a monopolistic, duopolistic, or competitive market structure, if regulatory policy does not connive with industry to weaken the criteria used to evaluate public service goals. Unfortunately, it seems that we are now in the midst of the worst of all possible worlds, as neither regulated monopoly, meaningful competition, or regulatory responsibility prevail. In this vacuous netherland, the power of the state and oligopolistic corporations collude to betray any meaningful commitment to people. Perhaps the best example of just how ludicrous state/corporate collusion can be and still claim to serve the public is represented by proposals in the United Kingdom. There, Oftel and BT talk about

> proposals . . . *for an outgoing calls barred service* . . . and a limited service where customers prepay for a certain value of calls to be made each month (*when reached, the line would revert to outgoing calls barred*). These *packages should help make the telephone more affordable and increase penetration rates.* (Office of Telecommunications, 1996, p. 4; emphasis added)

Despite Oftel and BT's obfuscation of the issues, transforming the telephone into a one-way communication system does not constitute a meaningful concept of universal service. Yet, it is just such redefinitions of communication that allow studies to show that competition does not cut people off from telephone service and that this may even increase levels of "universal service" as redefined. This is precisely the strategy adopted in an important OECD (1995a) study. If thinking about universal service is realistically portrayed by proposals now in favour with AGT, Bell, BT, the CRTC, Oftel, and so on, then what will universal access to the PANS (pretty amazing new services) of the heralded information highway look like? That is one of the questions pursued in the following chapter.

SUMMARY COMMENTS

Telecoms policy has become strategised and saturated with machinations of power, rather than open to the potentials of what people might do with the vastly powerful instruments of communication being introduced into society. This was evident in this chapter in at least three ways. First, the state has become an industrial state. As such, it is a Strong State that is, by and large, undemocratic—a political entity that works mainly to recalibrate society and industry to global imperatives that it helped unleash to begin with. The strong state has been conspicuous in successive efforts to shield new media from public interference; its intrusive interference before, during, and after CRTC hearings; by allowing private interests to usurp and drive the policy agenda; and, finally, by eliminating any provincial autonomy in electronic media.

Second, the elevation of competition to an end in itself is evident in the fact that it was born in Canada, not out of compelling evidence, nor recognised potential for sustainable, real competition, but because the CRTC came to believe in competition. It is not that there were not alternate paths or that competition could not be introduced in a sensible way. The CRTC struggled to reconcile competition and public service aims endlessly between 1976 and, 1987, before being forced to abandon its worthwhile initiatives by private and government interests who had aggrandised power over the years. As the Europeans had shown, and the CRTC had discussed prior to 1984, online services could develop in a competitive framework without abandoning public service aims or sanctioning unbridled/unsustainable network competition. Even from the narrow, albeit key, concern of price, Figure 6.3. shows that at least some attention was given to the costs of "competition" for the public until about 1992, when prices reversed their historical decline and began to climb.

Moreover, wedded to imprecise concepts of competition, the CRTC has been unable to muster a meaningful response to global market failure. As AT&T, BT/MCI, and a few others argue that global telecoms will be run by five PTOs in the not-too-distant future (and exert efforts to make this prophecy happen), a stable oligopoly in U.S. telecoms has settled in after 16 years of "competition," and the Canadian telecoms industry becomes aligned with either BT/MCI (Stentor), AT&T (Unitel/Banks), or Sprint (CallNet), it is time to stop mumbling about competition and get on with harnessing telecoms policy to more broadly felt goals. A choice is squarely on the telecoms policy agenda: namely, between the telecoms system in Canada being grafted onto the global telecoms oligopoly that is now in the making, or tempering the trend toward global consolidation in such a way as to continue with at least a relatively autonomous telecoms system in the country that can serve the interests of Canadian citizens, broadly defined.

With respect to so-called broadly defined goals, three proposals seem reasonable: one, that telecoms be depoliticised by removing the intrusive hand of the state and allowing control over the telecoms policy agenda to be returned to the CRTC and once again opened up for negotiation as to the ends desired and the practical means needed to obtain them. Second, this will require that the ongoing efforts to constrain universal service cease, and a commitment made to a more meaningful concept of communication that serves public and commercial needs in whatever way is most pragmatic. Third, the price of telecoms services should take as its guide at least two reference points. The least stringent criteria should be that no prices can rise faster than the CPI, and tariffs must be filed to avoid inflated prices from the start. A more stringent criteria should be based on the fact that transmission and switching costs for telecoms carriers are falling by at least 10% a year. Essentially, these two points set the 'bandwidth' within which prices can move.

The next chapter considers media reconvergence, that is, the forces bringing media together again and the prospects of new media for public life and private needs in Canada.

ENDNOTES

1. Of course, global news agencies are not new and have been around in modern form since at least the 1850s. The difference is related to the greater number of these agencies, the recomposition of their focus more exclusively on business-related news and services, and, as a result, how media and information are now inextricably weaved into the fabric of global capitalism so as to render the two mutually constitutive in an unprecedented way.

2. The U.S. regulatory framework started to distinguish between regulated and unregulated services with its Computer I decision in 1971. It was replaced in 1980 by the FCC's Computer II decision. The latter decision required structural separation between the telephone companies competitive and noncompetitive services. Yet another decision, Computer III in 1986, maintained the distinction between regulated (noncompetitive) and competitive (unregulated) services, but dropped the structural separation requirement (FCC, 1986). Competition would be secured by making parts of the telephone companies' networks available to would-be competitors on a nondiscriminatory basis (Mansell, 1993).

3. This was quite important because European privacy and data protection laws are usually considered to be much stronger than in the United Kingdom or North America, as they insist on prior consent for collection and third party use of personal information, the right to inspect personal information held in data banks, and so on.

4. The distinctions that these agreements try to draw among telecoms-network services, cable, and broadcasting is discussed in the next chapter.

5. Although I discuss these areas again in the next chapter, but with an eye to how they impact on the issue of media reconvergence, note that the GATS agreement may not be as powerful globally as CUFTA and NAFTA are regionally. This is because, interesting enough, it appears that even some of those within the telecoms industry and/or the global policymaking elite do not take them very seriously. During recent conversations with policymakers and PTO representatives in Singapore and the EC, I was told that despite the fact that their efforts to regulate online content services transgressed GATS measures, they would proceed nonetheless. Perhaps this is due to the fact that GATS is recognised as an interim measure on the way to full "liberalisation," as is now taking place under the auspices of the Negotiating Group on Basic Telecoms. Even before the GATS agreement was signed, the United States circulated a confidential proposal among Canadian negotiators and PTOs, and perhaps others, that staked out the conditions to include facilities-based competition in basic services.

6. Interestingly, AT&T had set up an office in Ottawa, the political capital of Canada (not one of the financial centres, such as Toronto or Montreal), in 1992. Such a choice of locations indicated not only a desire to get more involved in Canadian telecoms but also that it knew that the road to that end ran through the halls of Parliament as much as anywhere else. On another tangential point, also recall that Ted Rogers, Canada's "media mogul" behind the Rogers/Unitel venture, had made much of his communications empire as a result of changes to Canadian laws in 1968 that limited foreign ownership in the communication industries to only 20% of any one firm. It seems tragic, in a literary sense, that a corporate history that made as much out of government policy as anything else could culminate in the dispensation of those results to one of the largest telecoms empires in the world. Charles Sirois, director of the newly privatised Teleglobe, has recently suggested that all rules restricting foreign ownership of Canadian carriers should be eliminated, or reduced to a 49% limit.

7. The government privatized its 53% interest in March 1992, when it sold shares to Alouette Telecommunications, Inc., which is the Stentor group with the addition of the Canadian satellite manufacturer, Spar (Department of Finance, 1992). The largest participant is Bell Canada. Although one-third of Telesat was supposed to be held by "the public," no mention of this phantom group was made during the privatisation process.

8. Two measures of government spending reveal that it has not declined in the last decade or more, despite the so-called austerity programs, privatisation, and "deregulation." The first, a measure of government investment as a portion of all investment in the economy, reveals that government spending

rose between 1988 and 1993, from 21.8% to 27%. In addition, public spending as a percentage of the Gross Domestic Product has remained constant from the end of the 1970s (Statistics Canada, 1989-1994b, Table 23). Similar patterns prevail in the United Kingdom, where public spending as a percentage of GDP was exactly the same in 1995/96 as it was in 1978/79, 42.25% (Plender, 1997, p. 21). A read through the Government of Canada's 1996a publication, *Building the Information Society: Moving Canada into the 21st Century,* helps establish the claim that privatisation is less about reducing deficits and more about transforming how government intervenes in, creates, and expands telecoms markets. A review of that document reveals that government has earmarked $4.76 billion in funds to "move Canada into the 21st century," most of it in the short term, and a smaller amount to 1999. Most of it is funding for private industry, mainly the telcos, and is directed at expanding the technological infrastructure. As noted, the federal government is spending $3.2 billion on R and D, giving away $1 billion in tax credits, among other things. Of course, these are "partnerships," "stimulating," "preparing Canadian companies for the information age," "encouragements," and other thinly disguised covers for corporate welfare (see in particular, pp. 7-11). These are discussed further in the following chapter along with a discussion of funding for public access to new telecoms services.

9. The evisceration of the public sector is not unconnected to the CUFTA and NAFTA agreement provisions that redefine public crown corporations as monopolies and impose limitations on their methods of operation. As Mosco (1990b) states, redefining key instruments of public policy as monopolies delegitimates them, whereas other sections of the agreements wipe out any rational for having them to begin with, as they are forced to use "cost-based" pricing, penalised if they undertake any exemptions to promote "cultural policies," and brought under the watchful eye of Ottawa to ensure that they generally comply with the terms of the agreement (pp. 48-50; Canada, 1992, Article 1305).

10. The question of competition is discussed at greater length near the end of this chapter. For now, let it just be noted that although there may be 150 resellers, the fact that they account for only about $100 million in revenues out of $16 billion total network and services revenues (e.g., about .7% of all sales) suggests quite strongly that they really are on the "competitive fringes" of Canadian telecoms. Based on the figures available in Mozes and Sciadas (1995) with respect to large users and expenditures, it is possible to estimate that about 150 resellers compete for the accounts of between 200 and 500 large users—hardly the heartland of Canadian telecoms, although, as is shown shortly, this may admittedly be quite important for these few large beneficiaries of changes in Canadian telecoms policy. The basic question is really about whether or not public policy should be privatised to serve the needs of such a small number of large users (also see the discussion in Mozes and Sciadas, 1995, p. 85).

11. Broader questions about facilities-based competition *within* telecoms are deferred to a latter section of this chapter, and similar issues as they apply *across* the electronic media are treated in the next chapter.

12. Large firms were defined as those with over $5 million in annual revenues. No data was given with respect to how many of these there are in Canada, how much was spent on use of the PTN versus private networks, how much contribution to the overall economy they make, and so on (Mozes & Sciadas, 1995, p. 76).

13. These sources reported, for example, that Unitel was expected to lose $250 million in 1995 alone. Interestingly, the recent Unitel-related transactions have lead to the exodus of CP from telecoms. This is particularly interesting as it concretises the shift away from the "transportation" model of communication underlying much of this century's thinking about telecoms and symbolises the reintegration of communications and content/services that was the hallmark of telecoms for much of the last century (as described in Chapter 3). Babe (1990) also notes that Bell Canada has a significant stake in Montreal Trust Company, marking its foray into banking and finance affairs.

14. In the United Kingdom, Barclays Bank has been one of the leading interests holding shares in Mercury, the only major rival to BT.

15. See McQuaig (1995) for a critique of the "debt crisis" with respect to Canada.

16. Officials who most recently turned the stiles between government and industry include George Addy, former Director of Investigation and Research under the *Competition Act*, who went to AGT/Telus; Barbara McDougal, former Conservative Cabinet Minister now heads up AT&T's Canadian branch; and Nick Mulder, former Deputy Minister of Industry Canada, who has traded caps for a position with Stentor's regulatory affairs office. There are numerous others who have done the same and now fill the corporate offices of Unitel/AT&T, BCTel, and so on.

17. Although the proliferation of agencies may seem at odds with regulatory liberalisation, this fails to see, as Duch (1991) notes, that fragmentation of the state helps new interest constellations to form outside existing coalitions and to exploit endemic internecine rivalry among government agencies over the spoils of political power (pp. 236-243). Thus it is not odd at all that the abandonment of the telecoms monopoly has been followed by the rapid growth of new agencies, or that NAFTA and GATS promote the formalisation of regulatory agencies not their dismantling. The United Kingdom is a prime example: incessant bickering among the Department of Trade and Industry, the Office of Telecommunications Policy (Oftel), and the Monopolies and Mergers Commission has mostly benefited industry. This has also been true of France and Germany (OECD, 1988, pp. 37-38).

18. Although I have not referenced all of the Orders-in-Council used to vary or rescind the CRTC's Call Net decisions, the crucial dates are from October 1987 until March 1990, and the Order in Council numbers involved are P. C. 1987-606; P.C. 1988-265; P.C. 1988-2386; P.C. 1989-1238; and P.C. 1990-620.

19. By the logic of these observations, authoritarian states like Argentina, Chile, and Singapore, to name a few, are "better States" because they do not care about political legitimacy and other "frills" of a democratic polity. As such, they are more able to push through unpopular programs like privatisation, free trade agreements, regulatory liberalisation, and so on.

20. Section 9(3) of the *Telecommunications Act* (1993) states that "the decision of the Commission that a person is or is not an interested person is binding and conclusive," meaning that not only can the CRTC exclude people but also that, unlike every other section of the law, this cannot be appealed to Cabinet or the Courts.

21. The decision was precipitated by CRTC decisions allowing CNCP to interconnect with the telcos' local exchanges for its competitive data services. When AGT refused, it was challenged on the grounds that it had to comply with federal telecoms policy because telecoms was undisputedly under federal authority. Although the provinces resisted on the grounds that they had established defacto jurisdiction through a form of "squatter's rights," this was rejected. The British North America Act clearly identifies telegraphs as federal constitutional prerogatives, a fact confirmed in Toronto v. Bell (1905), Re Radio (1932), and many times subsequently.

22. It makes little sense to maintain a publicly owned PTO in light of the constraints imposed by "global trade regimes" and/or the strictures of regulatory liberalisation at home. Rather than limiting themselves to delivering a service that is 120 years old, it makes sense to allow private control of what was once an unbounded public resource. The only surprise, now that MTS is to be farmed out to the private sector, is that SaskTel has yet to be put up for sale. Resuscitating public ownership would mean redefining communication as something other than a commodity or tradable good on the stock market.

23. To the best of my knowledge, these proposals were never included in the final Constitutional reform package. Instead, they have been implemented through sector-specific legislative and policy changes, as is indicated with respect to telecoms. Even so, tinkering with the Constitution is pretty serious, and to even suggest writing these things into the supreme law under which people live is amazing. It also indicates the serious, as well as enduring, influence of the "crisis of democracy" thesis. Recall that such efforts proposed Constitutional reform to curtail the democratic distemper (McKay, 1983, p. 100; Rowley, 1983, pp. 53-61; see especially Crozier et. al. 1975, p. 63 for a description of what the "democratic distemper" is and for a discussion of how the excesses of democracy are embedded in the heart of western Constitutions and why this is dangerous).

24. Although proposals to change the price structure to favour business are usually justified on the basis of their function in the production of wealth, a factor presumed absent for residential users, two objections must be raised. First, although it is claimed that reduced business costs will be passed on to consumers, one must be sceptical. With bank profits in the range of 25% return on capital, and telephone companies only slightly below that, it is likely that any cost reductions would just further inflate profits rather than be delivered as a "consumer bonus." Second, considering that the home and people's expenditures are necessary to the reproduction of labour power, there is no compelling logic to favour business over the home for preferential pricing regimes on even the most economistic of grounds.

25. The CRTC, rather than looking for economies of scale and scope across the range of services offered by the telephone companies, limited its analysis to

whether or not long distance contained significant economies of scale. Essentially, instead of looking at telecoms as a system, the CRTC's method looked at the parts instead of the whole. Although this was inadequate, it is important to note two things. First, even this obscurantist methodological "trick" failed to support the CRTC's ideological preferences. Second, the capriciousness of the approach was revealed subsequently—as seen in the next section—when the CRTC spurned critics for using a similar method that basically hid any economies of scale or scope that might exist by looking at the telecoms system as a bundle of component parts, each imminently divisible.

26. The earlier Task Forces had already made this clear, stating that "competition would not be viable, . . . unless strong continued regulatory protections were provided" (Federal Provincial Task Force on Telecommunications, 1988, pp. 96-97).

27. This is one of the new mantras accompanying the new regime, repeated over and over again in order to justify almost anything (also see Regulatory Framework decision (94-19) (CRTC, 1994a, p. 19).

28. See Appendix One for a list of some of the recent mergers and acquisitions within telecoms and across the electronic mediascape. The list is not exhaustive but has been culled from a regular review of the U.K. business press, mainly the *Financial Times,* and the CEC (1995).

29. Note that MCI and the Stentor group already have extensive service contracts.

30. This, it can be recalled from Chapter 4, was exactly the strategy that had been used by Bell, and accepted by regulators, between 1914 and 1916 to decimate competition and to usher in the era of natural monopoly.

7 PURSUING THE HOLY GRAIL: INFORMATION HIGHWAYS AND MEDIA RECONVERGENCE

At the same time that government policymakers, TOs, and the "new coalition" were transforming the regulatory regime within telecoms during the 1980s and the first few years of the 1990s, they neglected the boundaries between telecoms, broadcasting, cable, and other electronic media. Only in the last several years has this reversed and efforts recalibrated to promote media (re)convergence. Although (re)convergence discretely entered the policy agenda near the close of the 1980s, such a potential was foreclosed by the *Broadcasting Act* (1991) and the *Telecommunications Act* (1993). Only the labour unions and publicly owned prairie telcos queried the wisdom of writing restrictions on convergence into the law during the hearings on the new telecoms law in 1992.

However, before the ink on the new telecoms legislation dried, the clarion calls for media (re)convergence were raised with a sense of dire urgency. Over a period of perhaps a year, reconvergence went from being the preserve of labour unions, prairie provinces, and the boondocks of government-sponsored studies to become an urgent matter of life and death. A new awareness suddenly found forceful expression in industry reports, government policy statements, and, of course, the popular media.

Symptomatic of the new sense of urgency attached to media reconvergence were statements made by the Stentor group of telephone companies, as they announced their Beacon initiative—a plan to spend $8.5 billion (cnd) to build a nation-wide, integrated broadband communication network (IBN) to be implemented by 2005. The program was crucial to the carriers in an era of competition, Stentor (1994) explained, but more importantly, and ominously, to the survival of the country as a whole. According to the *Beacon* proposal, released in 1994,

265

Canada must act now or get left behind. It is a *simple question of survival* in this fast-changing world. . . .

If we don't act quickly to make the information highway a reality, Canadian industry will fall steadily behind industries in other countries, Canadian employment will suffer and Canadian's standard of living will fall.

The information highway will accelerate the development of technologies and services critical to Canada's international competitiveness; *it will stimulate huge investment.* (emphasis added, p. 8)

The federal government agreed with this assessment. Survival, it claims, hinges on new media, wise policy, and communication industries cut loose from the shackles of the past. The message was reiterated in *Building the Information Society: Moving Canada into the 21st Century* (Canada, 1996a), a document that culminated the investigations of the Information Highway Advisory Council (IHAC), the CRTC and other government/ private sector initiatives over the last few years and inspired the new "convergence policy." According to the Government of Canada (1996a)

If we fall behind our major trading partners in building our Information Highway, its worldwide counterpart will come to Canada—later—and not the way Canadians want to see it.

Failure to seize the opportunity of using Canada's Information Highway will also result in reduced competitiveness and the loss of high-growth knowledge industries and high-quality jobs. The social costs . . . will be enormous. Our national cultural dialogue will languish and our governments will be less able to keep up with the . . . realities of the electronic age. (p. 3)

The popular press dutifully reported on these twists and turns in the development of information highway initiatives. Articles in the *Toronto Globe & Mail* containing the words "information highway" went from a trickle to some 513 stories in 1994 (Babe, 1996, p. 283). Likewise, stories in the *Ottawa Citizen* made reference to the "Internet," "information highway," or the "information super-highway" 395 times in 1994, 831 times in 1995, and nearly 1,500 times in 1996.

There was also marked agreement among industry statements, government policy documents and the press that the changes were driven primarily by technology. As a story from the *Economist* reprinted in the *Globe and Mail* waxed, "companies . . . have been transfixed by a vision of the profits to be made as *technology blends the telephone, the computer and the television*" (Bumps and potholes," 1994, p. A-16; emphasis added). On the other side of the Atlantic, a high-priced study by the consulting firm KPMG (1996a) prepared for the European Commission stated unconditionally that "[t]hroughout the world, information and communications *technologies are generating* an industrial revolution. *Technological developments are leading to the convergence* of audiovisual and telecommunications" sectors (pp. iii-iv; emphasis added). Despite the historical naiveté of this position, Stentor, the "new coalition" and government policymakers also endorsed the notion that it is technology that drives media *re*convergence (Canada, 1996a; Schultz & Janisch, 1993; Stentor, 1995).

It is claimed the progressive thrust of new technology, however, is still hindered by the reluctance of government to remove the heavy hand of regulation. Just behind the threat of cultural survival lurks yet another threat: the possibility that investment could be held back by government's failure to remove its intrusive hands from media markets. The message is clear: "Stentor companies invest approximately $4 billion a year in upgrading their networks and in related research and development. With greater regulatory freedom . . . *these investments would be increased significantly*" (Stentor, 1994, p. 14; emphasis added). A year later, Stentor (1995) again reminded government that "policy and regulatory uncertainty" were putting "telephone companies' investments . . . into doubt, which could undermine investor confidence" (p. 2). This was a call to rewrite electronic media laws, tout court, as a quid pro quo for investment. If electronic media policy was not totally revamped, Stentor members would plunge the country into information age hell. Obviously, the stakes were high.

The telephone companies and other new media providers were— as discussed in detail near the end of the chapter—not just striving for greater regulatory liberalisation across the entire electronic mediascape but new political and civil liberties. As Shultz and Janisch (1993) argued in a paper commissioned by Stentor, the carriers and all other electronic media should be given the "freedom to compete," and existing liberties shorn of "positive freedoms" in favour of "narrowly defined negative" freedoms (p. 9). In the scheme of things, the survival of Canada and investment in vital infrastructure were tied to new media freedoms for large corporations. As the following account shows, the government duly obliged, dismantling restrictions to cross-media ownership, allowing members of Stentor to line up for new media freedoms guaranteed under the *Charter of Human Rights and Freedom* (discussed later), and accepting that promotion of media (re)convergence "would stimulate investment and innovation in the new technologies and services critical to building Canada's Information Highway" (Canada, 1996a, p. 6). As a result, media policy went from preventing reconvergence to promoting it in a remarkably short time.

THE CALM BEFORE THE HYPE

The intense hype and threats of cultural survival of the mid-1990s contrasted sharply with the more austere and reflective first steps toward media reconvergence begun a few years earlier by the Canadian government and various policy agencies. Prior to 1994, there were only transitory ruptures in the status quo, as in 1989 when the Minister of Communications and Bell's de Grandpré publicly ruminated about the possibility of fostering telco/cable competition. Although Bell forever held this option in hand (Babe, 1990, pp. 136, 218), the brief publicness of this potential was quickly replaced with relative silence, a quiet that prevailed beyond the ripe opportunities to alter the status quo offered by the *Broadcasting Act* rewrite in 1991 and the *Telecommunications Act* two years later. Transitory ruptures in the consensus were more tactical threats and strategic rivalry then changes in policy. For the Minister of Communications, political points could be had by chastising cable companies for abusing their local monopolies, without doing much to curtail these abuses (Statistics Canada, 1995d, Table 3).[1] The telcos were interested in preempting further incursions by cable companies, especially Rogers, into telecoms, a potential widened by CRTC decisions opening local networks to some competition and tighter ties between Rogers and CNCP (CRTC, 1990).

The consensus began to unravel a bit further in 1991 with the publication of two DOC- and CRTC-sponsored studies. Both favoured eliminating obstructions to convergence but remained cautious in their recommendations as to when and how convergence could/should be brought about. One study noted that even after legal barriers were removed, network infrastructures would only slowly converge—technically and functionally—over a relatively long period of time, perhaps mainly after the year 2005. This study further noted significant economic barriers to convergence and development of IBNs, namely, the high cost of running fibre optic lines or a hybrid fibre/coaxial cable system into subscribers' homes, as well as the uncertain demand for the services distributed through such a network (Comgate, 1991, pp. 3, 21). Studies in the United States came to similar conclusions (Elton, 1992).

Although these issues are discussed further later, it can be added that the *un*economics of IBNs was buttressed by several experiments showing that people were quite unwilling to allocate more time and discretionary income to television, home shopping, online games, and other specialised services that the communications industry saw as the key drivers of the new media environment (Baldwin, McVoy, & Steinfield, 1996, pp. 63-71; KPMG, 1996a, pp. 82, 103-105). Moreover, the RBOCs, AT&T, and several publishers' attempts to commercialise videotext, gateway services, the picture phone, and so on, typically "fared miserably" and were either shut down quickly or allowed to expire silently outside the media spotlight (Baldwin, McVoy, & Steinfield, 1996, pp. 64-66; Shields, Dervin, Richter, & Soller, 1993, p. 565). In Canada, the joint Bell/government Telidon experiments, begun in 1975, were abandoned in 1983. They were only able to claim, at best, "a long series of half successes and half failures" (Proulx, 1991, p. 400). Bell's subsequent experiments with the Alex "gateway" service begun in 1988 was finally laid to rest in 1993.

SLIPPERY SLOPES AND ELECTRONIC PUBLISHERS ON THE INFORMATION HIGHWAY

Given the tepid support for telecoms network-based information and multimedia services, it is not surprising that nobody rushed out to dismantle the regulatory regime governing relations across the electronic mediascape. However, fractures turned into fissures throughout the early 1990s, as policy developments stealthily chipped away at the consensus supporting long-standing artificial divisions between electronic media. One such example was a decision in 1991 by the CRTC to allow Amtel Group, Inc. (AGI)—a company offering telephone and cable service in small, southern Ontario communities prior to the CRTC's 1969 policy statement prohibiting common carriers from owning cable systems except in rural and remote communities—to acquire a cable system in the Northern Ontario town of Simcoe (CRTC, 1991a, pp. 1-3). Although the decision did not establish any new principles, it did open the floodgates for a process of eroding media boundaries through an ever widening range of "exceptions to the rule."

The steady erosion of media boundaries continued apace a year later as the CRTC announced that it would consider telco/cable cross-overs in its upcoming regulatory framework decision. A year later, the new telecoms law shored up the boundaries between cable and telephony and the common-carrier principle that barred TOs from influencing the content of the messages they distributed, but gave the Commission the discretion to alter this requirement as it saw fit (Canada, 1993a, sec. 36).

The CRTC wasted no time using its discretion to open up a new range of exceptions to the general rule, as it allowed the BCE affiliate NorthwestTel to offer cable services in the Northwest Territories and the Yukon (CRTC, 1994b, 1995c),[2] spelled out the conditions under which telcos could conduct video-on-demand (VOD) experiments (CRTC, 1994c), and, crucially, in several pronouncements in 1994 and 1995, set out criteria the telephone companies would have to meet to offer video-dial tone (VDT), VOD, and near-VOD (NVOD) services and to hold broadcasting licenses (CRTC 1994a, 1995a, 1995b). By 1995, conditions were in place for reconvergence to move from the margins of Canadian communication toward the core.

The most important aspects of the CRTC's sweeping regulatory and policy changes with respect to media reconvergence are found in the *Review of Regulatory Framework* (94-19), *Competition and Culture on Canada's Information Highway* (1995a), and the *Implementation of Regulatory Framework* decision (95-21) (1995b). In the beginning, the Commission announced that it believed "telephone companies can play a useful role in the provision of new information services, including content-based services" (CRTC, 1994b, p. 32). This overturned the framework set out in the *Enhanced Services* decision a decade earlier and further eroded the common-carrier principle. Telecoms carriers were once again electronic publishers. Turning the tables against anyone thinking about challenging this outcome, the CRTC (1994a) warned "that there was a heavy onus on interveners seeking to restrict telephone companies from controlling the content of telecommunications services they provide" (p. 52). Continuing, it argued that

> competition, technology and the globalisation of markets have reduced concerns that any one supplier can control the provision of information services. Information is an unlimited commodity . . . . While various entities may control certain databases and various forms of information . . ., information is manipulated and disseminated far more rapidly than it is possible to control . . . . [T]elephone companies could make an important contribution to increasing the number and diversity of services, including services of an interactive or transactional nature, available to consumers. (p. 51)

The history of telecoms and online information services reviewed in this book does not support the CRTC's strategy of increasing the burden on those who would critique its or the telcos' preferred "world view." Although changes have no doubt occurred, these do not sweep away a record of abuses stretching across 150 years of telecoms history. Briefly, the history of "electronic publishers" (1846-1910) reviewed in Chapter 3, the decimation of competitive and independent telephone suppliers enroute to "natural monopoly" in 1915-6, usurpation of cable policy and regulation of media content by the telcos until 1977, and the failure of telcos to offer viable content services from the 1970s until the closing of Bell's Alex service in 1993, suggests that the recent flourishing of online content services associated with the Internet and so on has occurred despite the telcos' presence and certainly not from their participation. The mushrooming of online content services has been a result of technological changes, widespread interest in using the new technologies to overcome entrenched media practices, and regulatory policies, such as the *Enhanced Services* decision, which kept carriers out of content. Three other events in the recent history of electronic media also indicate why it may not be desirable to turn common carriers into electronic publishers: the use of familiar tactics by the telcos that jeopardize the survival of Internet Service Providers (ISPs); attempts to offset the poor economics of IBNs through a mass media model of development; and the long-term futility of trying to regulate network media through a hybrid electronic publisher/broadcast/common-carrier regime. Before turning to these concerns, however, it is necessary to consider the remaining efforts to dissolve the boundaries between electronic media.

During the just mentioned series of hearings the telephone companies pressed the CRTC to allow them into broadcasting and cable television. The telephone companies announced that they no longer wanted to be "common carriers pure and simple," to paraphrase de Grandpré's words to Parliament nearly three decades ago which helped usher in legislated media divergence. Although the CRTC postponed the matter, in 1995 it established the conditions under which the carriers could enter broadcasting. First, extending the logic established in the *Regulatory Framework* decision, the telcos would not be limited to carrying broadcast programming for others but could produce content themselves. Second, the telcos would not have to do this through a separate affiliate, a dubious concept used to shield one arm of a corporate organisation from another area in the corporate hierarchy.[3] Third, under the new policy all carriers—telcos, cable, satellite, wireless, and so on—will be regulated by the *Telecommunications Act* (1993) when providing telecoms services and the *Broadcasting Act* (1991) when offering broadcasting services. Thus, there would be reconvergence in facilities but continued separation of media along the lines of content (CRTC, 1995a, pp. 23-35).

Instead of eliminating the lines between different areas of the media, new government policy shifts the axis from distribution networks/technology to the level of content. On the one hand, the CRTC can continue regulating programming services according to the *Broadcasting Act* (1991) and thus pursue potentially worthwhile cultural policy goals with respect to Canadian content and so on. On the other hand, this exercise in line-drawing betrays the rhetoric of (re)convergence and opens new lines of media politics as various actors struggle over what should and should not be covered under the aims of cultural policy. The new policy also shifts media politics away from structural issues, which are usually considered to be less intrusive and susceptible to government interference with media freedoms, to content issues, which have traditionally come under government influence only narrowly and when absolutely necessary. In short, the new media policy increases the potential for those who own the means of distribution and government to control/influence the content of communication.

Inklings of problems were immediately evident, as the CRTC struggled over whether NVOD, VOD, and video games, for example, should be defined as programming and thus covered by the *Broadcasting Act,* or as something else and thus exempt from cultural policy obligations (CRTC, 1994c, 1995a, pp. 33-36). Such efforts had nothing to do with underlying technologies and everything to do with defining culture, markets, and relationships among the state, capital, and people. In the end, broadcast programs were defined as "a scheduled sequence of programming." Even though NVOD, VOD, and other types of services do not fit this definition, they too are covered by aspects of Canadian cultural policy (CRTC, 1995a, p. 33). Ignoring the potential of computer networking and online content provision by individuals, FreeNets— National Capital, Toronto, Vancouver, Victoria, and so on—and other noncommercial entities, the CRTC specifically excluded transactional services and online, nonprogramming content from any considerations of cultural policy (CRTC, 1994a, pp. 46-51).[4] Culture was defined, as a result, entirely within conventional state-centric terms and tied to the audiovisual sector. Although helpful in disguising the new dynamics unleashed by the government's decision to open the door to telcos becoming electronic publishers and broadcasters, this line-drawing exercise will be unsustainable in the long run—an issue returned to near the end of this chapter.

Implementation of the CRTC's media reconvergence policy will not take place immediately, but "as soon as barriers to effective competition in the local telephone business are removed" (CRTC, 1995a, p. 7). It is important to recall that when the CRTC speaks about competition, it does not mean real competition but only the legal potential for it. As such, the policy does not spell out the criteria of real competition or address economic barriers to competition. Instead, it removes legal and regulatory measures that impede competition and employs technical means to address what are essentially problems of economics, power, and politics. Competition means that the telcos must offer access to their facilities on an unbundled basis, allow co-location of transmission and switching facilities at their own switching centres, and grant competitors and content providers open access to the telcos' distribution network, the latter along the lines of a video dial-tone gateway through which content providers can access subscribers (CRTC, 1994a, pp. 31-52; 1995a, p. 13; 1995b, pp. 30-35; also see Wilson, 1996, pp. 10-11).

The method is intended to anchor common carriage in the network technology itself, instead of enforcing the principle through economic, organisational, and regulatory means. It assumes that building open access into the technology is a neutral means of arbiting the problems associated with the integration of content and carriage in comparison to the politicised arena of public policy and regulation. Critics, however, suggest the method just moves questions of politics, power, and culture further outside the purview of people by pretending that technology can fix problems of this sort (Mansell, 1993).

The new media policy does not eliminate concerns with cultural policy and the "public interest" but redefines what these are, who is responsible for them, and the measures that might be used to achieve such aims. Recent initiatives actually broaden the number of those responsible for meeting the cultural policy aims of the *Broadcasting Act* (1991), as well as formalises, and in some cases increases for the first time, the contributions that media players must make to the Canadian content production fund (see, e.g., CRTC, 1995d, p. 7). In this respect, the quid pro quo linking reconvergence to more money for cultural production has the appearance of being upheld. The new policy also strives to shield local telephone service subscribers from shouldering the costs of building a national IBN, although some of these charges can be assigned to the "utility category" (CRTC, 1995b, pp. 30-41). The CRTC has advised Stentor members to avoid trying to inflate the costs of local telephone service by shifting all the costs of the Beacon Initiative on to local subscribers, and instead to allocate most of these charges to the "competitive segments" of their accounts. Finally, the CRTC (1995a) culled some of the language from the heady days of cable media politics in the late 1960s and early 1970s, calling on

> parties . . . [to] come forward with innovative proposals for providing *community expression*, perhaps through incorporation of interactive community dialogue and vehicles for sharing information. Such proposals *should complement* the contribution made by existing cable operators through their community channels. (p. 46; emphasis added)[5]

Besides these measures, reconvergence as a whole was predicated on the notion that massive investments in new technologies, content, entertainment, and transaction services would soon follow regulatory changes to the benefit of the public. Apparently showing that this has been met, the government announced its "convergence policy" by pointing to "telephone and cable companies . . . poised to spend about $15 billion over the next 10 years to take advantage of new . . . opportunities" (Canada, 1996b, p. 1). Restrictions preventing foreign-owned TOs from obtaining broadcast licenses were ushered into media history with the announcement that doing so would translate into $11 million for content production in British Columbia and Quebec alone (Canada, 1996b, p. 5). In a climate of budget deficits, such moves appeared to represent a fiscally responsible state pursuing well-defined public policy goals through the market and succeeding.

Despite the erstwhile attempts of government to rapidly change media policy, there were times when it appears not to have moved quick enough. At such times, Bell, among others, took media law into their own hands. In 1995, for instance, Bell acquired part-ownership of Express Vu, a new Direct-to-Home (DTH) satellite broadcast service. A year earlier, Stentor members set up Multi-Media Incorporated (MMI), a content production company, before changes to the laws preventing telephone companies from participating in broadcasting. Rather than trying to regain control of media policy, the DTH and MMI ventures were legalised post hoc through decisions by the CRTC, several Orders-in-Council by His Excellency the Governor General in Council, and by legislative initiatives to change the laws preventing Bell Canada and the other telcos from holding a broadcast license (Governor General in Council, 1996a, 1996d; Industry Canada, 1996a, pp. 1-2).

With respect to the latter initiative, Industry Minister John Manley explained that "the rationale for keeping Bell out of the broadcasting business is no longer valid" (Industry Canada, 1996a, p. 1). The rationale itself was never discussed. Perhaps this was because the Minister might have looked a bit silly explaining that Bell no longer found it convenient to be "a common-carrier, pure and simple," as it proposed in 1967. It might have also been due to the fact that the communication industries are more concentrated than they have ever been, and that measures trying to sever the links between economic power, politics, and communication are as valid today as they have ever been.[6] Yet, such questions are no longer asked. There has been no investigation of media concentration for nearly 15 years, whereas from 1970 to 1983 there were four—all of which highlighted problems but failed to offer any remedies. Questions about ownership and control of electronic media have also been put "out of bounds" by reliance on *Competition Act* criteria that weigh attempts to regulate market power, mergers, and acquisitions against nebulous concerns about the cost of regulation, possible efficiency gains, and the effect of enforcement on technological innovation and the global competitiveness of the telecoms industry. As the former director responsible for enforcing the *Competition Act*, George Addy (1994, now of Telus) noted, the Act involves choosing between monopolies and concentrated market power, on the one hand, and their possible "social benefits," on the other (pp. 3-5). The impact of concentration on content, as in the financial support of production, diversity, plurality, and so on, are irrelevant. According to Addy (1994),

> The factors used by the Bureau in assessing mergers are deliberately very broad, to allow for a balancing of the pro- and anti-competitive effects of any . . . merger. They include an efficiency exception to allow mergers which would otherwise be prohibited because they substantially prevent or lessen competition. (pp. 3-5)

Of course this can be true. Yet, such vacuous statements can also obscure a great deal of abuse among those who claim to wield power in the "public interest." It can be asked, exactly what wouldn't these measures allow? Just what measure of efficiency does the Director have in mind: allocational efficiency, dynamic efficiency, or some other measure? Although Addy might not want to be encumbered by an overly prescriptive straight-jacket, it is is not unreasonable for people in a democratic society to have at least a clue what threshold might trigger efforts to prevent further concentration of communicative powers. As we have seen earlier as well, CRTC criteria are also vague and unhelpful on this matter. Canadian media policy seems to have slipped off the "democratic compass" and into obfuscatory regulatory proceedings and telecoms politics conducted behind closed doors. Communication systems cut from such ignoble cloth are unlikely to contribute to media freedom.

IS THE INFORMATION HIGHWAY HERE YET?

The "old" regulatory regimes governing electronic media have been dismantled and revamped. Almost all legal impediments to reconvergence have been removed and incentives put into place for developing the information highway. Given this, the following basic questions emerge: Is the Information Highway here yet? Is it coming? Do people want it?

With respect to the first question, the answer—from the view of expenditures on network modernisation—is no. In fact, if we look at the amount of money being put into network modernisation projects by the telcos it can be seen that expenditures are at an all time low!

In the early 1950s, the telephone companies were involved in extensive programs to extend the network, upgrade the local exchange, switch from manual to automated long-distance service, and build the trans-Canada microwave network. Annual expenditures reported for 1955 were 53.6% of annual revenues, a rate 16% higher than the previous year (DBS, 1957, p. 5). A decade later, investment had grown even higher, with over 60% of all revenues plowed into efforts to convert manual phones to the dial system, extend the long-distance network, and prepare the national microwave system for the introduction of colour television.

Investment was $78 for every line in operation (DBS, 1967, p. 6). By 1970, telcos had invested over $1 billion per year in network modernisation projects. Midway through that decade, the telephone companies poured 58.7% of annual revenues back into the network, or about $127 per subscriber (Statistics Canada, 1975a, pp. 510). This continued in the 1980s, especially in the prairies, as the telcos converted to digital and fibre optic technology in much of the long-distance network and portions of the local exchange. By the early 1980s, investment per subscriber in Canada was about $156, a rate higher than U.S. expenditures of $110 near the end of the decade (Davidson, 1991, p. 6). By 1990, network digitisation and fibre optic implementation in the prairies was more advanced than in any other country (SaskTel, 1991). The Stentor group completed much of a national fibre optic network using CCS7 digital switching equipment by the first part of the present decade. The new system was touted as an advanced network platform capable of supporting a plethora of services and superior to systems deployed in the United States during the 1980s using CCS6 analogue-based technology (personal correspondence, B. Gowenlock, Regulatory Affairs Advisor, MTS, Winnipeg, September 1, 1992; Telus, 1991).

Although investments began to taper off from the mid-1980s, the amount of money put into the PTN in the present decade has plunged. Amidst the public spectacles ushering in the "information age," telcos have spent less then ever on modernising the network. By 1991, investment levels fell to 25.6%, and by 1995, to 23.5%. Investment continued to fall between 6% and 11% for the two most recent years (*Globe & Mail Report on Business*, 1996, p. 162; OECD, 1991, p. 151; Statistics Canada, 1994a, pp. 13-14; 1996, p. 1). The dismantling of the media regulatory regime has not meant more money being poured into the so-called information highway, as promised by Stentor and the government. Instead, there has been massive disinvestment. This is illustrated in Figure 7.1.

If money spent is a good index of priorities, it appears that the Information Highway is not high on the telcos' list. Although this seems to be at odds with Stentor's "promise" to spend $8.5 billion in the next decade to connect 80% of Canadian homes to an IBN, such huge sums of money only make sense in historical and comparative context. There is no doubt that $8.5 billion is a great deal of money, but in historical and comparative perspective it is not. As a portion of revenues estimated to be about $188 billion over the 10-year life span of the Beacon Initiative, the amount is a pittance.[7] It is certainly not worth rewriting electronic media law in Canada. If the amount was $8.5 billion for each year of the program, it would just about equal the average between 1955 and 1980. However, this is not the case, as Stentor members boast of only spending about $4 billion per year (Stentor, 1994, p. 14; 1995, p. 7).

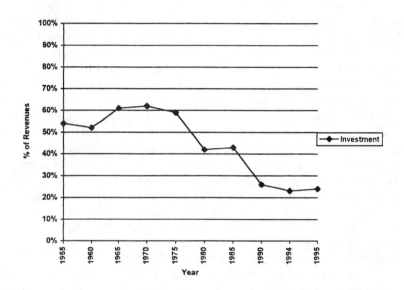

Figure 7.1. Telco investment in network modernisation (1955-1995)
Source: Dominion Bureau of Statistics (1957, 1962, 1967); *Globe & Mail Report on Business* (1996, p. 162); Statistics Canada. (1972-1996a).

It is surprising that commentators from across the political spectrum see the current hype about "information highway" initiatives as involving massive sums of money (Samarajiva, 1995, p. 2; Schiller, 1995, p. 4; Schultz & Janisch, 1993). As Samarajiva (1995) states, "enormous investments are being, or will be, made" (p. 2); Schiller (1995) also claims that "investment in telecommunications and information systems . . . has today begun to accelerate at a wholly unprecedented pace" (p. 4). Likewise, the CRTC (1995b) always mentions how its actions help "Stentor's Beacon Initiative, which entails a *substantial investment in broadband facilities*" (p. 2; emphasis added)—a point reiterated ad nauseum in the *Implementation of Regulatory Framework* decision (e.g., see, CRTC, 1995b, pp. 2, 28, 30, 33). Similar wisdom pervades almost every major government document and academic study published in the last two to three years on the topic.

This is perplexing in light of how the Commission previously approached proposals to invest huge sums of money in network projects. The Beacon Initiative looks very odd in relation to plans by Bell Canada introduced in 1978. Although the plan did not have a fancy public relations moniker, Bell (not Stentor) proposed spending $6 billion over a 5-year period (1978-82) to upgrade its network, expand digital capacity, and so on. The real value of such a plan today would be $10 billion, and if calculated over 10 years (e.g., the same length as the Beacon Initiative), it would involve expenditures of $20 billion—almost 2-1/2 times more than current proposals and funded from a much smaller revenue base. The CRTC (1978a), however, rather than gushing with enthusiasm, "expressed some concern . . . due to the fact that figures of this magnitude dictate with *inexorable logic* an ever-increasing revenue requirement and frequent rate applications" (p. 328; emphasis added). It also looked askance at the fact that funding for the modernisation bid was to come from ordinary subscribers, that many people were without plain telephone service, and, most importantly, that although the plan was designed mainly to serve the sophisticated needs of high-end users, Bell did not propose to pay for the project out of rate increases from its competitive services (CRTC, 1978a, pp. 327, 349-356).

The CRTC was not looking a gift horse in the mouth, but recognised the tendency for regulated monopoly telcos to "gold-plate" their networks, as investments could be added to the regulated rate base and spread across all subscribers. This is widely accepted now and used by enthusiasts of regulated contestable markets to promote abandoning the "old" regulatory regime. The CRTC still accepts part of this wisdom and has tried to prevent the costs of the Beacon Initiative from being assigned to those who will receive little benefit from it. Yet, although the agency insists on some of the expenditures being applied to the "competitive segments" of the telcos' accounts, it allows some costs to be assigned to basic telephone users (CRTC, 1995b, pp. 30-62). The complexity of cost allocation provides good reasons to remain skeptical about who will pay for the network upgrades that take place. Moreover, the CRTC appears to be trying to skirt the politics of cost allocation by eliminating public hearings previously used to review such projects in favour of internal staff analysis, although material submitted by carriers will still be on the public record (CRTC, 1995b, p. 39). Thus, as Stentor members obtain new powers to shape the communicative environment, the few pithy, nonprice-based communication channels previously linking people, technology, and economic actors are being wiped out.

The telcos basically promised government and citizens that they would spend less money than ever as a quid pro quo for a rewrite of Canadian media law. Astoundingly, the government complied. Government policymakers, thus, have not "sold the farm," they gave it away!

This is amazing, especially in light of the fact that the telcos have been well positioned to carry out such investments, as their profits over the last half decade have been higher than ever at between 14% and 20% (*Globe and Mail Report on Business*, 1996. p. 162; Industry Canada, 1995. p. 4).

From a different perspective, though, these observations are not so surprising. They reflect the fact that the planning horizon of private investors—perhaps in the range of two to three years—is shorter than the 5- to 20-year horizon of a legally protected PTO monopoly and government regulators. As such, investors are unlikely to support embedding extensive costs in an infrastructure whose lifespan will extend beyond their commitments. Thus, it is usual for investment to be low when network competition has been introduced, as in, for example, the United States and the United Kingdom, where network investment levels have hovered between 18% and 20% of revenues for several years now (OECD, 1991, 1995a). Even studies that set out to show the benefits of competition have only claimed that infrastructure competition has not harmed network modernisation, and that there is "no conclusive evidence that a diversion of investment has occurred" (OECD, 1995a, p. 19). In other words, the benefits of network competition for modernisation are unclear, and infrastructure competition may even lead to disinvestment, although this has not been proven conclusively yet. Events in Canada mirror this larger global context.

Accompanying competition—in the network and services—is a shift from dynamic efficiency to allocational efficiency. Infrastructure competition does not contribute to modernising and extending the telecoms network so much as intensify use of the PTN and increase the sensitivity of TOs to users capable of expressing their needs. On this point, the previously mentioned OECD (1995a) study is unequivocal: "liberalisation, through competition in price, quality and range of services, has stimulated greater utilization of networks" (p. 46). Given the ubiquity of the telecoms network in Canada and that Stentor finished a fibre optic, digital network at the beginning of the 1990s, there is not a strong need for intense investment in the infrastructure. Given the widely acknowledged history of "gold plating" the PTN,[8] that telcos may be investing less could be a "blessing in disguise"—if it were not for the fact that claims to the contrary were used to legitimate a near complete rewrite of media law. Finally, the lack of investment reflects, as the CRTC (1995a) notes, "uncertain consumer demand for interactive services, . . . video-on-demand" (p. 6) and other online services deliverable by a broadband PTN. This is the topic of the next section.

COMMUNICATION AND FREEDOM FROM COMPULSORY PARTICIPATION IN ELECTRONIC SPACE

> Consumers will not wait. . . . Over-managed or regulated competition . . . cannot be relied upon to produce world-class Canadian industries, or to produce for consumers what they want, when they want it, and at prices they are prepared to pay. (Stentor, 1995, pp. 1, 8)
>
> Competition will create—and, indeed, is already creating—a consumer-driven environment that will ensure the Information Highway meets the needs of all Canadians. (Canada, 1996, p. 5)
>
> Canadians must psychologically adjust to the changing economy. (quote from report prepared for the Government of Canada, cited in Shoesmith, 1995, p. 1)

Some Economic Considerations

Regulatory liberalisation, disinvestment, and the switch to demand-led markets betray a deeper shift in the logic of modernity. This shift is from dynamic innovation and the technocratic organisation of life as seen by the engineer and the long-term systems planner toward consumer sovereignty and demand-led lifestyles.

These shifts can be seen in telecoms economics in terms of the decline of a relatively homogenous offering of services—often characterised by the term POTS (plain old telephone service)—to a plethora of PANS (pretty amazing new services). An enlarged POTS-view includes services such as call waiting, call forwarding, voice mail, call blocking, caller ID, and so on. More importantly, this augers a metamorphosis of the telephone system into an infrastructure for delivering these services, as well as data retrieval, transactional and computer networking services, multimedia applications such as video games, and broadcast-like services such as NVOD, VOD, pay-per view, and so on. In this view, PANS are the services designed to meet people's communicative, entertainment, and informational needs, whereas the broadband communication system is the electronic nervous system of the "information society."

Much of the infrastructure for these services is already in place. As noted earlier, like many other economically developed countries, in Canada a digital, fibre network already connects most cities and provides the backbone for intracity networks (Melody, 1996, p. 246). With almost three-quarters of Canadian homes subscribing to cable television, there is an extensive broadband network connection to most homes (Industry Canada,

1995, p. 1). However, in terms of the telecoms providers, their inter- and intracity networks encircle central business districts and tie together dispersed neighbourhoods but do not extend into neighbourhoods or to homes or businesses. The cable companies lack the interactive networks stretching across cities, regions, or even the country, and will be hard pressed to develop this capacity because of heavy debt burdens (Baldwin, McVoy, & Steinfield, 1996, p. 15; Munk, 1995, pp. 42-44).

Connecting homes to a hybrid fibre-coaxial cable IBN[9] has been estimated as costing anywhere between $1,500 and $3,000 each (Comgate, 1991, p. 83; Gaz, 1995, p. 17).[10] Such costs do not include a terminal, which is valued between $700 and $3,000. Although computer terminals can serve as the interface between users and the network, it must be remembered that only about one-third of homes have computers, that just under one-quarter of these are networked, and that computer ownership remains the preserve of the well-off (Statistics Canada, 1996f, Table 1; Sympatico, 1996). As noted in the last chapter, the French dealt with this barrier to entry by giving away Minitel terminals. This will not happen in Canada. Recent announcements by the Manitoba Telephone System, IBM, Oracle, and others suggest that the barrier of expensive terminals might be surmounted by a cheap (about $500) terminal, albeit with limited functionality (Surtees, 1996, p. B6). This will be discussed further later.

The basic point to note for the moment is that the problems of IBNs are not technical but economic, social, and cultural. The huge cost of opening channels of communication between people, the network, and others means that a universal network would need to yield much more revenue from each user (Comgate, 1991, p. 83; Baldwin, McVoy, & Steinfield, 1996, pp. 113, 190-203; Elton, 1992, pp. 369-395). Estimates in Canada are that revenues generated from each subscriber would have to increase by 200%, or about $40 per month per subscriber, to make IBNs commercially viable (Comgate, 1991, p. 83). New techniques such as asymmetrical digital subscriber lines (ADSL) have recently been announced that could drive this cost down considerably. However, Baldwin et. al. (1996) conclude that ADSL technology has "very limited . . . capacity, costs as much per home as building a HFC network [,] . . . and is unlikely to be a viable large-scale or long-term way of offering video (pp. 118-119).

Because Stentor members have fibre network rings running within and between cities, but the cable systems have the coax link to people's homes, the telcos have insistently pressed the government to let them interconnect with the cable systems' subscriber drops. Although this is one way of cobbling together a hybrid fibre-coax system—and perhaps is even the most economic and "just" in a world of strategic rivalry and regulatory requirements compelling telcos to do the same for cable operators—the CRTC has spurned the telcos' requests on this matter (CRTC, 1995a, p. 17; Stentor, 1994, pp. 10-15; 1995, p. 6). This is crucial to Stentor, because unless the telcos can demonstrate sufficient demand for broadband services they cannot fund the "missing link" to subscribers out of basic/utility rates (CRTC, 1994a, p. 49). As shown next, neither Stentor nor any other telcos have demonstrated this, suggesting that IBNs will be subsidised by other means, for example, advertising and/or cheap low-function terminals, "marketed" as a luxury good, die a peaceful death, or fight for their lives through regulatory means—each is a distinct possibility. Although it is too early to know which will prevail, it is valuable to consider the range of issues at hand and the potential scenarios—the task of the following sections.

Information Highways: Who Wants Them?

The literature is full of "blue sky" scenarios and projections of gold mines awaiting those who tap into the burgeoning "global information economy." As such, it is not surprising that there are a plenitude of broadband experiments that have taken place recently, are still in progress, or planned to begin shortly. The KPMG (1996a) report on (re)convergence prepared for the EC discusses 10 trials recently concluded or still in progress in Europe alone, and 20 major projects taking place around the world (pp. 103-104). Straubhaar and Do (1996) list 37 experiments in 23 different countries on almost every continent (pp. 358-359). Several trials have recently concluded or are in the planning stage in Canada. A recent Canadian study has also considered the telecoms and information needs of small, medium, and large business users (Mozes & Sciadas, 1995). The results of these are briefly reviewed next, as are the responses that have been adopted as a consequence of what has been found.

With respect to business users, the study by Mozes and Sciadas (1995, p. 79)[11] found that for most businesses, telecoms expenses constitute a small amount of overall expenses and that such expenses are only very significant for large computer services firms. The only really significant "new" telecoms service used often by most businesses was the fax (73%). Data transmission was used by 19% of businesses "all of the time," whereas the corresponding patterns for other "new services" were as follows: discount long distance (42%), 800 service (14%), debit and calling cards (11%), cellular (29%), voice mail (13%), electronic text messages (7%), teleconferencing (2%), video conferencing (0%), and internet (3%) (p. 80). It was recognised, however, that a significant portion of large businesses had intensive telecoms needs. Computer service firms were also atypical (p. 82). Yet, among big users, many had their own private networks (or intranets, in the jargon now employed) (p. 85), so it is hard to imagine how their needs translate into demands on the PTN unless, of course, there is a vested interest by telecoms providers to get such heavy users back onto the network or by large users to "socialise" the costs of setting up their own networks (Mansell, 1993).

This is more than conjecture. On the one hand, private networks turn telecoms expenses into predictable fixed costs: they can be custom designed to meet exacting user needs and are supplied in a more competitively oriented market by Microsoft, IBM, SunSystems, and a host of global, national, and local Metropolitan and Local Area Network (MANs and LANs) providers. On the other hand, they are costly, do not eliminate the need to be connected to the PTN in order to connect with others, and can be plagued with interoperability problems due to a lack of standards. Thus, there is a distinct possibility that heavy users would like to migrate back onto the PTN in order to eliminate these problems, while also diffusing the costs of upgrading the PTN across society as a whole (Mansell, 1993).[12] As Baldwin et. al. (1996) note, "after a decade of implementing LANs that routinely transport data at 10Mbps," the lower level technologies such as ISDN found in the PTN are "not particularly exciting to business users" (p. 62). Hence the need to continue with separate networks or to force a convergence between exacting private needs and the PTN.

The problem, however, is that to build the PTN completely around IBN standard technology requires that there be either mass markets or at least sufficient demand in "consumer markets" to support its costly implementation. However, unlike Stentor's "consumers can't wait" populist appeal, research shows that people would prefer to wait, at least until broadband communication systems more closely mesh with their needs, or conversely, are rendered so cheap through various subsidies—the "free lunch"—that participation no longer exacts a heavy toll. As Melody (1996) notes, IBN trials have failed to identify significant demand for new services that require fibre cable connections. The KPMG (1996b) report is unequivocal: "Convergence is a long way from being a consumer driven phenomenon . . . . [R]evenues appear insufficient to justify the large and risky investment necessary to achieve full convergence" (pp. 4-5). Other studies came to the same conclusion.

One response to these findings has been to postpone or cancel future experiments or the planned implementation of services (KPMG, 1996a, p. 105). Kevin Wilson (1996, p. 25) notes that Bell Atlantic and US West have pulled applications pending before the FCC for various broadband services such as VDT, VOD, and so on. This, however, is a short-term strategy. In the long term, attention is riveted on the economic and cultural "barriers" to broadband communications and state/industry efforts to engineer conditions that can support new media markets.

As noted earlier, connecting people to broadband communication networks requires new revenue. However, analysts note that most people are not willing (or able) to spend more money and time on communication and entertainment services. New services will likely mean tradeoffs between existing media such as video rentals and film attendance, not a dramatic rise in new expenditures (Baldwin et. al, 1996, p. 202; Garnham, 1983, p. 324; Morley & Robins, 1995, pp. 34-35). The KPMG (1996c) study concluded that any expansion in "media markets" brought about by new media would be negligible (p. 6).[13] This is especially true considering that people often see new media services as luxury goods, which renders them discretionary and the first to go when budgets feel the pinch. This sensitivity to price changes does not auger well for the steady sources of new revenues needed to fuel the rapid deployment of IBNs. Finally, people's ability to allocate more resources to information services is constrained by large social changes such as declining incomes, longer work days, and the reduction of leisure time (Baldwin et. al., 1996, p. 207; Love & Poulin, 1991, pp. 4.1-4.11).

A more troubling problem for advocates of information highways is that people have not been impressed with the services offered by the many IBN trials conducted over the last decade or so. The summary of findings from IBN trials presented by Baldwin et. al. (1996) and KPMG (1996a) show that the communication industries' hoped-for increase in popular interest in VOD, NVOD, online video games, and other services has not, for the most part, materialised. The studies they survey indicate that people are willing to use VOD-based systems to order between two and three films a month and to use a few other services. However, the "economic value" to providers of such usage (between $6 and $12) does not produce near enough revenue to justify deploying IBNs. In addition, whatever demand exists confirms the "zero-sum" nature of media consumption, showing that use occurs in prime-time viewing hours and cuts into video rentals (Baldwin et. al., 1996, pp. 215-226; KPMG, 1996a, pp. 104-106). A few quotes from the KPMG study illustrates the idea that people's interests "deviate" from the core values on which the commercialisation of broadband services are premised: "users . . . showed a desire for diversity"; "demand for quality films"; "educational material was more popular than cartoons among children"; "VOD was commercially unviable in its present form"; "Consumers wanted more than just videos—they did not sell well"; and "VOD eats into video rental" (KPMG, 1996a, p. 105). Thus, people's lack of enthusiasm is not due to a lack of knowledge or a Luddite view of the new media, but a rejection of what "new media" have thus far offered (also see Shields, Dervin, Richter & Soller, 1993).

Laggards, Rumps, and Other Dangerous Impediments to Progress

Instead of changing the organisation, design, and delivery of communication networks to conform to people's expressed needs and patterns of communication, proponents of the new media industries have been horrified at the prospect of losing the biggest gold mine in modern history. To prevent new media from escaping the boundaries of market regulation, there is a state/industry-led shift to technology push programs, attempts at a kind of social/cultural engineering, and strategic evaluation of two commercial modes of delivering the "new media" services: mass marketing of a new mass medium versus the marketing of information services as "luxury goods." These are considered next.

There is an impressive gap between the rhetoric of a consumer-led revolution in communication services and the stark reality of frantic efforts to bring about the so-called information revolution as fast as possible. Instead of deferring to consumer sovereignty and letting IBNs die peacefully, meeting areas where adequate demand exists, or postponing them until conditions are more appropriate, there has been a decisive shift to strategies of sociocultural engineering and supply-driven introduction of information highways. The evidence resides in the language used to describe barriers to the new media, the origins of concepts used to analyze "problems" and to prescribe solutions, and in state/industry efforts to "accelerate the rate at which Canadians move onto the Information Highway" (Canada, 1996a, p. 24). The Bangemann (1994) report argued that the greatest "danger [is] that individuals will reject the new information culture and its instruments" (p. 6). Essentially, debate about whether new media instrumentation is necessary or desired has dropped from the agenda, displaced by the presumption, as Baldwin et. al. (1996) advocate, that "integrated networks must be built . . . . It is justification enough that it is possible. The social and economic benefits of high-speed communication in the computer age seem self-evident" (p. 303).

Despite wishful thinking, the benefits of "high-speed communication in the computer age" are not self-evident. However, rather than deferring to "consumer sovereignty," proponents of the "information age" attribute slack interest to a "[l]ack of understanding of the potential . . . of new telecommunication services . . . . This is [even] a problem for Business Services firms of all sizes" (Mozes & Sciadas, 1995, p. 92). People are thus formidable barriers to technical and economic advancement—a problem that must be surmounted. As Baldwin et. al. (1996) state, "fundamental changes in lifestyle" are needed, as "habit and lethargy are serious obstacles to marketing integrated broadband systems" (p. 190). Like the Bangemann report, these authors think that the gravest danger is that people might be so "overwhelmed by the options" that they could "reject the advanced services of integrated broadband networks . . . . Choosing what to do becomes a problem" (p. 384).

A report prepared by Burke Campbell for the Canadian government argues that "it may be psychology—not technology—that will enable Canadians to take advantage of the emerging information highway . . . . Canadians *must psychologically adjust to the changing economy*" (quoted in Shoesmith, 1995, p. 12; emphasis added). Those unable to make the "requisite psychological adjustments" face the sociocultural engineering apparatus of a state/corporate nexus bent on *"assisting the consumers desire* to have a flexible and responsive communications environment, especially when information-on-demand becomes part of everyday mentality" (quoted in Shoesmith, 1995, p. 12; emphasis added). Another report prepared for Industry Canada, but which never saw the light of day and can only be accessed under the Freedom of Information Act, illustrates the issues well. Under the heading of "freedom of choice," the report urges "government and business . . . [to] encourage consumer acceptance of new technologies" (IHAC, 1995, p. 7). This could be helpful, the report continues, as "Canadians . . . can be reluctant to embrace new technologies. In Canada, this technological disinclination could limit the . . . information highway as well as the speed with which it evolves. Canada's competitive position as a leader in high technology could also be at risk" (p. 3). According to the new thinking, domestic markets and the mind are launchpads for industries' foray into global markets, and unless they are recalibrated properly, cultural survival is at risk.

According to the new industrial/state complex, "a strategy is needed to ensure that all Canadians fully understand the value of emerging information technology" (IHAC, 1995, p. 4). The Bangemann Report (1994) is even more forceful: "A great deal of effort must be put into securing widespread public acceptance and actual use of the new technology. Preparing Europeans for the . . . information society is a priority task" (p. 6). KPMG (1996a) argues that "the *rump of users* may not change until *forced to do so*" (p. 120; emphasis added).

Although the impact of government/industrial coercion and the media campaigns behind social and cultural engineering efforts are uncertain and can fail miserably, it is important to look closely at the intellectual pedigree of some of the propaganda techniques that are being used. The intellectual origins of these efforts to resynchronise people's minds with the imperatives of the global information economy can be traced to similar efforts foisted on the "Third World" during the 1960s. A leading theorist was Everett Rogers. His theories provided some of the key intellectual props behind efforts to remove the purported psychological and cultural blocks behind the Third World's inability to industrialise. Recounting his ideas of that time, Rogers (1976) notes that "the route to modernisation was to transform the people, to implant new values and beliefs" (p. 218). His theory divided societies into innovators, early adopters, the majority, late adopters, and laggards. Based on these divisions, strategies were formulated to introduce new ideas about modern farming, birth control techniques, and so on to the innovators and early adopters, and then, through a "two-step flow" process, it was hoped that these ideas would trickle down to the rest of society. In the scheme of things, "leading sectors, . . . would spread their advantage to the lagging sectors . . . . Growth first, and . . . equality later" (Rogers, 1976, p. 217).

Rogers abandoned the theory around 1976 arguing that it did not work, had a narrow sense of development, wrongly manipulated people, correlated strongly with authoritarian governments, and so on. However, it appears that the theory now serves as a key prop behind social engineering efforts in Canada and elsewhere. The KPMG (1996a) study clearly has Rogers in mind when it refers to "innovators, early adopters, early majority, late majority and laggards" and the need to ensure that the new "technology establishes itself in people's minds. . . . [Once] this perception . . . is established take-off into a mass market can be rapid" (p. 93). Studies in the EC and United States are similar (Bangemann, 1994; Media Gruppe Munchen, 1996, p. 13; Shields, Dervin, Richter & Soller, 1993, p. 566).

The Industry Canada study by Campbell referred to earlier is also of this ilk, stressing the psychological blocks to "modernity." So, too, does modernisation theory permeate the banished IHAC working paper and its recommendations about how government and industry should deal with values, mindsets, and lifestyles that retard the information culture (IHAC, 1995, p. 8). There are obvious affinities between modernisation theories and the "crisis of democracy" thesis discussed throughout this book. Although the two were cut from the same cloth, until recently a division of labour saw modernisation theories applied to the Third World and the "crisis of democracy" to North America, Europe, and Japan. They have now "converged" around projects to promote and build information highways and societies on behalf of recalcitrant populations everywhere.

Modernisation theories have also encouraged states to act as model demonstrators of desired behaviour and to midwife change through injections of money, research, and development funding and technical expertise. The Canadian government excels at each of these. It presents itself as a "model user and . . . catalyst for the innovative use of the Information Highway throughout the Canadian economy" (Canada, 1996a, p. 27). It also "promotes the application of communications technology," "promotes a stronger science culture," acts "as a forcing house of change," and "stimulates demand for new services" (Canada, 1996a, p. 7; Industry Canada, 1994a, pp. 18-24; Communications Canada, 1987, p. 85).

The state is moving Canada into the 21st century by handing out large subsidies to the communication industries. The *Building the Information Society* (1996) paper alone identifies $4.76 billion allocated for forcing, promoting, and stimulating the vaunted information age culture, an amount conspicuously incongruent with concerns about the national deficit that are usually wielded to bludgeon the CBC, education, social welfare, and unemployment budgets, among other things.[14]

The Canadian government euphemistically claims that public subsidies for corporate actors "encourage new services," "stimulate information highway R&D," "prepare companies for the information age," "create strategic intelligence and alliances," "build technology partnerships," "realise social benefits," and so on (Canada, 1996a, pp. 5-19). One current example illustrating the ongoing alliance between Ottawa and industry is a government contribution of $141 million for the Advanced Satcom Initiative. The government claims the initiative will "place Canada at the forefront of the information economy and . . . to compete effectively in the rapidly growing domestic, regional and international markets for multimedia services" (Canada, 1996a, p. 7). The document also refers to "Industry Canada supporting and sharing the risk of the private sector as it undertakes the early development and commercialisation of . . . new satellite-based multimedia services" (p. 7). It also identifies $3.2 billion spent on research and development, tax credits of $1 billion, and an investment of over $120 million in CANARIE—the link to the global Internet that was transferred to BCE in 1997 and subsequently commercialised—among other things (pp. 8-9). Some money is also spent on projects that are more closely tied to public interests such as the recent $6 million fund created to build public access points to the Internet (Surtees, 1995b, p. A2). Yet, spending 1/800th the amount of all corporate subsidies on the one area where there really has been keen public interest, plus the privatisation of the Internet infrastructure in 1997, raise issues about the equity of federal budgetary priorities. This is discussed in greater detail later.

The opaqueness of these programs, and their ties to a state/industrial project of cultural transformation, are difficult to reconcile with any meaningful understanding of democracy, let alone the hyperbole regarding competition, deregulation, and free markets. They are particularly troublesome because government and corporate actors are busy altering the fabric of society, while refusing to acknowledge their role in shaping the conditions of life or allowing full democratic participation in these determinative processes. For all those free marketeers who have incessantly derided the paternalism of public broadcasters such as the CBC in favour of crass appeals to populism, their absolute silence with respect to the more forceful and penetrative form of paternalism represented by the socially transformative project of governments and industry vis-á-vis the information highway/age is conspicuous.

MASS MARKETS, LUXURY GOODS, AND UNIVERSAL SERVICE? THE BOUNDS OF PUBLIC DEBATE ON INFORMATION HIGHWAYS

Rather than confronting the unsupportive economic, social and cultural constraints that hinder the evolution of IBNs, multimedia, and online services, or state/industry efforts to orchestrate a supply-driven "information revolution," debates tend to take place under the umbrella of universal service. It seems that the concept offers a flexible rubric under which the liberal-conservative political spectrum can safely consider links between social stratification and communication, while avoiding the really troublesome issues. For those concerned about such links, the most appealing idea at first glance is to clamour for an expansion of universal service. Yet, this is too simple.

Naively pushing for an expansion of universal services ignores the fact that policymakers are already trying to get everyone hooked up and are willing to engage in quite extensive projects of social engineering and cultural transformation to bring this about. From human rights advocates to conservative politicians, there appears to be a broad consensus that everybody should be on the information highway. The American Civil Liberties Union lawyer who helped defeat the "communication decency" part of the *Telecommunications Act of 1996* recently argued that the most important civil rights issue of the decade is to get all Americans connected to the NII. Activist scholars such as Howard Frederick (1997) argue similarly, but on a global basis. Even conservative stalwarts such as Newt Gingrich advocate that youth should be given laptop computers and a free connection to the Net. Similar sentiments are found in Canada among public interest group advocates (Reddick, 1995). Such concerns are also prominent in government papers, in which people are promised "affordable access to essential Information Highway services . . . regardless of their income or geographic location" (Canada, 1996a, p. 23).

The only real disagreement seems to be about how broad universal service should be defined, who should administer it, and how it should be paid for. The debate is mainly about how to get everybody online, and whether services should be made affordable through regulation, an advertising-sponsored "free lunch," or market pricing of what is, essentially, a "discretionary" good. Given the stress on private sector development and competition, the first option is usually dismissed out of hand, or seen as a residual measure (Bangemann, 1994, p. 12; Canada, 1996a, pp. 23-24; CRTC, 1995, pp. 41-43; KPMG, 1996a, p. 143). By default, this retains only the mass media/free lunch and luxury goods options, or some combination thereof.

IBNs and the "New and Improved Free Lunch"

Given the lack of demand for, and the inelasticity of expenditures on, communication/information services, there is a real possibility that information highways, like every other mass media from the mid-19th century, will be given away "free," or heavily subsidised. In other words, broadband communications may be offered in the familiar fashion of the "free lunch," obtained by passive citizens as a quid pro quo for acquiescing their role in shaping the nascent media systems, abandoning the idea of communication as citizenship, and forfeiting control over personal data generated during the consumption of media services in "transactional space." There are four likely sources of the "free lunch" in emerging communicative spaces: personal data/privacy, advertising, cheap terminals, and private enclosure of the public good qualities of information.

Much research stresses the importance of privacy in electronic media space (Canada, 1996a, p. 25; CRTC, 1995a, p. 47; Samarajiva, 1995; Wilson, 1988). Despite concern, however, the issue inevitably confronts challenges by industry that privacy measures inhibit their rights to freedom of expression,[15] that there are close ties amid telecoms providers, banks, and online service providers that firmly implant a bias against privacy into the heart of the new telecoms, and last, that people may willingly forego personal data protection as an informal subsidy for cheap access to online services. The CRTC (1994a) recognises the latter potential, and has argued that whatever policies are adopted must not "significantly affect the economics of [broadband] services" (p. 84). Although the Commission has not yet made a determinative statement on this, its has indicated that it views privacy like any other commodity that can be bought and sold in the information age at desired levels and for a price.

As the CRTC dithers with privacy policy, online service providers are setting precedent, and defacto policy on the issue. A perusal of ISP contracts suggests that none guarantee privacy, nor forego the option of monitoring subscribers' use of the network for other than absolutely necessary network management functions. Because Bell Canada Enterprises (BCE) and the other Stentor members have moved aggressively into online services markets, it is useful to consider their practices.

Bell is not a newcomer to content services, despite the former common-carrier regime. For many years, the company has been linked by common ownership with InfoDirect, a database company that sells online access to information about Bell subscribers. More recently, and quick on the heals of changes that dismantled common carriage almost entirely, BCE and Stentor formed Sympatico/MediaLinx—a hybrid ISP, online content provider, and bandwidth wholesaler/retailer.[16] Because Sympatico has moved to become the largest ISP/online content provider in Canada, it is worthwhile to look at the standards it is establishing for privacy. A good indication is provided by the *Terms and Conditions* of its' users' contracts, which inform new subscribers that

> *MediaLinx has the right* to monitor the Sympatico Site electronically from time to time. . . . MediaLinx cannot insure or guarantee privacy for . . . users. It is recommended that this service not be used for the transmission of confidential information. . . . You authorise MediaLinx to collect from any party and to retain all relevant information relating to your use of the Sympatico Site, and you hereby authorize any party to provide us with such information. You understand and agree that unless you notify MediaLinx to the contrary by emailing us, *you . . . further authorize* MediaLinx to disclose . . . to any party with whom MediaLinx has business relations *all relevant information relating to your dealings with us and the Sympatico Site.* We will open and maintain a file in your name, which file will be kept at our head office. . . . *If you are dissatisfied with the Sympatico Site or with any terms, conditions, rules, policies, guidelines, or practices of MediaLinx . . . your sole and exclusive remedy is to discontinue using the Sympatico site.* (Sympatico, 1996, sec. 2-7; emphasis added)

The logic is impeccable: give up control over how information is collected and used or change the channel/supplier—the same kind of choice and consumption used by "old" media. Yet, what if other ISPs are similarly disrespectful of users rights? Moreover, the logic ignores the fact that users probably perceive online communication as the primary economic transaction, a perception that does not mesh with the reality that they are immersed in many "information markets" at once, most of which are below the threshold of awareness. Nonetheless, from the providers' perspective, the collection and sale of information is as much a part of the service as whatever users might think they are getting when signing into cyberspace (Samarajiva, 1995; Wilson, 1988). MediaLinx's use of "negative options" also signals its hope to preserve silence around these divergent views, because it is only in the silent gaps between users' perceptions and service provider actions that personal data markets can be maintained without interference. To do otherwise would open these issues to the politics of communication and privacy, or conversely, create pressures to put a price tag on the value of the hidden subsidy so that users could have a "choice" about whether they want to link privacy directly to their bank accounts.[17] As things now stand, the onus is on users to disrupt the normal flow of events, otherwise ISPs proceed as if consent has been given.

Although, the *Telecommunications Act* (1993) identifies respect for the "privacy of persons" as a priority policy aim, this is hedged against competing considerations linked to marketers' "freedom of expression" and the idea that privacy might involve excessive regulatory costs (Addy, 1994). Moreover, there are direct links between privacy and a more obvious source of an expanded "free lunch"—advertisers. Going one step further than the 'free lunch' scenario, one advertising agency is experimenting with paying people to view advertisements in return for the right to cull personal data. Cybergold's

> software gathers valuable demographic data from Web users who reveal their interests on a form, and then offers them individual menus of ads on CyberGold's Web site. Users must peruse each Web ad to its last page, then click on a special symbol to receive credit. (Ziegler, 1996, p. 10)

Although the outcomes of this experiment are admittedly far from certain, it is important for what it reveals. Three things stand out in particular: the cultivation of new frontiers in advertising; the enormous fear among advertisers that they may be losing control over people's attention; and finally, that the advertisement-supported new media "free lunch" and perhaps a willingness to pay people to use what is on offer suggests that problems about universal service—redefined as a connection to new media spaces and attention—may not be difficult to surmount.

Yet, as the Cybergold story itself notes, there are still barriers. For one, advertisers do not just want anyone, just those with the "right qualities." Some are skeptical about the idea of paying people for their attention, because, as John Uppgren of Gage Marketing Group in Minneapolis notes, "many high-end consumers . . . would pay money *not* to be subjected to ads" (Ziegler, 1996, p. 10). For those promoting the "free lunch" view of the new media, the biggest problem is that only the poor will attend the ad cluttered new electronic media spaces (Baldwin et. al., 1996, p. 239), whereas those who can afford to do so will buy themselves out of such miserable conditions. As media managers "work harder to . . . articulate the quality and value of their audiences for advertisers" (Opsitnik, 1990, p. 24), tensions will arise between attempts to transform electronic space into an advertising subsidised mass media versus efforts to maintain its "luxury good" profile in which those connected tend to be "married, between 35-54, well-educated, household income of $50,000 plus" (Sympatico, 1996).

The fact that advertisers will try to subsidise broadband communications is, as Schiller (1995) notes, "a virtual certainty." The Comgate (1991, p. 83) study for the CRTC referred to earlier claimed that advertising might have to be included as a new source of revenue to secure the economic viability of residential broadband services. The

Bangemann (1994) report similarly notes that "advertising will . . . be a necessary source of revenue" (p. 10). Baldwin et al. (1996), KPMG (1996a) and Media Gruppen Munchen (1996) have come to similar conclusions. Earlier studies suggested that advertising could provide up to 60% of all broadband network revenues, whereas transactional services would comprise 21% to 27% and end user fees less than 30% (Connell, 1994, p. 245).

For the "free lunch" proponents, online media present an unprecedented opportunity to target their messages with precision and accuracy (Samarajiva, 1995; Schiller, 1995; Ziegler, 1996). Although the hitherto open spaces of the new telecoms networks made it difficult to reach people and even threatened to upset the whole regime of production and consumption tied together through advertising-based mass media, new on-line media are being seen as a way of tightening the link between production and consumption. The new wisdom is reflected by the Chairman of Proctor and Gamble, Edwin Artzt, who urges advertisers to take "control of the environment . . . mold it to fit our needs . . . and make it work for us" (quoted in Schiller, 1995, p. 10). As Artzt notes, the "Number One priority" has to be "*to protect universal access to advertiser-supported media*. . . . If user fees replace advertising revenue, we're in serious trouble . . . . Remember consumers are on our side. They would rather have their *home entertainment free* (quoted in Schiller, 1995, p. 11; emphasis added).

However, as of now, the words of Artzt and others who support the "free lunch" approach to new media are more a rallying call than an accurate depiction of reality. The planned commercial colonisation of electronic space has yet to be fully unleashed. In some ways, the viability of the "free lunch" approach still remains open; it is not yet a done deal. Attempts to turn new media into an electronic shopping mall remain clumsy and uncertain, as advertising costs are still based on crude cost per thousand (cpm) measures linked to the number of hits, or impressions, registered on particular Websites or Internet search tools. In Canada, advertisers pay Sympatico/MediaLinx between $10 and $150 per thousand hits, depending on whether "impressions" are associated with a search engine—Lycos, WebCrawler, AltaVista, and so on—or one of the content services provided.[18] Most independent ISPs do not carry advertising at all.

There are several points that reveal the uncertainty still attached to the "free lunch" model. First, none of the top 100 advertisers in Canada advertised on the Internet in 1996, although recent surveys indicate that half of these plan to do so in the next year. Yet, even planned forays into emergent electronic frontiers will not initially be extensive: those indicating a desire to advertise suggest that only 1% to 3% of their budgets will be allocated to online media. Online advertising revenue currently remains modest—about $20 to $30 million—which is 10% of the estimated value of such advertising in the United States. Even the largest ISP in the United States, America OnLine (AOL), only derives 10% of its revenues from advertising and has just 50 advertisers at the time of writing (Sanders, 1996, p. 6).

Nonetheless, there are indications that this is ready to shift. There is a change under way in how subscribers to the Internet and other online services are being charged and a move from time bound pricing to a flat rate, although this has not been introduced at the time of writing by the major ISP providers in Canada. Sympatico/MediaLinx currently offers two kinds of accounts, both of which are usage sensitive. Yet, as the "free lunch" model is leaned on more heavily, ISPs are broadening their revenue sources. In the United States, AOL has announced that it will rely much more on advertising revenue and the sale of content with the advent of its' flat rate pricing scheme. The company expects to increase advertising revenue by 50%, to $60 million (USD), over the next year.

The "Free Lunch" and Industry Structure

The price of the "free lunch" is visible in the rapidly shifting structure of the new media industry. Whereas in 1995, the largest Canadian ISP was Istar, with 400 mainly small, independent ISPs, this is changing. The economics of the "free lunch" and the CRTC's new regulatory regime have fostered integration among network providers, ISPs, and content providers, as well as consolidation within the field of ISPs. These trends are discussed next.

The position of Sympatico/MediaLinx across the ISP and content provider domains, as well as the thrust of AOL into content provision and more advertising revenues, is part of a trend toward vertical and horizontal integration, or reconvergence of media ownership across former technology-based boundaries. As with Sympatico/MediaLinx services, the bundling of carriage, content, and Internet access is happening across North America, Europe, and perhaps globally. An agreement between IBM and Southam New Media, for instance, allows "Southam newspapers to comprise the default home page on selected IBM Internet access products" (Southam, 1995, p. 13). Even more spectacular alliances involved MCI (soon to be BT/MCI, or Concert) acquiring part of Murdock's NewsCorp, combinations between CNN, Time Warner, and USWest; Microsoft and NBC's joint lunge into online news and information services; and moves by Microsoft to bundle Internet access and content services into Windows '95 software. Although AOL, Compuserve, and Prodigy complained about the anti-trust implications of Microsoft's practices, they were inclined to obtain similar arrangements for themselves (Crane, 1996, p. 21; Kehoe, 1995, p. 14; Snoddy, 1995, p. 20). To this end, AOL moved closer to the German publisher, Bertelsmann, by giving the latter a 5% interest in AOL, and together they launched AOL/Bertelsmann in Europe.[19] In Europe, three of the largest publishers—Burda, Leo Kirch, and Pearson (owner of the *Financial Times*)—combined with AT&T to launch their own telecoms-based electronic services, Europe On-line (Dempsey, 1995. p. 20; KPMG, 1996c, Appendix 5, p. 5). BT has moved in this direction as well. BT's adroit merger with MCI tightens its links with Murdock's NewsCorp and Delphi On-line, a factor that may help it circumvent U.K. measures keeping it from holding a broadcasting license. Remarking on these trends, some think that the core of networked media may soon be dominated by half a dozen global carrier/service providers (Hart, 1995, pp. 46-8)—AOL, BT/MCI/Murdock, Compuserve, EOL/AT&T, Microsoft, and Prodigy— whereas others scramble to serve "niche markets" and/or to serve as local marketing agents for the small core of global providers.

These are not entirely new arrangements, however. In Canada, Southam has offered online services for 25 years—the Infomart/Dialog services with over 450 databases and other forms of content—in tandem with U.S.-based Knight Ridder and the California-based Dialog company (Infomart/Dialog, 1996). The change between the last 25 years and now is the ubiquity of trends, the reconvergence of carriage and content, regulatory neglect, and the trend toward turning electronic communicative spaces into the newest mass media. As Microsoft argued before the U.S. Department of Justice, current tendencies should not be impeded by regulatory authorities but embraced as a means of "expanding the market for online services" (Kehoe, 1995, p. 14). According to this view, bundling software, online access, and content into one package provides users cheap and convenient access to the new online media.

In Canada, the regulatory responses to such moves have been ambivalent. The new regulatory regime, as has been seen, is predicated on the idea that monopolistic control over content production and distribution is impossible. Moreover, the greater use of competition law has rendered such concerns superfluous. Indeed, after the recent review of Hollinger's take-over of Southam, which allowed the new company to control 40% of newspaper circulation, the Industry Minister claimed that competition policy offers no grounds to gauge the impact of mergers on content, questions of diversity and media freedoms. Content, according to Manley, just did not matter (Mosco, 1997).[20]

Similar concerns are apparent in Europe, as greater reliance on competition policy puts issues about the influence of ownership concentration on freedom of expression out of bounds (Hitchens, 1997). However, the trends are not uniform (discussed later), as some initiatives by the EC and European Parliament to regulate concentrated ownership, online advertising, European content, and universal service objectives, among other things, indicate (European Commission, 1996; Schenker, 1996a, p. 1).

There is no doubt that the linkages between content carriers, packagers, and providers may facilitate access to the new electronic spaces. This is especially true because lower prices may be brought about by the fact that content is simply dumped "online" for the cost of reproduction by content producers whose activities span various media. In addition, costs may be lowered by practices designed to neuter independents and competition, not by raising prices but by dropping them in a war of deep pockets. As Thomas Middlehoff of Bertelsmann multimedia, admits, "I reckon we will be subsidising the consumer . . . DM20 a month in the initial stages of AOL/Bertelsmann" (cited in Dempsey, 1995, p. 20). With respect to strategic rivalry and "price wars," U.S-based AOL was forced to adopt flat rate pricing and alternative sources of revenue only after Microsoft entered online services with prices that undercut existing ISP prices, in some cases by 200-300% (Hart, 1995, p. 47; Kehoe, 1995, p. 14). The key dilemma is not whether people will have access to online media but whether the Faustian bargain struck to achieve universal service will still make access worth having in the long-run.

The deep pockets needed to fund strategic rivalry and a war of attrition in electronic media space also begets actions that reinforce the consolidation of control in other areas of the new telecoms-network services environment. In other words, the cost of staying alive as an ISP drives independents and competitors into one anothers' arms. With profits driven below normal by the war of attrition, ISPs are consolidating, being bought out by others, or forced to shutdown. Thus, for example, even though Unipalm/Pipex was the United Kingdom's leading ISP, it was only able to secure a 4% profit[21] on revenues of $40 million (cnd). Rather than trying to stay afloat, it succumbed to a bid of $200 million by U.S.-based Uunet in late 1995 (Taylor, 1995, p. 17).[22] Thus, the same processes driving new media toward the "free lunch" model also propel consolidation, at least in the core of the "new" mass media market. Similar trends can be seen in Canada, as independents and the competition governing the evolution of ISPs and FreeNets since the start of the decade (Weston, 1994) are squashed to the meagre margins by the Stentor companies' Sympatico (140,000 subscribers), AOL (100,000 subscribers), Istar (60,000), and HookUp (50,000) (Angus Telemanagement, 1996, p. 2).

Prior to the move toward consolidation in the ISP sector, competition among small, independent competitors was the norm, with cities such as Vancouver supporting 15 to 20 ISPs and mid-size cities, such as Windsor, perhaps half a dozen providers. Even well into 1995, and prior to the entry of Stentor members or the large U.S.-based providers such as AOL, Compuserve, or Prodigy, the average ISP served 1,500 subscribers in what the CRTC, Bell, the Director of the Bureau of Competition Policy, and independent ISPs all described as a dynamic, innovative area of telecoms with rapid growth of up to 10% per month. Start-up costs were nominal at around $60,000 to $100,000, and the largest operating cost was the rental of the Centrex III digital line service from the telcos. Centrex charges for a typical ISP were between $13,000 and $25,000 per year (Courtois, 1995, p. 2; Darling, 1995, pp. 1-3; personal communication, M. Whatmore, president of Wincom, Windsor, Ontario, January 2, 1996).

Much of the independent sector tried to keep things this way, encouraging the CRTC and the Director of the Bureau of Competition Policy to prevent Stentor from entering ISP services. Their logic was simple: the telephone companies controlled access to the monopoly local network (which, as seen earlier, the CRTC still acknowledged would not be competitive in the near future), they had access to crucial information about the ISP's subscribers who had to go through the telcos to offer services, and the integration of online services with the incumbents' control over telephone services would give them undo advantage. Bell rejected the idea that the telcos could secure unfair advantages, pointing to strong ISP competition and the fact that bundling services did not confer an undo advantage but was standard practice among "mature players" in the industry such as AOL, Compuserve, Microsoft, and so on. The CRTC agreed, Stentor announced Sympatico/MediaLinx at the end of November 1995 and, whether by conspiracy or coincidence, a month earlier Bell and Telus unilaterally withdrew their basic network service (Centrex) that independents relied on and introduced another at 300% the cost of the previous infrastructure (Courtois, 1995, p. 2; Darling, 1995, pp. 1-3; Johnston & Buchanan, 1995, pp. 1-10).

Bell and Telus argued this was necessary because the ISP's use of the previous Centrex service was inappropriate. As they had done so many times in the past, Bell and Telus slipped effortlessly behind the veil of technological determinism to argue that the Centrex service was intended for voice rather than data communication. Of course, the ISPs rejected this. Not to be outdone, the ISPs called on their own version of technological mysticism, arguing that Centrex services covered basic communication services and that their operations fit under this definition more snugly than the enhanced computer-based service the telcos were trying to push them into using. Moreover, the telcos had marketed the service until October 1995, constructed ISP facilities based on Centrex technology in full awareness that they would be used to provide Internet access, and encouraged the ISPs to sign long-term leases (5 years). ISPs also pointed to recent CRTC decisions that revised Centrex tariffs to account for the heavy usage patterns of resellers and data dependent businesses with leased, private networks (Angus, 1995, pp. 3-5; Johnson & Buchanan, 1995, pp. 5-6). Obviously, the hyperbole about media reconvergence and technologies effortlessly commingling voice, data, and video services might make good fodder for the masses, but in the real world it does not cut muster when butting up against economic interests and the struggle for survival.

In the end, the CRTC allowed the telcos to introduce a new service for ISPs that was only 200% costlier, not 300%, than the old Centrex line. As one exasperated small ISP operator, Jonathan Levine (1995) bemoaned, it was clear that the CRTC had become "an ineffectual lapdog to the telephone . . . companies" (p. 1). Less strident ISP operators note that although these events have not wiped out independent ISPs, they did get rid of the "mom and pop" operations. It is also noted that remaining small- to mid-size ISPs persist at the whim of Stentor, and may even thrive for awhile as freeriders on the telcos' impressive advertising campaigns (personal communication, M. Whatmore, president of Wincom, Windsor, Ontario, January 2, 1996). Whatever the eventual outcome, neither the CRTC nor the Director of the Bureau of Competition have done their utmost to nurture competition in one of the only areas in which real competition actually existed. Instead, the ISP episode fills in another dimension of what policies designed to foster contestable markets, workable competition, and so on really mean: strategic rivalry among existing interests across the globe and previous media borders.[23]

The Content of the Free Lunch

As the financing and institutional machinations continue to struggle against the apparent uneconomics of broadband communication, the threshold questions in the end are those that deal with what kind of communication and content will occur on such systems. In communication systems characterised by enormous information capacity, the primary problems are how to get people's attention and how to feed the media systems' voracious appetite for content. Once again, such questions are accented by uncertain and clumsy efforts to find what will work to establish a commercially viable system and, in the Canadian context, complicated by cultural policy aims connected with Canadian content.

The problem of accessing people's attention is partially addressed through industry structure (vertical integration) and the linking of carriers with content providers. Linking carriers and content allows exclusive packages to be created and special menus formed to guide and direct people's attention along desired channels, with the potential for free exploration pushed to the margins of menu preferences. Essentially, the menu acts not just as part of the "free lunch" but as "free bait", luring people away from the uncertainty of "unfixed" time and space, towards the comforts of certainty provided by corporate or government actors. This approach is used by AOL, Compuserve, IBM/ Southam, Microsoft, Prodigy, Sympatico/MediaLinx and so on, as well as the Canadian government.

Canadian communication policy has used service tiers to give priority to Canadian content since 1971 and as provided for in the *Cable Television Regulations* (1986). This is being extended under the so-called information highway/reconvergence policy to build priority access to navigational systems employed by those who offer broadband communication services (Canada, 1996b, p. 2; CRTC, 1995a, p. 35). The use of menus and navigation systems could, then, be interpreted as merely updating long-standing cable policy. However, in the broader context of the new media policy—the narrow definition of culture as television, the expansion of the corporate broadcasting sector, and sociocultural engineering used to "bootstrap" citizens into the "information age"—such efforts take on a different hue. They problematically reinforce the "mass media" view of the new media and further steer and manipulate public consciousness toward goals that have, at best, dubious validity. Moreover, even from a narrower "strategic perspective," such mechanisms are unlikely to prevail in the context of global trade regimes covering electronic media—a topic covered in the last section of this chapter.

The reinforcement of the mass media view, again, although not yet a "done deal," can be illustrated by looking at Bell and Telus' broadband communication proposals now before the CRTC, and at how some think the voluminous bandwidth of IBNs will be partitioned for NVOD, VOD, pay-per view, and other forms of mass media. Bell's proposal plans to include 3,500 homes in London, Ontario and Repentigny, Quebec, whereas Telus' trial includes a similar number of homes in Calgary and Edmonton, Alberta. Both trials will use a hybrid fibre coax (HFC) system and offer telecoms and broadcasting services (although packaged differently in each case), so they offer a good opportunity to see what leading members of Stentor have in mind for the future of IBNs in Canada.[24]

Both trials will offer several community expression initiatives, cable television, public communication services, NVOD and VOD programming, and interactive services. The first aim seems to stem from the CRTC's exhortation to broadband providers to "come forward with innovative proposals for providing community expression" (CRTC, 1995a, p. 46). On this matter, Bell and Telus proposed to "distribute the community channel of the incumbent cable operators" and to put "computer terminals in publicly accessible locations" (CRTC, 1996a, p. 1). Surely, this is a rather meagre view of the potentials of the new media for community expression. It neither contributes in any way to expanding the terrain of cable access or media production in the local community, nor does it address various FreeNets or other nonprofit computer networking initiatives available in Canada, which have been recognised as a world leaders in opening up the new media to a broader swath of the public (Weston, 1994). Yet this is not surprising, given the policy record with respect to the computer networking community in Canada and the fact that the CRTC had just rendered a decision that narrowly circumscribed which public initiatives could apply for discounted tariffs from the carriers, namely health and educational institutions (CRTC, 1996b, pp. 1-2).

Despite the pithy view taken of the potentially worthwhile policy aim of expanding community expression, any effort along this line must really be seen as sop thrown to the crowds on the way to the services that Bell and Telus hope will pave the information highway with gold: broadcasting, NVOD, VOD, pay-per view, and so on. It was to these that the telcos drew the CRTC's attention after going through the obligatory "public service" list of community expression, Canadian content, and government parliamentary/legislative channels. According to Bell's proposal, "fees will vary with the package provided, and that its *intention is to price at approximately the same level as the incumbent cable company, for a comparable package of service*" (CRTC, 1996, p. 1; emphasis added). However, pricing "at approximately the same level" is not helpful when the idea is to lower prices by eliminating the monopoly profits that cable companies have extracted from subscribers for 20 years. Moreover the planned use of similar programming and pricing strategies is a recipe for ruinous competition, not sustainable and diversifying alternatives. Finally, it is crucial to consider what loading the system full of mass media-style programming does to the "inexhaustible bandwidth" that IBNs are suppose to offer.

Without getting too technical, an IBN offers 750 to 1,000 MHz, or more, bandwidth, which is enough room for 150 television channels, several thousand times the bandwidth of ISDN, and wildly beyond the capacity of ordinary telephone systems (Baldwin, et al. 1996, pp. 111-112; Connell, 1994, pp. 236-237). Although this bandwidth can be configured in endless different ways, certain strategies reveal how quickly bandwidth can turn into a scarce commodity if the "mass media" view of electronic space prevails.

The first example can be illustrated by NVOD services. NVOD services do not sit idly in a server waiting to be called into action (e.g., as in VOD) but continuously circulate in the system at 15, 30, 60, or whatever, minute intervals. Continuous circulation allows people to tap into a program at regular intervals. Baldwin et al (1996, p. 93) introduce a hypothetical case where 40 channels are used to circulate the top 10 films of the week at half-hour intervals. Given that the basic tier in a Canadian program schedule would take up perhaps 10 channels, this leaves 100 "possible channel spaces" remaining. However, this could quickly be reduced by another 40 channels should the top 10 films be rotated at 15 minute (rather than 30 minute) cycles, or should the strategy expand to include not just the top 10 films but the top 20 of the last month, and so on. Moreover, given the lack of finance to support new media production, the content would rely heavily on what is already distributed in video stores, on film, or that can be brought back to life from film studio and broadcasters' archives.[25]

Based on this scenario we can imagine the requisite Canadian content channels and NVOD, plus several pay-per view services, taking up perhaps 60 or so channels, or as Baldwin et. al (1996) note, nearly half the available bandwidth (e.g., from 50 to 450 MHz). According to their analysis, the remainder could be used to deliver VOD, a service in which individual subscribers get films and videos any time on demand. Because they explain it so clearly, the following is drawn directly from their discussion of VOD:

> Channels 61 to 120 (450 to 750 MHz) have been allocated for video on demand. When the first subscriber in a node orders a video-on-demand program, that program is modulated on channel 61 and routed down the fiber to that node [eg. the point at which neighbourhoods are connected to the local exchange]. A command is sent to the subscriber's addressable converter to tune it to channel 61, and only that customer will receive that program. As additional subscribers order programs, their requests will be placed on the next available channels (62, then 63, and so on). Simultaneously, other subscribers . . . may order different programs. In this example, the first 60 users of video on demand will receive their requested programming. If the node has 500 homes, about 12% of the potential subscribers can watch video-on-demand programming at any one time before getting . . . a busy signal. (p. 109)

It is reasonably clear that once basic, NVOD, pay-per view, and the one television channel per user mode of VOD (6MHz) commingle with integrated content packagers—IBM/Southam, Microsoft/NBC, AOL/Bertelsmann, Europe On-line/Pearson, Burda and Kirch/AT&T, Sympatico/MediaLinx, and so on—and the telcos' control of the local monopoly/duopoly distribution system, that available bandwidth could quite easily be driven toward scarcity. Of course, it would be foolish to argue that even this would not be a quantum increase in quantity and quality unprecedented in the history of mediated communication. It would also be churlish to claim that strategic rivalry among even the likes of the above-mentioned players could not prevent monopolistic control over information, knowledge, and public culture. Nonetheless, it is still true that such scenarios skew the evolutionary trajectory of new media down a well-trodden, but wider, mass media path, and that potential contributions of IBNs, or less grandiose systems such as ISDN (a prospect treated in the closing chapter), could more strongly contribute to decentralised, people-oriented communicative interaction and, thus, to more democratic communication and societies.

As things now stand, such potentials are being forgone while even the strategic goal of broadband mass media remains uncertain and illusive. Rather then considering the full range of possibilities, interviews with Sympatico/MediaLinx personnel indicate that most of the focus of service providers is on three current user types: browsers, infotainment seekers, and transactional service users. Browsers are currently the predominant type of user, but to ensure commercially viable IBNs, more infotainment seekers and, crucially, transactional service users are needed. So-called browsers use network communication mostly to look around, find information, watch what is going on in discussion groups, and so on. They seldom initiate communicative interaction or use transactional services such as stock market monitoring, banking services, buying and selling goods, discussion groups, and so on. It is claimed that if people continue to follow this line of use, the free lunch, mass media model of "information highway" development will implode as content providers and advertisers read inaction as a predilection against consumerist behavior.

Certain scholars claim this is exactly what is happening. At a recent meeting of the International Association of Mass Communication Research in Sydney Australia, many researchers seemed worried about what they referred to as the "lurkers." A more thoughtful scholar, however, was not dismissive and instead reflected on the fact that in the economic geography of electronic space a parallel structure of "virtual property" is emerging. In the virtual capitalism of electronic space only a relative few are "property owners" (e.g., those who own their own home page), have full interconnectivity, and are able to initiate and receive communications across the entire mediascape. Then there is a vast "propertyless" majority in possession of "dumb" desktop terminals (e.g., of the Oracle or early Minitel kind—discussed next), no home page, and accounts that allow them to browse websites and receive information but not to initiate communication and take a more active role in "informational space" (Sorensen, 1996, pp. 6-9).

In their myopic vision of the "free lunch" model of electronic mediaspace, some key players appear to be furthering exactly the thing that some claim may lead to the implosion of electronic space: people hardwired into the Net as propertyless browsers. This is clear in existing and emerging practices. First, it is apparent in current practices by signing up subscribers with minimal interactive capability; for example, they are unable to construct and control their own home page beyond a single page of biographic information (for the marketers??) and have little capacity to explore freely, because communication is tied strictly to one's bank account and/or strategically organized by corporate/ government-defined access menus (Sympatico, 1996).

More troublesome in the effort to give away access is the promotion of "stupid," cheap terminals with limited interactivity and almost no ability to communicate. This proposal is gaining in Canada, and included in Bell and Telus' broadband trials, and also in plans aired by MTS. As noted in a story about the latter, the stupid "Inbox" (the brand name)

> is a sort of poor person's Internet service. That is because it isn't capable of downloading large files or graphics—what a customer sees on a single TV screen is all he or she can retrieve during a session. . . . It is an enhanced entertainment unit. . . . [C]ustomers will be able to read electronic mail and search [browse] through MTS' Internet Yellow Pages directories. However, users will need to buy a computer keyboard if they want to compose and send e-mail messages with the system. (Surtees, 1996, p. B6)

The root problem begins with the fundamental uneconomics of broadband. A compounding problem is that the telcos like the idea because, as an MTS director notes, "the device puts the resources and complexity of computers in the telephone network, *where it belongs*" (Surtees, 1996, p. B6; emphasis added). Putting intelligence back in the network helps get large users of private networks/intranets back onto the PTN, and also weakens the competitive threat of private network builders aligned with powerful members of the computer industries such as IBM, Microsoft, and so on. This strategy is not just found in a single small Canadian telco but is part of a global struggle amid TOs and computer suppliers over the future of the "new telecoms" (Mansell, 1993). Discussions with a BT engineer confirms support for the "stupid interface" model among other global telecoms providers. A conference held by the French government-sponsored IDATE Institute in 1996 included a debate on the issue between Lawrence Ellison, the originator of the Oracle Computer ("InBox"), and Bill Gates of Microsoft.

The Oracle model would be a return to the "computer utility" model anticipated in the 1960s through the early 1980s, in which most intelligence is stored in the telecoms network or central computers. In this model, people use cheap terminals from home and have little interactivity with the facilities, programs, and services located online. Although for some this might be an acceptable way to avert a crisis of disenfranchisement in the capitalist "information age," it must be wondered if this is acceptable. In contrast, the "distributed intelligence" model allows ample "power" to sit on a person's desktop, but at a greater cost for the final interface between people and the network. Like most crucial sociological problems, especially those skewed toward a particular evolutionary path set by vested interests, this one is hard to solve.

Broadband Communications: Still a Luxury Good?

Of course, it is still possible that the mass market for broadband communications may not emerge, a prospect often admitted though seldom addressed. Here, I look at the possibility that IBNs will not be delivered as a free lunch after all, but as a luxury good. Three factors suggest that this might prevail: the "redlining" of poor districts to be cut off from new media infrastructures, the development of "information suburbs" versus information societies, and user profiles and the habitus of the "information professional" which make them the likely inhabitants of the "information suburbs" of the future.

In addition to disparities in access to basic and enhanced forms of communication in Canada (see Figure 1.1 in Chapter 1), similar patterns exist globally. A recent ITU report noted that 24 OECD countries, although only constituting 15% of the world's population, accounted for 71% of all telephone lines, whereas the other 85% of the world's people shared access to the remaining 29%. Fifty countries fall behind even the minimal rate of one telephone per 100 people recommended by the ITU in 1984 as a goal to be achieved (ITU, 1994, p. 10-11; Tarjanne, 1994, p. 2). Just as certain countries seem to fall off the map of global communication, so too may entire regions in North America be "cut out of the map" of planned IBN development. In this situation, even if people want the new media services, they may find that their TO has "redlined" their district. In the United States, the FCC was called on to avert this prospect by several groups who

> found indications of "electronic redlining" in the applications of four Regional Bell Operating Companies to construct video dialtone facilities. The . . . companies propose to bypass many lower income and/or minority communities in their initial deployment of video dialtone, while serving areas contiguous to those communities. This . . . amounts to a denial of a service which may be essential to the economic and social livelihood of the community that is redlined. (Campbell & Shwartzman, 1994, p. i)

The same studies found that adjacent, high income neighbourhood "nodes" were to be connected to broadband networks. Although many of the proposed plans included in these studies were eventually withdrawn, they nonetheless showed that in between mass marketing broadband and letting the information highway die a peaceful death, there lie other options that telcos may pursuit. Bell and Telus' choice to locate their broadband experiments in London, Repentigny, and the community of Lake Bonavista—all noted for their higher than usual incomes and the professional status of their citizens—suggest that such services may be initially marketed as a luxury good in Canada as well.

As luxury goods, IBNs could be freed from the constraints of income inelasticities and extreme price sensitivity, while also allowing users broader choice and more sensitivity to their interests and needs. Crucially, the much higher penetration of personal computers in households with more than $50,000 annual income means that users are not tied to dumb interfaces that hobble transactional services—banking, discussion groups, stock market monitoring, and so on. Moreover, residents of "information suburbs" are likely to have more appeal to advertisers than the masses of the "information society." Sympatico/MediaLinx (1996) and U.S. data provided in Baldwin et al. (1996) show that current Internet and interactive media users tend to be married men between 35-54, with some college or university education and a household income of $50,000 (p. 214).[26]

New media users also tend to be among those whose "habitus" includes more extensive use of computers and information services outside the home. There is likely to be significant overlap between such residents and the "information professionals" targeted for the last 25 years by online providers such as Infomart/Dialog. Infomart/Dialog (1996) has offered access to its over 450 databases to clients in law offices, hospitals, government offices, large manufacturing organisations, business and financial services industries, education, and so on for some time. Although speculative, it is likely that people with professional experience in the use of computers and data retrieval services may be more willing to use transactional services in the home. Recalling earlier discussions, it is these services that are considered to be key to the economic viability of IBNs, rather than the mass market made up of those derisively referred to as "lurkers."

Another practice favouring the evolution of IBNs as luxury goods is that some more "serious" independent ISP providers are thinking of combining with building contractors to build "intelligent communities." This is a novel prospect, suggesting that financing the "last HFC" mile to the home could be overcome by tucking it into the purchase price of a new homes. As mentioned earlier, the telcos have recognised the severity of this problem and relentlessly petitioned the CRTC to provide access to the cablecos' broadband drop to subscribers' home. However, in the ISP/building contractor model, telcos could build fibre to the node, as ISPs and builders extend the network from there to peoples' homes. Burying the $1,500 to $5,000 cost of making the connection in the purchase price of a new home could also relieve some of the pressure to subsidise the IBN luxury good from advertising or by invading people's privacy.

At the same time, however, such an approach would further divide electronic space, building 'information suburbs' rather than more inclusive "information societies." Yet, in an era when people escape public life by putting their kids in private schools, buy private health care, and live in guarded suburban enclaves, the prospect of "broadband Agora" amid the expanded free lunch does not look completely out of place.

THE FREE LUNCH AND THE ELECTRONIC FREE PRESS: COMMON CARRIERS, ELECTRONIC PUBLISHERS, OR BACK TO THE FUTURE

Who will speak in the "electronic Agora"? The answer will partially turn on which model of media development is ultimately adopted. Nonetheless, it is quite obvious that being connected to an advertising-saturated media space by way of a stupid interface will not be a boon for democratic communication. The "luxury good" model of growth, in contrast, might contribute to a sense of efficacy among users about their ability to shape the world in which they live, although this too might mirror existing sensibilities among different classes about their respective ability to influence the events—economic, political, and/or personal—impinging on their lives. Beyond these issues, the prospects for media freedoms in "new electronic media spaces" depends on how such freedoms are defined.

From Common Carriers to Editors

Telecoms providers now actively shape mediated electronic communication. This is occurring as telcos become, simultaneously, bandwidth wholesalers/retailers (carriers), content providers (publishers), and audiovisual producers and distributors (broadcasters). With this amalgamation of roles, common carriage is crumbling (Noam, 1994), replaced by a model of electronic publishing or a hybrid common carrier/electronic publisher/broadcaster model, as found in the history of telecoms and the press between, roughly, 1870 and 1910 (see Chapter 3). Whichever regulatory regime prevails, it is certain that new media markets are being accompanied by new economic, political, and civil liberties for telecoms providers.

Although there are obvious differences between today's era of media reconvergence and late 19th-century telecoms and press history, there are deep-seated parallels. In both eras, regulators have had to consider whether telecoms service providers are *active* or *passive* in the communication process, the *type of service* being offered, and if services are *public* or *private* in nature. Just as such distinctions determined if the telegraph would be regulated like the press or a common carrier, today they influence whether telecoms and/or computer network services will be regulated as publishers, carriers, or broadcasters.

A striking parallel to this early history is provided by two recent computer network cases in the United States, the first involving Compuserve and the latter Prodigy. In the first case, the Court determined that Compuserve "provided subscribers with computer related services forums including an on-line general information service or 'electronic library'" (cited in *Stratton Oakmonth, Inc and Daniel Prush vs. Prodigy Services Co.*, 1995, p. 4). The Court found that because Compuserve was not actively editing the material that it made available to subscribers, it was more like a common carrier and therefore not responsible for content within its "electronic libraries." In contrast, the Court argued in the latter case that

> Prodigy held itself out to the public and its members as *controlling the content* of its computer bulletin boards. . . . Prodigy . . . [was] clearly *making decisions as to content*, . . . *and such decisions constitute editorial control*. . . . Prodigy has uniquely arrogated to itself the role of determining what is proper for its members to post and read on its bulletin boards. (*Stratton Oakmonth, Inc. and Daniel Prush vs. Prodigy Services Co.*, 1995, p. 5; emphasis added)

Considerations of whether providers actively or passively intervene editorially in the communication process reflect a shift over the last decade from the carriage/content demarcation underlying previous models of telecoms regulation. This change has taken place mostly around issues raised by "dial-a-porn," and has captured the attention of several commentators concerned about how courts and regulators have welcomed a greater role for carriers in censoring content that would otherwise be constitutionally protected (Barron, 1993; Frieden, 1995; Samarajiva & Hadley, 1996; Samarajiva & Mukherjee, 1990).

As Samarajiva and Mukherjee (1990) note, Canadian telcos and regulators worked out a system behind closed doors whereby Stentor members would "police information services" for sexually oriented, racist, and/or other "nefarious" types of content (p. 330). Once carriers decided a service was undesirable, it was denied access to the network, regardless of its legal status. Similar trends occurred in the United States, where courts struck down unwieldy government attempts to regulate indecent sex-oriented services but eagerly sanctioned telco efforts to the same end. This was reflected in the precedent-setting *Sable* (1988) case, in which the Supreme Court declared "that while . . . the Constitution prevents Congress from banning indecent speech . . ., we do not hold that the Constitution requires public utilities to carry it" (quoted in Barron, 1993, p. 381). Barron (1993) claimed that Courts have engaged in extensive judicial activism, fabricating new rationales—the broadcast-like nature of online services, business judgment, enhanced services, State action and so on—that have vastly expanded the telcos' editorial judgment (pp. 386-387). Thus, just as radio broadcasters' usurped editorial control in the 1920s partially on the basis of the "Bolshevist Threat," those who own the distribution networks today, Courts, and regulators are again leaning on another "moral panic"—sex—to constrict editorial control over electronic space.[27]

The New Telcos: Editors, Publishers, Broadcasters or Carriers?

The scope of the telephone companies' "media freedoms" has expanded far beyond that which is incidentally attributable to the regulation of sex. In the United States, long-standing FCC regulations preventing telco/cable cross-ownership (except in rural areas) were struck down in 1993 as an infringement of the telephone companies' "First Amendment" speech rights (U.S. Court of Appeals, 1994). Thereafter, the *Telecommunications Act of 1996* gave carriers almost complete editorial discretion but tried to obligate telecom and computer network providers to take "good faith" measures to edit their networks according to broadcast indecency standards (*Communication Decency Act* (Title V), United States, 1996).[28]

Events in Canada have led in a similar direction, albeit working their way through the CRTC and Parliament more than through the courts. Canadian telcos can now obtain broadcast licenses,[29] and their entry into cable is imminent. Consequently, the telcos are obtaining new media freedoms under the *Canadian Charter of Human Rights and Freedom* (1982) and the *Broadcasting Act* (1991) (Canada, 1993b). As the Royal Task Force on Broadcast Policy (1985) noted,

> Freedom of thought, belief, opinion and expression, including freedom of the press and other media of communication is clearly the foundation of broadcasting as we conceive it in Canada. This principle has always been the cornerstone of the regulatory system. (Canada, 1985, p. 137)

As telecoms carriers gain new media freedoms they obtain greater ability to pick and choose who can access the PTN. Yet, even as the telcos put more emphasis on marketing bandwidth, providing content packages, and editing "on-line media space," they will still confront vestiges of common carriage embedded in the CRTC's video-dial-tone platform, among other places. As such, telcos do not have unbridled editorial rights and media freedoms. The issue now, however, is to define precisely where the telcos' media freedom ends and others' right to access the PTN begins. New media freedoms will likely give TOs an incentive to broadly interpret their editorial discretion and narrowly define common-carrier obligations. In the end, ill-defined editorial rights, hazy content distinctions, and new media freedoms offer the telcos enormous power to shape which services are central to the menus that organise online media space, which are peripheral, and which are excluded altogether.

There are several likely sources that may challenge the current effort to establish a hybrid regulatory regime in Canada. The first is smaller, independent, commercial and noncommercial content providers who may seek to establish a broader interpretation of public access to the "information highway" than is being offered by the telcos' pithy rendering of "community expression" and the CRTC's decision to limit discounted tariffs to public groups connected to education and health-related entities (CRTC, 1996a; CRTC, 1996b). This group could seek a broader expansion of what remains of common carriage, an enlarged definition of who constitutes the public, and a dynamic definition of cultural policy that embraces computer networking, information resources, and perhaps some new content services. This point is considered in the final chapter.

Current attempts to expand broadcast policy to embrace programming delivered by carriers could also face other challenges. As noted previously, SaskTel and the CRTC became embroiled in a tussle over whether NVOD and VOD should be classified as enhanced services or broadcasting services (Cohen, 1993). Although the CRTC and government prevailed in this dispute, they did so only by further mystifying the grounds on which different types of media content could be demarcated. Ottawa may have prevailed in this case because the telcos were willing to acquiesce in order to expedite their planned foray into multimedia, and as traditional broadcasters—Allercom, Astral Broadcasting, and the Canadian Association of Broadcasters (CAB)—sought to prevent their short-term extinction by having the CRTC regulate all audiovisual media under the *Broadcasting Act* (1991) (CRTC, 1994a, p. 47).[30] The CRTC, for its part, attempted to legitimate its new policy as carrying Canadian cultural policy into the 'information age'.

Although such a marriage of convenience may have been able to carry the day, it is not likely to be sustainable over the long run. Whatever the reasons, current policy is still based on trying to draw lines amid media signals that commingle in digital form and are carried down the same pipe. This state of affairs will likely whither in the near future as carriers—domestic and foreign—and new content providers seek to remove "on-line audiovisual services" from the rubric of cultural policy and into the enhanced services regulatory framework. This was what SaskTel was proposing to do, as it argued that NVOD and VOD were distributed on a point-to-point basis, to individuals, and over the telecoms network; as such, NVOD/VOD should be considered enhanced services, a move that would expand the carriers' position as "electronic publishers" and free them from the cultural policy aims of the *Broadcast Act* (1991).

Similar problems may be aggravated in the future as foreign providers seek market entry through NAFTA and GATS' sections covering enhanced services. Although NAFTA currently contains a "cultural exemption" clause (Article 1301, Canada, 1992), and the GATS allows countries to choose whether or not to include the so-called cultural industries,[31] the key question is will the distinction between cultural industries and enhanced services hold under the pressure of media reconvergence? The door opened in the United States by the courts and the *Telecommunications Act of 1996* (United States, 1996) for AT&T, RBOCs, MCI, Sprint, and others to offer content, suggests that the CRTC may be hard pressed in the near future to justify its attempts to "force-fit" new media into its cultural policy framework. Indeed, alliances between BT/MCI/NewsCorp, Time Warner/CNN/USWest, and others noted in this book render attempts to differentiate between media content highly circumspect. Given these conditions, and the close links between AT&T and Rogers, it is not difficult to imagine AT&T trying to provide NVOD and/or VOD services through Rogers' local cable networks or by tapping into Stentor members' local exchanges.[32] Similar conditions tie Stentor members to MCI/BT and thus indirectly to Murdock's NewsCorp.

Although neither NAFTA nor GATS compel services delivered over the telecoms network to be defined as enhanced services, they do offer fertile soil for those seeking to put new network-based media services beyond the reach of government regulators. Section 1310 of NAFTA, for instance, defines *enhanced services* as:

> those telecommunications services employing computer processing applications that:
>
> (a) act on the format, content, code, protocol or similar aspects of a customer's transmitted information;
>
> (b) provide a customer with additional, different or restructured information; or
>
> (c) involve customer interaction with stored information . . . (Canada, 1992).

This definition would not cover re-runs of old television programs broadcast over the telecoms network. Consequently, providers offering such a service would still be covered by Canadian broadcasting policy.

However, the NAFTA/GATS provisions would cover service providers such as AP/Dow Jones, Bloombergs, Infomart/Dialog, Reuters, and so on. These companies deliver images, data, and text accross national boundaries, "provide . . . customers with additional, different or restructured information," and require "customer interaction with stored information" (also see Intven, 1994, p. 54). The problem here is not that these services should be within the reach of Canadian regulators, but that by combining media forms—from television images to online data services—they muddle the boundaries between what is an enhanced service under international trade rules and the categories of programming services that the CRTC intends to regulate according to cultural policy aims. As the globalization of communications media forges ahead, such muddled boundaries between services that are and are not covered by "free trade" and "free flow" principles will be ripe for challenge. Should NAFTA and GATS' expansive definitions of enhanced services prevail in such a boundary dispute, the CRTC's attempts to regulate NVOD/VOD services in the name of cultural policy would fail. Canadian carriers would then have to offer enhanced service providers cost-based interconnection to the public telecoms network without imposing any "conditions [i.e., cultural policy obligations] . . . on access to and use of the public telecommunications services networks and services other than necessary" (TNC, 1993, Article 5.6). Among other things, this would eliminate the contribution of NVOD/VOD services to the Canadian content production fund.

On the one hand, the enhanced services provisions offer a convenient way of escaping Canadian media and cultural policies. On the other hand, however, shielding enhanced services from government regulation could expand the concept of an electronic free press. At a time when people are trying to carve out new institutional boundaries and legal regimes for new communication technologies, this concept of "negative freedoms" establishes an important minimal foundation for a transnational "electronic free press." This could be especially important in the United States where new legislation tried to impose onerous content responsibilities on telcos (Samarajiva & Hadley, 1996). Beyond the U.S. efforts to impose broadcast standards on telecoms—and similar efforts in Canada for different reasons—NAFTA and GATS could help overcome government restrictions on the free flow of information that has stifled political discourse.

Despite these potential positive contributions to media freedoms, however, it must also be noted that NAFTA/GATS provisions on telecoms and computer services are above all aimed at expanding information markets. Any contribution to media freedoms are incidental to this aim. In addition, even these residual benefits could be constrained by NAFTA/GATS sections covering public morals, or attempts by governments worldwide to regulate "offensive content" (Samarajiva & Hadley, 1996, pp. 18-19)—a catch-all phrase that could encourage governments to turn a blind eye to the suppression of political speech in some countries in return for favours in kind in others. Moreover, discussions with Canadian, EC, and Singaporean officials suggest that the WTO's telecoms Annex, unlike NAFTA's telecoms chapter, lacks authority. This could be due to the fact that it is ancillary to the WTO regime's ongoing efforts to expand the number of countries that have signed the Annex (only 30 countries signed in 1994) as well as efforts to formally include basic services and cultural industries in the WTO framework. In the meantime, governments appear able to establish telecoms policies that deviate from GATS requirements.[33]

Rather than democratising communication, it is more likely that the GATS agreement will serve to liberate the new media from attempts by governments or the public to influence the evolution of these new services in any way that threatens the commercial interests of the "electronic free press." Perhaps one of the best examples of the tensions between GATS requirements and national/regional communication policies is offered by the recent EC proposal to regulate new media. According to the proposed directive, regulations would standardise the authorization and licensing criteria of EC members and address issues regarding technical compatibility between networks and service providers, online advertising, market power, privacy, and universal service (EC, 1996, p. 5). Although the discussion pertaining to licensing was misguided and provisions about which services would be covered hazy, the focus on structural, not content, issues, as well as the "lightest regulation possible," did offer a workable basis for discussing the pertinent issues at hand (EC, 1996, p. 6).

The reaction from industry was swift and dogmatic. The EU Committee of the American Chamber of Commerce (1996), whose members include Dun & Bradstreet,[35] IBM, Microsoft, Time Warner, Uunet, and so on, stridently opposed the idea that "new communication services might be covered . . . including the Internet, on-line networks, video services, and other sources of information" (p. 4). The organisation took particular umbrage at the mention of monitoring "market power" or the idea that connections might be made between telecoms and the cultural policy aims "enshrined in the 1989 Television Without Frontiers Directive" (pp. 5-6). According to the EU Committee's position paper, "general authorizations should be strictly limited to *technical telecoms requirements*" (p. 5; emphasis added). The International

Communications Roundtable, whose members included the previously mentioned interests as well as Bertelsmann, Electronic Data Services, Reuters, Sony, and a few others, claimed the proposal "would cripple on-line services" (Schenker, 1996a, p. 1). Although criticisms of the attempt to draw lines between services that would be covered and those that would not were correct, the key point, Time Warner's Manuel Kohnstamm emphasised, was that "electronic services should not be subject to either broadcast or telecoms rules" (quoted in Schenker, 1996b, p. 30). Sir Frank Rogers (1995), chairman of the *The Telegraph*, a large daily newspaper in the United Kingdom, drew on the rich language of media freedom to point out in a letter to the president of the EC how:

> This proposal will, for the first time . . . impose licensing regimes on newspaper and magazine publishers for their on-line publications. . . . The freedom of the press will be jeopardised if any regulatory authority has powers over the publication of newspapers and magazines in whatever format . . . . Regulating access is depriving EU citizens of a crucially important liberty.

Although these comments are ignorant of the history of online media regulation (as noted in Chapter 3), they do demonstrate the extent to which "electronic publishers" want to keep new media free of communication policy and public interest debates. Although the incomplete nature of global communications policy allows Canada, EC members, and Singapore, among others, to tinker with bringing their media/cultural policies into the "information age," the tide is moving toward the globalisation of the "electronic publishing model." Canada's commitment to the sturdier legal framework of NAFTA's telecoms chapter (compared to the GATS telecoms Annex) demonstrates that such a model means forfeiting the ability to deal with the broad range of issues still under discussion in the EC. The CRTC's residual capacity to contest the classification of NVOD/VOD ("cultural exemption"[35] vs. enhanced service) is comparatively minor to the scope of the EC initiative. Even a triumphant defense of current media policy in Canada would be a hollow victory. Any effort to regulate online advertising,[36] extend universal service obligations to new media such as Internet, regulate the market power of ISP/online media such as AOL, Compuserve, IBM/Southam, Sympatico/MediaLinx, and so on, or to extend broader cultural policy obligations to the new media, would be severely constrained, if not impossible, under NAFTA.

SUMMARY COMMENTS

The telcos now enjoy similar standing in relation to civil liberties as their "mass media" predecessors. Broadly considered, the expansion of media freedoms side by side with new media markets reverses the conventional political-juridical wisdom that prevailed until the mid-1980s, which held the economy to be subordinate to the political sphere in democratic societies, as noted in Chapter 1 (*Klein and Law Society of Upper Canada*, 1985, p. 523). Such trends are also symptomatic of a broader amnesia regarding the troubled history of electronic publishing that preceded common carriage and the limited terms under which corporate actors were first admitted into modern society.

More narrowly considered, the new concept of media freedoms transforms, if not reverses outright, the position of content producers vis-à-vis common carriers. In a remarkably short period of time, formal telco involvement in content has gone from a few exceptional cases—gateway services, InfoDirect, the Telidon and Alex experiments, and so on—to an almost completely unbridled alignment between content production and distribution. As matters now stand, telcos can offer online services, censor "morally objectionable" content provided by others, and function as broadcast programmers, undertakings, and carriers. The boundaries between all of these activities and whatever remains of common carriage are blurry and perhaps a complete mystery. Such matters will only be clarified through what promises to be an intense period in the politics of Canadian telecoms.

Despite such massive transformations in the political and legal infrastructure of the "information age," much of the network infrastructure remains in disarray. The telcos are not investing in modernisation projects, there is slack demand for information highways, and the model of media evolution that will fit the constraints of commercial viability has yet to be determined.

The next and final chapter offers a different perspective on new media development. The proposals offered build on people's observable interests in new media and tries to breathe new life into concepts—community expression, cultural policy, demand-led supply of technologies and services, public access—that currently lay fallow within existing CRTC policy. I also suggest a more limited and less intrusive role for the Canadian state, increased reliance on competition to achieve and expand on media freedoms, and stresses the use of "appropriate technology," such as ISDN, rather than the chimera of IBNs. It is to these efforts that we now turn.

ENDNOTES

1. Telephone services by 1992 had fallen several points below the cpi. All items had risen by 27 points from the base year of 1986 (= 100), whereas cable television services rose almost 37 points. This was also coupled with efforts to restrict unaffiliated services access to cable networks as well as the use of "negative options" that loaded people up with, and charged them for, services that they had not requested, unless they specifically instructed the cable operator otherwise.

2. This decision was crucial in at least three respects. First, the CRTC initially rejected the application on the grounds that NorthwestTel had not sufficiently consulted with the communities where it planned to establish its systems, nor had it set out a clear timetable. The principle of community consultation is discussed further later, but for now it can just be noted that it is a novel idea that the telcos whose services have by and large been shielded from the Canadian public should have to consult with people only in remote areas. Perhaps such a novel principle could be expanded in other parts of the country without harming the impressive achievements of the people in northern communities. Second, the decision broadened the interpretation of the CRTC's 1969 common-carrier policy statement because that applied only to small carriers in rural areas. Although the systems were to be in rural and remote areas, NorthwestTel is not a small carrier. Finally, and most significantly, the decision claimed that NorthwestTel's parent, BCE, was "eligible to hold a broadcasting license, [since] section 7 of the *Bell Canada Act* [only] prohibits Bell from directly or indirectly holding a broadcasting license" (CRTC, 1994b, p. 4). This was a disingenuous use of corporate fictions and a narrow reading of the *Bell Canada Act* that was not consistent with the spirit in which the section had originally been written. Essentially, this opened the door for the largest telephone company to move into broadcasting through its parent company, rather than through a more explicit tackling of the issues. Subsequent legislative initiatives along this line are thus, cosmetic, basically formalising in public what has already been done through the back door. This is discussed in this chapter.

3. The structural separation mechanism, however, was required for those TOs (e.g., BCTel and Quebec Tel) that were foreign (US) owned, or that remained under public ownership (e.g., SaskTel and MTS). According to these arrangements, BCTel and Quebec Tel could own broadcasting outlets, but control would be separated by the appointment of an "all Canadian" board of directors, several independent directors, and an annual promise from the parent company, GTE, "declaring that there has been no influence or control exercised by those companies over the programming decisions of the broadcasting distribution subsidiaries" (Canada, 1996b, pp. 1-5). This mirrored a process undertaken earlier in the year under the *Broadcasting Act* that increased the amount of foreign ownership of Canadian broadcast outlets, ostensibly to give Canadian broadcasters access to foreign capital in order to increase the output of Canadian content (Governor General in Council, 1996c, PC 1996-479).

4. Demonstrating the politics of these new definitions, even before the CRTC announced its new policies it was engaged in a tussle with SaskTel over whether NVOD and VOD should be defined as telecoms services—and thus completely under the purview of the provincial, publicly owned telco—or as a broadcast program and thus under the authority of the CRTC and federal government. As SaskTel argued, VOD/NVOD programs were neither ordered sequentially or delivered to the public. They were ordered one by one by individuals "on demand." The government position was essentially that if it "looks, smells and tastes" like television, it is television. As discussed later such an "I know it when I see it" approach to legal questions has never faired well as a basis for law (personal correspondence between J. C. Meldrum, SaskTel and Avrum Cohen, CRTC, October 8, 1993).

5. Although this no doubt made the FreeNet and other public access groups' hearts race, the CRTC soon frustrated expectations that this proposal might be read in an expansive way as it announced that the telcos could give preferential rates for computer networking and other telecoms services only to the health and educational sector. This will be discussed further later.

6. This statement is based on the following: Nearly 50% of the cable industry is controlled by three companies, Rogers (23.3%), Videotron (14.6%), and Shaw (10.4%); 77 out of 110 daily newspapers in Canada are owned by three entities; Southam/Hollinger, Thompson, and Black (Southam/Hollinger, alone, accounts for 40% of newspaper revenues); and just two carriers—Bell Canada and GTE—account for 73% of all telecoms network and service revenues. Radio, in contrast, is far less concentrated.

7. The estimate is based on annual carrier revenues of $16.5 billion in 1995, and a growth rate of 3% per year. By the year 2005, this yields a figure of just over $21 billion in annual revenues. By adding the revenues for each year in between we can arrive at the figure of $188 billion.

8. When speaking to staff at the CRTC about these issues, they now generally agree that gold plating of the network took place on a large scale in the past.

9. A hybrid fibre coaxial cable (HFC) is simply a combination of fibre in most of the network and coaxial cable (the same technology used for cable television) in the last stretch to people's premises. As we will see, this is the technique being promoted in forthcoming broadband experiments conducted by Bell in Ontario and Quebec and Telus in Alberta.

10. Recent discussion in *Communications Weekly International* claim even higher figures, of between $2,000 and $5,000 US for fibre to the home, or 40 to 50% of this for fibre to the curb (Gaz, 1995, p. 17). Based on the figures of $1,500 to $3,000 introduced above, and a total of 18.2 million subscriber lines in Canada, the cost of building on HFC-based "information highway" can be calculated to be between about $27.3 billion and $54 billion. These sums should be compared with Stentor's proposal to spend $8.5 billion on its broadband initiative. Where will the rest come from?

11. As an aside, the study was very much interested in finding the existence of heavy usage of telecoms services, not an absense, as is clearly indicated by a read of the study and its recommendations.

12. Interviews with several staff members of the CRTC, Canadian telcos, and an engineer at British Telecoms have helped to inform the discussion.

13. This is different than in long-distance telephone service in which competition has led to more long-distance calls and thus a "bigger pie." In that scenario, incumbent TOs usually recover more than what they lose in market share through increases in overall revenues (OECD, 1995a, pp. 40-46).

14. Just to get a sense of magnitude, it can be noted that $4.7 billion is more than 10 times the amount of the CBC budget cuts of $417 million announced in 1996, and about one-half the sum collected in unemployment insurance each year.

15. Section 41 of the *Telecommunications Act* (1993) "prohibits . . . unsolicited telecommunications to the extent that the Commission considers it necessary to prevent undue inconvenience or nuisance, *giving due regard to freedom of expression* (Canada, 1993a, emphasis added). Also see the discussion of privacy issues and marketers "rights" during hearings held prior to the new legislation being enacted (Canada, Proceedings of the Standing Senate Committee on Transport and Communications, 1992).

16. For a discussion of an alternative approach by one proposed IBN provider in Canada, UBI, see Samarajiva (1995). According to his analysis, a combination of stringent privacy laws in Quebec, participation by the Post Office and other provincial government agencies, a commitment by the other participants in the proposed project to a "privacy code" worked up through personal interviews prior to beginning the trials, and several other factors have produced one of the most rigorous privacy policy regimes in the world. However, as he notes, the project has been postponed several times and may not get off the ground, although its lessons are still worthwhile.

17. Yet, even if the "free lunch" aspect or privacy were to be rendered transparent and individuated in the manner implied here, this would not be acceptable. Samarajiva (1995) is helpful when he notes that communicative spaces are public spaces, and like the "village green" cannot be sold off bit by bit to individuals. The value of the space is in its common enjoyment and use, its unpredictability, and the ability to establish communication with others. Selling "privacy" in individuated amounts fails to recognise that communicative relations, by nature, involve more than just one individual, and for any one person to "sell out" their privacy carries with it negative externalities that are brought forth in time and capture others who may or may not share their communicative partner's idea about where the bounds between the commercial, private, and social should be drawn.

18. The following is based on Sympatico (1996) website information and also several interviews with Sympatico/Medialinx personnel.

19. Compuserve has been aligned with IBM, Sears, and CBS since its debut, although CBS withdrew from the relationship several years ago.

20. The closest that Canadian policy has come to trying to deal with questions about links between ownership, control over distribution facilities, and editorial matters, is the CRTC's recent approval of Roger's acquisition of the largest magazine publisher in the country (also with press holdings) with the caveat that it ensure "a clear separation between itself and the editorial departments of its new publishing holdings" (Dalglish, 1995, p. 45).

21. AOL's profit was even smaller in 1995, at 3.1%, and in the first quarter of 1996, it posted a one-off loss of $354 million (Sanders, 1996. p. 6). Compare these figures with profit rates of between 15% and 25% for North American and European PTOs over the last five years.

22. Microsoft also owns 20% of Uunet.

23. The idea that communication policy does not really foster competition but strategic rivalry between global behemoths also meshes with the formation, in 1996, of the new Montreal-based Internet Law & Policy Forum (1996), which counts among its members Bell Canada, Telus, AT&T, BT, Cisco Systems, Deutsche Telekom, General Electric Information Systems, General Magik, Kong Kong Telecom, IBM, Mastercard International, MCI, Microsoft, Netscape Communications, Omnes-a Shlumberger/Cable & Wireless, Oracle, Premenos and Visa. In other words, these are the strategic rivals in the nascent global communications environment, although the group claims to represents the "*geographical and corporate diversity*" of the Internet. The task, according to the group's first press release, is to "build . . . a more predictable global environment." According to the group, "the Internet faces a confusing and potentially disabling range of national laws seeking to govern a global environment" (pp. 1-2, emphasis added). Obviously, such goals stand at odds with the lore of the Internet as a dynamic, even anarchic place, as well as with the potentials for small, independent, competitive providers such as ISP to persist and thrive. Essentially, it appears that the group desires moving rapidly toward the stabilisation of a global legal/regulatory regime to ratify the institutional arrangements pursued by its members over the last two years.

24. Unless otherwise stated, the following discussion relies on CRTC Notice of Public Hearing 1996-14 and Public Notice 96-37 (CRTC, 1996a). Although the present discussion takes place before any decision has been made, this does not matter because regardless of outcomes, the applications give a concrete expression of at least a couple of versions of what the telcos would like to see develop.

25. Hence the rush to acquire Hollywood film libraries and studios by other "software/content" providers and hardware manufactures, for example, Sony, Matsushita, and so on. Privatisation policy in Canada also supports this as government information is sold to the private sector. Other public cultural resources are also being digitalised and commercialised in conjunction with the private sector, or by the latter alone. These include the National Library of Canada collection, the National Archives of Canada, the National Museum of Science and Technology, the Canadian Museum of Civilisation, and the Canadian Museum of Nature, among others (Canada, 1996a, pp. 12-14; Mosco, 1997).

26. Households in the top 20% of income earners (56.6%) are more than four times as likely to own computers than the bottom 20% (13.7%), and eight times more likely to be connected to the Internet (Statistics Canada, 1996f, p. 10).

27. This is not an argument supporting pornography on the Net, or freer online distribution of obscene materials. Instead, it accepts that these are outside the ambit of free speech, but is critical of the idea that the state and

large corporations can work in the margins of the law to expand the range of unprotected speech.

28. The latter was subsequently struck down by the courts, although an appeal to the Supreme Court has been granted and is still pending.

29. Bell Canada still awaits final changes to the *Bell Canada Act* before it can do so, but meanwhile it can skirt these limitations through generous CRTC interpretations given to the Act which effectively excluded Bell's parent company, BCE, from its strictures. Regardless, Ottawa has announced that "the *Bell Canada Act* will be amended to enable Bell Canada to be eligible to hold broadcasting licenses" (Canada, 1996b, p. 3).

30. This issue is not unique to Canada but also applies to other areas where regulatory boundaries between broadcasting and telecoms prevail, such as Germany. In Germany, NVOD/VOD have also caused constitutional problems because of the Landers' (provinces) authority over broadcasting and the federal government's control over telecoms. The two levels of government are currently embroiled in discussions over how these services should be defined. A treaty embodying the results is expected in 1997 (KMPG, 1996c, p. 151).

31. It is quite significant that the GATS does not include a cultural exemption clause, as it means that even the weak measures Canada was able to secure in the FTA and NAFTA have not made it to the global level, that there is heavy pressure to eliminate this exception altogether and that, for the first time, the so-called cultural industries can be included in a global trade agreement. Thus, Hong Kong, India, Korea, Malaysia, Mexico, Singapore, the United States, the United Kingdom, and Thailand, among others, did include film, broadcasting, and so on—although some with important conditions—in the WTO's GATS agreement (Kakabadse, 1995, pp. 75-76).

32. This would also fit with efforts in the United States among the long-distance carriers—AT&T, MCI/BT, Sprint—to obtain partners among the large cable system operators who have extensive local networks. Thus, as in Canada, patterns in the United States suggest the emerging potential for duopolistic competition in the core of the local PTN, with perhaps a greater number of specialised CAPS (Carrier Access Providers) competing at the local level for large commercial and government accounts.

33. For example, Canada's policy with respect to NVOD/VOD could be at least challenged under the GATS provisions. Singapore, a GATS signatory, has established a policy of only licensing three ISPs and requires them to, at a minimum, censor a list of Internet Protocols (IP) (the address for Internet sites) proscribed by the Singaporean Broadcasting Authority for cultural, political, and religious reasons. Although such efforts would, as Singaporean officials acknowledged during interviews, abrogate Singapore's WTO commitments, nobody seems ready to challenge them as they seek to use the country as their "Asian region information hub." One can only assume that the real commitment is to economic, not political, civil, and media freedoms. EC policy that also contradicts GATS requirements, but for other reasons, is introduced next.

34. Dun & Bradstreet gained notoriety in North America during the early 1990s after trying to block U.S. labour unions' access to its online database of

corporate information, which the unions planned to use in wage negotiations, and so on. Presumably, one goal of public interest regulation might be to provide some form of nondiscriminatory access to such information resources, if only on a commercial basis.

35. Even if Canada were to succeed at having NVOD/VOD placed under the "cultural exemption" clause, because these two are new services, the United States and/or Mexico would be entitled to retaliate by "taking measures of equivalent commercial effect in response to [such] actions" (Canada, 1987a, Article 2005; also see Intven, 1994, p. 50).

36. As an article in *Communications Week International* noted, "limiting advertising will deter investors . . . slowing or even stopping the introduction of some services" (Schenker, 1996a, p. 1). Clearly, the electronic free press is strongly correlated to the mass media/free lunch model of new media evolution, a factor that coincides well with the press' historical reliance on advertising. Again, freedom of commerce cloaks itself in the morally compelling language of media freedoms first and foremost to expand the scope of information markets.

8 TOWARD A RESPONSIVE AND DEMOCRATIC MEDIA SYSTEM

INTRODUCTION

This chapter marks a change in the nature of presentation. An initial summary of key long-term historical trends is followed by an analysis of several policy issues. Each of these is followed by recommendations.

With the hindsight of 150 years of telecoms history, several persistent trends can be identified and used as a guide for communications policy for the new media. The first trend is that electronic media are driven by competition and uncertainty, on the one hand, versus incessant efforts to push media evolution toward oligopoly/duopoly/monopolistic patterns of control and the reduction of uncertainty, on the other. This was as true for the fate of the competing Bain, Cook/Wheatstone, House, and Morse telegraph systems at the hands of the American Telegraph Company, the Montreal Telegraph Company, Western Union, and so on, as it is today for independent online services and ISPs facing the strategic rivalry posed by AOL/Bertelsmann, IBM/Southam, Stentor/Smypatico, MediaLinx and so on.

Closely related to this trend is the pull toward vertical integration between carriage and content. The historical oscillation between common carriage, electronic publishing, or a hybrid combination of each (plus broadcasting, today) reveals that a satisfactory solution has yet to be found and that there have always been strong attempts by those who control distribution channels to influence the content flowing through them. Just as telegraph providers were aligned with the press, the stock market, and other content sources, so too are telecoms providers currently recuperating this pattern of control. In this light, the principle of common carriage brought about earlier this century at the insistence of disgruntled content providers, users, and regulators seems only to have offered a transitory respite from sought-after patterns of communication and control.

As these patterns reveal, governments neither sit idly by as the "night watchman" overseeing "free markets," nor do they single-handedly regulate the flow of historical events. In equal parts, states approve new constellations of power, while attempting to regulate excessive abuses of power. Just as the corporation was legalised as the motor of the industrial revolution—of which the American Telegraph Company, Canadian Pacific, Dominion Telegraph, Montreal Telegraph, Western Union, and so on, were early prototypes—today's carriers are also coming to enjoy retrofitted new media freedoms sanctioned by governments searching to build the "information economy/society."

Finally, although states and industry drive (commandeer) each successive "revolution," people have consistently held out hope that things could be different. Alongside this phenomenon, there has been an enduring politics of telecoms, whether as in liberal humanist ideas about the civilising effects of the telegraph and press, or more expansively as in the "radio movements" of the 1920s, the intense media politics accompanying the advent of "wired cities" in the late 1960s and early 1970s, or contemporary efforts to shape the evolution, organisation, and uses of the "new media."

This latest phase in telecoms politics is still unfolding. However, there already appears to be consensus that broadband networks are inevitable and desirable. Remaining disagreement focuses mainly on whether new media services should be made affordable through the advertising-sponsored free lunch, market pricing of a "discretionary" luxury good, or regulation. Few discussants take seriously the idea that a more radical potential is to remain disconnected from the transnational information grid, although such an option causes the greatest anxiety among those commandeering the information revolution (Bangemann, 1994; Canada, 1996a; KMPG, 1996; United States, 1994).

However, rather than dichotomising the options, perhaps the critical thing to think about is how choices about information use and electronic communication can be freed from the binds of class, compulsion, and the constraints of mass consumption, while at the same time maintaining people's freedom to choose a noninformation-intensive life. Problems of universal service and electronic connectivity seem to pale alongside these issues. The solutions to this dilemma are not easy, and they challenge communication scholars to find a space between Luddism and collusion with projects that uncritically promote expanded access to communication services. The key conundrum, it seems, is how to support a more meaningfully defined basket of universal services and participation in the choices that are shaping the evolutionary trajectory of new media while not contributing to state/industry-led "cultural modernisation" programs. In the following section, it is suggested that this puzzle can be addressed by focusing on more appropriate technologies than IBN-based "information highways" such as ISDN, by changing governments' role in communications policy, and by addressing commercial and public communication needs as a basis for building a sound, responsive, and equitable information infrastructure.

ISDN: AN APPROPRIATE COMMUNICATIONS INFRASTRUCTURE?[1]

Integrated Services Digital Networks (ISDN) stand half-way between plain old telephone service networks and the hoped-for information highways of the future. They are particularly appropriate in that they, for the most part, have already been built and because they more than adequately meet existing and emerging demands. As noted in Chapters 6 and 7, Stentor members built a cross-Canada network based on CCS7 network and switching technology during the 1980s. This ISDN platform was funded mainly from subscriber revenues set according to finance requirements negotiated between the telcos and the CRTC. ISDN is particularly suitable for meeting commercial and individual needs for facsimile, data transmission, voice mail, electronic messaging, teleconferencing, and Internet services, all areas in which demand exists, or, as in the case of the Internet, is exploding (Mozes & Sciadas, 1995, p. 90). Most studies concede that ISDN is appropriate for current and anticipated communication needs. Some even fear that its advent could postpone the development of IBNs altogether (Bangemann, 1994, p. 21;[2] Connell, 1994, p. 249; Elton, 1992; KPMG, 1996, pp. 129-310; Melody, 1996, pp. 254-258). As William Melody (1996) states,

> the vast majority of new information . . . services do not require . . . broadband enhancement, even in the US. Internet services, for example, do not require either an information superhighway or a fibre . . . connection to the user's PC. It runs on digital telephone lines. (p. 258)

It is only once requirements are placed on the infrastructure for services where there is little, if any, demand, that IBNs/information highways become necessary. Yet, even if the dubious aim is to promote another distribution network for television programs, it may be reasonable to allow telcos to interconnect with cable companies' broadband coax cable to overcome the costs of bringing broadband to the home. This could reduce the inefficiencies of building competing broadband networks when there is little demand for even one. It could also eliminate the "regulatory asymmetry" that lets cable operators connect with the PTN but not vice versa, as well as reduce the need for subsidies by advertisers, weak privacy standards, and "stupid terminals" to surmount the uneconomics of "information highways."

With an ISDN-compatible network already in the ground and paid for by all users, it could be relatively inexpensive to connect users to this network. The only remaining cost would be the terminal interface between subscribers' premises and the network, which is currently estimated between $300 to $1,000—depending on the sophistication of the interface desired (Bell, 1996). Despite the apparent viability of ISDN as the foundation for a universal digital public network, most Stentor companies have decided to market ISDN as an enhanced service. This is not necessarily unusual, as it is similar to patterns in the United States and the United Kingdom (Arlandis, 1994, pp. 224-239; Baldwin et al., 1996, pp. 205-206). However, this is not universal practice.

In Germany, in contrast, ISDN extends the basic PTN and is charged "at the same price as a regular phone line" (KPMG, 1996a, p. 118). A similar policy exists in France (Arlandis, 1994). Moreover, in France long-distance charges are based on the "postal pricing" system. Local calls are charged one rate and long-distance services charged at a uniform rate, regardless of distance—similar to letters sent by post. In contrast, Bell and other Stentor companies, as noted in Chapter 6, have proposed measured pricing for basic services[3] and, as just noted, are now marketing ISDN as a "luxury good." Bell recently announced discounted rates for its "Z@P" ISDN service of between $51 and $57 per month, plus a usage-sensitive charge for each hour of use (Bell, 1996).

Recommendations

1. ISDN should be made part of basic telecoms services and charged at the same price as basic telephone services, but subscribers who choose to use it should pay for the terminal interface.
2. Telcos should be given interconnection rights to cable companies' subscriber drops.
3. IBN/Information Highway Projects should be implemented only where demonstrable demand outstrips the capabilities of ISDN and without overreliance on vertical integration, advertising, privacy, and "stupid" terminal subsidies.

COMPETITION AND COMMUNICATION POLICY IN THE PUBLIC INTEREST

In addition to relaxing the push for IBNs, government communication policy needs to change its focus. Continued state and industry efforts to lead the "information revolution" and midwife IBNs into existence through massive cultural modernisation projects are not only ethically circumspect, but betray a model of development smuggled into the present from the days of the natural monopoly regime. The shift from the "old" to "new" telecoms should be furthered by promoting more intensive use of the existing ISDN infrastructure rather than advocating the extension and further modernisation of the PTN. Efforts along this line can be promoted by protecting real competition, as this usually leads to greater use of network facilities (OECD, 1995a).

Competition could be fostered by increasing opportunities for new providers to enter telecoms "markets" as well as by more diligently protecting competition where it already exists. In addition to allowing telco interconnection with cable networks, competition could be fostered by unbundling and identifying the stand-alone costs associated with the local exchange, the gateway between local and long-distance networks, and the long-distance network. Interesting ideas about how this might be done have been discussed by Gable (1995) and were introduced to the CRTC during its recent regulatory framework decisions by long-distance competitors and some public interest groups (CRTC, 1994a, pp. 17-27; 1995b, pp. 19-24). This would require reversing the recent trend of loading the local exchange with so-called "common-costs," which could help support sustainable competition in local and long distance. The point is not to make a fetish[4] out of competition, but to note that it can be usefully employed to the benefit of most subscribers if the proper conditions are put in place. In addition, the concepts of ONA/CEI, unbundling, co-location, and so on, should continue to be relied on by the CRTC as a means of fostering competition. However, these should not be seen as substitutes for regulation, but complementary to such efforts.

Moreover, it is important to protect competition where it exists and to move away from aims of merely making markets legally contestable. It has to be recalled that the services in which growth is the greatest and most dynamic are those that have been largely free of telco influence. The Internet, for example, was growing at up to 10% a month in 1995 before the introduction of the Stentor group's Sympatico-MediaLinx, whereas growth in the United States and Europe was similar before current attempts to turn online services into the newest mass media (KPMG, 1996a, p. 92). As Weston (1994), of the National Capital FreeNet in Ottawa, Canada, notes, "this inconceivable growth occurred despite the familiar observations that the Internet is difficult to access, hard to use, slow to respond, and . . . hopelessly disorganised" (p. 2). The point is that competition can promote more intensive use of the network infrastructure, yet may be unpredictable. In contrast to these possibilities, however, government policy has tended to undermine vibrant competition, especially when the benefits of this for controlled economic growth are uncertain.

Attempts to turn competition and uncontrollability into commercially regulated mass media could be overcome if the CRTC relied on transparent measures of market power and made tough decisions that might not permit those with entrenched positions into markets in which this is more likely to reduce rather than expand competition. Moreover, less emphasis on grandiose IBN projects and more on appropriate technologies such as ISDN to serve business and residential users could relieve some of the pressures that currently buttress entrenched economic and communicative power.

Current government/industry attempts to surmount the uneconomics of information highways will likely compound the problem of "market power," as TOs are compelled to exercise more control over revenue sources—advertising, bandwidth, content sources, and users; to organise online media space to give prominence to some content services over others; and to manipulate and guide the attention of users. These attempts to control content, channels, and attention, Hoffman-Riem (1996) points out, means that regulation will still need to protect the communications process from one-sided abuses of power (p. 333). In the current context, government policy is promoting irreconcilable goals: network competition and universal IBNs. Before competition and other aims can be properly promoted, it is necessary for government to relinquish its sponsorship of information highway projects.

However, attempts to move from the logic of dynamic technological innovation at the root of IBN projects, and the whole history of 20th-century telecoms regulation, in favour of promoting more intense use of the existing infrastructure through competition and greater sensitivity to user needs will be extremely difficult. Ironically, even current information highway terminology betrays the deep structural commitment to a focus on telecoms as just more "transportation capacity," rather than on services, content, and user needs. This also percolates throughout government policies that emphasise subsidies for infrastructure producers incomparably more than content services and network applications. Of the almost $5 billion in subsidies identified in the *Building the Information Society* document, only a pittance is tagged for content production and distributed computer networking programs.[5]

Analysts have long noticed the imbalance between media distribution and media production (Parker, 1991), but the magnitude of the problems have been amplified by information highway projects and recent government policy. More emphasis on competition and decentralised media production could help overcome this imbalance, although competition policy has little room for considerations that deal with the essence of communication, culture, and content. As noted previously, the Industry Minister of the Chretien Liberal government has candidly acknowledged this (Mosco, 1997), and other commentators have come to the same conclusion independently (Hitchens, 1997; Hoffman-Riem, 1996, p. 339). Competition policy ponders issues of efficiency, market power, and restraint of trade (Addy, 1994; Schultz & Janisch, 1993), not the diversity of speakers, the balance between speakers and listeners' rights, universal service, or factors that can distort the mediated communication experience (Hoffman-Riem, 1996, p. 338) such as the manipulation of access menus, the "free lunch" strategy (advertising, integration, privacy), or the "luxury good" model of new media evolution. In general, policy needs to shift from the reified transportation model of telecoms to a communication-based model that places greater emphasis on the quality of mediated communication experience, content, and factors that can distort mediated communication.

A set of proposals to curtail the state's role in communication could aim to reduce and redirect subsidies from hardware/transportation to software/electronic publishing, and promote more meaningful definitions of universal service, community expression, public access, and cultural policies. A redistribution of current subsidies to business might also obviate the need for the recent cuts of $417 million away from the CBC budget; enhance the availability of public information resources on an ISDN platform, rather than privatised data commercially available on information highways; and help to fund an expansive concept of universal service for those who need and want to use the available online media services.[6]

With respect to community expression, public access, and cultural policy, it is not funding that is needed so much as protection of commercial and noncommercial independent ISPs and FreeNets, among others, from the abusive practices of those in control of network facilities. Although funding is not the most pressing problem, the current meagre allocation of between $6 and $11 million to promote remote and rural access to the Internet could be increased considerably. A more robust interpretation of community expression, public access, and cultural policy might include ideas built into the *Broadcasting Act* (1991) with respect to the media system, including three pillars: a commercial sector, a community sector, and public sector (Royal Task Force on Broadcasting Policy, 1985). Such an approach would expand the CRTC's miserly definition of who is eligible for discounted tariffs (health and education) as well as Bell and Telus' stingy concept of "community expression" as the distribution of existing cable access channels and public terminals.

Setting aside a particular "public space" is vastly unlike granting access to those who request access on nondiscriminatory terms. Creating a vital civic sector would endorse the contributions that have been made by FreeNets to spreading computer networking to a broad public and in planting the seeds of commercial viability within a remarkably short period of time (CPSR, 1994; Weston, 1994). By 1995, as Reddick (1995, p. 20) noted, 17 FreeNets were used by some 150,000 to 200,000 people to obtain access to the Internet, computer networking organisations, electronic bulletin boards, and so on. This was a considerable portion of the estimated 600,000 users then "on-line."

One way of expanding on this success (and the precedent set in the NorthwestTel decisions covered in the last chapter) would be to maintain "public communicative spaces" where people can participate in their use and design through noncommercial means. It is through vested personal interests in the new media that vibrant, new communicative opportunities sprang to life over the last decade. Policy should acknowledge this and create an opportunity for such forms of investment to flourish in the future (see Computer Professionals for Social Responsibility, 1994; Weston, 1994). In addition to fostering a democratic communication system, such proposals would expand the definition of Canadian cultural policy beyond the narrow domain of television and radio. It would also enhance people's freedom to access public communicative spaces without the hassle of the free lunch version of the new mass media, which could then be allowed to proliferate in the vast majority of "online media space" with much less concern.

Recommendations

1. Policy should promote and protect real competition.
2. Competition should expand, not constrict, the quality of mediated communication.
3. Policy should shift from the "old" logic of dynamic efficiency associated with the transportation and natural monopoly model of telecoms to a "new" logic of allocative efficiency that is sensitive to user needs, the availability of content, use of the network, and the requirements of distributed "electronic publishing."
4. Communication and competition policy should promote structural diversity within the communication system. The new telecoms-based media services should consist of a commercial core, a community sector, and a public sector. Each should be as free of interference from the logic of the others as possible.

REDUCING GOVERNMENT INTERFERENCE IN COMMUNICATION

The increased emphasis on competition, the call to scale back and reallocate current subsidies, as well as the promotion of a vibrant community media sector, all portend a vast transformation in how the Canadian state intervenes in public and private life. In addition to calling for government to scale back the current levels of corporate subsidies, and to withdraw from duplicitous arrangements with corporate actors to change the fabric of Canadian society, efforts need to be undertaken to rein in the emergence of the strong state.

As Chapters 5, 6, and 7 in particular have shown, the processes of regulatory liberalisation and advancement of the "information revolution" have not diminished the role of the Canadian state in telecoms affairs, but vastly transformed and expanded the modes of government intervention. The strong state is visible in the efforts taken to shield new media from public interference (enhanced services decisions, CUFTA/NAFTA/GATS basic/enhanced decisions); efforts to manipulate regulatory proceedings, legal tools, and information distributed to the public as a way of ramming through predetermined policy aims; and by new policy instruments that allow government to intervene before, during, and after the CRTC's supposedly autonomous telecoms regulatory proceedings. The emergence of a strong state shielding, manipulating, and intervening in telecoms politics is disturbingly undemocratic and urgently needs to be redressed.

Recommendations

1. Adopt more open forms of communication policy with less government interference. The tendency to remove areas from the public arena, either through appeals to Cabinet Ministers, global trade agreements, or the telcos' construction plans, needs to be reversed. Those who shape the communicative environment in which people live must be open to the influence of the free flow of information and communication on their affairs.

2. The telecoms policy framework should be disconnected from information highway projects on ethical as well as economic grounds.

3. The *Telecommunications Act* sections allowing government to intervene before, during, and after CRTC hearings, should be replaced with a consultative procedure that allows the government to appraise the CRTC of relevant policy considerations (Canada, 1993a, sec. 9 to 12). Appeals of CRTC decisions should be to the

courts, not the Cabinet. Likewise, new measures allowing the CRTC to exclude interveners from telecoms proceedings should be eliminated (Canada, 1993a, sec. 9(3)).

COMMUNICATION POLICY IN GLOBAL CONTEXT

By necessity this last section of discussion and recommendations is even more general than the previous sections. Nonetheless, the discussion should still provoke some thought on connections between domestic and global communications policy as well as some plausible future directions for media policy in a global context. Three issues are raised: foreign ownership; the future of cultural and regulatory policies, and the insufficient balance between transnational economic institutions and other transnational agencies that draw on the normative regulatory functions of democratic politics and the sovereignty of popular public opinion. These points are discussed next, and then followed by recommendations.

Foreign Ownership

As earlier chapters have shown, there has been a close link between telecoms in Canada and foreign ownership, from the telegraph until the present. The role of foreign ownership has, of course, changed over time, especially as Bell Canada loosened and finally cut its links with AT&T, and again in the late 1960s when federal policy promoted Canadian ownership of telecoms, broadcasting, and cable systems. Although exceptions such as BCTel and QuebecTel remained, the general trend toward, and political support for, Canadian ownership of the media has been a solid aspect of policy.

　　　This is changing, especially under the pressure of WTO trade talks to liberalise foreign ownership restrictions. The general thrust of WTO proposals is that removing restrictions on foreign ownership will further the competitive policy objectives of the GATS, and that this is needed to expand the reach of that agreement beyond the purview of so-called "enhanced services" into "basic services" (Industry Canada, 1996b, p. 2451). In general, there seems to be support among Canadian policymakers and the telecoms industry to allow greater foreign ownership of telecoms providers in Canada, but not to eliminate restrictions altogether.

　　　Despite this general level of support, the means and ends relationship claimed between removing foreign ownership restrictions and competition is not logically clear. Removing foreign ownership rules can just as easily lead to mergers and acquisitions across national borders, and thus facilitate higher levels of concentration and less competition globally, as they can to the introduction of new telecoms providers within countries. For example, if AT&T was to buy out, merge, or establish a partnership with Rogers Communications in Canada in order to link its long-distance network with Rogers' local distribution system, this does little to enhance competition but much to consolidate duopolistic rivalry. On the other hand, if the aim is to increase competition, then AT&T would need to establish new operations in Canada, a move that could further competition as well as introduce new investment, jobs, technologies, and services. Of course, there are other policy concerns that bear on the issue as well, as will be seen next. The basic point, however, is that there is little reason to resist foreign ownership per se, but good grounds for being critical of current WTO proposals that confuse means and ends and are devoid of concern for broader issues in telecoms regulation and cultural policy.

National Cultural and Regulatory Policies

Throughout this book it has been argued that the CUFTA, NAFTA, and GATS all institute a form of transnational limited democracy that functions primarily to shield certain areas of the economy and new media services from the reach of people and telecoms policy. Yet, it has also been acknowledged that these trade regimes provide a minimum foundation for democratic communication in a global context as they prevent the intrusive hand of governments from interfering with the free flow of information across national boundaries. As such, it seems necessary to move beyond, not behind, that which has already been accomplished at the global level.

Perhaps the most important thing to do with respect to global telecoms policy is to jettison the distinction between basic and enhanced services. The distinction no longer makes sense, as domestic monopolies are cast out and the WTO advocates competition in all telecoms services. Moreover, the blurring of media and electronic information services boundaries by reconvergence limits the utility of the basic/enhanced regulatory framework. Finally, the constraints it imposes on public communication, regulation, and cultural policy are also anathema to democratic communication and politics.

A better way to proceed is offered by the EC's nonreserved services category. Such a framework offers opportunities to reconcile competition with broader ideas about what public communication as well as telecoms and cultural policies mean in the context of global electronic media spaces. Under such a framework it is possible to promote competition as well as to use regulatory and policy instruments to control market power, promote diversity, institute adequate privacy protection policies, implement universal service aims that are commensurate with the capacities of the new media and needs of citizens in the "information age," regulate advertising, and set aside limited areas of electronic media space for cultural policy goals.

Under this framework, not only would competition among infrastructure and service providers be allowed, but they would also enjoy editorial freedoms for much of the online media space so long as a certain proportion of available bandwidth was set aside for online public media spaces. Such media spaces could be used by people, nonprofit groups, and governments to further a number of aims such as promoting the spread of computer networking, access to public information, community expression, Canadian content, and noncommercial global communication. Under this arrangement, all users would be able to evade commodified media spaces, not just the information rich who need not rely on an advertising-subsidised "free lunch" that may characterise the emerging media spaces. Moreover, within this space of mediated public communication, it would still be possible to promote traditional cultural policies with respect to Canadian content. However, Canadian content would be just one pillar in a more broadly conceived idea of public space. Such an approach would maintain traditional aspects of Canadian media policy, broaden the scope of people and media production embraced by cultural policy, and, in so doing, could even enhance the legitimacy of cultural policy altogether as its roots extend beyond large institutions that are closer to centres of power than to people's everyday lives.

From Transnational Trade to the Globalisation of Democratic Communication

As mentioned in earlier chapters, although the state within democratic countries contains formal channels of communication between the rulers and the ruled, there are no links between the governors and the governed at the global level. The rules of global trade need to be supplemented by the normative regulatory functions of democratic politics, communication, and popular sovereignty. Again, the representative political and legal institutions of the European Union that have developed alongside efforts to harmonise the economic spaces of the continent may offer examples for North America and the world. In the EU, for example, developments in competition law that bear on the communication industries have to be reconcilable with sections of the *European Convention on Human Rights*, which establish diversity and other goals as aspects of media freedoms (Hitchens, 1997). Perhaps the move from limited democracy toward representative democracy within transnational organisations could draw on the European example. One measure in this respect might be more formal alliances between the United Nations and the emerging trade regimes and economic institutions. Such a closer alignment would begin, perhaps, to bridge the gap between economics, politics, and culture. Of course, such efforts would also need to draw more on citizens and civic groups, rather than being staffed exclusively with the same bureaucrats that fill trade offices.

Recommendations

1. Canadian foreign ownership rules for telecoms should be waived when and where doing so will increase competition, contribute to new network and services development within Canada, and the realisation of regulatory and cultural policy aims. Such rules should not be waived for mergers, acquisitions, or partnerships.
2. The basic/enhanced regulatory framework should be eliminated. The concept of nonreserved services in the EC offers good starting points for considering the future viability of regulatory and cultural policies in Canada.
3. A balance between economic imperatives and political and cultural goals needs to be reflected in global communications policies and institutional arrangements. Canadian policymakers should push for a reconciliation between the WTO, the ITU, the United Nations, and the United Nations Education Scientific and Cultural Organisation.

CONCLUSION

These proposals are incomplete and more suggestive than conclusive. However, it is obvious that vast changes in the economics, politics, and technologies underpinning the introduction of new media must be undertaken if positive outcomes are to be realised. Such shifts are needed urgently as decisions taken now set the new media on an evolutionary course that will be hard to dislodge in the future. It is one thing to equip media actors with new property and media freedoms and quite another to reverse this path at a subsequent date. As a trajectory of development is entrenched, potential alternatives will be eclipsed and largely disappear from view (Hoffman-Riem, 1996, p. 329). One hope for this book is that it will keep the potentials clearly in sight and fuel the discussion of what is needed, possible, and desired.

ENDNOTES

---

1.   The point of the next section is not to argue solely in favour of ISDN at the expense of all other distribution systems. Instead, the intent is to show that, at least with respect to the fixed wireline network, a universal ISDN-based public network may be more appropriate for the vast majority of users than broadband information highways.

2.   Even the Bangemann Report (1994) notes that "ISDN is particularly suitable for the communications needs of . . . a wide range of businesses" (p. 21), before slipping into an "IBN promotion" phase. The closest the Report comes to explaining why IBNs are needed instead of ISDN is through ill-defined references to the "next technological wave," "multimedia," and "interconnectivity with . . . cable television and satellite" (pp. 21-22). Why more television distribution channels are needed is never addressed, which is typical. Thus, as mentioned in the last chapter, it seems that one of the more compelling justification for IBNs, as Baldwin et al. (1996) noted, is that it is possible to build them.

3.   Measured service pricing should be rejected on economic and social justice grounds. From an economic perspective, the PTN represents a sunk investment. The irrelevance of volume, time, and distance to telecoms pricing is already apparent with more bandwidth intensive services such as the Internet, and will be even more so should NVOD/VOD services be delivered over the PTN at prices comparable to video store rentals and cable. How can measured service pricing for voice telephone service (32kbits/second) be justified when broadcasts using millions of bits of capacity are sent down the same line? As Connell (1994) notes, "traditional per-bit-kilometer rates would render video-on-demand hideously and practically expensive" (pp. 243-244), or voice communication would have to be so cheap that it would have to be given away.

4.   Indeed, in the present scenario, all competitors would be required to contribute to a universal service fund that would aim to expand, rather than contract, the concept of universal service, for those needing and wanting access to the new media. The general point, though, is that competition is to serve as a means of enhancing mediated communication, not detracting from it, as is the current trend. This proposal is somewhat similar to the logic of CRTC policy between about 1976 and 1987. This is discussed again later.

5.   Although it is difficult to tell with certainty, it seems that there is, at most, about $134 million for computer networking that can be identified. Yet, even $123 million of this is for infrastructure, namely the Canadian Internet backbone, and $6 to $11 million is earmarked for developing Internet access sites in rural communities (Canada, 1996a, pp. 9, 24; Surtees, 1995a, p. B2).

6.   Government and private carriers could contribute to this universal service fund. One way of linking the private sector's contribution with competition could be to let carriers pocket half their profits over the previously regulated level of 8%-12% while putting the remainder into the universal service fund.

APPENDIX 1:
MERGERS AND ACQUISITIONS
INVOLVING TELECOMS
COMPANIES

Date	Purchaser	Acquired Co./ Partner	Media Sectors Involved	Value of Deal/ % Acquired
1996	BT	MCI (final 80%)	Telecoms	$20bn
1996*	Cable & Wireless/ Mercury	Bell Cable, Nynex & Videotron	Telecoms, video, cable	$700m
1996	WorldCom	MFS	Telecom/ Network Services	$14bn
1996	Bell Atlantic	Nynex	Telecoms/ Cable	$51bn
1996	Southwest- ern Bell (SBC)	Pacific Telesis	Telecoms	$17bn
1996	US West	Continental Cablevision	Telecoms/ Cable	$1bn
1995*	AT&T, Bank of NovaScotia, Royal Bank, Dominion	UNITEL	Telecom/ Banking/ Finance Services	$N/A—33% (AT&T), 54% (Banks) Toronto
1995	MCI	NewsCorp On-line	Telecoms/pub/ broadcast/ on-line	$2bn—13.5%
1994	French Telecom/ Deutsch Telecom	Sprint	Telecoms	$4.2b—20%

1994*	Bell Canada Ent.	Express View	Telecoms/DTH Sat.	N/A—33%
1994*	Rogers/ UNITEL	MacLean-Hunter	Telecoms/Cable Pub/ Broadcast	$2.3b—100%
1994	LDDS	WilTel	Telecoms	$2.5b—100%
1994*	Sprint	Call-Net	Telecoms Enhanced Services	N/A—100%
1994	USWest	Wometco/	Telecoms/Cable GeorgiaCable	$1.2b—100%
1994	Bell Atlantic	Nynex Cellular	Telecoms	$13.0b—100%
1994	Air Touch	USWest Cellular	Telecoms	$18.0b—100%
1994	NexTel	One Comm	Telecoms	$.7b —100%
1994	AT&T	Unisource	Telecoms	N/A—N/A
1993	USWest	Time Warner Inc.	Telecoms/ Cable/ Film/Pub	$2.5b—23%
1993	NexTel	Motorola Mobile	Telecoms	$1.8b—100%
1993	Bell Atlantic	Iusacell	Telecoms	$1.0b—42%
1993	AT&T	McCaw Cellular	Telecoms	$12.0b —100%
1993	British Telecom	MCI	Telecoms	$5.3b—20%
1992*	AT&T	Rogers/UNITEL	Telecoms/Cable	N/A—20%
1992	Sprint	Centel	Telecoms	$2.9b—100%
1991	AT&T	NCR	IT Manufacture	$7.4b—100%
1991	Bell Atlantic	Metro Mobile	Telecoms	$2.5b—100%
1990*	Rogers'	Canadian National	Telecoms/ Cable	N/A—40%

* = Mergers/Acquisitions involving the Canadian communication industry.

Note: Derived and adapted from CEC (1995).

9 REFERENCES

Addy, G. N. (1994, March 29). *The Competition Act and the Canadian telecommunications industry*. Speech presented at the Institute for International Research, Telecommunications Conference, Toronto.

AGT. (1988). *1988 Annual report*. Calgary, Alberta: Author.

AGT v. CRTC and CNCP et. al. (1989). *Supreme Court Reporter*, pp. 225-302.

Anderson, M. (1994, April 7). The high-tech cold war heats up. *Financial Post*, p. A15.

Angus, I. (1995). *Bell Canada vs. Internet service providers: A review of the facts and issues*. Internet: http://www.angustel.ca

Angus Telemanagement Group. (1996). *Telecom Update, 61*(Dec. 2). Internet: http://www.angustel.ca

Arlandis, J., (1994). ISDN: A European prospect. In C. Steinfield, J.M. Bauer, & L. Caby (Eds.), *Telecommunications in transition* (pp. 223-235).

Atkins, D. J. (1994, May/June). Cable exhibition in the USA. *Telecommunications Policy*, 331-341.

Attali, J. & Stourdze, Y. (1977). The birth of the telephone and economic crisis: The slow death of the monologue in French society. In I. S. Pool (Ed.), *The social impact of the telephone* (pp. 97-111). London: MIT Press.

Atlantic Communication and Technical Workers (ACTWU). (1992). *Submission to the proceedings of the Standing Senate Committee on Transport and Communications, fifth proceeding on the examination of the subject matter of Bill C-62, an Act respecting telecommunications*. Unpublished speaking notes.

Attorney General vs. The Edison Telephone Company of London. *Queen's Bench, C.P., and Ex. Divisions* (1880), 6, pp. 244-263.

Babe, R. E. (1975). *Cable television and telecommunications in Canada*. East Lansing: Michigan State University.

Babe, R. E. (1990). *Telecommunications in Canada.* Toronto: University of Toronto Press.

Babe, R. E. (1995). *Communication and the transformation of economics.* Boulder, CO: Westview.

Babe, R. E. (1996). Convergence and the new technologies. In M. Dorland (Ed.), *The cultural industries in Canada* (pp. 283-307). Toronto: Lorimer.

Baldwin, F. G. C. (1938). *The history of the telephone in the United Kingdom.* London: Chapman and Hall. (Original work published 1925)

Baldwin, T. F., McVoy, D. S., & Steinfield, C. (1996). *Convergence: Integrating media, information and communication.* London: Sage.

Bangemann, M. (1994). *Europe and the global information society: Recommendations to the European Council.* Brussels: European Council.

Barbrook, R. (1995). *Media freedom.* London: Pluto.

Barlow, M. (1996, March). Class warfare: The assault on Canadian schools. Notes from a speech given at the British Columbia Teachers' Federation Public Interest Conference, Vancouver, BC.

Barnouw, E. (1982). *Tube of plenty.* New York: Oxford University Press.

Barron, J. A. (1993). The telco, the common-carrier model and the First Amendment: The dial-a-porn precedent. *Rutgers Computer and Technology Law Journal, 19,* 371-404.

Bartley, A. (1988). The regulation of cross-media ownership. *Canadian Journal of Communication, 13*(2), 45-59.

Bauer, J. M., & Steinfield, C. (1994). Telecommunications initiatives of the European Communities. In C. Steinfield, J. M. Bauer, & L. Caby (Eds), *Telecommunications in transition* (pp. 51-70). London: Sage.

Baxter vs. Dominion Telegraph Co., *Upper Canada Queen's Bench* (1874/1875), *37,* pp. 470-483.

Bell. (1996). *Pricing details: Z@P ISDN Service.* Internet: http://www.bell.ca

Bell Canada Enterprises (BCE). (1991). *Annual report: Leadership in telecommunications.* Montreal: Author.

Bell Telephone Company of Canada. (1893-1916). *Annual report.* Montreal: Author.

Benidickson, J. (1991). The Canadian Board of Railway Commissioners: Regulation, policy and legal process at the turn of the century. *McGill Legal Review, 36,* 1222-1261.

Benitez, R. (1992). *Privatisation of telecommunications services.* Geneva, Switzerland: Post Telephones and Telecommunications International.

Bercuson, D. J. (1990). *Confrontation at Winnipeg* (rev. ed.). Montreal & Kingston: McGill-Queen's University.

Bernard, E. (1982). *The long distance feeling: A history of the telecommunications workers union.* Vancouver: New Star Books.

Berry, P. M, Garton, G. R., Parkinson, G. D., Pyne, R. G., & Wallace, P. (1972). *Canadian Communication Law Review, 4,* 55-69.

Bird, B. (1992). Culture and communications: The ties that bind: Report of the Standing Committee on Communications and Culture. *Minutes of Proceedings and Evidence of the Standing Committee on Communications and Culture.* Ottawa: Ministry of Supply and Services.

Blondheim, M. (1994). *News over the wires: The telegraph and the flow of public information in America, 1844-1897.* London: Harvard University Press.

Board of Railway Commissioners. (1908, 1911, 1912, 1914a, 1915a, 1919, 1922). Report of the Board of Railway Commissioners for Canada. *Sessional papers of the Parliament of Canada.* Ottawa: J. De Labroquerie Tache, Printers to the King's Most Excellent Majesty.

Board of Railway Commissioners. (1910). The Western Associated Press v. The Canadian Pacific Railway Company's Telegraph and the Great Northwestern Telegraph Company of Canada. *Sessional Papers of the Parliament of Canada.* Ottawa: J. De Labroquerie Tache, Printers to the Kings Most Excellent Majesty.

Board of Railway Commissioners. (1913, 1916a, 1918). Telephone statistics. *Sessional Papers of the Parliament of Canada.* Ottawa: J. De Labroquerie Tache, Printers to the Kings Most Excellent Majesty.

Board of Railway Commissioners. (1915b, 1916b). *Judgments, orders, regulations, and rulings.* Ottawa: J. De Labroquerie Tache, Printers to the King's Most Excellent Majesty.

Board of Railway Commissioners. (1914b). Press telegraph tolls. *Sessional Papers of the Parliament of Canada.* Ottawa: J. De Labroquerie Tache, Printers to the Kings Most Excellent Majesty.

Bouwman, J. M., & Latzer, M. (1994). Telecommunications network-based services. In C. Steinfield, J. M. Bauer, & L. Caby (Eds.), *Telecommunications in transition* (pp. 161-181). London: Sage.

Boyd-Barrett, J. O. (1980). *The international news agencies.* London: Constable.

Briggs, A. (1977). The pleasure telephone: A chapter in the prehistory of media. In I. de Sola Pool (Ed.), *The social impact of the telephone.* Cambridge: MIT Press.

Bumps and potholes on the information highway. (1994, April 19). *The Globe & Mail,* p. A16.

Call Net Telecommunications, Inc. (1987, October). *Petition to the Governor in Council pursuant to Section 64(1) of the National Transportation Act. To revoke PC 1987 -2349 and to vary telecom decision CRTC 87-5.* Toronto, Ont.: Author.

Call Net Telecommunications, Inc. (1988, January). *Petition to the Governor in Council pursuant to Section 64(1) of the National Transportation Act. To Revoke PC 1987 -2349 and to vary telecom decision CRTC 87-5.* Toronto, Ont.: Author.

Campbell, A. J., & Schwartzman, A. J. (1994). *Petition for relief of Center for Media Education, Consumer Federation of America, United Church of*

Christ, National Association for the Advancement of Colored People, National Council of La Raza in the matter of unjust and unreasonable discrimination in the deployment of video dialtone facilities. [Filed with the FCC]. Washington, DC: Federal Communications Commission.

Canada. (1906a). An Act to incorporate the Grant Trunk Pacific Telegraph Company. *Acts of the Parliament of the Dominion of Canada,* 6 King Edward VII, Chap. 101. Ottawa: Samuel Edward Dawson.

Canada. (1906b). An Act to incorporate the Northern Commercial Telegraph Company. *Acts of the Parliament of the Dominion of Canada,* 6 King Edward VII, Chap. 101. Ottawa: Samuel Edward Dawson.

Canada. (1968). An Act respecting the Bell Telephone Company of Canada (Chapter 48). *Acts of the Parliament of Canada,* 27th Parliament, Second Session. Ottawa: Queen's Printer and Controller of Stationery.

Canada. (1979). Railway Act. *Revised statutes of Canada, c. R-2.* Ottawa: Supply and Services.

Canada. (1987a). *The Canada-U.S. Free Trade Agreement.* Ottawa: Minister of Supply and Services.

Canada. (1987b). An Act respecting the Bell Telephone Company of Canada. *Acts of the Parliament of Canada,* Ottawa: Minister of Supply and Services.

Canada. (1991). *Canadian federalism and economic unity.* Ottawa: Minister of Supply and Services.

Canada. (1992). *Canada-USA-Mexico North America Free Trade Agreement.* Ottawa: Minister of Supply and Services.

Canada. (1993a). The Telecommunications Act (Chapter 38). Statutes of Canada -1991-92-93. Ottawa: Minister of Supply and Services.

Canada. (1993b). Canadian Charter of Human Rights and Freedoms (S1/93-54). *Canada Gazette, Part II.* Ottawa: Minister of Supply and Services.

Canada. (1996a). *Building the information society: Moving Canada into the 21st century.* Ottawa: Minister of Supply and Services.

Canada. (1996b). *Competition and culture set to gain in convergence policy framework.* Ottawa: Minister of Supply and Services.

Canada, Committee of the Whole (1880). Bell Telephone Company of Canada Incorporation Bill. *Official Report of the Debates of the House of Commons.* Ottawa: Printer to the King's Most Excellent Majesty.

Canada, Consultative Committee on the Implications of Telecommunications for Canadian Sovereignty. (1979). *Telecommunications and Canada.* Ottawa: Supply and Services.

Canada, Department of Labour. (1907). *Report of the Royal Commission on a dispute respecting hours of employment between the Bell Telephone Company of Canada, Ltd. and operators at Toronto, Ont.* Ottawa: Printer to the King's Most Excellent Majesty.

Canada, House of Commons (1880a). An Act to incorporate the Bell Telephone Company of Canada. *Official Report of the Debates of the House of Commons.* Ottawa: Printer to the King's Most Excellent Majesty.

Canada, House of Commons (1880b). An Act respecting the Canadian Pacific Railway Company. *Official Report of the Debates of the House of Commons.* Ottawa: Printer to the King's Most Excellent Majesty.

Canada, House of Commons (1882). An Act to amend the Act incorporating the Bell Telephone Company of Canada. *Official Report of the Debates of the House of Commons.* Ottawa: Printer to the King's Most Excellent Majesty.

Canada, House of Commons. (1906, 1908, 1909, 1917, 1919, 1921, 1922, 1927, 1928, 1929, 1931, 1938, 1939, 1948, 1951, 1966). *Official reports of the debates of the House of Commons.* Ottawa: Printer to the King's Most Excellent Majesty.

Canada, House of Commons. (1978). *Royal Commission on corporate concentration.* Ottawa: Supply and Services.

Canada, House of Commons. (1981). *Royal Commission on newspapers.* Ottawa: Supply and Services.

Canada/Manitoba (1991). *Memorandum of understanding respecting telecommunications.* Winnipeg: Manitoba Government News Release.

Canada, Mulock Committee. (1905). Proceedings of the Select Committee on Telephones, Appendix A. *Journal of the House of Commons (Mulock Committee), 40.* Ottawa: Printer to the King's Most Excellent Majesty.

Canada, Proceedings of the Standing Senate Committee on Transport and Communications. (1992). *Examination of the subject matter of Bill C-62, an act respecting telecommunications,* 12-22. Ottawa: Canada Communication Group.

Canada, Senate of Canada. (1928). *Official reports of the Senate of Canada.* Ottawa: Printer to the King's Most Excellent Majesty.

Canada, Special Senate Committee on Mass Media. (1970). *The uncertain mirror (Vol. 1).* Ottawa: Queen's Printer.

Canada, Standing Committee on Transport and Communications, House of Commons (1967). *Minutes of proceedings and evidence (no. 3-14): Bill C-104, an Act respecting the Bell Telephone Company of Canada.* Ottawa: Queen's Printer and Controller of Stationery.

Canada, Standing Committee on Transport and Communications, House of Commons (1976). *Minutes of proceedings and evidence respecting the Bell Telephone Company of Canada.* Ottawa: Queen's Printer and Controller of Stationery.

Canadian Business Telecommunications Association (CBTA). (1992). *Notes for presentation to the proceedings of the Standing Senate Committee on Transport and Communications, fifth proceeding on: Examination of the subject matter of Bill C-62, An Act Respecting Telecommunications.* Ottawa, Ont.: Author.

Canadian Electrical Association: Proceedings of the first annual convention. (1892). *Canadian Electrical News, 2*(7).

Canadian interests pool patents for good of radio. (1923, August 14/15). *Toronto Star.*

Canadian Labour Congress (CLC). (1992). *Submission to the proceedings of the Standing Senate Committee on Transport and Communications, fifth proceeding on: Examination of the subject matter of Bill C-62, An Act Respecting Telecommunications.* Author.

Canadian Radio-television and Telecommunications Commission. (CRTC). (1969). *Public announcement–licensing policy in relation to common carriers.* Ottawa: Minister of Supply and Services.

Canadian Radio-television and Telecommunications Commission. (CRTC). (1971a). *Canadian broadcasting: A single system: Policy statement on cable television.* Ottawa: Author.

Canadian Radio-television and Telecommunications Commission. (CRTC). (1971b). *Annual report.* Ottawa: Minister of Supply and Services.

Canadian Radio-television and Telecommunications Commission. (CRTC). (1972). *Annual report.* Ottawa: Minister of Supply and Services.

Canadian Radio-television and Telecommunications Commission. (CRTC). (1976/1977). *Annual Report.* Ottawa: Minister of Supply and Services.

Canadian Radio-television and Telecommunications Commission. (CRTC). (1976a, January 8). Public notice: Applications for cable television services to certain areas of Manitoba. *The Canada Gazette, Part 1,* 131-139.

Canadian Radio-television and Telecommunications Commission. (CRTC). (1976b). *Telecommunications regulation–procedures and practices (preparatory statement).* Ottawa: Minister of Supply and Services.

Canadian Radio-television and Telecommunications Commission. (CRTC). (1977a). *Bell Canada, Tariff for the use of support structures by cable television licensees (Dec. 77-6).* Ottawa: Minister of Supply and Services.

Canadian Radio-television and Telecommunications Commission. (CRTC). (1977b). *Challenge Communications Ltd. v. Bell Canada (Dec. 77-16).* Ottawa: Minister of Supply and Services.

Canadian Radio-television and Telecommunications Commission. (CRTC). (1978a). *Bell Canada Increase in Rates (Dec. 78-7).* Ottawa: Minister of Supply and Services.

Canadian Radio-television and Telecommunications Commission. (CRTC). (1978b). *Telecommunications regulation–procedures and practices.* Ottawa: Minister of Supply and Services.

Canadian Radio-television and Telecommunications Commission. (CRTC). (1978c). *CN Telecommunications, Increase in Telephone Rates (Dec. 78-5)*. Ottawa: Minister of Supply and Services.

Canadian Radio-television and Telecommunications Commission. (CRTC). (1979). *CNCP Telecommunications: Interconnection with Bell Canada (Dec. 79-11)*. Ottawa: Minister of Supply and Services.

Canadian Radio-television and Telecommunications Commission. (CRTC). (1981a). *NorthwesTel Inc., general increases in rates (Dec. 81-4)*. Ottawa: Minister of Supply and Services.

Canadian Radio-television and Telecommunications Commission. (CRTC). (1981b). *Bell Canada, general increases in rates (Dec. 81-15)*. Ottawa: Minister of Supply and Services.

Canadian Radio-television and Telecommunications Commission. (CRTC). (1981c). *Terra Nova Telecommunications (Dec. 81-20)*. Ottawa: Minister of Supply and Services.

Canadian Radio-television and Telecommunications Commission. (CRTC). (1982). *Attachment of subscriber provided terminal equipment (Dec. 82-14)*. Ottawa Minister of Supply and Services.

Canadian Radio-television and Telecommunications Commission. (CRTC). (1984). *Enhanced services (Dec. 84-18)*. Ottawa Minister of Supply and Services.

Canadian Radio-television and Telecommunications Commission. (CRTC). (1985). *Interexchange competition and related issues (Dec. 85-19)*. Ottawa Minister of Supply and Services.

Canadian Radio-television and Telecommunications Commission. (CRTC). (1987a). *Resale to provide primary exchange voice services (Decision 87-1)*. Ottawa: Minister of Supply and Services.

Canadian Radio-television and Telecommunications Commission. (CRTC). (1987b). *CNCP Telecommunications-application for exemption from certain regulatory requirements (Decision 87-12)*. Ottawa: Minister of Supply and Services.

Canadian Radio-television and Telecommunications Commission. (CRTC). (1990). *Resale and sharing of private line services (Dec. 90-3)*. Ottawa: Minister of Supply and Services.

Canadian Radio-television and Telecommunications Commission. (CRTC). (1991a). *Clearview Cable TV Ltd (Dec. 91-840)*. Ottawa: Minister of Supply and Services.

Canadian Radio-television and Telecommunications Commission. (CRTC). (1991b). *Request of Telecommunications Workers Union for a stay of six proceedings (Dec. 91-1)*. Ottawa: Minister of Supply and Services.

Canadian Radio-television and Telecommunications Commission. (CRTC). (1992a). *Competition in the provision of public long distance voice services and related resale and sharing issues (Dec. 92-12)*. Ottawa: Minister of Supply and Services.

Canadian Radio-television and Telecommunications Commission. (CRTC). (1992b). *Submission to the proceedings of the Standing Senate Committee on Transport and Communications, fifth proceeding on: Examination of the subject matter of Bill C-62, An Act Respecting Telecommunications.* Author.

Canadian Radio-television and Telecommunications Commission. (CRTC). (1994a). *Review of regulatory framework (Dec. 94-19).* Ottawa: Minister of Supply and Services.

Canadian Radio-television and Telecommunications Commission. (CRTC). (1994b). *Mackenzie Media, Ltd. Performance Communications, Nortwestel Cable, Inc. (Dec. 94-706).* Ottawa: Public Works and Government Services Canada.

Canadian Radio-television and Telecommunications Commission. (CRTC). (1994c). *Exemption order respecting experimental video on demand programming undertakings (Dec. 94-118).* Ottawa: Public Works and Government Services Canada.

Canadian Radio-television and Telecommunications Commission. (CRTC). (1995a). *Competition and culture on Canada's information highway.* Ottawa: Public Works and Government Services Canada.

Canadian Radio-television and Telecommunications Commission. (CRTC). (1995b). *Implementation of regulatory framework: Splitting of the rate base and related issues.* Ottawa: Public Works and Government Services Canada.

Canadian Radio-television and Telecommunications Commission. (CRTC). (1995c). *Local service pricing options.* Ottawa: Public Works and Government Services Canada.

Canadian Radio-television and Telecommunications Commission. (CRTC). (1995d). *Mackenzie Media, Ltd. Northwestel Cable Inc., Nortwestel Cable, Inc. (Dec. 95-897).* Ottawa: Public Works and Government Services Canada.

Canadian Radio-television and Telecommunications Commission. (CRTC). (1996a). *Notice of Public Hearing CRTC 1996-14; Telecom Public Notice 96-37.* Ottawa: Public Works and Government Services Canada.

Canadian Radio-television and Telecommunications Commission. (CRTC). (1996b). *CRTC rules in favour of more affordable telecommunications options for health and education sectors* [news release]. Ottawa: Public Works and Government Services Canada.

Canadian Transport Commission. (CTC). (1975). *Report in the matter of whether the Canadian Transport Commission should award costs to parties that appear before it and more particularly to some intervenors under certain circumstances* (August 19). Ottawa: Supply and Services.

Carey, J. (1989). *Communications as culture.* Boston, MA: Unwin Hyman.

Carnoy, M. (1984). *The state and political theory.* Princeton, NJ: Princeton University Press.

Carroll, W. K. (1986). *Corporate power and Canadian capitalism.* Vancouver: University of British Columbia.

Carsberg, B. (1987). Regulation of British Telecom: A reply to Beesley, Laidlaw and Gist. *Telecommunications Policy, 11*(3), 237-242.

Cashman, T. (1972). *Singing wires: The telephone in Alberta.* Edmonton, Canada: Alberta Government Telephone Corporation.

Christians, C. G. (1995). Communication ethics as the basis of genuine democracy. In P. Lee. (Ed.), *The democratisation of communication* (pp. 5-91). London: World Association for Christian Communications.

Clarke, A. B. (1929/1930). *Wire line systems for national broadcasting* (Reprint B-456). New York: Bell Telephone Laboratories.

Clarke, H. D., LeDuc, L., Jenson, J., & Pammett, J. H. (1991). *Absent mandate: Interpreting change in Canadian elections* (2nd ed.). Toronto: Gage Educational Publishing.

Cobb, C. (1996, May 13). Spicer says Cabinet sold out consumers. *Ottawa Citizen,* p. A3.

Cochrane vs. The Exchange Telegraph Company. *The Times Law Reports* (1895-6), *12,* pp. 197-99.

Cohen, A. (1993, October 8). Correspondence with J. C. Meldrum, vice president and corporate counsel, SaskTel. Unpublished letter.

Colonial Office and the Authorities in Canada and British Columbia. (1864-66). *Telegraphic communication between Canada and the Pacific (Continuation of Parliamentary Paper, No. 438, of Session 1863)* (Correspondence relating to the affairs of Canada, Irish University Press series of British Parliamentary Papers). Shannon, Ireland: Irish University Press.

Comgate Engineering Ltd. (1991). *The effect of changing technology on telecommunications and cable networks and the impact upon services in the nineties (Final report prepared for the CRTC).* Ottawa: Author.

Commission of the European Communities (CEC). (1987). Toward a dynamic European economy–Green Paper on the development of the Common Market for telecommunications services and equipment (COM (87)290 final. Brussels: Author.

Commission of the European Communities (CEC). (1990). Commission directive on competition in the markets for telecommunications services (90/388EEC). *Official Journal of the Commission, 192*(10). Brussels: Author.

Commission of the European Communities (CEC). (1995). *Green paper on the liberalisation of telecommunications infrastructure and cable television networks.* Brussels: Author.

Communication Workers of Canada (CWC). (1984). *History of CWC: A fact sheet.* Ottawa: Author.

Communications Canada. (1987). *Communications for the twenty first century.* Ottawa: Minister of Supply and Services.

Communications Canada. (1988). *Regulatory impact analysis statement regarding Order in Council P.C. 1987-2349.* Unpublished document.

Communications Canada. (1992a). *Government extends Teleglobe Canada mandate.* Ottawa: Communications Canada News Release.

Communications Canada. (1992b). *Telecommunications in Canada: An overview of the carriage industry.* Ottawa: Author.

Computer Professionals for Social Responsibility. (1994). Serving the community: A public interest vision of the National Information Infrastructure. Internet: gopher:// gopher.cpsr.org:70 /00/ cpsr/nii_policy

Congress asks postponement of telephone rate increase. (1952, January). *Congress Journal,* p. 19.

Connell, S. (1994). Broadband services in Europe. In C. Steinfield, J. M. Bauer, & L. Caby (Eds.), *Telecommunications in transition* (pp. 236-264). London: Sage.

Court rejects appeal. (1975, October 10). *Winnipeg Tribune,* p. 13.

Courtois, B. A. (1995). Correspondence with A. J. Darling, Secretary General of the CRTC regarding Part VII Application by Mr. Gary Reuter re Bell Canada and Sygma Joint Marketing. Internet: http://www.angustel.ca

Cox, R. (1992). Global perestroika. In R. Milliband & L. Panitch (Eds.), *New world order?* (pp. 30-43). New York: New Left Review.

Crandall, R. W. (1990). Entry, divestiture and the continuation of economic regulation in the United States telecommunications sector. In G. Majone (Ed.), *Deregulation or re-regulation? Regulatory reform in Europe and the United States* (pp. 118-152). London: Pinter.

Crane, A. (1996, June 11). Partners cast the Net wide. *Financial Times,* p. 21.

Crockett, B. (1991, January 14). Packet switching fees under fire in Canada. *Network World, Inc.* (Nexis Lexis), p. 27.

Crozier, M., Huntington, S. P., & Watanuki, J. (1975). *The crisis of democracy: Report on the governability of democracies to the Trilateral Commission.* New York: New York University.

Cyberspace Research. (1996). *The central index of Canadian WWW servers.* Internet: http://www.csr.ists.ca/w3can/welcome.html.

Dalglish, B. with Fulton, E. K. (1995, January 2). Cable booster: Ted Rogers wins federal approval for his Maclean Hunter bid. *Maclean's,* 44-45.

Danielian, N. R. (1939). *AT&T: The story of industrial conquest.* New York: Vanguard.

Darling, A. (1995). Correspondence to G. Reuter and B. C. Courtois Re Bell Canada and Bell Sygma Joint Marketing. http://www.angustel. ca

Davidson, W. H. (1991, January 24). Telecommunications take-off: While the U.S. dithers, other nations are aggressively modernising to compete. *LA Times,* sec. 4, p. 6.

Davis, A. (1994). *Telecommunications: The decentralized view.* New York: St. Martins Press.

Dawson, D. A. (1972). *The Canadian Radio-Television Commission and the consumer interest.* Hamilton, Ontario: Canadian Consumer Council.

Demont, P. (1996, May 3). Manitoba Tel on block in $750M share issue. *Financial Post,* p. 1.

Dempsey, J. (1995). On-line giant stirs. *Financial Times,* p. 20.

Department of Communication. (DOC). (1971a). *Concept of a telecommunications carrier–Telecommission Study 1(c).* Ottawa: Author.

Department of Communication. (DOC). (1971b). *Analysis of relationships between the functions of common-carriers and those engaged in broadcasting–Telecommission Study 1(d).* Ottawa: Author.

Department of Communication. (DOC). (1985, May) *Confidential brief presented to the federal Cabinet.* Author.

Department of External Affairs. (1992). *Market studies on telecommunications equipment and systems in Mexico.* Ottawa: Latin Affairs Division, Department of External Affairs.

Department of Finance. (1987). *Government shares in Teleglobe to be sold.* Ottawa: Department of Finance News Release.

Department of Finance. (1991, October 23). *Telesat Canada legislation tabled.* Ottawa: Department of Finance News Release.

Department of Finance. (1992, March 24). *Government shares in Telesat Canada to be sold to Alouette Telecommunications, Inc.* Ottawa: Department of Finance News Release.

de Sola Pool, I. (1983). *Technologies of freedom.* Cambridge, MA: Harvard University Press.

Dewe, J. (1863). *Canadian postal guide: Containing the chief regulations of the Post Office.* Montreal: E. Pickup.

Direct United States Cable Co. v. Anglo-American Telegraph Co. et al., *Newfoundland Law Review* (1876/87), 6, pp. 1-52, affirmed House of Lords, Judicial Committee of the Privy Council, February 14, 1877.

Dominion Bureau of Statistics (DBS). (1957, 1962, 1965, 1967, 1969). *Telephone statistics.* Ottawa: Queen's Printer and Controller of Stationary.

Dominion Telegraph Co. vs. John Silver and Abraham Martin Payne, *Reports of the Supreme Court of Canada* (1882/83), 10, pp. 238-276.

Duch, R. (1991). *Privatising the economy: Telecommunications policy in comparative perspective.* Ann Arbor: University of Michigan Press.

Electric Frontier Foundation. (1994). *Open network platform: Public policy for the information age.* Washington: Author.

Electrical companies pool their patents. Financial Post (Toronto), August 23, 1923.

Electrophone (nd). Advertisement for home information and entertainment servie by telephone in London, England (circa 1988 to 1902). Post 30/1532B (file 1). London: British Telecom Archives.

Ellis, J. (M.P.) (1988, August 22). Correspondence with Sid Shniad of the TWU regarding Bill C-130 to implement the Free Trade Agreement. Author.

Elton, M. C. J. (1992). The U.S. debate on integrated broadband networks. *Media, Culture and Society, 14,* 369-395.

European Commission. (EC). (1996). Proposal for a European Parliament and Council Directive on a common framework for general authorisations and individual licenses in the field of telecommunications services. *Official Journal of the European Communities,* No. C. 90/5, 27. 3. 96.

EU Committee of the American Chamber of Commerce. (1996). *Position paper on the Commission proposal for a directive on a common framework for general authorizations and individual licenses in the field of telecommunication services* [Unpublished paper]. Brussels, Belgium: Author.

Exchange Telegraph Company vs. Gregory & Co. *Queen's Bench Divisions, Court of Appeals* (1895), 1, pp. 147-158.

Exchange Telegraph Company vs. Howard and the London and Manchester Press Agency. *The Times Law Reports* (1906), 22, pp. 375-78.

Federal Communications Commission. (FCC). (1938). *Proposed report: Telephone investigation.* Washington, DC: United States Government Printing Office.

Federal Communications Commission. (FCC). (1983). *Market structure (phase II) (Dec. 82-579), 93 FCC 2d (p. 241).* Washington, DC: United States Government Printing Office.

Federal Communications Commission. (FCC). (1986). *Third computer inquiry (Dec. 86-252).* Washington, DC: United States Government Printing Office.

Federal Communications Commission. (FCC). (1988). *Telecommunications policies of foreign governments (Dec. 88-71).* Washington, DC: United States Government Printing Office.

Federal Communications Commission. (FCC). (1991). *Action in docket case: Commission proposes video-dial-tone policy* (No. DC-11979; CC Docket 87-266). Washington, DC: Government Printing Office.

Federal Provincial Task Force On Telecommunications. (1986). *Examination of telecommunications pricing and the universal availability of affordable telephone service: Report.* Ottawa: Minister of Supply and Services.

Federal Provincial Task Force On Telecommunications. (1988). *Competition in public long-distance telephone service in Canada.* Ottawa: Minister of Supply and Services.

Festinger, J. (1994). *Parameters of cable sovereignty. Communications law and policy: Current issues.* Toronto: The Law Society of Upper Canada.

Financial Times. (1983, November 20-23).

Fleming, S. (1880). *Report and documents in reference to the Canadian Pacific Railway.* Ottawa: Maclean, Roger & Co.

Fleming, S. (1882). *Memorandum in reference to a scheme for completing a great inter-colonial and inter-continental telegraph system by electric cable across the Pacific Ocean.* London: Sir Joseph Causton and Sons. (Pre-1900 Canadiana Microfiche)

Fleming, S. (1902, February 28). *Cheap telegraph rates. Address delivered at the annual meeting of the Canadian Press Association.* Ottawa, Canada.

Flichy, P. (1995). *Dynamics of modern communication: The shaping and impact of new communication technologies.* London: Sage.

Frederick, H. (1997). Mexican NGO computer networking and cross-border coalition-building. In M. Bailie & D. Winseck (Eds.), *Democratising communication?: Comparative perspectives on information and power* (pp. 255-286). Cresskill, NJ: Hampton Press.

Frieden, J. (1991). Invested politics: The politics of national economic policies in a world of global finance. *International Organisation, 45*(4), 425-451.

Frieden, R. (1995). Contamination of the common carrier concept in telecommunications. *Telecommunications Policy, 19*(9), 685-697.

Gabel, D. (1995). Pricing voice telephony services: Who is subsidising whom? *Telecommunications Policy, 19*(6), 453-464.

Galbraith, J. K. (1967/1977). The technostructure and the corporation in the new industrial state. In M. Zeitlin (Ed.), *American society, inc.* (2nd ed., pp. 202-213). Chicago: Rand McNally College Publishers.

Galbraith, J. K. (1992). *Culture of contentment.* New York: Oxford University Press.

Galtung, J. (1994, January 20-23). *State, capital and civil society: A problem of communication?* Paper presented at the 6th Annual MacBride Roundtable , University of Hawaii, Manoa.

Garnham, N. (1983). Toward a theory of cultural materialism. *Journal of Communication, 33*(2), 314-329.

Garnham, N. (1990). *Capitalism and communication.* Newbury Park, CA: Sage.

Garnham, N. (1995). Comments on John Keane's "Structural transformations of the public sphere". *The Communication Review, 1*(1), 23-25.

Gates, B. (1992a, March 23). Consumers will be big winners in CRTC verdict. *The Financial Post* (Lexis Nexis), p. s5.

Gates, B. (1992b, September 21). LD choice promises bonanza in services: Competition forcing phone firms to innovate. *Financial Post* (Lexis Nexis), p. T1.

Gaz, D. (1995, September). The local loop: Place your bets. *Communications Week International,* pp. 17, 20.

Giddens, A. (1993). *The Gidden's reader* (P. Cassell, ed.). Basingstoke, UK: Macmillan.

Gill, S. (1992). The emerging world order and European change: The political economy of European union. In L. Panitch & R. Miliband (Eds.), *Socialist register* (pp. 157-196). London: The Merlin Press.

Globe and Mail, Report on Business (1996, July). Toronto: Author.

Globerman, S., & Booth, P. (1989). The Canada-U.S. Free Trade Agreement and the telecommunications industry. *Telecommunications Policy, 13*(4), 319-328.

Goodhart, D. (1988). Bonn to go ahead with limited deregulation of telecoms. *Financial Times* (Nexis/Lexis), p. 2-1.

Government of Manitoba. (1974). *Broadcasting and cable television: A Manitoba perspective.* Winnipeg: Communications and Information Services Division.

Governor General in Council. (1976). Order setting aside certain broadcasting licenses issued by the CRTC-P.C. 1976-2761. *Canada Gazette, Part II, 110*(23), 3285.

Governor General in Council. (1982a). Order Varying Telecom Decision CRTC 81-13-P.C. 1982-2558; *Canada Gazette, Part II, 116*(17), 2882

Governor General in Council. (1982b). Order Varying Telecom Decision CRTC 81-26-P.C. 1982-2581; *Canada Gazette, Part II, 116*(17), 2881

Governor General in Council. (1982c). Order Varying Telecom Decision CRTC 81-20-P.C. 1982-2580; *Canada Gazette, Part II, 116*(17), 2885.

Governor General in Council. (1982d). Order Varying Telecom Decision CRTC 81-15-P.C. 1982-2350; *Canada Gazette, Part II, 116*(18), 2998.

Governor General in Council. (1982e). Order varying Telecom Decision CRTC 81-4-P.C. 1982-2579; *Canada Gazette, Part II, 116*(17), 2880.

Governor General in Council. (1983). Order Varying Telecom Decision CRTC 83-417-P.C. 1982-3224; *Canada Gazette, Part II, 117*(21), 4015.

Governor General in Council (1985). Direction to the CRTC (Ineligibility to hold broadcast licenses)-P.C. 1985-2108. *Canada Gazette, Part II, 119*(14), 3058-3060.

Governor General in Council. (1988). Order varying CRTC Telecom Decisions 87-5 and 87-14–P.C. 265. *Canada Gazette, Part II, 122*(5), 1245-1247.

Governor General in Council. (1990). Order varying CRTC Telecom Decisions 88-9–P.C. 1990-620. *Canada Gazette, Part II, 124*(8), 1342-1344.

Governor General in Council. (1994). Canadian telecommunications common carrier ownership and control regulations, P. C. 1994-1772. Unpublished copy of the Order-in-Council.

Governor General in Council. (1995). Order varying CRTC Telecom Decision 95-21-P.C. 1995-2196. *Canada Gazette, Part II, 130*(1), 96-98.

Governor General in Council. (1996a). Order declining to set aside or to refer back to the CRTC certain decisions respecting various undertakings. P.C. 1996-353. *Canada Gazette, Part II, 130*(7), 1177.

Governor General in Council. (1996b). Order declining to set aside or to refer back to the CRTC certain decisions respecting various undertakings. P.C. 1996-354. *Canada Gazette, Part II, 130*(7), 1178

Governor General in Council. (1996c). Direction to the CRTC (Ineligibility of Non-Canadians) P.C. 1996-479. *Canada Gazette, Part II, 130*(9), 1296-1300.

Grant, J. C. (1991). Making it to the global major leagues. In D. W. Conklin & L. Deschenes (Eds.), *Canada's information revolution* (pp. 41-53). Canada: The Institute for Research on Public Policy and Canadian Workplace Automation Research Centre.

Habermas, J. (1975). *Legitimation crisis.* Boston: Beacon.

Habermas, J. (1984/1987). *The theory of communicative action* (volumes 1 and 2). London: Heinemann.

Habermas, J. (1989). *Jurgen Habermas on society and politics.* Boston: Beacon.

Hardt, H. (1992). *Critical communication studies: Communication, history, and theory in America.* New York: Routledge.

Harris, N. H. (1969). Contractual terms of cable television pole agreements in Canada. *Canadian Communication Law Review, 1,* 185-203.

Hart, K. (1995, September). On-liners catch the next wave. *Communications Weekly International,* 46-48.

Hawkins, R. (1995, May). *Global ambitions and regional realities: Extending the information and communication infrastructure to a waiting world.* Paper presented at the Telecommunicacoes e Competitivadade Conference, Rio de Janeiro, Brazil.

Hayek, F. (1986). Economic freedom and representative government. In J. Donald & S. Hall (Eds.), *Politics and ideology* (pp. 23-26). Milton Keynes, UK: Open University.

Heilbroner, R. L. (1969). *The worldly philosophers* (3rd. ed.). New York: Simon & Schuster.

Held, D. (1987). *Models of democracy.* Stanford, CA: Stanford University Press.

Hills, J. (1986). *Deregulating telecommunications: Competition and control in United States, Japan and Britain.* Westport, CT: Quorum Books.

Hills, J. (1991). Liberalisation of telecommunications in Britain and its impact on the residential and small business consumer. (Evidence of Professor Jill Hills in response to CRTC Telecom Public Notice 1990-73).

Hills, J. (1993a). Telecommunications and democracy: The international experience. *Telecommunications Journal, 60*(1), 21-29.

Hills, J. (1993b). Back to the future: Britain's 19th century telecommunications policy. *Telecommunications Policy, 17,* 186-199.

Hitchens, L. (1997). The European Commission and the regulation of media ownership and control: Possibilities for pluralism? In A. Sreberny-Mohammadi, D. Winseck, J. Mckenna, & O. Boyd-Barrett (Eds.), *Media in global context* (pp. 207-219). London: Edward Arnold.

Hoffman-Riem, W. (1996). New challenges for European multimedia policy. *European Journal of Communication, 11*(3), 327-346.

Holcombe, A. N. (1911). *Public ownership of telephones on the continent of Europe.* Boston & New York: Houghton Miffin.

Holoday, M. (1995). New media technologies and media education. *Media Asia, 22*(1), 181-192.

Horwitz, R. B. (1991). The First Amendment meets some new technologies: Broadcasting, common carriers and free speech in the 1990s. *Theory & Society,* 22-73.

Huyek, J. N. (1978). *The phone book: Working at the Bell.* Sudbury, Canada: BMI.

Humphreys, P. (1990). The political economy of telecommunications in France. In K. Dyson & P. Humphreys (Eds.), *The political economy of communication* (pp. 209-227). New York: Routledge.

Industry Canada. (1994a). *The Canadian telecommunications service industries: An overview.* Ottawa: Author.

Industry Canada. (1994b). *The Canadian Information Highway: Building Canada's information and communications infrastructure.* Ottawa: Minister of Supply and Services.

Industry Canada. (1995, February). *The information economy in Canada: Fact sheets. Paper presented at the Information Society Conference of the G7,* Brussels.

Industry Canada. (1996a). Government moves to amend Bell Canada Act. Ottawa: Author. (also http://info.ic.gc.ca/ic-data/announcements/news-releases/1996english/e_09_19.html.

Industry Canada. (1996b, August 24). Telecommunications Act and Radiocommunication Act, Notice No. DGTP-008-96–Review of Canadian telecommunications policy in the context of global trade developments. *Canada Gazette, Part 1,* 2450-2452.

Informart/Dialog. (1996). *Informart/Dialog rate schedule.* Toronto: Author.

Information Highway Advisory Council. (1995). Consumer awareness and involvement on the Canadian information highway [not released; obtainable under Access to Information Act request]. Ottawa: Information Canada.

Information Technology Advisory Council (ITAC) (1992). *Presentation to the proceedings of the Standing Senate Committee on Transport and Communications, fifth proceeding on: Examination of the subject matter of Bill C-62, An Act Respecting Telecommunications.* Ottawa: Author.

Ingersoll Telephone Co. v. Bell Telephone Co. of Canada, *Dominion Law Reports* (1917), *31,* pp. 49-66.

Innis, H. A. (1951). *The bias of communication*. Toronto: University of Toronto.

Innis, H. A. (1972). *A history of the Canadian Pacific Railway*. Newton Abbot: David and Charles. (Original work published 1923)

International Telecommunications Union (ITU). (1994). Report on the state of world telecommunications. *ITU Newsletter*, 1, 9-12.

Internet Law and Policy Forum (1996, October 1). New international forum launched to address critical internet law and policy issues [press release]. http://www.osc.edu

Intven, H. (1994). Traffic rules on Canada's information highways: The regulatory framework for new cable and telephone services. *Communications Law and Policy: Current issues*. Toronto: The Law Society of Upper Canada.

Jackson, T. (1995, September 22). Giant bows to colossal pressure. *Financial Times*, p. 13.

Jackson, R., & Jackson, D. (1990). Politics in Canada: Culture, institutions, behaviour and public policy (2nd ed.). Scarborough, Ontario: Prentice Hall, Canada.

Janisch, H. (1986). Competition in telecommunications. *Ottawa Law Review, 18*, 581-624.

Janisch, H. (1989). The Canada-U.S. Free Trade Agreement: Impact on telecommunications. *Telecommunications Policy, 13*(2), 99-103.

Johnston, D. (1995, June). Speaking notes for Professor David Johnston, Chair, Information Highway Advisory Council, at Net '95, Ottawa.

Johnston & Buchanan, Solicitors (1995). Correspondence to A. J. Darling, Secretary-General CRTC, re Internet Service Providers vs. Bell Canada: Application for interim and final relief. http://www.angustel.ca

Juneau, P. (1972). Transcript of speech before the Canadian Association of Broadcasters. Appendix to J. Morris. The CHNS case: An emerging Fairness Doctrine for Canada? *Canadian Communications Law Review, 4*, 1-53.

Jussawalla, M. (1989). Overview of thoughts expressed on information technology and economic interdependence. In M. Jussawalla, T. Okuma, & T. Araki (Eds.), *Information technology and global interdependence* (pp. 2-23). Westwood, CT: Greenwood.

Kakabadse, M. A. (1995). The WTO and the commodification of cultural products: Implications for Asia. *Media Asia, 22*(2), 71-77.

Keane, J. (1991). *The media and democracy*. London: Polity.

Kehoe, L. (1995, August 9). Microsoft undercuts rivals with new online service. *Financial Times*, p. 14.

Kelley, D., & Donway, R. (1990). Liberalism and free speech. In J. Lichtenberg (Ed.), *Democracy and the mass media: A collection of essays* (pp. 66-101). Boston, MA: Cambridge University Press.

Kesterten, W. H. (1967). *A history of journalism in Canada.* Toronto: McClelland and Stewart.

Khan, R. A., & McNiven, J. D. (1991). *An introduction to political science* (4th ed.). Scarborough, Ontario: Nelson Canada.

Kieve, J. (1973). *The electric telegraph: A social and economic history.* Newton Abbot: David and Charles.

Klein and Law Society of Upper Canada. (1985). *Dominion law reports (4th ed.), 16,* 489-542.

Kolko, G. (1963). *The triumph of conservatism.* New York: The Free Press.

KPMG. (1996a). *Public policy issues arising from telecommunications and audiovisual services–main report.* Brussels: European Commission.

KPMG. (1996b). *Public policy issues arising from telecommunications and audiovisual services–summary report.* Brussels: European Commission.

KPMG. (1996c). *Public policy issues arising from telecommunications and audiovisual services–appendices.* Brussels: European Commission.

Krommenacker, R. (1991). Multilateral services negotiations: From interest lateralism to reasoned multilateralism in the context of the servicisation of the economy. In E. U. Petersmann & M. Hilf (Eds.), *The new GATT round of multilateral trade negotiations: Legal and economic problems* (pp. 455-453). Boston: Kluwer.

Levine, J. (1995). Thanks, but I've chosen AGT as my mortal enemy. Internet: http://www.canuck.com/AGT/

Lichtenberg, J. (1990). Introduction. In J. Lichtenberg (Ed.), *Mass media and democracy.* New York: Oxford University Press.

Liebling, A. J. (1961). *The press.* New York: Ballantine Books.

Lippman, W. (1956). *The public philosophy.* New York: Mentor Books.

Locke, J. (1963). *Two treatises of government.* New York: Mentor Books. (Original work published 1689)

Love, R., & Poulin, S. (1991). Family income inequality in the 1980s. *Canadian Economic Observer,* 4.1-4.11.

MacDonald's record: The readers' view. (1988, February 29). *The Financial Post,* p. 1.

Macpherson, C. B. (1985). *The rise and fall of economic justice.* Oxford: Oxford University Press.

Magdoff, H. (1992). Globalisation—to what end? In R. Miliband & L. Panitch (Eds.), *Socialist register* (pp. 44-75). London: Merlin.

Manitoba Telephone System. (1991). *People of service.* Winnipeg, Canada: People of Service.

Manitoba Telephone System. (nd). *Current issues in long distance telephone regulation.* [Internal company document]. Winnipeg, Canada: Author.

Manitoba telephone surplus. (1946, May 10). *Winnipeg Tribune,* p. 6-1.

Manitoba to be in the vanguard of "visionary communications". (1979, July 13). *Winnipeg Tribune,* p. 12.

Mansell, R. (1988, September). Telecommunications network-based services. *Telecommunications Policy*, 243-255.

Mansell, R. (1993). *The new telecommunications: A political economy of network evolution.* California: Sage.

Mansell, R., Holmes, P., & Morgan, K. (1990). European integration and telecommunications: Restructuring markets and institutions. *Prometheus, 8*(1), 50-66.

Marotte, B. (1991). Record bank profits come under fire: Real rate of growth in out of line, analyst says. *Ottawa Citizen* (Lexis Nexis), p. B12.

Marshall, T. H. (1950). *Citizenship and social class, and other essays.* London: Cambridge University Press.

Marx, K. (1977). *Capital (Vol. One).* New York: Random House.

Mattelart, A., & Mattelart, M. (1992). *Rethinking media theory.* Minneapolis: University of Minnesota.

Mattelart, A., & Stourdze, Y. (1985). *Technology, culture and communication: A report to the French Minister of Research and Industry.* New York: North Holland.

Mather, F. C. (1953). The electric telegraph and public order during the Chartist Period, 1837-48. *History, 37,* 40-53.

Mavor, J. (1917). *Government telephones.* Toronto: Mclean Publishing.

McCarthy, J. (1993). The idea of a critical theory and its relation to philosophy. In S. Benhabib, W. Bon, & McCole. (Eds.), *On Max Horkheimer* (pp. 127-152). Cambridge: Massachusetts Institute of Technology.

McChesney, R. (1990). *Off-limits: An inquiry into the lack of debate concerning the ownership, structure and control of the mass media in U.S. political life.* Unpublished manuscript.

McChesney, R. (1997). The communication revolution: The market and the prospect for democracy. In M. Bailie & D. Winseck (Eds.), *Democratizing communication?: Comparative perspectives on information and power* (pp. 57-80). Cresskill, NJ: Hampton Press.

McKay, D. (1983). The political economy of economic policy. In B. Jones (Ed.), *Perspectives on international political economy* (pp. 93-117). London: Frances Pinter.

McMahon, R. C. (1996). Cost recovery and statistics Canada. *Government Information in Canada, 2*(4), np.

McNulty, J. (1988). The political economy of Canadian satellite broadcasting. *Canadian Journal of Communication 13*(2), 1-15.

McQuaig, L. (1995). *Shooting the hippo: Death by deficit and other Canadian myths.* Toronto: Viking.

Media Gruppe Munchen. (1996). *Market survey of on-line services: A comparison of 10 national and international systems.* Unterfohring, Germany: Author.

Melody, W. H. (1994). The information society: Implications for economic institutions and market theory. In E. Comor (Ed.), *The global political economy of communication* (pp. 21-36). New York: St. Martins Press.

Melody, W. H. (1996). Toward a framework for designing information society policies. *Telecommunications Policy, 20*(4), 243-259.

Mill, J. S. (1947). *On liberty.* New York: Appleton, Century Crofts. (Original work published 1859)

Mody, B., Bauer, J. M., & Staubhaar, J. (Eds.) (1995). *Telecommunications politics: Ownership and control of the information highway in developing countries.* Mahwah, NJ: Erlbaum.

Mody, B., & Tsui, L. S. (1995). The changing role of the state. In B. Mody, J.M. Bauer, & J. Staubhaar (Eds.), *Telecommunications politics: Ownership and control of the information highway in developing countries* (pp. 19-200). Mahwah, New Jersey: Lawrence Erlbaum.

Morley, D., & Robins, K. (1995). *Spaces of identity: Global media, electronic landscapes and cultural boundaries.* London: Routledge.

Morris, R. J. (1972). The CHNS Case: An emerging Fairness Doctrine for Canada? *Canadian Communication Law Review, 4,* 1-53.

Morton, E. H. (1975). *Developing public libraries in Canada, 1535-1983.* Halifax, Nova Scotia: Dalhousie University Library and Dalhousie University School of Library Service.

Mosco, V. (1988). Toward a theory of the State and telecommunications policy. *Journal of Communication, 38*(4), 107-124.

Mosco, V. (1989). *The pay-per society.* Norwood, NJ: Ablex.

Mosco, V. (1990a). *Transforming telecommunications in Canada.* Ottawa: Centre for Policy Alternatives.

Mosco, V. (1990b). Toward a transnational world information order: The Canada-United States Free Trade Agreement. *Canadian Journal of Communication, 15*(2), 46-63.

Mosco, V. (1996). *The political economy of communication.* London: Sage.

Mosco, V. (1997). Marketable commodity or public good: The conflict between domestic and foreign communication policy. In G. Swimmer (Ed.), *How Ottawa spends, 1996-97.* Ottawa: Carleton University Press.

Mozes, D., & Sciadas, G. (1995). The demand for telecommunications services. *Service Indicators, Statistics Canada (cat. no. 63-016),* 1st quarter, 73-96.

Mueller, M. (1993). Universal service in telephone history. *Telecommunications Policy, 17*(5), 352-369.

Mumford, L. (1963). *Technics and civilization.* New York: Free Press. (Original work published 1934)

Munk, N. (1995). Canadian communications mogul Ted Rogers is under attack from powerful rivals. Will AT&T ride to his rescue? *Forbes, 155*(9), 42-44.

Mustafa, M. (1993). Methods of sale of state-owned telecommunications enterprises. *Telecommunications Journal, 60*(9), 345-353.

Myrvold, B. (1986). The first hundred years: Toronto Public Library (1883-1983). In P. F. McNally (Ed.), *Readings in Canadian library history* (pp. 65-73). Ottawa: Canadian Library Association.

National Anti-Poverty Organisation. (NAPO). (1987). *Rate restructuring.* Ottawa: Public Interest Advocacy Centre.

Nationwide busy signal for `phones. (1953, May 2). *Financial Post,* p. 53.

Negroponte, N. (1995). *Being digital.* London: Hodder & Stoughton.

Nelson, B. (1969). Econometrics and applied economic analysis in regulatory decisions. *Journal of Contemporary Law and Economic Problems, 34*(2), 330-339.

Nichols, M. E. (1948). *The story of the Canadian Press.* Toronto: Ryerson.

Noam, E. (1994). Beyond liberalisation II: The impending doom of common carriage. *Telecommunications Policy, 18*(6), 435-452.

Noll, A. M. (1996, April 24). Aren't we glad they broke up Bell? *Los Angeles Times,* p. B-9.

Noll, R. A., & Owen, M. (1983). *The political economy of deregulation.* Washington, DC: American Enterprise Institute.

Nora, S., & Minc, A. (1978). *The computerisation of society.* Massachusetts: MIT Press.

Norman, P. (1995, August 9). Bonn unveils new plan for telecom reform. *Financial Times,* p. 2.

Northern Electric Ltd. (1923). *Report to shareholders.* Toronto & Montreal: Author.

Offe, C. (1984). *Contradictions of the welfare state.* Cambridge: Massachusetts Institute of Technology.

Offe, C. (1996). *Modernity and the state.* Cambridge, UK: Polity.

Office of Telecommunications. (1996). Oftel makes progress on Universal Service Policy. *Oftel News, 34,* p. 4.

Opsitnik, J. (1990). Monday memo. *Broadcasting, 119*(19), 24.

Organisation for Economic Cooperation and Development. (OECD). (1988). *The telecommunications industry: The challenges of structural change.* Paris: Author.

Organisation for Economic Cooperation and Development. (OECD). (1990). *Performance indicators for the public telecommunication operators.* Paris: Author.

Organisation for Economic Cooperation and Development (OECD). (1991). *Universal service and rate restructuring in telecommunications.* Paris: Author.

Organisation for Economic Cooperation and Development (OECD). (1995a). *Telecommunications infrastructure: The benefits of competition.* Paris: Author.

Organisation for Economic Cooperation and Development (OECD). (1995b). *Price caps for telecommunications*. Paris: Author.

Pacific Cable Committee (1899). *Reports, minutes of proceedings, and correspondence presented to both Houses of Parliament*. London: Her Majesty's Stationery Office.

Parker, I. (1990). Options in telecommunications regulation. *Canadian Journal of Communication, 15*(2), 33-45.

PCs put move on phones in west. (1990, October 20). *Calgary Herald*, p. A3.

Pettrazinni, B. (1993). The politics of telecommunications policy reform in developing countries. *Pacific Telecommunications Teview, 14*(3), 4-23.

Penner, N. (1973). *Winnipeg 1919: The strikers' own history of the Winnipeg General Strike*. Toronto: James Lewis and Samuel.

Perry, C. R. (1977). The British experience 1876-1912: The impact of the telephone during the years of delay. In I. S. Pool (Ed.), *The social impact of the telephone* (pp. 69-96). London: MIT Press.

Phone devices to be regulated. (1977, April 5). *Winnipeg Tribune*, pp. 3-7.

Pike, R., & Mosco, V. (1986). Canadian consumers and telephone pricing. *Telecommunication Policy, 10*(1), 17-33.

Plender, J. (1997, January 17). An accidental revolution. *Financial Times*, p. 21.

Porat, M. U. (1978). Communication policy in an information society. In G. O. Robinson (Ed.), *Communications for tomorrow: Policy perspectives for the 1980s* (pp. 8-27). New York: Praeger.

Post Office. (1870-80). *Exchange Telegraph royalties: Extracts from correspondence regarding license of January 1872* (File I). From *Exchange Telegraph Co. License: Part 1*. London: British Telecom Archives, post 30/253B.

Post Office. (1876). *Report for the Select Committee on Post Office (Telegraph Department)*. London: Her Majesty's Stationery Office.

Post Office. (1879-1881). *MacMahon's Telegraphic News Agency: Royalties and extracts from correspondence* (File 1). From *Exchange Telegraph Co. License: Part 1*. London: British Telecom Archives, post 30/253B.

Post Office. (1882-1907). *Exchange Telegraph Company: Royalties and applications for reductions* (File VI). From *Exchange Telegraph Co. License: Part 1*. London: British Telecom Archives, post 30/253B.

Post Office. (1898). *Report for the Select Committee on Telephones*. London: Her Majesty's Stationery Office.

Proulx, S. (1991). The videotex industry in Quebec: The difficulties of mass marketing telematics. *Canadian Journal of Communication, 16*(3/4), 399-408.

Province of Canada. (1852). Electric Telegraph Companies Act, 1852. *Statutes of the Province of Canada*, 16 Vict., Cap. 10. Quebec: Stewart Derbishire and George Desbarats.

Pugliese, D. (1992, December 10). Uncrowning achievement. *The Ottawa Citizen*, p. A5.

Raboy, M. (1990). *Missed opportunities.* Toronto: University of Toronto.

Racine, P., Mozes, D., & Kennedy, H. (1992). *Managing competition and regulation.* Ottawa: Department of Communication.

Re Radio Communication in Canada, Attorney General of Quebec v. Attorney General of Canada et. al. (1932). *Times Law Reports, 48,* 235.

Read, D. (1992). *The power of news: The history of Reuters.* New York: Oxford University Press.

Reddick, A. (1995). *Sharing the road: Convergence and the Canadian information highway.* Ottawa: Public Interest Advocacy Centre.

Rens, J. G. (1993). *L'empire invisible: Histoire des télécommunications au Canada, de 1846 à 1956* [The invisible empire: A history of telecommunications in Canada, 1846-1956]. Sainte-Foy, Québec: Presses de l'Université du Québec.

Restrictive Trade Practices Commission (RTPC). (1982). *Telecommunications in Canada, Part III: The impact of vertical integration on the equipment industry.* Ottawa: Minister of Services and Supply.

Rideout, V., & Mosco, V. (1997). Communication policy in the United States. In M. Bailie & D. Winseck (Eds.), *Democratizing communication?: Comparative perspectives on information and power* (pp. 81-104). Cresskill, NJ: Hampton Press.

Rogers, E. (1976). Communication and development: The passing of the dominant paradigm. *Communication Research, 3*(2), 213-240.

Rogers, F. (1996, November 10). *Correspondence with Mr. J. Santer, President of the European Commission* [Unpublished letter]. London: Publishers' Council.

Roman, A. (1990). The telecommunications policy void in Canada. *Canadian Journal of Communication, 15*(2), 96-110.

Romaniuk, B. (1992). *Comments before the proceedings of the standing Senate Committee on transport and communications, fifth proceeding on: Examination of the subject matter of Bill C-62, an act respecting telecommunications.* Ottawa: Canada Communications Group.

Rowley, C. K. (1983). The political economy of the public sector. In B. Jones (Ed.), *Perspectives on international political economy* (pp. 17-63). London: Frances Pinter.

Royal Commission on National Development in the Arts, Letters and Sciences. (1951). *Report of the Royal Commission on National Development in the Arts, Letters and Sciences, 1949-51.* Ottawa: Printer to the King's Most Excellent Majesty.

Royal Task Force on Broadcasting. (1985). *Report of the Task Force on Broadcasting Policy.* Ottawa: Minister of Supply and Services.

Ruggles, M. (1994). *The audience as reflected in the medium of law.* Norwood, NJ: Ablex.

Samarajiva, R. (1995, September-December). *Interactivity without surveillance? Lessons from the proposed UBI network design.* Paper presented at the 23rd Annual Telecommunications Policy Research Conference, Solamans, MD.

Samarajiva, R., & Hadley, P. D. (1996, August). *Online content regulation: The interaction of domestic and supranational law.* Paper presented at the International Association of Mass Communication Research, Sydney, Australia.

Samarajiva, R., & Mukherjee, R. (1990). Information services and the intelligent network: Policy implications from the US and Canadian experience. In D. Henderson (Ed.), *ASIS '90: Proceedings of 53rd ASIS annual meeting* (pp. 326-333). Medford, NY: Learned Information.

Sanders, J. (1996, November 11). America On-Line posts loss after big charge. *Wall Street Journal*, p. 6.

Sangster, J. (1978). The 1907 Bell Telephone strike: Organising women workers. *Labour, 3*, 109-130.

Saskatchewan, Department of Telephones (SaskTel). (1908-1991). *Annual reports.* Regina: Saskatchewan Government Telephones.

Saskatchewan. (1985a). Strategy for the development of rural Saskatchewan: *Report of the Task Force on Rural Development.* Regina: Government of Saskatchewan.

Sayer, A. (1995). *Radical political economy: A critique.* Oxford, UK: Blackwell.

Saywell, J. T. (1960, 1966). *Canadian annual review.* Toronto: University of Toronto Press.

Schact, J. N. (1985). *The making of telephone unionism, 1920-1947.* New Brunswick, NJ: Rutgers University Press.

Schenker, J. (1996a, March 18). Proposed law would cripple on-line service, providers say. *Communications Weekly International, 1*, 34.

Schenker, J. (1996b, February 5). On-line providers protest European license scheme. *Communications Weekly International, 1*, 30.

Schiller, D. (1995, October). *Ambush on the I-Way: Information commoditisation on the electronic frontier.* Speech delivered at the British Columbia Library Association Information Policy Conference, Vancouver, BC.

Schiller, H. (1989). *Culture Inc.* New York: Oxford.

Schiller, H. (1986). *Information and the crisis economy.* New York: Oxford University Press.

Schultz, R., & Janisch, H. (1993). *Freedom to compete.* Ottawa: Bell Canada.

Science Council of Canada (SCC). (1991). *Sectoral technology strategy series.* Ottawa: Minister of Supply and Services.

Scott, J. M. (1972). *Extel 100: The centenary of the Exchange Telegraph Company.* London: Ernest Benn.

Shefrin, I. H. (1993). North American Free Trade Agreement: Telecommunications in perspective. *Telecommunications Policy, 17*(1), 14-26.

Shields, P., Dervin, B., Richter, C., & Soller, R. (1993). Who needs "POTS-plus" services. *Telecommunications Policy, 17*(3), 563-587.

Shoesmith, J. (1995). Infobahn study demands change. *Computing Canada, 18*(2), 1.

Sloan Foundation. (1971). *On the cable: The television of abundance.* New York: McGraw-Hill.

Smith, J. (1991). Canada's privatisation programme. In J. Richardson (Ed.), *Privatisation and deregulation in Canada and Britain: Proceedings of a Canada/UK colloqium, Gleneagles Scotland* (pp. 35-47). Toronto: Institute for Research on Public Policy.

Smith, R. L. (1972). *The wired nation—cable television: The electronic communications highway.* New York: Harper and Row.

Smythe, D. (1977). Communications: Blindspot of Western Marxism. *Canadian Journal of Political and Social Theory, 1*(3), 1-27.

Smythe, D. (1981). *Dependency road.* Norwood, NJ: Ablex.

Snoddy, R. (1995, August 10). NewsCorp and MCI form on-line alliance. *Financial Times,* p. 20.

So you can't get a `phone? (1953, November 21). *Financial Post,* p. 25.

Sorensen, B. (1996, August). *Let your finger do the walking: The space/place metaphor in on-line computer communication.* Paper presented at the International Association of Mass Communication Research, Sydney, Australia.

Southam. (1995). *Annual report.* Don Mills, Ontario: Author.

Stahl, W. A. (1995). Venerating the black box: Magic in media discourse on technology. *Science, Technology and Human Values, 20*(2), 234-258.

Statistics Canada. (1972-96a). *Telephone statistics.* Ottawa: Supply and Services.

Statistics Canada. (1989-1994b). *Private and public investment in Canada.* Ottawa: Minister of Supply and Services.

Statistics Canada. (1990, 1992, 1994c). *Family expenditure in Canada.* Ottawa: Minister of Supply and Services.

Statistics Canada. (1995b). *Consumer prices and price indexes.* Ottawa: Minister of Supply and Services.

Statistics Canada. (1996b). The information technology sector: A profile. *Statistics Canada's On-line Daily* (05. 12. 96). Internet/Email (godfrey@stcinet.statcan.ca): Statistics Canada.

Statistics Canada. (1996c). *Household facilities by income and other characteristics.* Ottawa: Minister of Supply and Services.

Stentor Telecom Policy, Inc. (1992). *Petition to the Governor in Council to vary a section of telecom decision CRTC 92-12.* Unpublished manuscript.

Stentor Telecom Policy, Inc. (1994). *Stentor's vision statement.* Ottawa: Author.

Stentor Telecom Policy, Inc. (1995). *Consumers will not wait.* Internet: http://www.bell.ca/bell/eng/iway/compet.htm

Stratton Oakmonth, Inc and Daniel Prush vs. Prodigy Services Company. (1995). Supreme Court of New York, Index number 31063/94 (3 October, 1994). Internet: gopher:// gopher.cpsr.org:70/00 /cpsr/free_speech/s0_v_prodigy_1995.txt

Straubhaar, J., & Do. J. (1996). Multinational full service networks. In T. Baldwin, D.S. McVoy, & C. Steinfield (Eds.), *Convergence: Integrating media, information and communication* (pp. 353-378). London: Sage.

Streeter, T. (1987). The cable fable revisited: Discourse, policy, and the making of cable television. *Critical Studies in Mass Communication, 4*(2), 174-200.

Surtees, L. (1994a). *Wire wars: Unitel's fight for telecommunications control.* Toronto: Prentice Hall.

Surtees, L. (1994b, April 6). Stentor seeking broadcast rights. *Globe & Mail,* p. A13.

Surtees, L. (1995a, December 21). Inter-city phone rate cuts killed. *Globe & Mail,* p. A1-2.

Surtees, L. (1995b, December 21). Ottawa grants $6-million for rural Internet plan. *Globe & Mail,* p. B2.

Surtees, L. (1996, May 22). Manitoba to test Internet TV box. *Globe and Mail,* p. B6.

Sympatico. (1996). *About Sympatico: Terms and conditions, advertising, services.* Internet: http://www1.sympatico.ca/

Tarjanne, P. (1994, January). *The missing link: Still missing?* Paper presented at the 16th annual Pacific Telecommunications Conference, Manoa, Hawaii.

Taylor, P. (1995, October 12). Uunet bid values Unipalm at £97 m. *Financial Times,* p. 17.

Teichrob, C. (1992, October 8). Unfinished business. Paper presented to the Financial Post Conference on Telecommunications, *Telecommunications in Canada—Can you put me through to the 21st century?* Toronto, Ontario.

Telecommunications Workers Union (TWU). (1988). *The Mulroney Trade Agreement—A threat to Canada's telephone system?* Burnaby, BC: Author.

Telecommunications Workers Union (TWU). (1989, March .15). *Letter between Sid Shniad, TWU, and M. Fernand Belisle, Secretary General, CRTC* Burnaby, BC: Unpublished letter.

Telecommunications Workers Union (TWU). (1992). *Brief to the Standing Senate Committee on Transport and Communications, fifth proceeding on: Examination of the subject matter of Bill C-62, An Act Respecting Telecommunications.* Burnaby, BC: Author.

Telecommunications Workers Union v. CRTC et. al. (1988a, May 27). Federal Court of Appeals Court File No.: A-498-88, Stay of Proceedings. *National Reporter, 86*, pp. 324-328.

Telecommunications Workers Union v. CRTC et. al. (1988b, October 14). Federal Court of Appeals Court File No.: A-498-88, Judgment. Unpublished decision.

Telesat. (1991). *1991 Annual report.* Ottawa: M.O.M. Printing.

Telus. (1991). *1991 Annual report.* Canada: Smith and Associates.

The choral union concert. (1881, December 16). *Ottawa Citizen*, p. 2.

Thompson, J. (1995). *Modernity and media.* Cambridge, UK: Polity.

Thompson, R. L. (1947). *Wiring a continent: The history of the telegraph industry in the United States, 1832-1866.* Princeton, NJ: Princeton University Press.

Tomlinson, J. (1991). *Cultural imperialism: A critical introduction.* London: Pinter.

Tonnies, F. (1955). *Community and association* [Gemeinschaft and gesellschaft]. London: Routledge and Kegan Paul. (Original work published 1887)

Toronto v. Bell Telephone Co. (1905). *Canadian Law Journal. XLI*, p. 371.

Trade Negotiations Committee (TNC). (1993). *Final Act embodying the results of the Uruguay Round (General Agreement on Trade in Services— Annex on telecommunications).* Geneva: GATT Secretariat.

Trebilock, M. J. (1977/78). Regulations and the consumer interest: The Canadian Transport Commission's cost decision. *Canadian Business Law Journal, 2*, 101-113.

Trebing, H. M. (1995). Privatisation and the public interest: Is reconciliation through regulation possible? In B. Mody, J. M. Bauer, & J. D. Straubhaar (Eds.), *Telecommunications politics: Ownership and control of the information highway in developing countries* (pp. 309-339). Mahwah, NJ: Erlbaum.

Union leader hopeful. (1950, June 9). *Winnipeg Tribune*, p. 1

United Kingdom. (1868). The Telegraph Act, 1868. *Statutes of the United Kingdom*, 31-2 Vict., Cap. Cx. London: George E. Eyre and William Spottiswoode.

United Kingdom. (1869). The Telegraph Act, 1869. *Public General Statutes*, 32-3 Vict., Chap. 73. London: George E. Eyre and William Spottiswoode.

United Nations. (1948). *Universal Declaration of Human Rights.* Geneva, Switzerland: United Nations.

United States. (1994). *Administration White Paper on Communications Act reform.* Washington, DC: Government Printing Office.

United States. (1996). *Telecommunications Act of 1996.* Washington, DC: Government Printing Office.

United States Court of Appeals (4th Circuit) (1994). *The Chesapeake and Potomac Telephone Company of Virginia, et. al. v. United States of America and National Cable Television Association* (nos. 93-240, 93-241). Internet: Bell Atlantic Gopher Server.

United States v. Western Electric Company, Inc. et al., Defendents. United States District Court, Dist. of Columbia, 1991. 767 *Federal Supplement.* 308-333.

United States v. Western Electric Company et al., United States Court of Appeals, District of Columbia, 1990. 900 *Federal Reporter.* 2d. 283-311.

United States v. Western Electric Company et al., Defendents. United States District Court, Dist. of Columbia, 1988. 714 *Federal Supplement.* 1-23.

United States Senate Committee on Commerce, Science, and Transportation (1991). *Telecommunications Equipment Research and Manufacturing Competition Act of 1991: Report on S. 173.* Washington, DC: Government Printing Office.

United States, Subcommittee on Communications of the Committee of Commerce, Science and Transportation (1988). *International telecommunications issues.* 100th Congress, 2nd Session, Washington, DC: U.S. Government Printing Office.

United States Senate in Committee of the Whole. (1926). *Regulation of radio communication* (67th Congress, Rd. 124497). Washington, DC: Government Printing Office.

Veblen, T. (1924). *Absentee ownership and business enterprise in recent times: The case of America.* London: George Allen and Unwin.

Verschelden, L. (1980). *The attachment of subscriber provided terminal equipment.* Ottawa: Canadian Federation of Communication Workers.

Voge, J.P. (1986). A survey of French regulatory policy. In M. Snow (Ed.), *Marketplace for telecommunications: Regulation and deregulation in industrialised democracies* (pp. 115-125). New York: Longman.

Walkout won't hit here. (1958, March 15). *Winnipeg Tribune,* pp. 19, 23.

Webster, F. (1995). *Theories of the information society.* London: Routledge.

Weston, J. (1994, November). *Old freedoms and new technologies: The evolution of community networking.* Paper presented at the Free Speech and Privacy in the Information Age symposium, University of Waterloo, Canada.

Whitaker, R. (1977). The liberal-corporatist ideas of Mackenzie King. *Labour, 2,* 137-169.

White House's blue ribbon scrutiny of telecommunications. (1991, May 27) *Broadcasting,* p. 23.

Willis calls for probe of telephone set-up. (1956, March 3). *Winnipeg Tribune,* p. 15.

Wilson, K. (1988). *Technologies of control.* Madison: University of Wisconsin Press. Wilson, K. (1992). Deregulating telecommunications and the problem of natural monopoly. *Media, Culture and Society, 14,* 343-368.

Wilson, K. (1992). Deregulating telecommunications and the problem of natural monopoly. *Media, Culture and Society, 14,* 343-368.

Wilson, K. (1993). The paradox of competition. In R. De La Garde, W. Gilsdorf, & I. Wechselmann (Eds.), *Small nations big neighbour: Denmark and Quebec/Canada compare notes on American popular culture* (pp. 193-216). London: John Libbey.

Wilson, K. (1996, August). *Canada's new regulatory framework: Convergence, competition, and the information highway.* Paper presented at the International Association of Mass Communication Research, Sydney, Australia.

Winston, B. (1995). How are media born and developed. In J. Downing, A. Mohammadi, & A. Sreberny-Mohammadi (Eds), *Questioning the media* (2nd ed., pp. 54-74). London: Sage.

Ziegler, B. (1996, November 15-6). Will cyber advertisers pay for attention? *Wall Street Journal,* p. 10.

AUTHOR INDEX

SUBJECT INDEX